Word and Music Studies

Essays on Performativity and on Surveying the Field

WORD AND MUSIC STUDIES
12

Series Editors

Walter Bernhart
Michael Halliwell
Lawrence Kramer
Suzanne M. Lodato
Werner Wolf

The book series WORD AND MUSIC STUDIES (WMS) is the central organ of the International Association for Word and Music Studies (WMA), an association founded in 1997 to promote transdisciplinary scholarly inquiry devoted to the relations between literature/verbal texts/language and music. WMA aims to provide an international forum for musicologists and liteary scholars with an interest in intermediality studies and in crossing cutural as well as disciplinary boundaries.

WORD AND MUSIC STUDIES publishes, generally on an annual basis, theme-oriented volumes, documenting and critically assessing the scope, theory, methodology, and the disciplinary and institutional dimensions and prospects of the field on an international scale: conference proceedings, collections of scholarly essays, and, occasionally, monographs on pertinent individual topics.

Word and Music Studies: Essays on Performativity and on Surveying the Field

Edited by
Walter Bernhart
in collaboration with Michael Halliwell

Amsterdam - New York, NY 2011

The paper on which this book is printed meets the requirements of "ISO 9706: 1994, Information and documentation - Paper for documents - Requirements for permanence".

ISBN: 978-90-420-3463-1
E-Book ISBN: 978-94-012-0745-4
©Editions Rodopi B.V., Amsterdam - New York, NY 2011
Printed in The Netherlands

Contents

Introduction v

Performativity in Literature and Music

Tobias Janz
Performativity and the Musical Work of Art.. 1

David Francis Urrows
Text vs. Act:
The *Bearbeitungsfrage* and the 'Romantic Baroque' 17

Robert Samuels
The Act of Performance as Mahlerian Topic 35

Katia Chornik
Politics, Music and Irony in Alejo Carpentier's Novel
La consagración de la primavera (*The Rite of Spring*) 53

Delia da Sousa Correa
Musical Performativity in the Fiction of Katherine Mansfield 71

Walter Bernhart
Rhythmical Ambivalence of Poetry Performance:
The Case of Elizabethan Verse 87

Adrian Paterson
"Music will keep out temporary ideas":
W. B. Yeats's Radio Performances 101

Axel Englund
'The Invisible' / 'The Inaudible':
Aspects of Performativity in Celan and Leibowitz 121

Simon Williams
Romantic Opera and the Virtuoso 143

Lawrence Kramer
Sexing Song:
Brigitte Fassbaender's *Winterreise* 157

Michael Halliwell
Vocal Embodiment and Performing Language
in *Waiting for the Barbarians*:
Philip Glass's Adaptation of J. M. Coetzee's Novel 173

Bernhard Kuhn
Operatic Hyperreality in the Twenty-First Century:
Performance Documentation in High-Definition Quality 191

Emily Petermann
Jazz Novels and the Textualization of Musical Performance 211

Mario Dunkel
Charles Mingus and Performative Composing 229

Katrin Eggers
Wittgenstein and Schoenberg on Performativity of Music
as Method for Philosophy 243

Surveying the Field

Peter Dayan
Seeing Words and Music as a Painter Might:
The Interart Aesthetic 265

David Mosley
Milan Kundera's Polyphonic Novels and
the Poetics of Divestment 279

Notes on Contributors 291

Introduction

The essays collected in this volume of Word and Music Studies, the thirteenth of the series, are all versions of papers read at the Seventh International Conference of the International Association for Word and Music Studies (WMA) held at the University of Music and Performing Arts Vienna in June 2009. As has been a regular practice of by now almost fifteen years in organizing WMA conferences, a special topic was chosen for the main section of the conference, which this time – appropriately so, in view of the inviting Vienna institution – was 'Performativity in Words and Music'. In addition, a smaller section of the conference was devoted to the topic of 'Surveying the Field', which is another regular feature of WMA conferences.

The choice of the main topic, 'Performativity in Words and Music', needed little justification, as a substantial part of recent reflections in the humanities had been devoted to the performance aspect of cultural activities, particularly in the arts. This reorientation of scholarly interests in the arts, trendily called the 'performative turn', has yielded significant contributions to an increasingly refined understanding of artistic processes, and specifically what has been labelled the crisis of the work concept has sharpened our awareness of the need of finding the 'proper' object of such scholarly investigation, which cannot be exclusively, as in most traditional studies, the written "monuments of unaging intellect".

While general discussions of performativity have generated essential re-conceptualizations concerning the ontological dimension of the issue (which are partly reflected in Tobias Janz's contribution to this volume), yet what has been largely missing so far, particularly from an intermedial point of view, is a set of careful case studies from a wider range of artistic genres and historical phases which can give detailed insight into consequences of addressing issues of performativity in the arts. Specifically, such topics as the various effects of particular performative conditions and situations on the constitution of meaning (in the widest sense), or the successful integration of performative elements into the fabric of artefacts can only be discussed fruitfully on the basis of a close examination of pertinent individual examples. The focus of the case studies collected in this volume is obviously on performative activities in music and literature, whereby

– interestingly so – as music is the more 'performative' of the two art forms, stressing the performative side of literary products frequently implies an approach of literature to music: the perspective of performativity strengthens the intermedial link of the two art forms.

Tobias Janz, in his theoretically oriented contribution "Performativity and the Musical Work of Art", sees a limitation in conceptions/ approaches which try to draw a clear line between the concepts of work and of performativity and argues in favour of an extended work concept, against recent attempts at altogether abandoning it. Basing his argument on positions taken earlier by Paul Bekker, Theodor W. Adorno and, more recently, Albrecht Wellmer, he discusses the methodological consequences of such an extended work concept for analytical and historiographical scholarly practices.

In his essay on "Text vs. Act: The *Bearbeitungsfrage* and the 'Romantic Baroque'", David Urrows looks into the history of the contemporary debate on 'work' vs. 'performance' and discusses the issue of Bach transcriptions as it was hotly argued over in the later nineteenth century. The scholarly Bach-Gesellschaft, holding an emphatic view of 'works' being totally manifested in 'texts', was an early defender of notions of 'authenticity' and *Werktreue*, against the views of an 'interpretive', 'artistic' school around Robert Franz, including such prominent performing artists as Franz Liszt or Ignaz Moscheles, who despised the "millstone of text" and practiced romantic freedom of individual expressiveness in their performances.

Robert Samuels draws attention to another case of pervasive performativity in the later nineteenth and earlier twentieth centuries by discussing "The Act of Performance as Mahlerian Topic". His issues are the theatricality and the physicality of performances as reflected in Gustav Mahler's music as well as representations of performances and the presence of songs in his symphonies, all these foregrounding the act of performance as part of Mahler's musical cosmos.

A group of essays in this volume addresses the presence of musical performances on the diegetic level in works of narrative fiction. In "Politics, Music and Irony in Alejo Carpentier's Novel *La consagración de la primavera* (*The Rite of Spring*)", Katia Chornik demonstrates how the performance of specific musical works, such as Stravinsky's famously scandalous piece referred to in her and Carpentier's titles, or "L'Internationale", is successfully put to use for a political purpose.

Delia da Sousa Correa's contribution on "Musical Performativity in the Fiction of Katherine Mansfield", also discussing the presence of musical performances on the plot level – here of Mansfield's short stories – and stressing their function of affective intensification, additionally shows how the stories themselves 'perform' music insofar as their writing, including typographical suggestions, reflects features of oral musical performances.

The fact that literary texts in their graphic representation generally do not encode those prosodic features which are relevant for their oral presentation, and this fact's consequence of a fundamental freedom in the recitation of verse, are reflected in Walter Bernhart's contribution "Rhythmical Ambivalence of Poetry Performance: The Case of Elizabethan Verse". This essay attempts a (linguistically informed) reconstruction of highly contrastive (formal/'artificial' vs. rational/ 'natural') styles of verse performance practiced during the Elizabethan period, which are backed up by references to contemporary written documents and mirror conflicting art-ideological positions of the time.

A closely related sequel to this essay is Adrian Paterson's contribution "'Music will keep out temporary ideas': W. B. Yeats's Radio Performances". Yeats's radio broadcasts have hitherto been largely unexplored regarding the light they throw on the poet's views of poetry. Yeats's chantlike style of verse delivery with its strict observation of identifiable rhythmical and intonational features attests to the intense attention the poet gave to sound, and demonstrates his conviction that oral performance is of unquestionable importance for poetry.

In "'The Invisible' / 'The Inaudible': Aspects of Performativity in Celan and Leibowitz", Axel Englund focuses on late poetry by Paul Celan as read aloud by the poet himself and as set to music by the dodecaphonic composer René Leibowitz, and investigates the consequences of these performative acts for the poetic meaning. While Celan's reading matches the poems' sense of imperfection and erasure by giving prominence to sound over sense, Leibowitz's twelve-tone musical settings demonstrate symmetry, coherence and perfection, which are alien to the poems. However, sung performances of the settings show inaccuracies in the singing, which is a common and unavoidable practice yet works against the essential illocutionary meaning of Leibowitz's music: "Every performance potentially distorts that which is performed." Thus, following Schoenberg, Adorno and Celan, it can be argued that to radically withdraw altogether from sensual materialization is the best way to guarantee preserving the poetic and musical essence of the work.

Another group of essays in this volume concentrates on the issue of 'voice' in musical performance. Simon Williams discusses "Romantic Opera and the Virtuoso" and by looking at three exceptional singer-artists of the nineteenth century (Giuditta Pasta, Maria Malibran, and Adolphe Nourrit) identifies a variety of styles, represented by them, of how to put the operatic voice to either a statuesque or a dramatic use in performance, an insight reminiscent of Bernhart's findings in his contribution.

In his essay "Sexing Song: Brigitte Fassbaender's *Winterreise*", Lawrence Kramer analyses the famous mezzo-soprano's fascinating re-reading of Schubert's song cycle as one reflecting the transgression of the speaker's conventional masculine role of mourning and anxiety by adopting a courageous feminine stance of protest and defiance. This re-reading sheds a bright light on the fact that performance plays an important role in establishing artistic meaning and, as in this particular case, can even fundamentally overrun traditional interpretations.

Michael Halliwell, in "Vocal Embodiment and Performing Language in *Waiting for the Barbarians*: Philip Glass's Adaptation of J. M. Coetzee's Novel", asserts that voice manifests the emotional core of opera yet, by inspecting Glass's Coetzee opera, also observes a tension between voice as a verbal signifier and as a material presence, which may lead to a distortion of the linguistic meaning in the vocal utterance. Thus, voice in performance is on the one hand in the service of dramatic representation but on the other also introduces an element of distancing the audience from the drama.

A very special effect on audiences is produced by HD broadcasting, a recent form of operatic performance practice, as Bernhard Kuhn investigates in "Operatic Hyperreality in the Twenty-First Century: Performance Documentation in High-Definition Quality". In this practice, which is a hybrid form involving opera performed on stage, performance documentation for television, and film opera, the work – here exemplified by Franco Zefirelli's La Bohème – is experienced by the audience as being 'hyperreal', which implies (in terms of Umberto Eco and Jean Baudrillard) that it is experienced as more real than it is in the opera house. In this type of performative activity the performance widens the range of experiences and 'meanings' over that offered by traditional communication channels.

Two contributions deal with the subject of performance and jazz. Emily Petermann's investigation of "Jazz Novels and the Textualization of Musical Performance" discusses musical performances in novels by, e. g., Toni Morrison, Albert Murray, or Xam Wilson Cartiér, both – as Chornik's essay does – on the diegetic level and as structural models for the narrative. Oral delivery devices and specific linguistic behaviour, such as gossip, are imitated and evoked in the texts, and narrator roles in the novels reflect the roles of performing and improvising solo jazz players. In this way the typical tension in jazz between a fixed text and the idea of spontaneity is mirrored in literary narrative.

This tension is even more strongly demonstrated by Mario Dunkel in "Charles Mingus and Performative Composing". Typically for the 1950s, Mingus abandoned traditional forms of musical notation and instead practiced the art of "performative composing". This spontaneous form of composition consisted in acts of collaborative activity in performance with his fellow musicians in which Mingus even used his body as a compositional medium to create the musical 'work' as a form of spontaneous self-expression.

A process of meaning generation, in its way strikingly similar to Mingus's, is expounded by Katrin Eggers in her essay, "Wittgenstein and Schoenberg on Performativity of Music as Method for Philosophy". Ludwig Wittgenstein and Arnold Schoenberg shared a sceptical attitude towards systematic methods of establishing meaning and instead propagated a performative, operational practice of meaning production, whereby the processes of poetic and musical performativity became models for the 'new method' of philosophic reflection.

The theme of performativity in literature and music proved to be so multifaceted and inexhaustible at the WMA Vienna conference, and some of the issues raised asked for further critical elaboration, so that it was felt to be reasonable to continue discussing it at the next WMA conference. The topic of 'voice' was considered a particularly fertile and compact area of investigation, so it was decided to concentrate on it at the 2011 conference, held at Santa Fe, NM.

In the section 'Surveying the Field' of the Vienna conference, two papers offered new perspectives on issues of general interest in word and music studies. In "Seeing Words and Music as a Painter Might: The Interart Aesthetic", Peter Dayan widens the intermedial angle of word and music studies and discusses the major art forms of music, literature, and visual art from the perspective of a globally conceived

'Interart Aesthetic'. With the eyes of this aesthetic approach, the media specificity of the individual art forms is transcended, and what it sees as a fundamental characteristic of the arts is a specific affinity and attraction among them which finds expression in the liability of the individual art forms to reflect on themselves in terms of the other art forms, a condition based on romantic notions of the inexplicability of art.

David Mosley's essay on "Milan Kundera's Polyphonic Novels and the Poetics of Divestment" attempts a reconsideration of one of the central issues of word and music studies, the musicalization of fiction, and in particular, polyphony in fiction. While the position taken by Calvin Brown, Steven P. Scher, Werner Wolf, and others that, from a descriptive perspective, fiction cannot be polyphonic, is not put into question, the contribution, however, argues for the existence of narrative polyphony from an ontological perspective, grounded in the experience of reading.

The success of the Vienna conference was largely due to its excellent organization, for which thanks need to go to Gerold W. Gruber from the Institute for Analysis, Theory and History of Music of the University of Music and Performing Arts Vienna; Gerold was an indefatigable and graciously energetic host. Thanks are also due to Fred van der Zee from Editions Rodopi for his unflagging and tireless support of Word and Music Studies to keep its profile in unchangedly good shape. Michael Halliwell deserves special thanks for his always competent and prompt help in editing this volume when there was need for help. Last but not least this book would not be able see the light of day without the technical expertise of Katharina Bantleon, who has once again skilfully seen to it that the manuscript should find a form that is acceptable in the intricate world of desktop publishing.

Graz, autumn 2011   Walter Bernhart

Performativity in Literature and Music

Performativity and the Musical Work of Art

Tobias Janz, Hamburg

> While the musical work of art and its performance have long been considered as two separate ontological objects, in recent years, following Theodor W. Adorno and Albrecht Wellmer, a discussion has emerged in German-speaking musicology about a definition of the musical work of art which comprises the performative dimension of music as an irreducible aspect of the work itself. This discussion not only tries to acknowledge the constitutive function of sound and time as the medial dimensions in which music is taking form, posing highly complicated methodological problems for the analysis of music; it also develops a new sensitivity for the historicity of the work of art. The paper discusses those methodological and historiographic problems and also further implications of such a conception of the musical work of art.

The concept of the musical work and the ontological status of musical works have posed problems in the philosophy of music and in the musicological practice long before the so-called 'performative turn' in cultural studies. Nonetheless, for a long time the historiography and interpretation of music have been depending on a concept of music which was based almost exclusively on the written text of music, the published score, and on written documents, especially those by composers themselves. As a consequence, the architectural structure of a piece of music and the spatially fixed dimensions of pitch and rhythmic value have been much more important for the understanding of a piece than the ephemeral elements of sound, intensity, expression and modifications of musical time. One hundred years of recording history raise the question of a scholarly approach to recorded performances but, in general, the recently developed discipline of performance analysis has not significantly modified the established view of the musical work of art. The distinction between work and performance remains untouched, since the (often computer-based) analysis of, for instance, rubato, sound and articulation of a given performance mostly refers to the performative aspects of the individual performance only, as clearly distinguished from the structure of the work, which remains considered an objective entity.

What I plan to present in the following are some considerations about the question of how this often unreflected distinction between the work concept and the concept of performativity may be overcome and replaced by an integrative approach to the subject. My topic will therefore, at first, be the relation – or non-relation – of the traditional work concept and the concept of performativity as developed in literary and cultural studies. In this I am not so much interested in the general ontological problems of the topic, and also not in its socio-historical dimension, i. e., in the emergence of the traditional work concept around 1800 (or perhaps centuries earlier) and its (supposed) decline in the twentieth century – two aspects, which have been discussed intensively in recent years. The problem can be reduced to two questions: what kind of an object do we face in the historiography and analysis of music when we take the performative aspect of music as an essential element of our subject? And what are the consequences of such a view for our work as music analysts and music historians? Concerning the first question, my aim is not so much to propose a new approach to the topic, but rather to refer to some of the recent contributions in the German-speaking discussion, namely Albrecht Wellmer's conception of the musical work as developed in his recent book, *Versuch über Musik und Sprache* (2009). Concerning the second question, I will round up my paper with some speculations about a (still to be written) history and the analysis of musical works as performative phenomena.

1. Work and Performativity as Incongruous Opposites

A preliminary remark: in the German-speaking discussion there are two different terms related to the English term 'performativity': 'Performanz', which is associated with Austin's speech act theory, the history of the self and the gender debate; and 'das Performative', which is basically associated with performance art and certain aspects of the performing arts. Although both terms and their applications overlap in several respects, this paper will focus on 'das Performative'.

The concept of performativity has always been in some kind of tension with the work concept. The emergence of discourse about performativity in the arts seems to be closely related to the 'crisis of the work concept' which has been an essential topic in the performing arts at least since the 1950s. In art forms in which the crisis of the work concept has led to an outright abandonment of the whole concept, as in the fluxus movement, in conceptualism or performance art, the tension between work and performance seems to have completely disappeared. In art forms which still depend on the performance of works in the traditional sense this tension poses new methodological problems, as long as the work concept no longer seems reliable yet the discipline of performance analysis remains underdeveloped and is unable to reach the level, not to say replace, the highly differentiated methods of music analysis, or better, work analysis. Furthermore, in practice, performance analysis and work analysis in most cases refer to different phenomena or aspects of music: if a performance is thought of as the realisation of a work – of a play, an opera, a piece of music –, the analysis of the performative dimension commonly refers to elements related only to one particular performance and not to the work as independent from an individual performance, i. e., to the voice, the body and the real-life presence of the performers and their actions, the actual sounding and operating of musical instruments, the actual environment in which the performance is taking place, and even the reaction of the audience, at least as long as this reaction has to be considered as an essential and not an accidental part of the event. Work analysis, on the other hand, is always associated with the stability of its object – an object independent from the contingency of singular performances; for example with the stability of a text as an object to which the actual performance refers, yet without having any influence on the configuration of the object itself. Thus, it is common to see the work and its performance in some kind of a complementary relation.

By contrast, for Erika Fischer-Lichte, who is one of the foremost exponents of an aesthetics of performativity in Germany (see 2004), performativity and the work of art mutually exclude each other, at least as aesthetic concepts. Because performativity is bound to the peculiar moment of the event, it cannot be thought of as a stable object. It cannot even be observed after its occurrence since every attempt to preserve a performance on tape, video or some other media creates an object which is already something else; an object, in which the performative dimension is already mediated and thus transformed into a different thing. Therefore – as Fischer-Lichte argues – it would be misleading to call a performance a work of art – a proposal Hermann Gottschewski has made in his book *Die Interpretation als*

Kunstwerk (1996). For Fischer-Lichte, a performance may use the text of a work as an instrument or as a starting point, a performance may also be preserved in the form of a text, but the performance itself belongs to a different ontological category: it is an event which can only be experienced in its temporal and spatial presence. Whether the performance is a performance *of* a work, i. e., a performance referring to a work, or an autonomous performance without a work basis, makes no real difference in view of an aesthetic of performativity. What matters, for example, in Frank Castorf's production of Dostoyevsky's *The Idiot* is what happens on stage, or between stage and audience, and not the qualities of Dostoyevsky's novel as a literary text, or its plot. Applied to the performance of a musical work, this would mean that in the moment of the performance only the actual presence of the music, the gestures of the performers, and the feedback loop between stage and audience will constitute the aesthetic environment as experienced by the participants. It makes no difference whether it is Keith Jarrett performing a free improvisation or Maurizio Pollini performing Chopin's b-Minor Sonata, for both the improvisation and the sonata are experienced as events that are acoustically and emotionally present in time, not as the text, the ideal or intentional object to which the performance may refer. Considered as a work, the sonata becomes an object which can be observed, analysed, interpreted, and historically contextualized regardless of the contingency of the singular performance, although at the expense of all the aspects that distinguish a performance from a score (and which, as Fischer-Lichte would argue, only make real and vital music out of a score), i. e., regardless of its presence in time, the expression and the materiality of the sound.

In this perspective the aesthetic of performativity and the conventional work concept appear as incongruous opposites. Considering a piece of music as a work (as is common in musicological practice) means to exclude the aesthetic presence of the piece in terms of an experienced reality. The existence of this dimension is not denied, but it is rated as accidental. Considering the piece as a performance means to forget about its existence in texts and as historical documents (and even in recordings). Thus, to adopt the position of an aesthetic of performativity, for a music historian, would mean to deal with actual performances, not with texts and documents as materializations either of works or performances. I will return to this problematic perspective at the end of this paper. At this point of the discussion we can observe that an aesthetic of performativity as radical as it has been outlined so far will lead a music historian dealing with music into a difficult situation: he has to choose between the text or score, which, however, is clearly devaluated in comparison with the live performance, or the performance, which, however, is observable only in its temporal and spatial presence. In addition, as an analyst of performances he will be confronted not with one central object but with a plurality of objects which are difficult to manage.

2. Ideology and Ideological Criticism: Performativity and Work in Historical Perspective

The work concept has often been criticized for its ideological suppositions, for instance, for being a bourgeois phenomenon only relevant within a limited cultural context. But it has to be conceded that Fischer-Lichte's *Ästhetik des Performativen* is equally based on ideological (and also political) foundations. At first it seems to be a reaction against a set of practices, methods and values that dominated the arts and the humanities since the nineteenth century: a reaction against the self-confident assurance of an ever-present wealth of cultural heritage, the canon of sacrosanct masterworks; a reaction against a conservative historicism that valued the great achievements of the past higher than the ephemeral products of the present; a reaction against a critical discourse that is based on interpretation and hermeneutics rather than on aesthetic experience; a reaction against a form of criticism that is focussed only on the meaning and the referential quality of signs and therefore neglects the materiality, sensuousness and physicality of art, in other words, the performing arts. However, in view of postmodernism, which forms the background of the 'performative turn' as observed in the arts since the 1960s by Fischer-Lichte, the aesthetic of performativity seems also to be a reaction against a culture that is more and more dominated by the media. In this respect, insisting on performativity also seems to be an attempt to regain an element of the authentic, of the real, of the pure being of existence from the alienating forces of modernism. Performativity thus appears as one of the ways of deconstructing the concept of the autonomous work of art, in this respect comparable to intertextuality or the cultural-historical contextualisation of artworks.

There is no doubt that reactions against the alienating forces of modernism in favour of appreciating aesthetic presence have been a driving force in the arts not only since the 1960s, but already since the beginnings of aesthetic modernism itself. Richard Wagner's criticism of taking drama as pure literature and his ideas about the presence of the real-life human body with all its natural qualities on the opera stage (as articulated in his essays on art written in the Zurich exile) can be seen as early invocation of the performative against forms of art that are caught in representation and alienation. Certainly, Wagner's dramas, in his own view, are not performances in terms of the post-dramatic theatre (see Lehmann 1999), but 'works' in a more emphatic sense, applied to the opera, which until the mid-nineteenth century or even later was far from being dominated by the narrow work paradigm, predominantly applied to symphonies and sonatas. Nevertheless, Wagner did not write his dramas for an imaginary museum but for actual productions on stage. In general, the musical culture of the nineteenth century shows the work concept and performativity often more intertwined as it might appear in retrospection. The shift from an era of great composers still alive and often performing their own compositions to an era of great performers performing mostly works by dead composers, which took place at the end of the nineteenth century and was effective throughout the twentieth century (concomitant with the development of recording techniques and their commercialization), it seems has intensified, or has perhaps even created, the gap between the idea of an abstract, permanent musical work of art and its ephemeral performance. This coincided with the rise of the still young discipline of musicology, which concerned itself – far into the twentieth century – mainly with the examination of musical texts and music-historical documents, yet scarcely with contemporary performances or compositions.

3. The Dialectics of Work and Performativity:
Bekker, Adorno, Wellmer

Although early musicology from its inception in the early twentieth century was mainly focussed on written documents, the aesthetic and philosophical discussion of the work concept has from early on dealt with the complicated relation between the textual and the performative dimensions of music. Already in 1916, Paul Bekker suggested a work concept and a concept of musical form that anticipated some of the recent discussions about performativity in music. In the first chapter of *Das deutsche Musikleben*, Bekker argued (cf. 1916: 17–19) that musical form cannot be seen – as it is generally is – in the structure of themes and motives of a composition, but rather in the perception of the 'material' ("Materie") of a 'sound image' ("Klangbild"). The perception is effected by the environment ("Umwelt") of the sound image, and only in such an environment the acoustic material turns into form. The form of music – as Bekker explains – is a result of relations between material and environment. There is no musical form without perception in a certain environment, but, in addition, there has to be something performed in the environment that can become the form of the perception. Thus, in Bekker's concept of musical form the composer is disempowered in two respects, firstly, because his intended form depends on the specific circumstances of the environment in which his 'work' is becoming musical form – it depends on the acoustics and the character of the performance space, the audience as part of the environment, and the individual perceptions by the members of the audience; and secondly, because the presentation of his work needs 'alien forces' ("fremde Kräfte"), namely the performers, who can only be controlled to a certain degree. Thus, as Bekker concludes, the composer is not the exclusive creator of the musical form, he is only the one who 'guides' and 'instructs' the performers when they create the actual sound image. Basically, Bekker's argument aims at establishing a sociology of music, replacing or complementing the then dominating work- or composer-centred music history and music theory. His critical reformulation of the work concept assigns to society an essential role not only in the reception or production of music, but also in the emergence of the music itself – an emergence that is considered decidedly performative. It is interesting to see how Bekker's description of a performance anticipates some of the qualities Fischer-Lichte emphasizes in her aesthetic of performativity – not only the performance itself, but the environment and the feedback-loop between audience and performers as well; yet he still concedes the composer and his work the constitutive role of an instructor of the performance.

Although it was innovative and opened new perspectives not only for the sociology but also for the historiography of music, Bekker's work concept did not find much resonance in musicology. Rather, it did find criticism. Giselher Schubert pointed out the absence of normative criteria that would allow a differentiation between successful and unsuccessful realizations of a musical form (see 1970). Two performances of a Mahler symphony may lead to two completely different musical forms, but how can we distinguish between an aesthetically adequate and a failed performance without criteria that lie outside the performance, criteria like the structure or the meaning of the piece, which cannot be drawn from the individual performances?

Bekker did not say much about this no doubt relevant aspect, and it took some time until at the end of the last century the topic of musical performance and its relation to the work concept attracted more interest in musicological discourse. Between Bekker's *Das deutsche Musikleben* and Schubert's criticism, Theodor W. Adorno produced a large body of sketches and drafts which were supposed to become a 'Theory of Musical Reproduction' (*Theorie der musikalischen Reproduktion*), a book which Adorno never finished but whose collected materials have been published as part of the edition of Adorno's posthumous writings in 2001 (see 2001). Although Adorno maintained a marked concept of the musical artwork, many of these sketches deal with the sociological background which Bekker considered essential for the emergence of musical form in a performance. Characteristically these are often sketches marked by Adorno as "sehr wichtig" or "zentral". That the work concept is essential for Adorno is already demonstrated by the vocabulary he uses for the performative dimension, which was the central concern of his planned book. Adorno never uses the term 'Aufführung' (the German equivalent for 'performance'), using instead the term 'Interpretation', or more often the very unusual term 'Reproduktion'. Both 'Interpretation' and 'Reproduktion' seem closely related to a fact which is not the actual performance, i. e., close to the text to be interpreted, or to the work to be reproduced *in* a performance. In addition, we associate 'Reproduktion' with the mere technical reproduction of an artwork, which thus tends to imply a more or less pejorative attitude towards performativity, or at least implies its inferior status. Nevertheless, Adorno never considers the work as an absolute object that is completely independent from the dimension of performativity. In fact he proposes a work concept which is at the same time a concept of musical performance, showing these two different aspects as dialectically intertwined. Adorno's position can be summarized as follows: the text of a score is neither only an instruction for the performer (as Bekker argued) nor the representation of the intention of the composer. Rather the text is considered as a kind of a substitute representing the meaning ('Sinn') of the work, its content ('Inhalt'), and its truth. Yet it is not the task of the musical 'reproduction' – as one might guess – to present and decipher this once given and unchangeable content. The music – as Adorno underlines – is not 'in possession' of that content. By using a frequently applied metaphor, Adorno characterizes the content ('Gehalt') of music as the process of the sedimentation of content. This underlines a processuality of his work concept in contrast to its traditional conception as a stable, unchangeable entity and can be linked to a central idea of Adorno's *Ästhetische Theorie*, namely, the idea of the basically processual character of the artwork, which links the artwork to the general processuality of history. Works of art "are alive" in history, Adorno says. Not only the attitude towards the work changes in time, the work itself changes its appearance:

> If the artwork is nothing fixed and definitive in itself, but something in motion, then its immanent temporality is communicated to its parts and whole in such a fashion that their relation develops in time and that they are capable of cancelling this relation. If artworks are alive in history by virtue of their own processual character [i. e. the process of aesthetic experience], they are also able to perish in it. [The changing attitude of individuals towards works] is external with regard to what transpires in the works themselves: the dissolution of layers, one after the other, which was unforeseeable in the moment of the work's appearance; the determination of this transformation by their emerging and increasingly distinct law of form; the petrification of works that have become transparent, their decrepitude, and their falling silent. Ultimately their development is the same as their process of collapse. (Adorno 1970/2004: 235)

This is one of the points where Albrecht Wellmer's recent contributions to the discussion of the work concept tie in. As he is a pupil of Adorno, Wellmer's work concept is always close to Adorno's *Ästhetische Theorie*. On the other hand, Wellmer tries to find a concept which is appropriate also for artistic developments since the 1970s, i. e., especially for the arts after the so-called 'performative turn'. In his recent book, *Versuch über Musik und Sprache*, Wellmer has a long chapter about John Cage and indeterminate art, which are subjects that also play a decisive role in Erika Fischer-Lichte's *Ästhetik des Performativen*. Thus, Wellmer's interest in the work concept can be read as an attempt to make Adorno's aesthetics compatible with today's aesthetic discourse. At the same time, Wellmer's study is a plea for adhering to a normative work concept even with regard to art forms in which textuality is replaced by the temporal and spatial presence of an event (cf. 2009: 134). Thus, Wellmer's work concept is also an implicit criticism of authors who too readily abolish the work concept in favour of performativity or with a background of ideological criticism.

At the risk of oversimplifying Wellmer's complex and dense argument, I will try to outline some of its main elements (see ibid.: 125–165). With Adorno, Wellmer considers the work of art as an essentially historical phenomenon ("geschichtliches Phänomen"). From Adorno Wellmer also adopts the expression of the 'processuality' of the work of art and thus sets off his work concept from a traditional one which conceives of the work as an unchangeable object that is bound to a specific historical context, i. e., the time of its composition/publication. As for Adorno, for Wellmer works are no historical documents. They rather unfold their content over time in the processes of performance, aesthetic experience and verbal interpretation. As this content can never be fixed, ultimately verbalized or completely understood – Wellmer quotes Adorno's remarks about the incomprehensibility, or "Rätselcharakter", of artworks –, this process is an infinite process. Wellmer refers to the early romantic conception of art as an infinite medium of reflection ("unendliches Reflexionsmedium"). He further argues that works underlie the 'différance' in terms of Jacques Derrida, that is to say, the meaning of a work is subject to a process of continuous suspension and retention.

It is an important aspect with regard to the topic of performativity that Wellmer's work concept includes the dimension of performativity in several respects. Like Paul Bekker, Wellmer argues that a musical work in an emphatic sense of the word only emerges in a performative situation, although it can never be reduced to its performativity. Furthermore, Wellmer proposes a strongly normative meaning of the work concept, which links the emergence of a work to the success of an aesthetic experience. The musical work has not only to be performed to become a work in the strict sense of the word; it also has to be experienced aesthetically. A successful aesthetic experience is itself at least partially performative, although it is no performance itself as it is not public but rather the individual experience of a subject. Yet the aesthetic experience is characterized by a 'performative attitude' ("die performative Einstellung der ästhetischen Erfahrung"; ibid.: 125), which means that the aesthetic experience is engaged in the production of something that is more than a mere emotional reaction of the subject. Thus, according to Wellmer, the work has its place somewhere between subject and object, between performance, aesthetic experience and the historical matter which is reflected both in the performance and the aesthetic experience. The object status of the work is the point to which we refer in the discourse about the work – a point which cannot be claimed by only one of the sides, by one of the different elements and processes that are engaged in the emergence of the work. The gist of Wellmer's argument is that this point, to which we refer in the discourse, does not only exist in the performance and the experience of traditional works; it also exists in the experience of performances in terms of performance art:

> Yet it is justified to talk of 'works' also with regard to forms of art which, in the narrower sense, have an event character. If one takes the concept of art to be what I have just explained, art becomes a form of being, 'made' with aesthetic claims, that is capable of becoming the object of a successful aesthetic experience; in this situation the 'object character' of a work is not tied to a specific degree of permanence but shows itself in the fact that it – i. e., the work – is located in a public space *between* subjects who have an aesthetic experience and is an 'object' to which these subjects refer in their discourse and to which they can come back, as it were.[1]

Unlike Fischer-Lichte, for whom performativity makes the traditional boundaries between subject and object, between the aesthetics of work production and of reception, dispensable, Wellmer adheres to the conception that an aesthetic experience is always bound to an object of experience. A complete immersion in the event, dissolving the distinction between production and experience, between subject and object, would be a completely different experience, perhaps something like a Dionysian trance in Nietzsche's terms, but not an aesthetic experience, which always implies a certain distance to its object, allowing it to become an object of reflection and an object of aesthetic discourse. (Even Fischer-Lichte is engaged in nothing else when, in

---

[1] "Jedoch kann man auch mit Bezug auf die im engeren Sinne ereignishaften Formen der Kunst von 'Werken' sprechen. Wenn man den Begriff des Kunstwerks so versteht, wie ich ihn gerade erläutert habe, dann ist das Kunstwerk dasjenige mit ästhetischem Anspruch 'gemachte' Seiende, das Gegenstand einer gelingenden ästhetischen Erfahrung zu werden vermag; wobei die 'Objekthaftigkeit' eines Werks nicht an einen bestimmten Grad von Permanenz gebunden ist, sondern sich darin zeigt, daß es – das Werk – in einem öffentlichen Raum *zwischen* ästhetisch erfahrenden Subjekten lokalisiert ist, ein 'Objekt', worauf sich diese Subjekte im Diskurs beziehen und gleichsam zurückkommen können." (Wellmer 2009: 134; my translation)

her *Ästhetik des Performativen*, she writes long hermeneutic interpretations of various performances.)

4. Consequences

To sum up what has been said: Wellmer's work concept is an attempt to open up the concept for a dimension, namely that of performativity, which has been essential for the contemporary arts since the 1960s and which seems to be incompatible with the traditional work concept. However, Wellmer's extension of the traditional work concept tries to maintain elements which on the other hand seem to be incompatible with an aesthetic of performativity in terms of Fischer-Lichte, e. g., the object status, the aesthetic value and the repeatability of a work (i. e., the possibility of going back to it as an object in the aesthetic discourse), the distinction of work and performance, and not least the historicity of works.

Wellmer's work concept may be less attractive for a discussion of performance art, but – as I understand it – it can be highly attractive for the historiography and the analysis of music that belongs to the era of the work paradigm, i. e., art music at the latest from the eighteenth century onward. To conclude, I will try to outline some of the methodological consequences and perspectives which an extended work concept according to Wellmer can open up.

1. To me, a first aspect of interest is the perspective which an extended work concept opens up for the analysis of sound, expression, and the physicality of music. These aspects can now be considered not as something outside the work proper, as in some way related to the structure of the work, or as in some way performing its structure. They can rather be considered as an essential part of the musical form and thus be included in the analysis of the work. Instead of the traditional descriptive distinction between pitch and duration as the 'workly' aspects of music, and tone colour and expression as aspects which belong to the performance, there would be the normative distinction between a successful or adequate realisation of a rhythm, motive, or orchestral timbre, and an unsuccessful or inadequate realisation of these elements, a failed realisation which disturbs the aesthetic experience. To be sure: to make such a distinction is not easy and requires, amongst others, a critical close reading of the piece. Such

a close reading is possible in two directions: starting from the score and explaining how the piece should be performed, how it should sound, how it should be shaped in time; or starting with a given performance and explaining why its musical form allows for a successful aesthetic experience, or why it does not. It would be even more difficult to historicize the performative shape of a work, i. e., not to judge from a present-day and – at least partially – subjective point of view, but to reconstruct the norms and values which shaped a work in a given historical performance. Since the meaning of a work – as we have seen – is neither fixed in the text of the score nor in period documents, which represent the (supposed) intentions of the composer, but is historically changeable, the task would be to recover the norms and values of the period to which the given performance belongs. Thus, historical analysis in a strict sense would require the contextualization of the performed work in terms of a history of listening and a history of performing.

2. The second aspect which I think is of interest is the perspective which an extended work concept opens up for the historiography of music. A fusion of work analysis and performance history, or performance analysis and work history, could lead to a historiographical model placed in between the traditional approaches of work history and reception history. If the term work history stands for a history of historic events, for example, the year 1803 as the year of Beethoven's *Eroica* or 1859 as the year of Wagner's *Tristan und Isolde*, and if reception history is understood as transferring the meaning implied in a work from the date of its composition to the date of its reception, thereby leaving the information and the form of the work basically unchanged, a history based on an extended work concept would accommodate the fact that not only the circumstances of reception are subject to historical change but also the object which is being received. The reception of Beethoven in the 1940s – for example the compositional reception of Beethoven by Béla Bartók – is never directly the reception of pieces which are historically located at the time around 1800, but of a historical process in which not only its object changes but in which levels of meaning are added, possibly unknown at the time of the composition of the pieces. Above all, the reception of a musical work is always mediated through performances as the actual generators of musical form, whether live performances or recordings. Writing the history of a work would thus mean to trace the historical

process in which the work unfolds and thereby changes its content. Again, this would require an extension of the traditional historiographical methodology by elements of a history of performance and a history of listening.
3. A third and last aspect is closely related to what has already been said: if every experience and every reception of a work depends on actual performances, the work of the musicologist highly depends on the performativity of music. Hans Joachim Hinrichsen has pointed to this very influential but little reflected fact, showing, e. g., how the musicological image of Bach in the late nineteenth century or Thrasybulos Georgiades's interpretation of Schubert's music are to a certain degree mirrors of contemporary performance practice rather than accounts of Bach's or Schubert's music 'by itself' (see Hinrichsen 2000). This insight could be used for a self-reflection of the discipline, either in terms of a critical history of the discipline (including its performative background) or in terms of a general reflection on the performative a priori of musicological practice. However, the insight that every interpretative or analytical engagement with a musical work is highly dependent on actual performances – perhaps one's own performances – should not preclude one from this engagement for the reason that such a dependency would contaminate the historical objectivity one feels committed to as a music historian. A mere positivistic approach to music, abstaining from any critical and subjective engagement, may result in a higher level of objectivity, however, at the expense of all the elements which make the historiography of music also an aesthetically relevant affair. To abstain from one's own aesthetic experience and its implied performative attitude would mean to reduce the musical work in its textual and performative dimensions to the status of mere documents. Paradoxically, the consequence would be a music history in which the aesthetic phenomenon for which the term 'work' stands has no longer a place.

References

Adorno, Theodor W. (1970/2004). *Aesthetic Theory*. Trans. Robert Hullot-Kentor. London: Continuum. (German orig.: *Ästhetische Theorie*. Frankfurt am Main: Suhrkamp).

— (2001). *Zu einer Theorie der musikalischen Reproduktion: Aufzeichnungen, ein Entwurf und zwei Schemata.* Ed. Henri Lonitz. Frankfurt am Main: Suhrkamp.

Bekker, Paul (1916). *Das deutsche Musikleben*, Berlin: Schuster & Loeffler.

Fischer-Lichte, Erika (2004). *Ästhetik des Performativen.* Frankfurt am Main: Suhrkamp.

Gottschewski, Hermann (1996). *Die Interpretation als Kunstwerk: Musikalische Zeitgestaltung und ihre Analyse am Beispiel von Welte-Mignon-Klavieraufnahmen aus dem Jahre 1905.* Laaber: Laaber-Verlag.

Hinrichsen, Hans Joachim (2000). "Musikwissenschaft: Musik – Interpretation – Wissenschaft". *Archiv für Musikwissenschaft* 57: 78–90.

Lehmann, Hans-Thies (1999). *Postdramatisches Theater.* Frankfurt am Main: Verlag der Autoren.

Schubert, Giselher (1970). "Aspekte der Bekkerschen Musiksoziologie". *International Review of the Aesthetics and Sociology of Music (IRASM)* 1: 179–186.

Wellmer, Albrecht (2009). *Versuch über Musik und Sprache.* Munich: Hanser.

Text vs. Act
The *Bearbeitungsfrage* and the 'Romantic Baroque'

David Francis Urrows, Hong Kong

When the Bach-Gesellschaft was founded in 1850, could its organizers have known that their 'objective' actions and intents would not be taken kindly by much of subjectively-minded musical Europe? Within the decade, a polemical public debate about the *Bearbeitungsfrage* (issue of arrangements and transcriptions) arose around the very nature and goals of the emerging discipline of musicology. Early editors such as Phillip Spitta and Friedrich Chrysander often found critical support for their work in progressive figures such as Joachim, Brahms, and Eduard Hanslick. The opposition was led by the composer Robert Franz, and supported by (among others) Franz Liszt. They derided the 'most recent alliance' of Spitta and Chrysander, characterizing them as mere 'archeologists', musical incompetents who were vandalizing great art and producing useless, unperformable editions. In the period 1860 to 1890, Franz's 'artistic' school (which included his acolytes, Julius Schaeffer, Albert Hahn, and Otto Dresel) published rival editions of Baroque works with full scores, vocal scores, and instrumental parts, some of which were still in print well into the 20th century. By the end of the 19th century, the debate had died down, along with its principal authors. But the issues raised remained, as the tensions surrounding performances in the past fifty years by Glenn Gould and Angela Hewitt may remind us.

1.

Those familiar with musicological literature over the past twenty years will recognize at once that the title of my article is adapted from Richard Taruskin's 1995 collection of essays, *Text and Act: Essays on Music and Performance*. I might state at the outset that I do not agree with everything Professor Taruskin has ever said or written, nor do I share all of his views on music history, composition, or aesthetics. However, his ideas about performance and the nature of performance are close to mine. I identify in him at least a kindred spirit, if not quite a brother-in-arms. In basing the title of my short inquiry into the old and largely forgotten debate about the *Bearbeitungsfrage* on his provocative book, I hope it will not be felt that I am trivializing his closely-argued thesis[1].

Taruskin's ideas on performance and performance practice cannot, in fact, be briefly summarized. There is a danger in attempting such a summary. Taruskin's essays and other writings cover a very wide range of topics and employ a wide variety of approaches. In a summary, important ideas, nuances, and details are apt to get lost. The intellectual content of his strongly-argued positions is at risk of being diluted to the point of ineffectiveness. Nevertheless I have to assume that, nearly two decades on, Taruskin's position is by now well-enough known. His writings are accessible to anyone, especially those outside the discipline of musicology who want to know more.

If I am reading him correctly, then, in the essays collected in *Text and Act*, Taruskin fundamentally attacks the cherished concept of so-called 'authenticity' in music and performance practice. This authenticity, whether it refers to performances of music of the Baroque and earlier eras, or in fact any historical period, is for Taruskin nothing more than a catch-all term by which mere taste in performance style has been mistaken for some sort of objective truth. In the hands of academics – in collusion with recording companies dependent upon a star system – the concept of 'authentic performance practice' has grown since 1950 uncritically into a "hegemonic discourse" through which is embodied "a whole wish-list of modern(ist) values, validated in the academy and the marketplace alike by an eclectic, opportunistic reading of historical evidence" (Taruskin 1995: 5). Taruskin maintains that what we have called 'authenticity' is fundamentally a modernist, positivist obsession: the idea that "restoration – 're-imagining' something old – is ideally a better accomplishment than participating in the creation of something new" (ibid.: 9).

Taruskin traces the 'authenticity' movement back to the beginning of the 20th century, and to the figure of Arnold Dolmetsch (1858–

---

[1] Taruskin even appears to deny that the inquiry I am conducting here has much value when he writes that "[b]ecause the current practice of 'authenticity' entails so many anachronisms, a mere account of its origins (in romanticism, in *Werktreue*) can neither explain it nor even adequately characterize it", and claims further that there is "an incompleteness of an account of 'the ideology of authenticity' that focuses on its nineteenth-century manifestations" (1995: 16). My goal, however, is somewhat different and I make no claims to completeness. I also dispute the idea that this "mere account" does not go some way towards explaining how we got to where we are today.

1940). Dolmetsch, in Taruskin's words, "bequeathed a mythology to which many still unreflectingly subscribe" (ibid.: 145), a mythology "that cast a hated 'present' that even by the time of its casting was receding into the past, against a 'past' that was actually a constructed dogmatic fiction, created in the present" (ibid.). An isolated figure, "Dolmetsch and the musicians of his age stood as it were back to back; and as his life went on he adopted more and more the embattled and bitter tone of a voice crying in the wilderness – a tone that has remained characteristic of many of his heirs" (ibid.: 144). Before Dolmetsch, Taruskin refers vaguely to an 'antiquarian' period in musicology, and he appears to have had little interest in the origins of authenticity in the 19th century *per se*. Nevertheless, this is where the ideological debate over text and act began, in the formative decades of the discipline of musicology.

In the 1990s, Taruskin's campaign (if I may so characterize it) received a boost from the writings of Lydia Goehr, professor of philosophy and aesthetic theory at Columbia University[2]. Goehr's 1992 book, *The Imaginary Museum of Musical Works*, dealt with the regulative concept of 'works of music' which, she proposes, came into being only around 1800. She identifies Beethoven's Symphony No. 5 in C minor as one of the first 'works', in the sense of a reified *Werk* of which the composer was conscious while composing it; and which was so recognized by his contemporaries, and subsequently by posterity as such. Prior to this, asserts Goehr, composers composed – that is, they composed *music* – but did not really think of this as the production of autonomous 'works' – it was just *das Solo, die Musik, das musikalische Stück*, depending on how much of it was being referred to, or played. The ontological identification of specific 'works' led to a canon of a special class of such works – timeless works, masterworks – and the emerging concept of *Werktreue* – 'fidelity to the work' – which characterized both the increasingly sacramental tone taken in consideration of such works, as well as to the conducting approaches of such unlikely partners as Mendelssohn and Wagner. This reflected a major shift in relationships and paradigms. "The only duty of liberated composers", writes Goehr,

---

[2] It may or may not be deemed relevant to know that her father is the composer Alexander Goehr (b. 1932) and her grandfather the composer Walter Goehr (1903–1960).

was to make it possible for performers to fulfill their role; they had a responsibility to make their works performable, and they did this by providing complete scores [in the sense of giving every possible notational direction for a complete performance]. This duty corresponded to the need [...] for reconciliation of the abstract (the works) with the concrete (the performances). The comparable duty of performers was to show allegiance to the works of the composers [...]. Thus, the effective synonymity in the musical world of *Werktreue* and *Texttreue*; to be true to a work is to be true to the score. (1992/2007: 231)

Taruskin, commenting on Goehr's writing, similarly observes that this

Romantic notion of the autonomous, transcendent artwork [also] entailed a hierarchized, strictly enforced split between emancipated creators [the composers], beholden (in theory) to no one but the muse, and selfless curators [editors, publishers, and performers] sworn to submission. The producers of timeless works are the gods, exulting in their liberation from the world of social ("extramusical") obligation and issuing peremptory commands. The recipients of the commands are the Nibelungs, bound scrupulously to carry out the master's intentions for the sake of their glory, their own lives pledged to a sterile humdrum of preservation and handing-on. (1995: 10)

Thus, on the one hand Goehr's conceptualization brings us to a mid-19th-century point where we have 'works' and a kind of moral imperative to be faithful to the composer's (apparent) intentions and, above all, to the letter rather than the spirit, as well as to revere the text of the sacralized work; while on the other hand Taruskin's thesis takes for its start a *fin-de-siècle* point at which a mythologized past became tyrant over any interpretive present. What happened in the – let us say – fifty years between these two points? That is precisely what has arrested my attention: I propose here to at least begin to show how this lacuna has resulted from a failure (perhaps it is more of an omission) to consider one of the great musicological debates of the later Romantic era, the *Bearbeitungsfrage*, which is too late chronologically for Goehr, and seemingly not relevant in and of itself for Taruskin, given his meta-view of the authenticity debate.

2.

Most debates of a scholarly sort grow gradually, and out of a kind of friction between amorphous bodies. But in the quite exceptional case of the *Bearbeitungsfrage,* we can pinpoint exactly when this began. It began on the 15th of December, 1850. The year 1850 marked the 100th anniversary of the death of J. S. Bach; and the 15th of December was the date of the founding of the Bach-Gesellschaft in Leipzig. The goal of the Bach-Gesellschaft – whose membership included the cantor of St Thomas' Church, Moritz Hauptmann (1792–1868), Otto Jahn (1813–1869), C. F. Becker (1804–1877), and Robert Schumann (1810–1856), later joined by Ignaz Moscheles (1794–1870), Julius Rietz (1812–1877), Phillip Spitta (1841–1894), and Wilhelm Rust (1822–1892) – was to publish within fifty years of the date of founding all the known works of Bach in a critical edition[3]. This critical edition was to be free from editorial accretions; it was to give information as to the sources of the music, and criticism of those sources, as well as studies of the handwriting in the manuscripts chosen. In a word, it was to be 'scientific'. For this reason, the term for the new discipline which grew up with the early critical editions was *Musikwissenschaft*.

The Bach-Gesellschaft scores were to differ from the sorts of editions available in the mid-19th century, which were to a greater or lesser extent *interpretive* editions. In these interpretive editions, editors freely chose their sources and imposed their own views on both the text and upon performance directions. These matters included the actual pitches, which could be changed at will, if the editor simply thought a mistake had been transmitted (consulting sources was deemed irrelevant). The Lied composer Robert Franz (1815–1892), speaking in 1881 of his forthcoming edition of Handel's *Messiah* (for which his colleague, the German-American composer Otto Dresel [1826–1890], provided the piano arrangement), told his friend, Wilhelm Waldmann:

> Ich bin erstaunt gewesen, welche Fehler sich in den vorliegenden Ausgaben finden, die gröbsten Schulschnitzer, – neun Arien habe ich bereits ändern müssen; alle Welt hat das so ohne weitere Gedanken hingenommen und ich selbst habe ja früher nach diesen Ausgaben drei bis viermal den „Messias" aufgeführt.[4] (Waldmann 1894: 66)

---

[3] There had been earlier, but unfinished attempts at a complete edition by Hoffmeister und Kühnel (1801–1804) and C. F. Peters (1837–1865) (see Lehman 2004).

[4] 'I was astounded at how many errors are in the previous editions, the clumsiest mistakes of beginners – I've already had to change things in nine of the arias; everyone has just accepted them without any further thought, and I myself have performed *Messiah* three or four times from these editions.' (This, and all subsequent translations, are my own.) The Franz-Dresel edition of *Messiah* was published in Leipzig by Kistner in 1885.

Moreover, the addition of fingerings, ornaments, dynamics, articulations, and other expressive indications were part and parcel of the interpretive editor's task. In the case of music prior to the 19th century, the interpretive edition also had to deal with the following issues: continuo accompaniment, obsolete instruments, and non-standard notational practices.

The Bach-Gesellschaft, under the direction of Hauptmann, Spitta, and later Rust, decided to cut the Gordian knot involved in making such decisions, and publish scores as they appeared in Bach's manuscript, if available, or as they had been transmitted as far as the mid-19th century. Manuscripts were compared, where possible, and deviations and differing readings noted. Beyond just publishing the works of Bach, the agenda of the Gesellschaft was to use this new critical edition – that is to say, to use the *text* – to elevate the 'science' of musicology to something on par with literary and fine art studies. To do this, they sought to make the texts of the works alone the reification of the work, a literature of music. In a sense, pieces of music which the composers had not necessarily thought of as 'works', to follow Goehr's argument, were now being retroactively reified under the influence of the *Werkprinzip* (work concept).

To this end, the scores of the Bach-Gesellschaft were printed in as biblical or sacramental a format as their academic aims allowed for. Fraktur title pages evoked the visual-emotional impact of old liturgical manuscripts and books; while extremely large and unwieldy quarto volumes, usually bound expensively in leather, were useless for anything but library study. They were truly to be monuments – *Denkmäler* – to genius, a sacramental offering given by these musical-museum curators with the level of care usually bestowed upon the Holy Scriptures.

However, such an attitude did not sit well with many of the members of the original Gesellschaft. Monuments are there to be revered, not to be made use of. Divisions based on opposing opinions appeared almost immediately within the group. One of the chief complaints concerned the extent to which the edition would cater for practical music-making. And this is where the *Bearbeitungsfrage*, not unexpectedly, emerged: a decision was taken not to issue performance materials – vocal scores, choral scores, instrumental parts –, and as a result several members, including Schumann and Moscheles, resigned in protest. Here we see the beginning of a struggle of text vs. act: even as the first volume, edited by Hauptmann and containing Cantatas 1 to

10, was published in December 1851, the whole enterprise was close to falling apart.

This polarization hardened over the next twenty years into two competing camps: on one side the Gesellschaft, funded by the Prussian Ministry of Culture (of which Spitta was a Secretary), his erstwhile nemesis, Friedrich Chrysander (1826–1901, who began the Handel *Gesamtausgabe* in 1856 at his own expense) and supported by progressive figures such as the violinist-composer Joseph Joachim (1831–1907), Brahms, and Josef Rheinberger (1839–1901), as well as critics in Berlin and Vienna and the publishing house of Breitkopf und Härtel; and on the other side a disenfranchised group of idealists who derided the Gesellschaft for losing the works themselves in the texts. Subsequently, the Gesellschaft and its followers were characterized derisively as the "archeological" school, who "seem[ed] to delight to dig in the entrails of the deadest of the dead to find some questionable jewels", as Otto Dresel later archly remarked in a letter to John Sullivan Dwight (1868). It was also darkly rumored that the Gesellschaft was nothing of the kind: it was just a front for a publishing venture of Breitkopf und Härtel, whose large financial risk had been assumed by gullible subscribers.

The position of the Bach-Gesellschaft need not be recounted here in detail. After all, it eventually led to present-day musicology and by the widespread acceptance of its theoretical positions, attitudes, and by sheer tenacity, won out over the 'artistic' school, although, as we have already seen, the issues which formed the basis of the debate continue to be raised, in different and newer contexts, by scholars such as Taruskin and Goehr. As early as 1879, a popular writer on musical topics, Wilhelm Riehl (1823–1897), commented on its rising hegemony with some bemusement when he made the following observation about the period between the second and fourth editions of his *Musikalische Charakterköpfe*:

> Seit den fünfzehn Jahren [...] ist unsere Musikgeschichte gelehrt geworden, ja noch mehr, sie wurde teilweise sogar wissenschaftlich, und man schreibt jetzt die Biographie eines alten Musikanten nach derselben Methode der Quellenforschung, wie das Leben eines Königs und Kaisers, und edirt Bach's Werke nach denselben Regeln der philologisch-diplomatischen Kritik, wie den Cicero oder Thukydides.[5] (1857/1879: vii)

---

[5] 'In the past fifteen years, music history has become a learned field, and what's more, it has become in large part scientific, and one now writes the biography of an

On the other side, Moscheles and his supporters, who included Franz Liszt[6] and Robert Franz, sought to distance themselves as far as possible from the erroneous path of the Gesellschaft, and identified themselves as the 'artistic' school, that is, the school where art (subjective, emotive reasoning) was not eliminated in exclusive favour of an objective, positivist, and 'scientific' text-based approach[7]. They found their saviour in the figure of Robert Franz, who during the last forty years of his life was the centre of the *Bearbeitungsfrage*, which became a running controversy over the Bach-Gesellschaft and other ventures, such as the critical editions of Handel and Palestrina, and the many *Denkmäler*, which followed in the next decades[8]. Franz dedicated himself to single-handedly crafting a library of competing editions which contained what the 'artistic' school felt made the music of the

---

old composer with the same approach to sources and research as the lives of kings and emperors, and one edits Bach's music with the same rules of diplomatic philology as you would with Cicero or Thucydides.' In mentioning 'fifteen years', Riehl is here referring (in the Preface to the fourth edition of his book) to the second edition of 1862. My thanks go to my colleague, Sanna Pederson, of the University of Oklahoma, for bringing this interesting appraisal to my attention.

[6]   Liszt's aesthetic opposition to the enterprise did not stop him from being an original subscriber to the Bach-Gesellschaft edition. Goehr identifies him as a major figure in the establishment of the *Werkprinzip* (cf. 1992/2007: 205f.). This is nonetheless a fraught contention. While he certainly contributed to the building of the musical 'museum' of great works, he would have been a very idiosyncratic 'curator', given his attitudes towards *Werktreue* as evinced in his hundreds of transcriptions of other composers' works. For more on this topic, see my article on Liszt (Urrows 2008), as well as Pedroza (2010).

[7]   That this purported objective/subjective opposition is still with us can be seen in some of the reactions to Taruskin's writings. Quoting an editorial written by Roland Jackson ("Performance Practice and Its Critics – The Debate Goes On", see 1991), Taruskin notes that Jackson "opposes 'the search for objective reality' to my 'subjectivism'". But Taruskin goes on to point out that "he [Jackson] might seem to be committing the ancient error Adorno debunked so long ago in his dear old screed against dogmatic performance practitioners of yore: 'Objectivity,' he scolded, 'is not left over after the subject is extracted.'" (1995: 37)

[8]   Other important critical editions which followed the Bach-Gesellschaft, included: Handel (1856), Palestrina (1862), Beethoven (1862), Mendelssohn (1874), Mozart (1877), Chopin (1878), Schumann (1880), Schubert (1884), Schütz (1885), *Denkmäler deutscher Tonkunst* (1892), *Denkmäler der Tonkunst in Österreich* (1894), Lassus (1894), Berlioz (1899), Schein (1901), and Victoria (1902). The preponderance of near-contemporary figures of the 19th century is nonetheless telling.

Baroque accessible, both in a practical and an emotional sense, to contemporary performers and listeners. His work, and his writings on the subject, attracted many like-minded musicians for whom only in this mediation of text moving towards performance did the 'work' really reside[9].

The editorial approach of the 'artistic' school included not only the publication of vocal scores and instrumental parts, but was most clearly seen in the handling of continuo realizations. The early Gesellschaft-scores avoided realizing the continuo at all; later series, such as Chrysander's Handel edition, stuck to a bare-bones, simplistic approach (known then as *accords plaqués*), which raised caustic reactions from the 'artistic' school. A single unharmonized note in the bass could stir up a hurricane of invective from Franz's partisans, chief among them Julius Schaeffer (1823–1902) and Albert Hahn (1828–1880):

> Nach dem papstischen Canon der Cardinals-Weisheit Spitta's, des Secretairs der Preußischen Academie, welche ein simples, accordisches Darstellen der vorhandenen Ziffern predigt, würde der beliebige Extemporirer an der Orgel oder am Clavier sofort mit dem *d* hinein zu plumpen haben [...]. Bach dachte allerdings nicht daran, daß einstmalen zwei so gefährliche musikalische Ignoranten wie Spitta und Crysander [sic] es verstehen würden [...].[10] (Hahn 1877: 41)

Then there was the contentious question of 'filling in' the thin Baroque orchestral textures with so-called 'additional accompani-

---

[9] So ignored has the *Bearbeitungsfrage* been in English-speaking countries that the last substantial writings on the topic were published in the late 19th century by William Foster Apthorp (1848–1913), a student of Otto Dresel and a well-regarded music critic in Boston, who was on friendly terms with Robert Franz: "Additional Accompaniments to Bach and Handel's Scores" (1878), and "Two Modern Classicists" (1893). Both of these originally appeared in the magazine, *The Atlantic Monthly*, and were later edited and included in Apthorp's *Musicians and Music-Lovers and Other Essays* (1894). Two more recent and important articles on the topic of Robert Franz and his *Bearbeitungen* are both in German: Sasse (1986) and particularly Gutknecht (1993). These also address many of the issues raised here, and in much greater musicological and theoretical detail, though from a 'pre-Taruskin' point of view.

[10] 'Following the pontifical decrees of that Cardinal of Wisdom, [Phillip] Spitta, the Secretary of the Prussian Academy, who preaches the gospel of a simple, chordal realization of the figured bass, the poor continuo player (improviser) at the organ or clavier would have to make do with just the D as written [...]. In any event, Bach never thought of it that way, as those two dangerous musical ignoramuses Spitta and Chrysander would immediately suggest [...].'

ments', after the precedent of Mozart's 1789 revision of Handel's *Messiah*, and Mendelssohn's 1829 adaptation of the *St. Matthew Passion*[11]. Not surprisingly, the Bach-Gesellschaft camp denounced these practices as 'painting over the Old Masters' ("Überpinseln alter Gemälde" – the phrase was Chrysander's; qtd. Gutknecht 1993: 231[12]). But the additional accompaniments – added parts for wind and brass instruments, as well as a fully realized continuo part, often a *concertante* part for the organ – were necessary in 'artistic'-school *Bearbeitungen* for two reasons.

The first of these reasons was to solve the twin problems of obsolete instrumentation, and to enlarge the tonal mass of the orchestra to balance with the large-scale choruses typical of the 19th century. Franz explained the general purposes and rationale as follows:

> Eine vollständige Aufführung nach der Originalpartitur ist aber unmöglich, weil dieselbe hin und wieder nach dem früheren Gebrauch nur Skizzen gibt, welche erst durch die hinzutretende Orgel volles Leben und volle Entwicklung finden sollten, an anderen Stellen aber nicht mehr gebräuchliche Instrumente aufführt oder der Instrumentalstimme Aufgaben stellt, die heutzutage unlösbar sind.[13] (Franz 1864: 28)
>
> [...] um dem Chore eine feste Haltung zu geben oder einzelne besonders bedeutungsvolle Motive hervorzutreten zu lassen, darauf Stimmen der Originalpartitur zu verdoppeln; an anderen Stellen – besonders in den Arien [...] war der Versuch zu machen, die harmonische Füllung im polyphonen Stile der ganze

---

[11] I briefly raised and discussed some of these issues in my article, "'Life on a higher pedestal'" (Urrows 2003).

[12] Also see Franz's reply in his 1871 'open letter' to Eduard Hanslick: "Es ist keineswegs dasselbe, ein fertiges Gemälde zu überpinseln und die von dem Urheber einer musikalischen Komposition offengelassenen Lücken nach seinen gegebenen Andeutungen auszufüllen." (1871/1910: 55. 'To paint over a finished portrait is in no sense the same thing as filling up the empty spaces in a musical composition, following the indications already given by its creator.')

[13] 'A complete performance from the original score is simply impossible, as, following the norms of earlier practice, here and there the score gives but sketches which can only find their complete expression and development through the organ part, while elsewhere obsolete instruments are required, or pose insoluble problems with regard to orchestration.' 'Sketches' ("Skizzen") must be here understood to mean the standard Baroque two-line score of melody and figured bass, not actual sketches for a composition. In the 19th century these two-line scores seemed to be only the outline, or sketch of a composition, and as such, incomplete. Thus, the imperative for the *Bearbeitungen*.

Komposition, also in frei geführten, das thematische Material aufnehmend Stimmen zu geben.[14] (Ibid.: 29)

The other major goal was to fill what Konrad Sasse identified as 'an emotional void' ("eine emotionale Leere") in music of the Baroque era and earlier, which 'was particularly deeply felt by people of the 19th century'. This emotional void, or gap, arose from the fact that whereas Baroque composers had relied for aesthetic and emotional effect on a modulation and ambitus of register and dynamics, the Romantic era relied on a modulation of instrumental colour and timbre, which was completely lacking in most of these scores. Sasse put forth his views in this way:

> Nachdem die Generalbaßpraxis und die ornamentale Verzierungskunst aufgegeben oder wenigstens stark reduziert worden waren, entstand in der Wirkung der alten Musik eine emotionale Leere, die den Menschen des 19. Jahrhunderts zwar in besonderem Maße auffiel, die jedoch [...] auch im 20. Jahrhundert bemerkt wurde. Um die emotionale Leere auszufüllen, bedürfte es ersatzweise einer Verbreiterung des Klangspektrums, die nun auf anderem Wege eine farbliche Vielfalt bot.[15] (1986: 49)

A look at one of Franz's *Bearbeitungen* will show how he reconciled all this (see *Examples 1* and *2*).

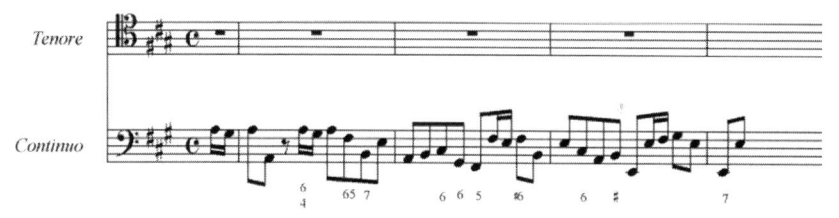

Example 1: J. S. Bach, bars 1–4 of the tenor aria, "Der Glaube ist das Pfand der Liebe", from the Cantata BWV 37: Wer da gläubet und getaufft wird. *From the Bach-Gesellschaft Edition, Vol. 7, ed. Wilhelm Rust (1857).*

---

[14] 'To make the choir parts more secure, or to pick out some noteworthy motive; further, to double parts in the original orchestration; at other points – especially in the arias [...] the intention was to provide a harmonic infilling in the polyphonic style of the whole work using thematic material freely selected from the melodic voices.'

[15] 'As the practice of continuo realization and ornamentation was either given up or at the very least much less widely employed, there came to be an emotional void (perceived) in early music, which was particularly deeply felt by people of the 19th century, and which however [...] was also noticed in the [early] 20th century. In order to fill this emotional void it was necessary to compensate by expanding the tonal spectrum, which now summoned up a variety of colours through a different process.'

Example 2: Robert Franz's Bearbeitung *of bars 1–4 of "Der Glaube ist das Pfand der Liebe", from the Cantata BWV 37:* Wer da gläubet und getaufft wird *(Bach ca. 1867).*

In 1875, the debate was further inflamed when Chrysander and Spitta founded the Leipziger Bach-Verein, which proceeded to publish supra-rival vocal scores and instrumental parts to challenge Franz's rival editions. And so, like an *ourouboros* devouring its own tail the debate seemed as if it would never end. The continuo realizations in the scores edited by the Spitta-Chrysander camp were criticized for musical and aesthetic reasons by Franz and his associates. Voice-leading errors, parallel fifths and so on, were ridiculed in print as 'student errors' ("Schulfehler"[16]). And far from what the 'artistic' school assumed were the rich contrapuntal lines in Bach's own continuo realizations, the thin, *accords-plaqués* realizations in the Leipziger Bach-Verein editions suggested only 'puritanical Quakers dipping their brushes in Chrysander's barrel of whitewash, in order to smear these masterful outlines with just a bit of "organ-tone"'[17].

Somewhere in between these extremes was the critic Eduard Hanslick (1825–1904). In 1869 Hanslick took the point of view of a practicing musician, who, while respecting his academic colleagues, saw the dangers of a 'philological faithfulness to the letter' of the text, through which 'purists' (*Puristen*) and 'artistic zealots' (*Kunstzeloten*) might 'destroy the living organism of music'[18]. It is most interesting to consider Hanslick's emotional-aesthetic reaction to the *Bearbeitungsfrage* in light of his reputation and, above all, his *Vom Musikalisch-Schönen* of 1854. Franz's camp, nevertheless, despised critics such as Hanslick, as well as the influential Berlin critic, Gustav Engel, who sat on the fence in this way. Engel, for example, was no more than

> [...] ein typischer Repräsentant derjenigen Kritiker [...], welche mit dem Strom schwimmen. Sein Herz ist dort, wo das Publikum schwärmt, also vor allen Dingen, z. B. bei Sängerinnen ganz Feuer und Flamme; wo das Publikum sich um nichts kümmert, bei allen ernsten Fragen in Bach'scher Musik, z. B. ist er dagegen vollständig ununterrichtet.[19] (Hahn 1877: iii)

---

[16] In discussing one of the volumes which Chrysander had issued in his Handel edition, Franz groused: "Leider kann der Tonsatz jener 32. Lieferung von dem Vorwurfe, dergleichen nicht zu rechtfertigende Schulfehler in Masse gebracht zu haben, schwerlich freigesprochen werden." (1910: 57. 'Regrettably, the musical composition of this thirty-second volume cannot escape accusations of being loaded with a great number of utterly unjustifiable student errors, which can hardly be excused.') This ("Schulfehler") was a term which he used frequently in his recurring criticism of the early critical editions.

[17] "[...] als puristischer Quäker den Maurerpinsel in Chrysanders Kalkfass getaucht und die herrlichen Skizzen nur mit 'Orgelfarbe' überschmiert hätte" (Hahn 1877: 2).

[18] "[...] die lebendige Wirkung eines musikalischen Kunstwerk aufgrund ihrer 'phlilologischen Buchstabentreue' zerstören würden" (Gutknecht 1993: 231, quoting Hanslick from Chrysander 1869: 387).

[19] 'A typical representative of the sort of critic who goes with the flow. His heart is in whatever the audience is crazy about, especially when they're all worked up over some female singer. In matters that the musical public doesn't care about, for example all the really serious questions about Bach's music, he is in contrast completely uninformed.' Franz's major offensive against Hanslick was the 1871 "Offener Brief

The *Bearbeitungsfrage* also took on moral and religious dimensions. The 'artistic' school understood that a refusal to accept the need for (their) *Bearbeitungen*, that is, to allow Bach's music to be brought again into a performative context by doing (and doing correctly) what they said Bach himself would have done, was the relinquishment of a moral imperative: the musical equivalent of atheism, perhaps even atheism itself. There had to be something atheist, felt Franz, about editions of the most evangelical of musical works – the cantatas and other sacred vocal works of Bach – which discouraged or impaired their performance. Text was in great danger of triumphing over act. The synonymity between *Werktreue* and *Texttreue* was already manifest, only here to be true to the score was to be true to the work. But this was heresy for the 'artistic' school. Albert Hahn, in his polemical 1877 study of Franz's edition of Bach's Cantata 37[20], began with the declaration, "Wir leben in einer Zeit des Unglaubens" – 'we live in an age of unbelief' (1877: i[21]). This unbelief was for Franz's camp a characteristic of the 'most recent alliance' ("jüngste Alliance"; ibid.: iii) of Chrysander, Rust, and Spitta. To them, the 'archeological' school embodied nothing more than a 'false [...] dilettante-ish, [and] school-master-ish doctrine'[22]; they indulged in 'most trivial equivocations' ("allertrivialsten Concessionen"; ibid.: iii) and hid behind a lack of belief, which betokened a lack of artistic conviction. If music had, as Robert Franz believed, been going steadily downhill since Beethoven, then the music of Bach offered a redemptory escape route, which the Bach-Gesellschaft, in his view, was doing everything possible to obstruct.

3.

The adversaries in the *Bearbeitungsfrage* each cast the other in the character of a hated 'present' and sought refuge in their own concep-

---

an Eduard Hanslick", in which he laid out publically and at considerable length his position on the *Bearbeitungsfrage*. Nevertheless, Hanslick maintained cordial relations with Franz throughout his life.

[20] BWV 37, *Wer da gläubet und getaufft wird*.

[21] This sentence is the entire first paragraph of Hahn's pamphlet, printed in type larger than the body of the work.

[22] "[...] falsche [...] dilettantische Schulmeister-Doktrin" (Hahn 1877: 1).

tions of the 'past'. What does the *Bearbeitungsfrage* have to tell us, then, about text vs. act?

First, the fact that Franz misinterpreted Baroque aesthetics and superimposed his own, Romantic, aesthetics on these works, should not be held against him. To make these works performable, he made the right choices for the 19th century, though not for later times[23]. Performativity was very much what these editions were about: and that is probably why they were still in use well into the 20th century, especially in the United States. Apthorp was even urging Franz, shortly before his death in 1892, to provide 'additional accompaniments' for the B Minor Mass, for performance by the Handel and Haydn Society in Boston (cf. 1894/1972: 243f.). (Franz rather wisely declined[24].)

Second, the Bach-Gesellschaft and the Leipziger Bach-Verein were two of the organizations which certainly laid the foundations of modern musicology. But they also brought with them troublesome notions of 'authenticity', *Werktreue*, and *Texttreue*, which resonate, complicate, and perplex to this day. And the 'victory' of the Spitta-Chrysander camp had something of a Pyrrhic quality, at least until the after time of Dolmetsch:

> Zwar hat die 'historisch-philologische' Partei den vermeintlichen Sieg davongetragen, aber ins Konzertleben gewirkt hat sie nach vorliegenden Untersuchungen keineswegs. Im Gegenteil: die Liszt-Wagner Orchesterkultur war wohl vor allem daran schuld, daß nicht nur die altbekannten Bearbeitungen weiterhin und fast ausschließlich musiziert wurden, sondern auch neue Bearbeiter hervortraten.[25] (Gutknecht 1993: 247)

---

[23] For a more general look at the issue of transcription, and for a discussion of Liszt's transcription of Franz's Lieder, see my article "Conscientious Translation: Liszt, Franz, and the Phenomenology of Lied Transcription" (2008).

[24] The Franz arrangements did not really go entirely out of favor until well after World War One. For more on this, see the articles in *Bach Perspectives. Volume Five* (Crist, ed. 2003) by Broyles, Greer, Owen, and especially Dirst, who comments favorably on Franz's "radical but immensely popular solutions to the problem of continuo realization in editions of Bach's sacred vocal works" (2003: 31–33).

[25] 'While it is true that the supposed victory was carried off by the "historical-philological" camp, they in no sense had any real effect on concert life. On the contrary: the orchestral culture of Liszt and Wagner was above all responsible for the fact that not only were these established arrangements continually and almost exclusively performed, but also that new arrangers came to the fore.'

Gutknecht goes on to mention Otto Reubke (1842–1913), Hans Richter (1843–1916), Max Reger (1873–1916), Philipp Wolfrum (1854–1919), and Felix Mottl (1856–1911), as conductors and composers who either continued to use Franz's *Bearbeitungen*, or went a step further and made their own. To this list we could easily add Edward Elgar (1857–1934), Thomas Beecham (1879–1961), Hamilton Hardy (1879–1941), and Leopold Stokowski (1882–1977), all of whom carried the 'artistic' tradition and its aesthetic reality onward into the 20th century, and even into living memory[26].

Finally, when a philologically pure approach to editing became accepted as the norm in the early 20th century, this led to the search for a philologically pure approach to performance, typified in the early 20th century by Dolmetsch. The text having been fetishised, the next logical step was to fetishise instruments themselves, and then the often arcane techniques required to play them, leading to a situation where the only performative value left is what Taruskin identifies as "restoration". And it has been typical of the past century that this "restoration – 're-imagining' something old – is [considered] ideally a better accomplishment than participating in the creation of something new" (Taruskin 1995: 9).

The struggle to keep the act of performance from suffocating under the millstone of text is an old one, as Robert Franz, and later Glenn Gould, and more recently Angela Hewitt have found out, among many others. It is only through a clearer understanding of its origins that we can explain how we got to where we are today.

References

Adorno, Theodor W. (1955/1981). "Bach Defended Against His Devotees". Samuel and Shierry Weber, eds. and trans. *Prisms*. Cambridge, MA: MIT Press. 133–146. (German orig.: *Prismen. Kulturkritik und Gesellschaft*. Berlin/Frankfurt am Main: Suhrkamp).

---

[26] As a 14-year-old music student in 1971, I met Stokowski backstage in the Green Room of Avery Fisher Hall after a performance of *Messiah* (my organ master, Allen Sever, had accompanied the oratorio). I mention this only to show how long this 'tradition' survived, at least in the person of its last major practitioner.

Apthorp, William Foster (1894/1972). *Musicians and Music-Lovers and Other Essays.* New York, NY: Scribner's (Reprint: Freeport, NY: Books for Libraries Press).

Bach, J. S. (1857). *Cantata BWV 37: Wer da gläubet und getaufft wird.* Wilhelm Rust, ed. Leipzig: Breitkopf und Härtel.

— (ca. 1867). *Cantata BWV 37: Wer da gläubet und getaufft wird.* Robert Franz, ed. Leipzig: Leuckart.

Crist, Stephen A., ed. (2003). *Bach Perspectives. Volume Five: Bach in America.* Urbana, IL/Chicago, IL: University of Chicago Press.

Chrysander, Friedrich (1869). "Was Herr Professor Hanslick sich unter 'Kunstzeloten' vorstellt". *Allgemeine musikalische Zeitung* 49: 387–389.

Dirst, Matthew (2003). "Doing Missionary Work: Dwight's Journal of Music and the American Bach Awakening". Crist, ed. 15–35.

Dresel, Otto (1868). Unpublished letter to J. S. Dwight, 3–11 December 1868. Boston Public Library, Department of Rare Books and Manuscripts and Special Collections. Shelf mark ms.C.1.7. no. 31. By permission of the Boston Public Library.

Franz, Robert (1864). "Vorbemerkung zu Joh. Seb. Bach Magnificat (in D-dur) bearbeitet von Robert Franz". Franz (1910). 28–30.

— (1871). "Offener Brief an Eduard Hanslick". Franz (1910). 45–72.

— (1910). *Gesammelte Schriften über die Wiederbelebung Bach'scher und Händel'scher Werke.* Ed. R. Bethge. Leipzig: Leuckart.

Goehr, Lydia (1992/2007). *The Imaginary Museum of Musical Works.* Rev. ed. Oxford: OUP.

Gutknecht, Dieter (1993). "Robert Franz als Bearbeiter der Werke von Bach und Händel und die Praxis seiner Zeit". Musketa/Traxdorf, eds. 219–247.

Hahn, Albert (1877). *Johann Sebastian Bach's Cantate "Wer da gläubet und getaufft wird" bearbeitet von Robert Franz.* Königsberg: Verlag der Expedition der Tonkunst.

Jackson, Roland (1991). "Performance Practice and Its Critics". *Performance Practice Review* 4/2: 113.

Lehman, Karen (2004). *Die Anfänge einer Bach-Gesamtausgabe: Editionen der Klavierwerke durch Hoffmeister und Kühnel (Bureau de Musique) und C. F. Peters in Leipzig 1801–1865. Ein Beitrag zur Wirkungsgeschichte J. S. Bachs.* Leipzig/Hildesheim: Georg Olms Verlag

Musketa, Konstanze, Götz Traxdorf, eds. (1993). *Robert Franz (1815–1892): Bericht über die wissenschaftliche Konferenz an-*

läßlich seines 100. Todestages am 23. und 24. Oktober 1992 in Halle (Saale). Halle: Händel-Haus.

Pedroza, Ludim R. (2010). "Music as *Communitas*: Franz Liszt, Clara Schumann, and the Musical Work". *Journal of Musicological Research* 29/4: 295–321.

Riehl, Wilhelm (1857/1879). *Musikalische Charakterköpfe: Ein kunstgeschichtliches Skizzenbuch*. 4th ed. Stuttgart: Cotta.

Sasse, Konrad (1986). *Beiträge zur Forschung über Leben und Werk von Robert Franz 1815–1892*. Halle: Händel-Haus.

Taruskin, Richard (1995). *Text and Act: Essays on Music and Performance*. Oxford: OUP.

Urrows, David Francis (2003). "'Life on a higher pedestal': Otto Dresel's Bach Club (1883–1890)". *American Choral Review* 45/1: 1–4.

— (2008). "Conscientious Translation: Liszt, Franz, and the Phenomenology of Lied Transcription". D. F. Urrows, ed. *Essays on Word/Music Adaptation and on Surveying the Field*. Word and Music Studies 9. Amsterdam/New York, NY: Rodopi. 135–160.

Waldmann, Wilhelm (1894). *Robert Franz: Gespräche aus zehn Jahren*. Leipzig: Breitkopf und Härtel.

The Act of Performance as Mahlerian Topic

Robert Samuels, Oxford

Although Mahler never wrote an opera, his experience as an opera director informs his use of performance as a 'topic' of his musical discourse.

Mahler's use of theatrical effects is the first method of foregrounding performance as an act. Examples are found in the First Symphony (the introduction) and the Second Symphony (the use of offstage instruments).

The physicality of performance is deliberately exposed by Mahler's choices in instrumentation and the demands he makes of the players. The use of the 'hammer' in the percussion section of the Finale of the Sixth Symphony shows physicality exploited in a violent gesture.

Performance can also be represented by the music. Examples are found in the Fifth and Sixth Symphonies. In the song "In diesem Wetter", Mahler represents the human voice through his use of the singer's voice.

This leads to the subject of the incorporation of song within Mahler's symphonies, which ranges from the incorporation of voices to the quotation of Mahler's own or other songs, to more elusive and general references to song.

In conclusion, performance as a topic demonstrates an emergent category of meaning within Mahler's symphonies in the moment that they are themselves performed.

Introduction

Gustav Mahler (1860–1911) was a quintessentially Viennese performing musician. In his ten years as Director of the *Hofoper* (1897–1907) he epitomised the figure of the conductor-composer, a celebrity whose physical appearance was the subject of newspaper cartoons and caricatures (sometimes affectionate, often the indicators of anti-Semitic ridicule), and whose expressive (to many, excessive) style on the podium was as much a part of his persona as the acknowledgement of his musical brilliance. Performance was therefore an act essential to his public image, both in the straightforward sense that his professional life revolved around performances in the Opera House and with the Vienna Philharmonic, and in the sense that his life was represented as itself a kind of performance.

It has often been remarked on as curious that Mahler, for all his fame as an opera director, never attempted to compose an opera himself, after a few aborted projects of his student days. His compositional output, almost entirely consisting of songs and symphonies, is however a constant engagement with two aesthetic concerns which are as it were in dialogue with the director of opera. First there is the late-nineteenth-century romantic's desire for expressivity, transferred (or perhaps transposed) from the expressive articulation of the characters on the operatic stage to the compositional persona that expresses itself within the symphonic discourse. Second there is a constant foregrounding of performance as an act. These two poles can be seen as a 'constellation', to use a term of Theodor Adorno's, in constant dialectic with each other.

This essay seeks to investigate some of the ways that the act of performance becomes a 'topic' within Mahler's music, principally in the orchestral symphonies. I am using 'topic' here as a semiotic term, one which has become widespread in critical writing since its use by Kofi Agawu in his influential *Playing with Signs: A Semiotic Interpretation of Classic Music* of 1991. Agawu glosses topics or *topoi* as "subjects of musical discourse" (ibid.: 17), and although his study is restricted to late-eighteenth-century and early-nineteenth-century examples, he acknowledges that the "extroversive semiosis" which topics unleash is not confined only to this period. Few have doubted that Mahler's music is suffused with extroversive reference, and indeed early critical attacks on him tended to centre on this, for instance the charge of 'banality' which was attached to his frequent stylistic allusions to military or popular music. This supposed banality, which Arnold Schoenberg devoted an entire article to dismissing ("Gustav Mahler"; 1975: 449–471), is part of Mahler's eclecticism, another element in the Adornian 'constellation' mentioned above.

Performance as a topic carries some sense of self-referentiality, since performance is also an act necessary to the realisation of these signifying moments. Mahler the opera director can perhaps be seen in the similarity between representing performance within performed music, and the use of diegetic song in opera (a subject central to another influential 1991 study, Carolyn Abbate's *Unsung Voices*). My aim here is not to repeat the theoretical speculations of my previous contribution to Word and Music Studies, however (see Samuels 2010); rather, I want to explore how Mahler exploits some of the possibilities that performed music offers to foreground the act of performance.

The Theatricality of Performance

One thing that Mahler's career in the opera house gave him was an acute awareness of the extent to which the symphony was a stage spectacle. Its dual nature as a huge public event and as a summit of the 'absolute music' so prized by nineteenth-century aesthetics creates a kind of fissure exploited by Mahler from his first engagement with the genre. His First Symphony effectively poses the question of what a symphony is meant to be: is it absolute music, to be opposed to programmatic or stage works, or is it something similarly dependent on the extra-musical? Is it, perhaps, something more like a novel, as Mahler's elaborately literary programme note for its second performance in 1894 seemed to imply, giving it the title *Titan*, suggesting that it was in some way doing in sound what Jean Paul's novel of that title was doing in prose[1]? The symphony as a public statement, whose theatricality is intrinsic to its capacity to create narrative, was an idea to which Mahler responded throughout his composing career. In the First Symphony, it animates the very opening, as the lengthy introductory section, more than three minutes of 'musical prose' over an unchanging A in the bass, eventually gives way to the first subject, the melody of Mahler's own song "Gieng heut' Morgens über's Feld". Adorno rightly compared this to the raising of the curtain after an overture (cf. 1992: 4f.).

If the opening of the First Symphony foregrounds the musical discourse as drama, the role of the individual players as performers is even more prominent in the Second Symphony, in which Mahler uses instruments placed offstage. Their first entry, early in the huge final movement, shares with the opening of the First Symphony its use of Wagnerian *Naturlaut* effects, sounds which unavoidably suggest programmatic interpretation. Here, the unseen instruments are horns, their connotation being the sylvan world of Oberon or Diana. Mahler's ear for acoustic effect plays with the subtle difference of timbre, yet similarity of dynamic, between horns actually played as loudly as pos-

---

[1] This programme for the First Symphony is reproduced and discussed in Franklin (1997: 88–91).

sible, yet muffled and invisible through their offstage placement, and the oboe and trumpets played as softly as possible onstage, as *Example 1* shows[2].

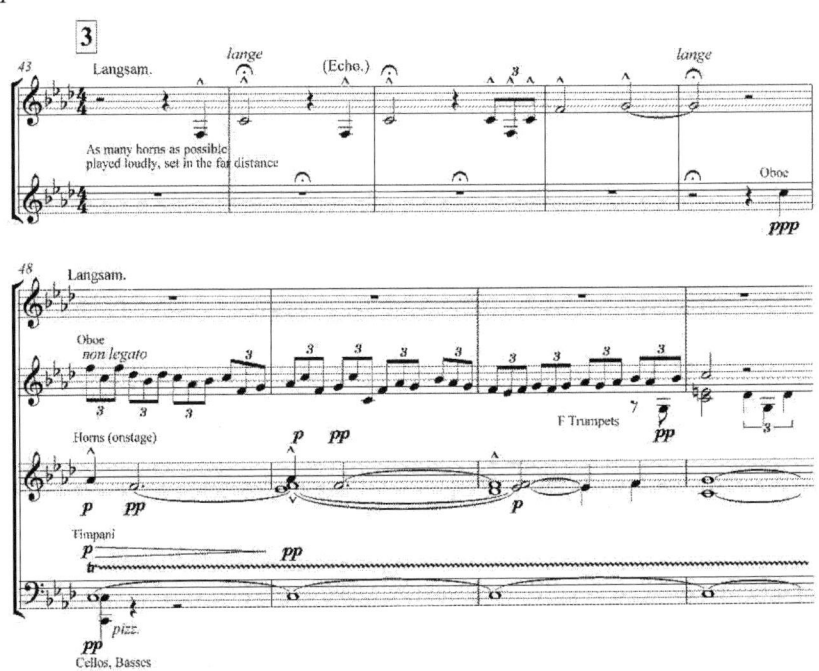

Example 1: Mahler, Symphony No. 2, movement V, reduction of bars 43–51 showing first entry of offstage horns.

The passage is rich with allusive power, but its semiotic possibilities depend on the physical arrangement of the performance space, and the evident bodily effort of the apparently disembodied off-stage players; the sounds alone (for a modern listener, this significantly includes the sounds of a recording or broadcast) cannot convey the meaning painstakingly constructed by Mahler's performance directions. Offstage singers and instruments occasionally feature in opera, such as the offstage ensemble that accompanies Orpheus's first aria, "Chiamo il mio ben", in Gluck's *Orfeo ed Euridice* (1762). For an 1895 performance of Beethoven's Ninth Symphony in Hamburg, before his appointment in Vienna, Mahler contemplated placing wind instru-

---

[2] Mahler's performance direction in the score reads: "Hörner in möglichst großer Anzahl sehr stark geblasen, und in weiter Entfernung aufgestellt".

ments offstage for the "Alla Marcia" episode in the finale. He abandoned this idea, probably anticipating a horrified reaction from critics; when he added instrumental doublings to Beethoven's orchestration for performances of this work in Vienna in 1900, he was obliged to justify this apparent sacrilege on the grounds that he was respecting Beethoven's artistic intent, in an extended programme note (these controversies are recounted in La Grange 1999: 232–237). Both instances confirm his beliefs both in the programmatic or narrative dimension of the symphony, something which Beethoven established perhaps more than any earlier composer, and also in the symphony as a performance occasion requiring and exploiting its theatrical possibilities for dramatic effect.

This concern for the visual effect of the symphonic performance is evident again at what is perhaps the most striking auditory moment of the symphony, the entry of the choir at RH 31, b. 472 in the last movement, with words by Klopstock, "Aufersteh'n, ja aufersteh'n, wirst du, mein Staub, nach kurzer Ruh!" ('Rise again, yes you will rise again, my mortal dust, after brief repose!'). The similarity with the introduction of voices in the final movement of Beethoven's Ninth Symphony has been noted since the work's premiere, and indeed was an anxiety to Mahler as he composed it; as with the earlier work's use of Schiller's "Freude, schöner Götterfunken" ('Joy, bright divine spark'), the choir's aspirational and consolatory words confirm a dramatic and narrative curve already established by musical means. What is noticeable in this context is how carefully again Mahler arranges the theatre of the moment. It is preceded by a much more extended development of the *Naturlaut* music from the first offstage entry given above in *Example 1*, once again involving a dialogue between offstage forces played loudly (not just horns this time, but trumpets and a kettledrum as well) and onstage woodwinds played quietly: a flute and piccolo imitate birdcalls. The choir then enters, marked "Langsam. Misterioso." ('Slow. Mysterious.') at the dynamic level *ppp* and with the second basses required to sing a *ppp* contrabass B flat; Mahler even adds a footnote to the score "für das Studium" ('for purposes of study') to explain why this unbelievably difficult note must not be transposed up an octave to double the first basses as this would destroy the balance of the passage. Mahler was so concerned that the entry of the choir should be nearly imperceptible that he suggested in a letter to Julius Buchs, who was to conduct a performance of the work in 1903, that the choir should stand up well in advance of their entry, to avoid the undesired theatrical effect of their sudden and literal 'rising' just before the enunciation of the word "Aufersteh'n" (Letter of 25 March 1903, printed in Martner 1979: 268–270).

The point I wish to make through these examples is that the physical presence (or absence) of the players is integral to the symphonic drama in this movement. When the offstage players return to the stage to join the rest of the horns (which they do whilst the choir sings the passage just described), they are instructed, with another typically Mahlerian performance direction, to play "mit aufgehobenem Schalltrichter" ('with bells raised'), as much a promotion of their physical as their musical importance. These detailed performance directions, which amount to stage directions, serve to create distance between the performers and the music they perform. Instead of functioning indistinguishably from their instruments, they become visible agents in the narrative being portrayed within the music; a role much closer to that of a singer in an opera than to the conventional assumed invisibility of orchestral players.

The Physicality of Performance

Although the theatricality of performance just exemplified in the case of the Second Symphony demonstrates Mahler's sensitivity to the nature, constraints and possibilities of the performance occasion without which his music could not be heard (at the time of its composition), this is still some way from showing how performance becomes a topic in the Mahlerian symphonic narrative. The use of offstage versus onstage sounds, which incorporates the musicians into the drama of the Second Symphony making them 'players' in the theatrical sense, is one example of an aspect of performance deliberately exploited by Mahler in other ways. This is the nature of performance as a physical act, one that involves effort, risks failure, and depends upon the body. A remark made to Natalie Bauer-Lechner, Mahler's devotee and companion in the years before his marriage, demonstrates this:

> If I want to produce a soft, subdued sound, I don't give it to an instrument which produces it easily, but rather to one which can get it only with effort and under pressure – often only by forcing itself and exceeding its natural range. I often make the basses and bassoon squeak on the highest notes, while my flute huffs and puffs down below. (Bauer-Lechner 1980: 160)

An example of this deliberate foregrounding of the physicality and difficulty of performance is the use of the solo double bass as melody instrument in the slow movement of the First Symphony, where it opens the movement with the folk tune "Bruder Martin". As with the performance direction "mit aufgehobenem Schalltrichter", the seamless identity of player, instrument and music is disrupted by the foregrounding of the physical effort and control required to produce the sound. There are other places where one can detect some version of the "huffing and puffing" of Mahler's comment above; but there are also at least two further ways in which the physicality of performance may enter the symphonic discourse.

The first method employed on occasion by Mahler is to inscribe the physical act within the symphonic narrative. To explain my meaning, one of the best-known and theatrical 'special effects' will serve as an example, the use of the 'hammer' in the finale of the Sixth Symphony. Mahler does not specify exactly what this percussion instrument should be, and the implement used varies according to the conductor's and percussionist's interpretation of his description "Kurzer, mächtig, aber dumpf hallender Schlag von nicht metallischem Charakter" ('Brief, powerful, but non-reverberant blow of a non-metallic sort'). This sounds more like a headsman's axe than anything one might usually call a 'hammer', and that is part of the point. For the first performance (in Essen) Mahler had made a large wooden crate stretched with cowhide, to be struck with a wooden mallet; unfortunately, the effect was comically insufficient in volume, and the enormous instrument remained unused at the back of the stage, the bass drum apparently being used instead[3]. Mahler calls for the 'hammer' to strike just three times in the course of the movement. In her memoir published in 1940, nearly thirty years after Mahler's death, his wife Alma describes the third hammer-stroke as "the death-blow" (Mahler-Werfel 1947/1990: 100), and equates the three hammer-strokes with three disasters in Mahler's life: the death of their daughter Maria, his loss of the post of Opera Director in Vienna, and the diagnosis of the heart condition that eventually led to his terminal illness. These events actually all occurred in 1907, a year after the Symphony's premiere and publication, and three years after its completion; nevertheless, Mahler himself apparently shared some of Alma's superstitious foreboding, since he deleted the third of the

[3] See the description of this instrument in La Grange (1999: 406f.).

hammer-blows from the printed score (it is restored in most modern performances). In some respects, the deletion hardly seems to make any difference to the music of the finale, since this third stroke (at b. 783, seven bars before RH165) can hardly be perceived within the huge volume of sound produced by the full orchestra (including eight muted horns, six muted trumpets, four trombones, tuba, timpani and snare drum) playing *f*, *ff* or (for the strings) *fff*. Indeed, Mahler's deletion may have been in response to Richard Strauss's complaint that Mahler's orchestration made the hammer inaudible. Alma, however, in describing this third hammer-blow as the "death-blow" had perceived something that Strauss missed, namely that the hammer participates in the symphony as part of the work's narrative journey towards catastrophe, but visually and symbolically rather than only acoustically. The audience does not need to hear the axe fall if they can see it being wielded, the violence of the gesture being confirmed by the overwhelming power of the orchestra.

It is worth pausing over the question of what constitutes musical meaning in a gesture of this sort. As a redundant addition to the other percussion sounds at this point, the hammer-blow does not carry 'denotative' meaning in the way that a functional harmonic chord or similar event can be considered as doing. And its near inaudibility renders it devoid of 'connotative' meaning as well (this is the thrust of Strauss's objection to the orchestration). But it is not meaningless – Mahler's superstitious decision to delete it, and subsequent conductors' consistent decisions to reinstate it, more or less confirm the fact. Its force is much more what Roland Barthes described as a 'third meaning' – a semiotic category he invented in his analysis of Sergei Eisenstein's film technique (significantly, of what he termed its "orchestration"), to explain how certain moments (for Barthes) appeal directly to the body for their signifying force ("The Third Meaning"; see Barthes 1977: 52–68).

To return to Mahler's Sixth Symphony: the hammer-blows are far from the only violent gestures in this movement, which is the most unremittingly bleak in the whole of Mahler's oeuvre. The 'third meaning' produced by the physicality of performance more or less emblematises mob violence in another climactic passage (see *Example 2*).

Example 2: Mahler, Symphony No. 6, movement 4, reduction of bars 385–389.

Here the orchestra seems to attack tonality itself in its aggression, amplifying the tritone E / B flat by building a dominant seventh chord on each note of the tritone (resulting in a bitonal six-pitch collection, bars 386f.), and then doing the same with the tritone A / E flat (bars 388f.). Violence has become a topic of the symphonic narrative here, and performance is foregrounded as the condition of its articulation.

Representation of Performance

Theatricality and physicality are two aspects of performance which break down the distinction between the production of the sound and the content of the musical work; both intersect with a third category of possible semiosis, which is the potential of music to *represent* performance. I remarked above regarding the theatre created by the use of offstage instruments in the Second Symphony (see *Example 1*) that the horn of Oberon or the retinue of Diana the divine huntress are part of the rich "allusive power" of these bars. This is, obviously enough, because the unseen horns are a *representation* of the sounds of huntsmen blowing fabulous horns; and this representational role is all the more true because of the theatrical contrivance of the staging and the evident physical effort involved in the production of the literally distant sound.

Diegetic performance, and in particular diegetic song, is another technique familiar in opera (one thinks of Orfeo's song before Proserpina, or the onstage band at Don Giovanni's banquet) but much less exploited by symphonies, especially before the nineteenth century. As Mahler's career progressed, he became more confident in creating moments of diegesis within symphonies, where performance is represented by the music. The offstage instruments in the Second Symphony have the status of a 'special effect'; not so later examples which evoke performance diegetically, and therefore as a topic. One notable instance of this is an episode from the middle of the immense Scherzo movement of the Fifth Symphony (see *Example 3*).

Example 3: Mahler, Symphony No. 5, Scherzo, bars 307–319.

There is a sense in which any scherzo movement carries an overtone of diegetic performance, since its roots in dance forms are more clearly audible than in the other movements of a symphony; this aspect of the genre is exploited by composers (from Berlioz onwards) who convert its speeded-up minuet rhythms into genuine waltzes, often with associations of sexual danger and social impropriety. Here, though, Mahler is inserting a strange kind of waltz into a movement already full of several different waltz types. Constantin Floros detects Austrian, French and Russian waltzes as distinguishable types within this movement, and he is also convinced that these participate in a symphonic narrative:

> All those who view Mahler's symphonies as models of "pure, absolute music" like to refer especially to the Fifth. [...] Whoever adheres to this opinion, however, does not realize the nature of the Fifth, which, like all of Mahler's music, makes a statement – one that is based on an *inner* programme that is kept secret. [...] Regarding the idea for the Scherzo, Mahler advised Bauer-Lechner "It is mankind in the bright light of day, at the zenith of life" [Bauer-Lechner 1980: 173]. Later he also gave this movement features of a dance of death and with that the meaning of *media vita in morte sumus*. (1993: 141f.)

The instrumentation in *Example 3* is reduced to chamber-like sparseness, with pizzicato strings and a solo bassoon (solo oboe and horn join later in the episode); the texture resembles the kind of small group that might be found in a ballroom, and the depiction of performance within the symphonic performance is inescapable: Adorno describes it as "the remembrance of something never heard before [...] the archetype of the shadowy in Mahler" (1992: 103).

Another depiction of performance occurs in the Andante of the next symphony, the Sixth. The passage in question is the varied reprise of the main theme of the Andante immediately after the first episode in an overall slow rondo form[4]. As in the Fifth Symphony, Mahler reduces the orchestral texture to chamber-like forces with just strings and harp accompanying the solo horn, whose line is an amalgamation of the lied-like "zart, aber ausdrucksvoll" ('tender, but expressive') original version of this melody, and the *Naturlaut* allusiveness of the horn (see *Example 4*).

---

[4] I discuss the form of this movement in some detail in Samuels (1995: 20f.).

Example 4: Mahler, Symphony No. 6, Andante, bars 28–32.

Like the previous example, this is a section within a section: the passage given earlier as *Example 3* is described by Floros as a section within the second trio of a scherzo-and-double-trio form (1993: 150f.). It seems that diegetic depiction works best as something reserved for the most interior sections of an overall form.

Example 5: Mahler, Kindertotenlieder, *No. 5, "In diesem Wetter", vocal line at the beginning of first three stanzas.*

Contemporary with the composition of the Fifth and Sixth Symphonies was the creation of Mahler's most intensely subjective song cycle, *Kindertotenlieder* ('Songs on the Death of Children', 1901–1904). Although the performing forces in the song cycle are much smaller than those of the symphony, the melodic and harmonic similarities between them have been often noted (see for instance my previous contribution to this book series, Samuels 2010). Beyond these connections in terms of technique, Mahler creates and exploits in the song cycle an identification of the human voice as a performing instrument and the voice represented in the text, effectively another example of diegetic signification similar to the examples from the symphonies just discussed. The way that vocal expression becomes a topic of the music is seen best in the final song of the cycle, "In diesem Wetter" ('In such a storm'). The first half of this song sets the first three stanzas of Rückert's poem (the second half sets the final stanza), and the development of the poem's text can be traced through the setting of the opening lines of each stanza (see *Example 5*).

The scenario of this poem is that of a bereaved parent inside the family home during a storm (this song contains one of the finest of all musical depictions of a raging storm, one that was for instance clearly influential on Benjamin Britten's *Peter Grimes*). The parents' immediate thought is that they would never have permitted the children out in such weather, and this leads to the realisation of loss in the fact that the children have gone for ever. The first line of each stanza expresses the instinctive anxiety of the parent, and what is of interest from the context of this chapter is how Mahler's setting works to efface the distinction between diegetic representation of the protagonist's state of mind and physical expression of emotion.

The lines from the first stanza are set mostly to a monotone on D: "In diesem Wetter, in diesem Braus, / nie hätt' ich gesendet die Kinder hinaus" ('In this weather, in this storm, / I would never have sent the children out'). The one leap comes at the end, on "hinaus", as the voice jumps a seventh to the upper D. The disposition of the line seems to mime the poetic protagonist's voice, holding it steady despite extreme emotion, until the realisation that the children have gone causes a momentary loss of control. In the second stanza, Mahler advances this index of emotion within the line: the move from D to E (on "nie hätt' ich" in the first stanza) is brought forward to "Wetter". And at the end of the line, significantly on the word "Kinder", the singer's voice breaks out of the octave between d^1 and d^2 for the first time. This process is then intensified in the third stanza: the pitch shape D–E–G (which underlay "nie hätt' ich gesendet" in the first stanza) is used for both "in diesem Wetter" and the next phrase, "in diesem Graus" ('in this horror'), and the leap beyond the bounds of the octave on "Kinder" is more chromatic, spanning a diminished octave from f^1 sharp to f^2 natural.

The cumulative effect of these passages is a depiction of hysteria overtaking initial emotional control. The singer, whose craft is after all to employ extreme control of the human voice in the service of *re-presenting* sometimes dramatic or extreme emotional states, is invited to court actual loss of control in the third stanza as he or she follows Mahler's performance directions, with the sudden crescendos to *ff* followed by the quiet sobbing of the line marked "klagend" ('lamenting'). A performance which accords with the score of this song has to rely on another of Roland Barthes's categories of bodily involvement in the text, that of the 'grain of the voice' (see Barthes's essay of that title, 1977: 179–189). Barthes's 'grain' is not unlike his 'third meaning'; it escapes both denotative and connotative signification, but if it is absent, if the singing voice sounds too 'perfect', too much like an impersonal, machine-like instrument, then the essence of the song is lost.

Songs within Symphonies

The kinship between Mahler's use of instruments in the Fifth and Sixth Symphonies and his use of the human voice in "In diesem Wetter" serves as an introduction of my final category of the transformation of the role of performance in his music from enabling condition to topic of discourse. This is the use that Mahler makes of song as a component of his symphonic world. Some examples have already been discussed above: the use of the melodies of Mahler's own song "Gieng heut' Morgens über's Feld" and the folk song "Bruder Martin" in the First Symphony; the introduction of voices in the Second Symphony, with the illustrious forerunner of Beethoven's Ninth Symphony as a necessary invocation. Because songs have words, and words carry articulate meaning (usually at least), the human voice inescapably brings questions of signification, and usually some suggestion of narrative, into the symphony. The examples just cited show Mahler exploiting this in two different ways, which mark out a spectrum within which there are many possibilities. Klopstock's ode in the Second Symphony is indeed close to Beethoven's use of Schiller, using voices to articulate the previously non-verbal signification of the music, and (both in Beethoven and Mahler) to close the narrative with a moment of utopian transcendence and triumph. The examples from the First Symphony are quite different; although the words of the songs whose melodies are used are not irrelevant, the signifying force is one of representation rather than articulation. What they bring to the symphonic narrative is not the meaning of their words (the knowledge of which is not essential to comprehending their function), but their tone, musical imagery (in the case of "Gieng heut' Morgens") and genre (in the case of "Bruder Martin"). Once again, Mahler is playing with the possibilities offered by multiple potential sources of musical meaning; what in Umberto Eco's semiotic theory (see 1976) are termed multiple 's-codes' affording potential readings to the listener: the code of harmonic and formal syntax and grammar, the code of text-setting in vocal music, the code of representing music through allusion and indirect quotation. As with the examples of representing performance discussed above, Mahler's use of songs as referents within his symphonies became more subtle as time went on, and the later symphonies, in which the manner of reference to song as a topic becomes much more elusive, provide perhaps the most interesting examples of this method of signifying. I have previously commented in detail on the case of the Adagietto movement of the Fifth Symphony (cf. Samuels 2010: 40–44). In this short 'song without words' which serves as an introduction to the Rondo-Finale, Mahler subsumes the sound-world of the *Kindertotenlieder* and *Rückert-Lieder*, and the generic associations of the intimate love-lyric (the movement was composed as a wordless tribute to Mahler's newly-betrothed Alma), into the narrative of the symphony. At this level of semiotic richness, the topic of performance is at its most potent: the symphony quite literally performs the song as a serenade to Alma whilst also narrating it as an episode within a story of more general and universal scope.

Conclusion

Performance as a topic of musical discourse unleashes some of the most complex possibilities of musical meaning-making. To return to the example of the hammer-blows in the finale of the Sixth Symphony, these signify simultaneously at all three levels of the typology of sign types created by the founder of American semiotics, Charles Sanders Peirce, and explored in relation to musical meaning by Naomi Cumming in her ground-breaking *The Sonic Self* (2000). The hammer-blow as a violent physical act signifies via Peirce's category of 'firstness'; this is a level at which what Peirce terms the 'quality' of the sound signifies, without the need for any interpreting convention, and also in a way which draws attention only to itself, rather than pointing towards something else. But the hammer-blow also signifies in other ways: as a part of the narrative curve of the Sixth Symphony, it signifies by pointing to something else (what Alma terms "the death-blow" in describing the third hammer stroke, see above). This is an example of Peirce's 'secondness', in which the hammer plays a particular role in this individual work, as a 'singular sign' or 'sinsign'. Peirce's 'thirdness' refers to signs which he calls 'legisigns' whose signification stems from a set of enabling conventions, in other words signs which require pre-existent knowledge on the part of the listener to understand their meaning. The hammer-blows appear at first not to fall into this category, since they are so unusual an addition to the percussion section of the orchestra. However, Richard Strauss's reported complaint that Mahler fluffed his climactic points does refer exactly to a set of conventions governing symphonic form – in semiotic terms, Alma heard first and foremost a symphonic hero-narrative, and so wanted to affirm the primacy of the hammer as sinsign; whilst Strauss was out of sympathy with Mahler's construction of the overall musical form, and wanted to complain at its articulation as legisign.

The brief sketch of sign function above does not exhaust the ways that the hammer-blows signify within the categories of sign described by Peirce's system. My intention was to gesture towards the complexity of signification involved, and to argue that this is inextricable from the establishment of performance itself as a musical topic. There are dimensions to this complex polysemy, though, that seem to me to go beyond even Peirce's ramified typology. To move away from the specific example of the hammer-blows in the Sixth Symphony, the topic of performance produces meanings that arise out of the combination of these rich, simultaneous fields of potential meaning, but which cannot be reduced to them. This is something discussed by Cumming as "emergent meaning":

> [...] the musically embodied subject can display features that are in some ways at odds with one another, but which together create a newly compound (if unstable) affect. To say that this affect "emerges" in the play of signs is to call upon a term that is part of everyday language, and yet which cannot retain its semblance of ordinariness when placed in a philosophical context. (2000: 240f.)

Cumming's exploration of the nature of the 'musical subject' is one of the great themes of her book. Performance as a topic is one which necessarily foregrounds the nature of the subject embodied within the musical text, and hence problematises the question of subjectivity within the musical work. Meaning emerges from performance as the topic engages the listener on multiple levels simultaneously, refusing to be reduced to any one of them. This emergent meaning escapes from Peirce's threefold typology of sign function, just as the 'third meaning' of moments of Eisenstein's films, or the 'grain' of Charles Panzéra's voice escape from Roland Barthes. But this elusive, emergent and yet potent meaning, the meaning of performance, is what Mahler seeks to enact through the very performance of his works.

References

Abbate, Carolyn (1991). *Unsung Voices: Opera and Musical Narrative in the Nineteenth Century*. Princeton, NJ: Princeton UP.

Adorno, Theodor W. (1992). *Mahler: A Musical Physiognomy*. E. Jephcott, trans. Chicago, IL: University of Chicago Press. (German orig.: *Mahler: Eine musikalische Physiognomie*. Frankfurt am Main: Suhrkamp, 1960).

Agawu, Kofi (1991). *Playing with Signs: A Semiotic Interpretation of Classic Music*. Princeton, NJ: Princeton UP.

Barthes, Roland (1977). *Image – Music – Text*. Stephen Heath, trans. London: Fontana.

Bauer-Lechner, Natalie (1980). *Recollections of Gustav Mahler*. Peter Franklin, ed., Dika Newlin, trans. London: Faber. (German orig.: *Erinnerungen an Gustav Mahler*. Leipzig et al: Tal Verlag, 1923).

Cumming, Naomi (2000). *The Sonic Self: Musical Subjectivity and Signification*. Bloomington, IN: Indiana UP.

Eco, Umberto (1976). *A Theory of Semiotics*. Bloomington, IN: Indiana UP. (Italian orig.: *Trattato di semiotica generale*. Milan: Bompiani, 1975).

Floros, Constantin (1993). *Gustav Mahler: The Symphonies*. Vernon Wicker, trans. Portland: Amadeus Press. (German orig.: *Gustav Mahler III: Die Symphonien*. Wiesbaden: Breitkopf, 1985).

Franklin, Peter (1997). *The Life of Mahler*. Cambridge: CUP.

La Grange, Henry-Louis de (1999). *Gustav Mahler Volume 3. Vienna: Triumph and Disillusion (1904–1907)*. Oxford: OUP.

Mahler-Werfel, Alma (1947/1990). *Gustav Mahler: Memories and Letters*. 4th ed. Donald Mitchell, Knud Martner, eds., Basil Creighton, trans. London: Sphere. (German orig. of the 4th ed.: *Erinnerungen an Gustav Mahler / Gustav Mahler: Briefe an Alma Mahler*. Donald Mitchell, ed. Frankfurt am Main: Ullstein, 1978).

Martner, Knud, ed. (1979). *Selected Letters of Gustav Mahler*. Eithne Wilkins et al., trans. London: Faber.

Samuels, Robert (1995). *Mahler's Sixth Symphony: A Study in Musical Semiotics*. Cambridge: CUP.

— (2010). "Mahler within Mahler: Allusion as Quotation, Self-Reference, and Metareference". *Self-Reference in Literature and Music*. Walter Bernhart, Werner Wolf, eds. Word and Music Studies 11. Amsterdam/New York, NY: Rodopi. 33–50.

Schoenberg, Arnold (1975). *Style and Idea*. Leonard Stein, ed. London: Faber.

Politics, Music and Irony in Alejo Carpentier's Novel *La consagración de la primavera* (*The Rite of Spring*)

Katia Chornik, London

> Political and musical subjects have a prominent presence in the work of Alejo Carpentier (1904–1980), a noted Cuban writer and music critic who coined the concept of 'the real marvellous' ('lo real maravilloso') and exerted a crucial influence on the writers belonging to the so-called Latin American Boom. The present study deals with the performative effects of music upon Carpentier's political fiction and the ways in which music performance is used to convey political ideology. Focusing on the 1978 novel *La consagración de la primavera* (*The Rite of Spring*), in which Stravinsky's *The Rite of Spring* has a central role, this article discusses the ironies that result from a politicised interpretation of the ballet and the ideological contradictions produced by performances of the militant song "L'Internationale".

Following the fiftieth anniversary of the Cuban Revolution in 2009 and the bicentenary of the start of political emancipation of Spanish American countries from Spain in 2010, it seems fitting to examine Alejo Carpentier's recurring use of political revolutions in his novels.

El reino de este mundo (1949, *The Kingdom of this World*) deals with the Haitian Revolution that led to the abolition of slavery and the establishment of the first Latin American free republic at the turn of the nineteenth century. Crucially, ritual chanting incites slaves to begin revolutionary actions against their white masters[1]. *El reino* was a product of Carpentier's trip to Haiti, where he conducted extensive research on Voodoo music. It was in the Prologue to this novella where he first conceptualised the notion of 'the real marvellous' ('lo real maravilloso'), widely acknowledged as the beginning of literary Magical Realism.

El acoso (1956, *The Chase*) deals with the 1930s student-led revolution that overthrew Cuban dictator Gerardo Machado, in which Carpentier personally participated. For the author, that revolt 'was heroism for the sake of heroism, it was outrage, it was rebellion for

---

[1] For a study on Voodoo chants in Carpentier's *El reino de este mundo*, see Birkenmaier (2004).

the sake of rebellion', adding that *El acoso* 'is the story of a wasted effort'[2]. To accompany the useless political sacrifices and anti-heroic story of the main character of this novella, Carpentier uses Beethoven's *Eroica* Symphony, a work that has long been taken as an emblem for the hope of freedom and escape from tyranny. The *Eroica* is significant in terms of the structure of *El acoso* too. Carpentier attempted to parallel the length of the symphony with both the timeframe of the action and the time it takes to read it. He also tried to integrate the model of sonata form, deliberately directing readers to these analogies[3].

In opposition to the portrayal of politics without purpose in *El acoso*, the novel *La consagración de la primavera* (1978, *The Rite of Spring*) presents a triumphant depiction of the Cuban Revolution[4]. Carpentier stated that in this novel, he aimed to 'give expression to *the epos* of a revolutionary epoch in the world, concerning Latin America and my country'[5]. *La consagración* responds to his own call to turn current socio-political events into literary topics, as explained in his essay "Problemática de la actual novela latinoamericana" (1964):

> [W]here there are strata of humanity present, in conflict, ascending or descending, in misery or opulence, in bankruptcy or prosperity, the subject matter becomes epic material for the novelist. [...] Important events are happening [...] and the novelist must place himself in the front row of spectators. [...] There, in the expression of the boiling of that human plasma, lies the authentic epic material for our novelist. Those who could follow the Cuban Revolution closely could well understand that, and in the following years, they began [...] to write novels that prove to be epic.[6]

---

[2] "[...] era el heroísmo por el heroísmo, era la indignación, era la rebelión por la rebelión [...]. [*El acoso*] es la historia de un esfuerzo inútil" (Carpentier 1963/1985: 92).

[3] For a study of Carpentier's analogies with musical form and musical time, see Chornik (2007).

[4] *La consagración de la primavera* is published in French as *La danse sacrale* and in German as *Le Sacre du printemps*. It is yet to be published in English. Translations given in this article are mine.

[5] "[...] expresar *el epos* de una época revolucionaria en el mundo, en lo que concierne a América Latina y a mi país" (qtd. Osorio 1980/1985: 486).

[6] "[...] donde hay bloques humanos en presencia, en pugna, en ascenso o descenso, en miseria u opulencia, en quiebra o encumbramiento, la materia a tratar, para el novelista, se torna materia épica. [...] Grandes acontecimientos se avecinan [...] y debe colocarse el novelista en primera fila de espectadores. [...] Ahí, en la expresión

Central to *La consagración de la primavera* is Stravinsky's *The Rite of Spring*. This piece is widely considered revolutionary for its bursting rhythmic irregularities and groundbreaking harmony. In the novel, it is used as a means to express not only innovative aesthetic ideas but also revolutionary political impulses. The latter conveys much irony, for *The Rite* grew out of, and was re-absorbed into, Western capitalist culture. Moreover, Stravinsky held strong anti-revolutionary political views. After the victory of the Bolsheviks, he became a resentful tsarist patriot, recoiling into a hard-line monarchism (cf. Taruskin 1996: 1514). He also had sympathy for fascism, as seen in a letter he wrote to the music critic Alberto Gasco: "I don't believe that anyone venerates Mussolini more than I. To me, he is the *one man who counts* nowadays in the whole world. [...] He is the saviour of Italy and – let us hope – of Europe." (Qtd. Paddison 1993: 306)

Crucial to this and other ironies that emerge out of *La consagración* is the reader's knowledge of composers, musical works, performers and socio-political contexts referred to in the text, on which Carpentier relies.

1. The Militant *Rite*

The story of *La consagración* is set against some of the most significant historical events of the twentieth century, culminating with the failed U. S. invasion of the Bay of Pigs. Vera, the heroine, is a White Russian ballerina working for Diaghilev's Ballets Russes. Despite her anti-revolutionary views, she gets involved with a left-wing intellectual named Jean-Claude. Vera makes a trip to Benicassim (eastern Spain) to visit the Frenchman, who has enrolled as a militiaman with the International Brigades against Franco. There she meets Enrique, a bourgeois Cuban architect also fighting against Franco who later becomes her partner. After the death of Jean-Claude, Vera and Enrique flee war-devastated Europe to settle in Cuba, where she develops a social-artistic project involving the creation of a new cho-

---

del hervor de ese plasma humano, está la auténtica materia épica para el novelista nuestro. Bien lo entendieron aquellos que pudieron seguir de cerca el proceso de la Revolución Cubana y comienzan [...] a escribir novelas que resulten épicas." (Carpentier 1964/1990: 43f.)

reography for Stravinsky's *The Rite of Spring* with Afro-Cuban dancers.

Vera first thinks about *The Rite* during her train journey to Spain through the Pyrenees. Her head whirls with thoughts about The Chosen One (in Stravinsky's ballet, the character that is sacrificed to the God of Spring in order to gain his benevolence) as she gets closer to the battlefield where Jean-Claude lies wounded. 'They all cried ... And I also feel like weeping, at this moment, surrounded by awakening travellers', thinks Vera mournfully[7]. Once she recovers from the shock produced by the death of Jean-Claude, Vera returns to working life with renewed spirit, performing in a number of Diaghilev's productions. When the Ballets Russes begin rehearsing *The Rite of Spring* – 'whose score was already played everywhere, but which, as a ballet, continued to be a failed work'[8] – The Chosen One returns to her mind, this time directly linked to her own traumatic experiences with political revolutions:

> [...] when I was getting close, marking the steps, towards The Chosen One of today [...] I could not see *the one who was to die*, but the one who suffered her death in lifetime, who would embrace, cry, sob for it, a hired mourner of herself, as I would take on, cry, sob, during solitary nights in my hotel, my despair caused by an idea – the *Idea*, the eternal *Idea*, religious or political, always tied to the existence of a sacrifice, the *Idea* to which I was paying my own tribute without having ever accepted it.[9]

Vera sees herself as the victim of an unjust fate to which she has not surrendered. Her sacrifice is not anchored in an ancient tribal world nor does it defy the dark forces of nature, but is an all-too-present

---

[7] "Lloraron todos ... Y yo también tengo ganas de llorar, en este momento, rodeada ya de viajeros que despiertan." (Carpentier 1978/1998: 97)

[8] "[...] cuya partitura se tocaba ya en todas partes, pero que, como ballet, seguía siendo una obra malograda." (ibid.: 307) Here Vera seems to be a mouthpiece for Stravinsky, who preferred *The Rite* as a concert work and was unhappy with the original 1913 production. The composer highlighted that *The Rite* "exists as a piece of music first and last." (Stravinsky 1921: 9)

[9] "[...] al acercarme, marcando los pasos, a la Virgen Electa de hoy [...] no veía a *la que iba a morir*, sino a la que padecía su muerte en vida, que la asumía, la lloraba, la sollozaba, plañidera de sí misma, como yo asumía, lloraba, sollozaba, en las noches solitarias de mi hotel, mi desesperanza causada por una idea – la *Idea*, la eterna *Idea*, religiosa o política, unida siempre a la existencia de un sacrificio, *Idea* a la que estaba pagando el tributo de mí misma sin haberla aceptado jamás." (Carpentier 1978/1998: 309)

destiny that threatens to continue till eternity. It is the power of her own imagination that liberates Vera from her sorrows:

> I continue marking the steps of the *Danse sacrale*, but after the final chord, bizarrely brought by the flutes' chromatic scale, I think about a second ballet which could begin here, one never written, and which perhaps never will be written: the Gods are not satisfied with the sacrifice. They ask for more. [...] And the past sacrifice will be forgotten [in order] to organise a New One, as there will always be good reasons to do so ... And I interrupt my daydream about that imaginary ballet, complementary to the other one, which would be, really, the never-ending ballet, [while] feeling, one morning, rebellious and hard, suddenly liberated from depression and stress.[10]

Once settled in Cuba, Vera is invited to witness a ritual Afro-Cuban ceremony taking place in a deprived area of Havana, which instantly revolutionises her artistic thought. She first thinks about staging *The Rite* with non-professional Afro-Cuban dancers, revealing a clichéd statement of racial prejudice towards blacks – that they have a 'natural' sense of rhythm reflecting their 'primitive' nature:

> Here *The Rite of Spring* could be staged, with people like the ones we have just seen dancing. With what they have inside, with their sense of rhythm, there would be little to add. They would quickly understand Stravinsky's rhythms, and one would see a dance truly subject to elementary and primeval pulses, very different from the choreographic monstrosities we have seen so far.[11]

Vera persuades the untrained dancers to take part in an experiment in her studio: to improvise to a recording of *The Rite of Spring*. Their response to Stravinsky's music prompts her to take on her long-dreamed project to create a new choreography for the ballet. Through *The Rite*, not only does she defy the apartheid-like social order of pre-

---

[10] "Sigo marcando los pasos de la *Danse sacrale*, pero, al sonar el acorde final, extrañamente traído por una cromática de flautas, pienso que aquí podría empezar un segundo ballet, jamás escrito, y que acaso no se escriba nunca: los Dioses no se dan por satisfechos con el sacrificio. Piden más. [...] Y se olvidará el pasado sacrificio para organizar uno Nuevo, pues buenas razones habrá siempre en ello ... E interrumpo mi divagación en torno a ese imaginario ballet, complemento del otro, que sería, en verdad, el ballet del nunca acabar, sintiéndome, una mañana, rebelde y dura, repentinamente liberada de la depresión y del agobio." (Carpentier 1978/1998:309–311)

[11] "Aquí podría montarse una *Consagración de la primavera* con gente como la que acabamos de ver bailar. Con lo que llevan dentro, con su sentido del ritmo, habría poco que añadir. Entenderían muy pronto la rítmica de Stravinsky, y se vería una danza realmente sometida a pulsiones elementales, primordiales, bien distintas de las birrias coreográficas que hemos visto hasta ahora." (Ibid.: 399)

revolutionary Cuba by working with black dancers, but she also becomes sensitised to the economic inequalities and the harsh political climate of Fulgencio Batista's dictatorship[12]. During the 1950s, as the political atmosphere in Cuba thickens, Vera abandons her *Rite* project as she finds endless difficulties in realising it. The Cuban Revolution has a redeeming effect on Vera, who eventually accepts a historical fate 'whose fundamental ideas coincided with those of the grand and only Revolution of the time'[13]. After Enrique's brave participation in the Battle of the Bay of Pigs, Vera finds the inspiration to take up her *Rite* project again.

2. "L'Internationale": Utopia and Showcase

Intertwined with Stravinsky's composition is "L'Internationale", a militant anthem written by the French woodworker Eugène Pottier (1816–1887) during the Paris Commune, and set to music by the Belgian composer Pierre Degeyter (1848–1932). This song was adopted world-wide by communist, socialist, social democrat and anarchist movements, and became the official anthem of the Soviet Union until 1944. Commonly sung with the hand in a clenched fist, the song is a stirring call to build a new society, as the chorus tells:

> C'est la lutte final:
> Groupons-nous, et demain,
> L'Internationale
> Sera le genre humain.[14] (Pottier 1966: 101)

For Vera, "L'Internationale" is a shadow that follows her everywhere. As a young child, she hears it sung by Bolsheviks. She and her family escape the October Revolution to settle in France. There she hears the anthem sung by the dancers of Diaghilev's troupe and later by the supporters of the French Popular Front. When she visits Jean-Claude

---

[12] Vera's social-artistic initiative bears certain resemblance to the dance project *Rhythm is it!*, in which hundreds of children and teenagers coming from disadvantaged areas of Berlin danced to *The Rite* performed by the Berliner Philharmoniker under Simon Rattle. For more information about this project, see Bleek (2003[?]).

[13] "[...] cuyas ideas fundamentales coincidían con las de la grande y única Revolución de la época." (Carpentier 1978/1998: 765)

[14] "Then comrades, come rally / And the last fight let us face / The International / Unites the human race." (Pottier/Degeyter 1932: 1)

in Spain, she hears "L'Internationale" sung by the celebrity American black singer and actor Paul Robeson with the participation of a multitude of partisans in many languages. (Carpentier here presupposes an informed reader who knows not only that the real-life Robeson was the first major singer to perform African-American folk songs and spirituals on an international stage, but that he was overtly involved with the socialist cause and anti-colonialist movements, regularly performing for the poor and the oppressed[15].) On hearing Robeson's performance, Vera feels

> taken over by the masculine impetus of a revolutionary song loaded down with history. And it is History which leads me – I think – as, by profound conviction, because of the trauma undergone in childhood, I reject – I loath – any idea of revolution.[16]

When a partisan asks her whether she is moved by "L'Internationale", she coldly replies: 'Well, anthems are always impressive. They come with their load of collective emotion', and adds with derision: 'I am very moved by *God Save the Tsar*.'[17] Despite her ideological reservations about "L'Internationale", Vera is deeply impressed by the powerful and mystical artistry of Robeson, seeing this in terms of a Kantian sublime: '[...] in the giant Paul Robeson I found a different power, that of firm belief, totally independent of the words that he was conveying: the power of art, of transcendent eloquence, magnificent, universal and timeless.'[18]

In Robeson, Vera finds the overwhelming charisma and inspiration which she once admired in the acclaimed Russian ballerina Anna

---

[15] During the Spanish Civil War, Robeson actively supported the International Brigades against Franco, performing in Benicassim and other locations (cf. Boyle/ Bunie 2001: 383). For Robeson's music repertoire, see Pencak (2002) and Hagopian (2002), for his political activities, see Foner, ed. (1978).

[16] "[...] arrastrada por el másculo ímpetu de un canto revolucionario cargado de historia. Y es la Historia, la que me lleva – pienso – ya que, por convicción profunda, por el trauma recibido en la infancia, rechazo – aborrezco – toda idea de revolución." (Carpentier 1978/1998: 262)

[17] "Bueno: los himnos siempre son impresionantes. Vienen con su carga de emoción colectiva, a mí me emociona muchísimo *Dios salve al Zar*." (Ibid.: 269)

[18] "[...] en el gigante Paul Robeson hallaba yo otra fuerza de convencimiento, totalmente independiente de las palabras que acarreaba: fuerza del arte, de la elocuencia trascendida, magnificada, universal y sin tiempo." (Ibid.: 259)

Pávlova, her all-time model. She fantasises about the two artists dancing and acting a scene from Shakespeare's *Othello*:

> An impossible, exotic *pas de deux*, absurdly incongruous, but harmonious nevertheless, realised in my imagination, between the black giant whom I saw here, and the ethereal Mallarmesque swan that lived in my memory, and even more now that the grandson of slaves, at the request of English and Yankee listeners who were eager to hear him in a brief dramatic action, addressed the invisible whiteness of Desdemona – dying swan, identified with Anna dancing her own death – in the topmost monologue of the Shakespearean tragedy:

> *It is the cause, it is the cause, my soul;*
> *Let me not name it to you, you chaste stars!*
> *It is the cause. Yet I'll not shed her blood,*
> *Not scar that whiter skin of hers than snow,*
> *And smooth as monumental alabaster.*
> *Yet she must die, else she'll betray more men.*[19]

(As an actor, the real-life Robeson excelled in the title role of *Othello* and in the musical *Show Boat*. The real-life Pávlova's most famous role was the Dying Swan, subject of innumerable postcards. She became a renowned figure while working for the Imperial Russian Ballets, before she escaped the Bolshevik Revolution. Despite her association with Diaghilev's groundbreaking Ballets Russes, Pávlova danced mainly to a conventional classical and romantic musical repertoire – allegedly she turned down the lead role in Stravinsky's *The Firebird* because she thought the music was too complicated. Carpentier's readers might recognise that Pávlova's artistic interests, her relations with audiences and her political consciousness were very different from Robeson's.) The lines from *Othello* recalled by Vera, recited by Robeson in the particular context of the anti-fascist struggle, appear to point to political commitment and sacrifice rather than conveying the themes of love and jealousy of the original play. One may suggest that this scene signals the moment when the heroine begins to question her own conservative political views. The lines

---

[19] "Un imposible, exótico *pas de deux*, contrastado hasta el absurdo, aunque harmonioso a pesar de todo, se concertaba en mi imaginación, entre el gigante negro que aquí veía y el etéreo cisne mallarmeano que habitaba mi recuerdo, y más ahora que el nieto de esclavos, a pedido de oyentes ingleses y yankis [sic], deseosos de escucharlo en una breve acción dramática, se dirigía a la invisible blancura de Desdémona – Desdémona, cisne agónico, identificado con Anna bailando su propia muerte – en el monólogo cimero de la tragedia shakesperiana: [...]." (Carpentier 1978/1998: 259)

from the play may also be linked to the fundamental notion of the sacrifice to the collective in Stravinsky's original *The Rite of Spring*. Years later, Vera's own reinterpretation of *The Rite* with Afro-Cuban dancers plays a key part in her ideological transformation, from staunch anti-revolutionary to supporter of the Cuban Revolution. As a consequence of her radical changes, Pávlova falls from her imaginary pedestal:

> And today I would look at that portrait [Pávlova's] once again, realising that a change in the way of contemplating it had occurred in me overnight. [...] I suddenly thought that she, the Incomparable, would have hated the show [Vera's *Rite*] that, after years of effort, I was to present to the world.[20]

Subsequently, following her husband's revelation of sexual betrayal, a heart-broken Vera flees to the most isolated corner of Cuba, where she plans to lead an eventless life. She is unaware that the country is on the brink of a socialist revolution, naively thinking that there, "L'Internationale" '*in truth, had never been heard*'[21]. She soon hears the anthem sung by supporters of the Cuban Revolution, which she will eventually embrace.

"L'Internationale" is of key significance to the hero's story. On his journey to the Spanish battlefield, Enrique first comes across "L'Internationale" in the hustle and bustle of a train station:

> "L'Internationale", enormous, multitudinous, terrifying, from platforms full of people, and in the wagons which now begin to roll, sounding solemn, overwhelming – like a *Magnificat* sung in a high-vaulted nave, on the *organum* of the locomotive that, with a long whistle, sets off for the Pyrenees.[22]

Like Vera, Enrique attends Robeson's concert in Benicassim and is particularly touched by his performance of "L'Internationale". This experience will have important repercussions after he leaves Europe. Once settled back in Cuba, Enrique travels to the U. S. to buy archi-

---

[20] "Y hoy miraba ese retrato [de Pávlova] una vez más, dándome cuenta de que un cambio se había operado en mí de la noche a la mañana en la manera de contemplarlo. [...] Pensaba de repente que ella, la Incomparable, habría detestado el espectáculo [*La consagración* de Vera] que, tras de un esfuerzo de años, iba a presentar al mundo." (Carpentier 1978/1998: 574)

[21] "[...] *para decir la verdad, no se había oído nunca*" (ibid.: 651).

[22] "[...] enorme, multitudinaria, tremebunda, en andenes repletos de gente, y en los vagones que ya empiezan a rodar suena, solemne, sobrecogedora, *La Internacional* – tal *Magnificat* cantado en nave de altas bóvedas, sobre el *organum* de la locomotora que, con un largo silbido, toma el rumbo de los Pirineos." (Ibid.: 226)

tecture publications and music scores for Vera. In New York City, he meets up with his frivolous cousin Teresa and takes her to a restaurant frequented by members of the American avant-garde. Enrique shows some frustration when his cousin, on hearing Edgard Varèse at work next door, questions whether his music – 'panting and spasmodic roaring from an enormous though unidentifiable wounded animal'[23] – has any artistic value at all. Varèse's music is still in the background at the point when Teresa decides to drag Enrique to the Rainbow Room, a luxurious cabaret frequented by the jet set. He greatly enjoys the vaudevillian combination of song, dance, magic tricks and stripping. Yet his mood changes dramatically at the end of the show, as he tells us how

> the orchestra, with a certain solemnity, began to play a piece which to me was extremely familiar, tremendously familiar, dramatically familiar. But, no. It couldn't be. Here? In the Rainbow Room? I had drunk something, and mixing wine and whisky had been a bad idea. I must have got the wrong music. It must be something by Tchaikovsky (maybe that martial Scherzo in the *Pathétique*...), or, perhaps, I don't know, something by Wagner (I can't quite recall that march from *Tannhäuser* right now...) [...]. But no, no, no, no! There are no doubts now. There are no doubts. And twenty-four girls enter, all of the same look and height, cast in the same mould, wearing ermine hats, red jackets, red-striped skirts, red boots, and begin dancing symmetrically, in an almost military manner: back to the dance floor, dividing into two rows, groups crossing, geometrical figures – then they line up again, divide into two rows again, the groups cross back again, they make more geometrical figures, then they turn again and again, marking time, before a final deployment and line-up. And they raise the left fist ... And the audience of the rich, of the wealthy, of film stars [...], the whole of show-business Broadway, of advertising, of trade, the members of Boards of Directors and PR heads, who have gathered here tonight, they clap, clap, clap, endlessly. And the conductor makes a sign to his musicians. *Bis. Bis. Bis.* And so they play it again. And there is no possible doubt. It is *that*.[24]

---

[23] "[...] bramidos jadeantes, espasmódicos, de un enorme aunque inidentificable animal herido." (Carpentier 1978/1998: 418)

[24] "[...] la orquesta, con cierta solemnidad, empezó a tocar una música que me era sumamente conocida, tremendamente conocida, dramáticamente conocida. Pero, no. No podía ser. ¿Aquí? ¿En el Rainbow Room? Había bebido algo, y la mezcla de vino y wisky [sic] era muy poco recomendable. Debo haberme equivocado de música. Debe ser algo de Tchaikovski (acaso ese *scherzo* marcial de la *Patética* ...), o, tal vez, de Wagner (no recuerdo bien, en este momento, la marcha de *Tannhäuser* ...) [...]. Pero no, no, no, no. No hay dudas ahora. No hay dudas. Y entran veinticuatro *girls*, todas iguales en pinta y estatura, cortadas por el mismo patrón, llevando bonetes de armiño, casacas rojas, faldas listadas de rojo, botas rojas, y empiezan a bailar

Enrique's account of the piece he knows so well yet cannot name conveys obvious dramatic irony, as the reader quickly realises that *that* is "L'Internationale". He first thinks of Wagner's and Tchaikovsky's marches, which are of undoubted musical similarity and share with "L'Internationale" a vital, majestic and triumphant character. The audience of the cabaret, which Enrique perceives as ideologically despicable, reminds him of the uses of these composers by certain non-socialist societies: Wagner by the Third Reich and Tchaikovsky by the Russia of the Tsars. (Throughout the novel, the music of Wagner and Tchaikovsky is associated with negative events and political attitudes. Wagner's operas are linked to fascism, for instance in the discussion of American opera productions during the Second World War [cf. Carpentier 1978/1998: 418f.]. Tchaikovsky's *1812 Overture* signals anti-revolutionary attitudes [cf. ibid.: 269; 653], and his Fifth Symphony is the background against which Vera learns about the death of Jean-Claude [cf. ibid.: 305].)

When Enrique finally recognises "L'Internationale", he experiences a dreadful ideological dissonance as he hears it in the most distant and inappropriate context he can imagine for it. The perversely trivialised cabaret version violently clashes with his memories of the impetuous combatants singing along with Robeson. The dancing-girls are fake protesters who do not incite their audience to arise nor to build a new socialist society. Instead of addressing hungry workers, the girls amuse the rich, achieving a disturbing subversion of the original utopian message of the song. The anthem's rebellious lyrics are not sung, yet the performance tradition of raising the left fist is incorporated in the coercive choreography, which evokes totalitarianism[25].

---

simétricamente, de modo casi militar: vuelta a la pista, división en dos filas, cruce de grupos, figuras de geométrica ordenación – y vuelta a la pista, re-división en dos filas, re-cruce de grupos, re-figuras, y más vueltas y revueltas, marcando el paso, hasta un despliegue y alienación final. Y levantan el puño izquierdo ... Y el público de ricos, de adinerados, de estrellas de cine [...], el todo Broadway del *show-business*, de la publicidad, de los negocios, la gente del patronato y de las relaciones públicas, que aquí se ha congregado esta noche, aplaude, aplaude, aplaude, interminablemente. Y el director de orquesta que hace una seña a sus músicos. *Bis. Bis. Bis.* Y vuelve a escucharse lo de antes. Y ya no hay duda posible. Es *eso.*" (Carpentier 1978/1998: 420f.)

[25] The incongruous message produced by the cabaret performance may find a contemporary parallel in the 2007 rap version of Richard Makela, aka Monsieur R

The play on utopia and capitalism in this scene recalls Bertolt Brecht's satirical treatment of political themes, particularly in the final scene of *The Rise and Fall of the City of Mahagonny* (1927–1929), co-written with Kurt Weill. This opera is about an amusement town called Mahagonny, where money alone rules. The town is founded to provide satisfaction and pleasure to people, and is finally destroyed by those same desires. In the end, while the city perishes in flames, the characters march carrying placards with inscriptions such as "For The Prolongation Of The Golden Age", "For Property", "For The Buying And Selling Of Love", "For Freedom For The Rich" and "For Brute Stupidity" (Brecht 1929/1997: 63–65). Carpentier, in the satire on the travesties of capitalism in the Rainbow Room scene, seems to reverse Brecht's concept of defamiliarisation (*Verfremdung*) as he does not cause alienation but hilarity[26].

Enrique is so altered by the misuse of "L'Internationale" that he needs to leave the cabaret, dragging Teresa with him. On their way to their hotel, they have a sharp ideological disagreement over the song:

"Do you know what has just been played here? 'L'Internationale'!" – "So what?" – "'L'Internationale' by Degeyter; the one that Paul Robeson sung for us in Benicassim; the one that was chanted, in twenty languages, by the combatants of the International Brigades." – "So what?" – "'L'Internationale'. The title says everything." – "So what?" – "That, damn it, can't be sung in a cabaret. I never believed that I'd see such a thing. Just thinking about it makes my blood boil." – "But it seems OK to me. You know that, sooner or later, we – the rich – will get screwed. So it's better if we get used to hearing 'L'Internationale'". – "But not like this. And especially not in the Rainbow Room. Also, I see a bad omen in this: those who so easily accept what they loathed yesterday, will be the first ones to renounce, tomorrow, what they applaud today. 'L'Internationale' was not made for them." ... We were speeding in a taxi, to the hotel: "To know what

---

(2007). Here, all stanzas are declaimed over a typical rap rhythmic backing, and the refrain is sung by the chorus girls in a hilariously sensual manner. As a result, the original militant character of the song is washed out. More generally, the genre of rap, which has become a thriving multi-million industry in the last decades, is easier to identify with commercial attitudes than with revolutionary ideals.

[26] According to Brecht, contradictory social reality should be portrayed in a shockingly unnatural manner in order to alienate the viewer. He called his work 'socialist realist' despite his experimental political aesthetics diverging from the homonymous Soviet doctrine, which aimed to represent the socialist struggle in a positive way according to canonical models.

'L'Internationale' means you have to have known hunger, exploitation, misery, unemployment."[27]

In her black-humour response to Enrique's objection to the cabaret "L'Internationale", Teresa is suggesting that the revolutionaries will usurp the power of the rich ruling class. Obviously, the rich cannot get used to "L'Internationale" because their privileged status is in contradiction with the ideological content and purpose of the song. Following Enrique's diatribe against the capitalist audience of the cabaret, Teresa calls his bluff and dares him to demonstrate his commitment to the socialist utopia:

> – "But I don't believe that you have known much in the way of hunger and misery in your life. You sang 'L'Internationale' in Spain, but it seems to me that you haven't sung it for a long time." – "That's why I am nothing. Neither bourgeois nor proletarian. Neither fish nor fowl." [...] "Are you still angry?" – "I can't help it." "We saw the twelve o'clock show. They will repeat it at two, with the same 'L'Internationale' at the end. You still have time." – "For what?" – "To go there, to throw a bomb. It would blow up the whole Rainbow Room, and it would be a magnificent apotheosis, with fireworks and everything." – "I'm not a terrorist, I don't have bombs, nor would I throw them if I had them. Nothing is achieved by throwing bombs." Teresa, with an uninhibited gesture, took her shoes off: "Good. As you don't want to blow up the Rainbow Room, come to bed with me."[28]

---

[27] "'¿Sabes lo que acaba de tocarse aquí? ¡*La Internacional!*' – '¿Y qué?' – '*La Internacional* de Degeyter; la que nos cantó Paul Robeson en Benicassim; la que fue coreada, en veinte idiomas, por los combatientes de las Brigadas Internacionales.' – '¿Y qué?' – '*La Internacional*. El título lo dice todo.' – '¿Y qué?' – 'Que eso, carajo, no es para que se baile en un cabaret. Jamás creí que vería semejante cosa. Es que, de sólo pensarlo, se me revuelve la sangre.' – 'Pues, a mí me parece muy bien. Tú sabes que, tarde o temprano, los ricos tendremos que jodernos. Por lo tanto, más vale que uno se vaya acostumbrando a oír *La Internacional*.' – 'Pero no así. Y menos, en el Rainbow Room. Hay, en todo esto, una frivolidad, una novelería, que me indignan. Además, veo un mal agüero en ello: quienes con tanta ligereza aceptan lo que ayer aborrecieron, serán los primeros en renegar, mañana, de lo que hoy aplauden. *La Internacional* no se hizo para ellos.' ... Rodábamos ya en un taxi, hacia el hotel: 'Para saber lo que significa *La Internacional* es necesario haber conocido el hambre, la explotación, la miseria, el desempleo.'" (Carpentier 1978/1998: 421f.)

[28] "–'Pues, yo no creo que tú hayas conocido muchas hambres y muchas miserias en tu vida. Cantaste *La Internacional* en España, pero me parece que hace tiempo que ya no la cantas.' – 'Por eso es que no soy nada. Ni burgués ni proletario. Ni chicha ni limonada, como se dice.' [...] '¿Te sigue la rabia?' – 'No puedo remediarlo.' – 'Vimos el *show* de las doce. Lo repetirán a las dos, con la misma *Internacional* en fin de espectáculo. Todavía tienes tiempo.' – '¿De qué?' – 'De ir allá, a tirar una bomba. Volaría el Rainbow Room entero, y sería una magnífica apoteosis, con fuegos

Unable to show his heroism to Teresa and reconcile his ideological frustrations, Enrique resigns himself to making love to her, marking the beginning of an affair of a quasi-incestuous nature which will last many years. (Wagner having been already invoked in Enrique's erroneous musings on the cabaret performance, the cousins' relationship brings to mind his *Ring* cycle. These operas feature various adulterous and incestuous lovers including Wotan's illegitimate children Siegmund and Sieglinde, whose offspring Siegfried loves Brünnhilde, the banished Valkyrie and Wotan's daughter.)

For Enrique, being immersed in the luxurious world of the Rainbow Room – 'the most affluent atmosphere I had ever breathed in'[29] – does not seem to pose a problem at first. After the politically-twisted performance of "L'Internationale", that same space turns knotty, reflecting his own ideological conflicts. Teresa, light-hearted, perceives and reacts to the anthem very differently. She exploits the irony conveyed by the performance in a particularly close-to-the-bone manner, unmasking the contradictions between her cousin's upper-class background and his revolutionary raptures, preaching and actions. Naturally, Enrique does not accept her defiant suggestion that he return to the dance hall to destroy it, and feels pushed into admitting the uselessness of his political endeavours: 'nothing is more annoying than another's correct apprehension of unwelcome evidence'[30].

Immediately following the triumph of the Cuban Revolution, the cousins meet up at the mansion of their aristocratic aunt, who has just left for Miami. Teresa persuades her lover to try out their aunt's bed, 'an unpolluted couch'[31]. The cousins' affair, triggered by their disagreement over the Rainbow Room "L'Internationale", is 'consecrated' in the bed of their anti-revolutionary aunt. While Teresa undresses, she asks, "'Listen ... Didn't Wagner compose something called *The Consecration of the House*?" – "That was Beethoven.

---

artificiales y todo.' – 'Yo no soy terrorista, no tengo bombas, ni las tiraría si las tuviese. Nada se consigue con tirar bombas.' Teresa, con gesto desenfadado, se quitó los zapatos: 'Bueno. Ya que no quieres volar el Rainbow Room, acuéstate conmigo.'" (Carpentier 1978/1998: 422)

[29] "[...] la más millonaria atmósfera que yo hubiese respirado nunca" (ibid.: 420).

[30] "[...] nada resulta tan irritante como la acertada visión ajena de una molesta evidencia" (Ibid.: 424).

[31] "[...] un lecho impoluto" (ibid.: 716).

You're mixing everything up tonight."[32] The original Spanish title of the novel, *La consagración de la primavera*, allows the confusion with Beethoven's little-known overture, *Die Weihe des Hauses* (*The Consecration of the House*, 1822), and also preserves the religious connotations of the original title of Stravinsky's work, which is translated into Spanish as *La consagración de la primavera* (hence the title of the novel). Teresa thinks of a very respectable piece by Beethoven but incorrectly attributes it to Wagner, whose works contain several pairs of illicit lovers. Enrique shows an impressive erudition when remembering the correct title of Beethoven's obscure overture, which contrasts with his mistaking of "L'Internationale" for Wagner and Tchaikovsky during the cabaret show when the performance context impacts so strongly on what his ears can tell him. Now, although he can correctly attribute *The Consecration of the House* to Beethoven, Enrique does not notice that the title of the overture suggests Stravinsky's ballet about the ritual killing of a sacrificial virgin, even though his wife Vera has been working on this piece for many years.

3. Conclusion

The performance of music plays an important role in Carpentier's political fiction. In *La consagración de la primavera*, it is intricately tied to revolutionary politics and generates layers of irony in relation to events inside and outside the novel.

The scene at the Rainbow Room cabaret illustrates Carpentier's use of performance as a platform to convey irony and ideology. There is dramatic irony in the hero's mistaken identification of the militant song "L'Internationale" with Wagner and Tchaikovsky, which derives from the music as it is being divorced from the words. The musically-informed reader can appreciate the undoubted musical similarity between the socialist anthem and the marches by Wagner and Tchaikovsky, and also the clash between the revolutionary message of the song and the ideologies associated with the former composers. There is a level of situational irony, where the anthem is used as a showpiece in a nightclub, which embarrasses and angers

---

[32] "'Oye ... ¿Wagner no compuso algo que se titula *La consagración de la casa*?' – 'Fue Beethoven. Esta noche lo enredas todo.'" (Ibid.: 717)

Enrique. Another level of irony, shared by the hero and the reader, is the clash between Paul Robeson's idealistic performance of "L'Internationale" earlier in the novel and the commodified version of the same music in the cabaret. The conflict between revolutionary ideals and commercial entertainment produced by the cabaret version of "L'Internationale" results in an unexpected ironic outcome: Enrique falling for his capitalist cousin Teresa. Their sexual relationship is reminiscent of Wagner's incestuous characters and may be interpreted as a critique of the decadence of capitalism. There is further irony in Teresa's confusion of titles of musical works by Wagner and Beethoven, and in Enrique's missing of the religious connotations of the original title of Stravinsky's ballet.

The heroine's social-artistic *The Rite of Spring* project with Afro-Cuban dancers is fundamental to her conversion from staunch anti-revolutionary to supporter of the Cuban Revolution. Through *The Rite*, Vera becomes sensitive to the racial and economic inequalities of Batista's regime. The Cuban Revolution and the impulses conveyed by "L'Internationale" have a positive effect on her, as she is finally able to bring her artistic project to fruition.

An informed reader with knowledge of the political attitudes of Stravinsky and the composition and performance history of his *Rite* may recognise the irony in Carpentier's use of this piece to convey left-wing impulses. The defeat of capitalism and the possibility of moral change in *La consagración* may appear ironic to the contemporary reader, given the collapse of socialist regimes beginning with the fall of the Berlin Wall and the profound ideological crisis that Cuba presently experiences. This is an additional irony that Carpentier could not possibly have foreseen.

References

Birkenmaier, Anke (2004). "Carpentier y el Bureau d'Ethnologie Haïtienne: Los cantos vodú de *El reino de este mundo*". *Foro Hispánico* 25: 17–33.

Bleek, Tobias (2003[?]) [online]. "Making of the Project". *Rhythm Is It*. http://www.rhythmisit.com/en/php/index_flash.php?HM=2&SM =1 &CM=2. [05/03/2009].

Boyle, Sheila Tully, Andrew Bunie (2001). *Paul Robeson: The Years of Promise and Achievement*. Amherst, MA: University of Massachusetts Press.
Brecht, Bertolt (1929/1997). *The Rise and Fall of the City of Mahagonny*. Trans. W. H. Auden, Chester Kallman. Eds. John Willett, Ralph Manheim. Collected Plays Series 2/3. London: Eyre Methuen.
Carpentier, Alejo (1963/1985). "Entrevista en Radio Televisión Francesa". *Entrevistas: Alejo Carpentier*. Ed. Virgilio López Lemus. Havana: Letras Cubanas. 72–97.
— (1964/1990). "Problemática de la actual novela latinoamericana". *Ensayos*. Obras Completas Series 12. Mexico City: Siglo Veintiuno. 11–44.
— (1978/1998). *La consagración de la primavera*. Ed. Julio Rodríguez Puértolas. Madrid: Castalia.
Chornik, Katia (2007) [online]. "Musical Analogies in Alejo Carpentier's *El acoso*". *International Association for Word and Music Studies*. http://wordmusicstudies.org/forum2007/forum1.htm. [09/05/2008].
Dorinson, Joseph, William Pencak, eds. (2002). *Paul Robeson: Essays on His Life and Legacy*. Jefferson, NC: McFarland.
Foner, Philip S., ed. (1978). *Paul Robeson Speaks: Writings, Speeches, Interviews 1918–1974*. London: Quartet Books.
Hagopian, Kevin Jack (2002). "'You Know Who I Am!': Paul Robeson's Ballad for Americans and the Paradox of the Double V in American Popular Front Culture". Dorinson/Pencak, eds. 167–179.
Osorio, Manuel (1980/1985). "La vida es la materia misma de la escritura". *Entrevistas: Alejo Carpentier*. Ed. Virgilio López Lemus. Havana: Letras Cubanas. 483–495.
Paddison, Max (1993). *Adorno's Aesthetics of Music*. Cambridge: CUP.
Pencak, William (2002). "Paul Robeson and Classical Music". Dorinson/Pencak, eds. 152–159.
Pottier, Eugène Edmé (1966). *Œuvres complètes*. Ed. Pierre Brochon. Paris: François Maspero.
—, Pierre Degeyter (1932). "The International". *The Workers' Song-Book*. London: The Workers' Theatre Movement. 1.
R, Monsieur (2007) [online]. "L'Internationale". *Russian Anthems Museum*. http://media.vad1.com/temporary_url_20070929kldcg/internationale_2007-fr-monsieur_r_2007.mp3. [15/03/2009].

Stravinsky, Igor (1921). "Interview with Stravinsky: His Aims and Methods. Music and its 'Subjects'. *The Rite* and its Two Ballets". *The Observer* (3 July): 9.

Taruskin, Richard (1996). *Stravinsky and the Russian Traditions: A Biography of the Works through* Mavra. Oxford: OUP.

Musical Performativity in the Fiction of Katherine Mansfield*

Delia da Sousa Correa, London

Katherine Mansfield, who lived from 1888 to 1923, was a pioneer of the Modernist short story. She was the one writer of whom Virginia Woolf admitted envy, and thirty or so years after her early death, was hailed by Elizabeth Bowen as the "missing contemporary" who had altered "for good and all our idea of what goes to make a story" (1957: 15)[1]. This essay is about musical performance in Mansfield and also about the 'performative' in the sense that her stories perform rather than merely invoke musical analogy. It arrives at a sense of 'performativity in words' that is rather different from that originally conceived by the philosopher J. L. Austin in that it incorporates the notion of affect: a sense of performativity in literature fundamental to Mansfield's writing and much other[2].

Katherine Mansfield settled in London in 1908, leaving behind her native New Zealand. Both whilst at home in Wellington, and during a period as a pupil at Queen's College, London, she was a serious student of the cello, apparently divided as to whether music or writing would form her chosen career. "If I let the bow ever so softly fall / – – – The magic lies under my hand", she wrote of her beloved instrument

---

* This essay is an extended version of an article on "Musical Performance in Katherine Mansfield's Stories" that appeared in *Katherine Mansfield Studies* 3 (September 2011): 21–34. I am grateful to Edinburgh University Press for permission to make use of this material here.

[1] Assessing her still-crucial development of a particular strand of the short story, Bowen wrote:

> We owe to her the prosperity of the 'free' story: she untrammelled it from conventions and, still more, gained for it a prestige till then unthought of. How much ground Katherine Mansfield broke for her successors may not be realized. Her imagination kindled unlikely matter; she was to alter for good and all our idea of what goes to make a story. (1957: 15)

[2] According to the Philosopher Stanley Cavell, this is an elaboration that ought to be made of the philosophical theory of performative language, as well as to the employment of the concept by literary critics (cf. 2005: 155–191; also 5 and 16–20). For a discussion of the interrelation between the performative and affective 'force' of language see Eve Kosofsky Sedgwick (2003: 90).

in 1903 ("This Is My World"; 1989: 1). She became a writer, subsequently selling her cello for a fraction of its worth to pay her bills[3]. But she was a writer for whom performance, especially musical performance, was significant to a degree that was more acute, and specific, than for most literary Modernists despite their conscious efforts at correspondences with other art-forms. Indeed, Mansfield's experience as a musical performer was to give her use of musical analogy in her writing a precision which arguably had a formative and salutary influence on Virginia Woolf's development of a writer of musicalised prose (cf. Manhire 2011: 51–66)[4].

One of the ways in which this musical specificity is evident is in Mansfield's confident use of musical terms; her aim for her writing, for example, was always to find "the middle of the note", the correct intonation sought by a string player or singer (1997: 2/137; 1984–2008: 1/205). Mansfield's early letters and notebooks convey how important music was to her. During 1907, on a camping trip taken in New Zealand before her longed-for return to London, her letters and notebook entries also show her turning to musical analogy to convey her responses to the Urewera landscape, ranging from the musically specific "booming sound" of the Huka Falls, which "rises half a tone about each minute [...] but never ceases" to an account of travellers who, perched on a rock against a violent sunset and above a raging river, sit "fiercely almost brutally thinking – like Wagner" (1984–2008: 1/35; 1997: 1/145)[5].

Mansfield's early writings are also full of invocations of music, and a novel draft, *Juliet*, written in 1906, included detailed accounts of musical performance: Juliet, the heroine, is transported by the exquisite playing of a young cellist and follows him to London, where she is ravaged by his fellow music student who has inflamed his passion-

---

[3] "Definitely I have decided not to be a musician – its not my forte, I can plainly see. The fact remains at that – I must be an authoress." [1907] Notebook entry (1997: 1/123).

[4] Vanessa Manhire contrasts Mansfield's confident technical knowledge of music with Woolf's less directly-informed allusions to music (despite her more privileged access to musical performance).

[5] For a discussion of Wagner's importance for Mansfield see da Sousa Correa (2011a).

ate feelings for Juliet whilst playing Wagner and Chopin at the piano[6]. Although, in this essay, I discuss stories that overtly dramatise musical performance, Mansfield's published fiction contains relatively few explicit accounts of music, compared with early works like *Juliet*. In this respect, she seems particularly to exemplify how, in Modernist writing, the specific references to musical repertoire and performance typical of nineteenth-century fiction give way to a self-consciously 'musical' literary technique.

Performance is certainly a term that can appropriately be transposed to literature when describing Mansfield's concentrated and perfectly timed stories, and she wrote with musical performance very consciously in mind. "I chose not only the length of every sentence, but even the sound of every sentence", she recorded of her 1920 story, "Miss Brill", "I read it aloud [...] just as one would *play over* a musical composition" (1984–2008: 4/165). The Modernist scholar Sydney Janet Kaplan sees an early engrossment with musical practice as fundamental to the "passion for technique" that Mansfield identified in herself as a writer (1991: 203f.): "Out of technique is born real style, I believe", Mansfield declared, "[t]here are no short cuts" (1984–2008: 4/173).

Mansfield's letters following her arrival in London in 1908, especially those written to her lover, the violinist Garnet Trowell, reveal her intense ongoing interest in musical performance. In Wellington, she had met the Venezuelan pianist Teresa Carreno and was invited to visit Carreno when she came on tour to London where Mansfield felt "staggered" by her concert performance, "the last word in tonal beauty and intensity and vitality" (ibid.: 1/64)[7]. She much enjoyed their subsequent discussions of "Music in Relation to Life" and "of the splendid artist[ic] calling" (ibid.: 1/68). She herself wrote lyrics for which Trowell's brother Arnold composed music, at one point requesting that they should be set "with strange Macdowell, Debussy chords" (ibid.: 1/80). It had above all been the "tone" of Carreno's playing which excited Mansfield and, in a letter written in

---

[6] For an account of *Juliet* and its relationship to Mansfield's later fiction see da Sousa Correa (2011a).

[7] Carreno's programme for her recital at the Bechstein Hall on the date of this letter included Liszt's transcription of Schubert's "Der Erlkönig", Beethoven's Waldstein Sonata and compositions by Chopin, Schubert and MacDowell (cf. Mansfield 1984–2008: 1/65, fn. 4).

1908 whilst she was still sharpening her spurs as a writer, she declared her plan "to write – and recite what I write – in a very fine way" (ibid.: 1/84). To this end she intended to develop a new style of recitation in order "to study *tone* effects in the voice [...]. *Tone* should be my secret – each word a variety of tone", she wrote (ibid.). This interest in the "*tone* effects in the voice" was fundamental to the innovative prose style that she developed for her fiction where meaning is often conveyed by the ways in which the rhythmic and symbolic disposition of language combine to create the tone of her stories. Both her experience as an instrumental player and her interest in voice underpin Mansfield's literary technique. As Elizabeth Bowen declared, "[w]ords had but one appeal for her, that of speakingness" (1957: 15)[8].

Mansfield's letters to Garnet Trowell show her experimenting with many of the Modernist literary techniques that she was later to employ in her stories, often fuelled by the sense of a shared passionate responsiveness to music which seemed to open up a sense of unlimited possibilities to be lived and imagined, "Oh, Music, Music – Oh, my Beloved – the *worlds* that are ours – the *universes* that we have to explore" (1984–2008: 1/88). This letter, the last in a sequence of long intimate letters before Garnet's parents intervened to terminate his relationship with Mansfield, includes an intensely auditory account of the launch of a battleship which she had attended the day before. She describes crowds of onlookers below the ship on a "brilliant" but windy day, and, towering above them, the lines of ship-builders assembled on deck, all silent "while the choir & sailors sang a hymn" from a platform, the sound of their voices "crying in the wind" prompting "[s]trange visions" of "victories and defeats – death – storm" (ibid.). A rush of phrases strung on dashes which convey the swift sequence of thoughts and impressions, the "dramatic effect" that has "caught" together the writer, the different sections of the crowd, the weather, sky, sea and ship, the future and the past, into a breathlessly animated stream of consciousness:

> And all the time we heard inside the ship a terrible – knocking – they were breaking down the supports, but it seemed to me almost symbolical as tho' the great heart of the creature pulsated – And suddenly a silence so tremendous that

---

[8] "She uses no literary shock tactics. The singular beauty of her language consists, partly, in its hardly seeming to be language at all, so glass-transparent is it to her meaning" (Bowen 1957: 15).

the very wind seemed to cease – then a sharp, wrenching sound, and all the great bulk of her swept down its inclined plank into the sun – and the sky was full of gold – into the sea – which waited for her. The crowd cheered, screamed – the men on board, their rough faces – their windblown hair – cheered back – In front of me an old woman and a young girl – the little old women, whose grand uncle had been in the fighting Temeraire – trembled & shook and cried – but the girl – her flushed face lifted – was laughing. (Ibid.)

And this same letter quite specifically confirms the musicality of the imagination that has been inspired to this performance in words, as Mansfield describes a dream on the night following the ship launch in which she and Garnet attended a Tchaikovsky concert where, "in a violin passage, swift & terrible – I saw to my horror, a great flock of black, wide winged birds – fly screaming over the orchestra – it's rather strange – waking I can see that – too, in much of his music – can't you?" (Ibid.)

As the ready transitions between the arts of drama, music and writing in her plans for a new art of recitation indicate, Mansfield was a writer with an acute capacity to take on board the aesthetic and technical concerns of other art forms. Music was of particular importance, but 'performance' is a principle that informs Mansfield's work in a wider sense, and this extends to her engagement with film and painting, as well as with music, drama and the written word. Scholars interested in relationships between her writing and the visual arts have claimed her in turn as a Fauvist and an Impressionist, for example. Others have noticed the radical extent to which her writing internalised the long-shot, close-up, jump-cut techniques of the new art of cinema, long before other Modernists descended from their lofty disparagement of this vulgar form of entertainment (Mansfield even acted as a film extra while she was living in London). Her peculiar ability to engage with the technical and performance practices of art forms other than her own is perhaps relevant to the rather extraordinary degree to which she continues to influence artistic performances today: writers as various as Elizabeth Bowen and Ali Smith have been conscious of her influence and she has been the subject of numerous dramatic performances and works in visual media[9].

Music and drama obviously go hand in hand in her conception of literary practice, and her own comic-dramatic gifts are recorded in

---

[9] Some of which may be seen on the Katherine Mansfield Society website: http://www.katherinemansfieldsociety.org/.

Leonard Woolf's autobiography. "I don't think anyone has ever made me laugh more than she did in those days", he recalled, recounting how

> [s]he would sit very upright on the edge of a chair or sofa and tell at immense length a kind of saga, of her experiences as an actress or of how and why Koteliansky howled like a dog in the room at the top of a building in Southampton Row. There was not the shadow of a gleam of a smile on her mask of a face, and the extraordinary funniness of the story was increased by the flashes of her astringent wit. (Qtd. Tomalin 1988: 180f.)

The performed musicality of Mansfield's prose emerges not only in its lyricism, rhythmic complexity and wealth of auditory allusion, but also in the highly comic sense of timing that structures her characteristic blend of dialogue and free indirect discourse. The comic-dramatic gifts with which she entertained her friends are certainly on display in the stories that satirise musical performance, including "Mr Reginald Peacock's Day", which was published in *Bliss and Other Stories* (1920). Reginald Peacock is a singing master who wants his entire life to be a bravado performance, and will admit the right of nothing but applause to intrude upon him. He has secured a wife – implicitly a plain-ish pea-hen in this story full of symbolic allusions to birds – who sees to all his practical needs, but Peacock feels only resentment of her as an onslaught against his artistic sensibilities.

Peacock's day begins as quite a performance on Mansfield's part as on his ('performative' too in the manner in which it engages the creative capacity of its reading audience). As his bath-water runs, Peacock indulges in fantasies about his adoring pupils and tries out his voice with a setting of a Meredith poem to which "even the bath tap seemed to gush stormy applause" (145)[10]. His operatic ablutions continue with Wagnerian hyperbole as he dries himself "singing while he rubbed as though he had been Lohengrin tipped out by an unwary Swan and drying himself in the greatest haste before that tiresome Elsa came along" (145). As Peacock, true to his name, admires himself in the glass, his vanity, to his mind, is no such thing, but a "thrill of purely artistic satisfaction" (146).

At breakfast he opens an adulatory letter in violet ink from a female admirer "as gracefully as if he had been on the stage" (147). "I

---

[10] All page reference to Mansfield's stories are to the 1981 Penguin edition of *The Collected Stories of Katherine Mansfield* (based on a 1945 edition prepared by John Middleton Murry for Constable).

cannot go to sleep until I have thanked you again for the wonderful joy your singing gave me this evening", it begins, continuing with several lines of swooning vacuity before extolling Peacock for "doing a great thing. You are teaching the world to escape from life. P.S. – I am in every afternoon this week." (147f.)[11] Peacock proceeds to give lessons to a succession of adorable – because adoring – young women. As with the Lohengrin metaphor, Mansfield's mode of third-person free indirect discourse means that the irony of her portrayal is part and parcel of the flow of narrative via which Peacock's ludicrous fantasies about the world, and the narrator's satire on the paucity of his imagination are conveyed in the same words. Having arrived "blushing and shy", his first pupil "parted her pretty lips and began to sing like a pansy" (148f.). Pupil number two, the Countess Willkowska, comes bearing violets and leaves trembling, having been exhorted to "confess" herself in her singing (150). An abjectly adoring pupil number three promises to send him a poem about *her* feelings about his singing the night before. "Dear lady, I should be only too charmed", are his parting words to all his pupils, and ultimately, this phrase is all he is capable of drunkenly parroting to his wife, when he wakes her on his return late that night from a further – he thinks – 'artistic' triumph: "He was an artist. He could sway them all. And wasn't he teaching them all to escape from life? How he sang! As he sang, as in a dream he saw their feathers and their flowers and their fans, offered to him, laid before him, like a huge bouquet" (152) – or like a huge peacock's tail, the reader might think, having the benefit

---

[11] This letter, as the editors of Mansfield's collected letters point out, parodies a letter that Mansfield herself sent to her cello teacher Thomas Trowell in 1907 beginning "I cannot let you leave without telling you how grateful I am and must be all my life – for what you have done for me – and given me. You have shown me that there is something so immeasurably higher and greater than I had ever realised before in Music – and therefore, too, in Life". There is also something parodic about the original letter, in which Mansfield seems to enjoy trying out hyperbolic declarations: "I must tell you that [...] you changed all my life – – – And Music which meant much to me before in a vague desultory fashion – is now – fraught with inner meaning", and a Germanic continuous tense: "Please I want you to remember that All my life I am being grateful & happy and proud to have known you" (1984–2008: 1/25, fn.1). At the same period, Mansfield was composing rhapsodic letters to Trowell's cello-playing son Arnold (also known as 'Tom' Trowell, including a letter in German praising a composition of his in a string of – possibly ironic – Romantic clichés: "so wunderbar schön – so träumerisch – und auch so sehnsuchtvoll" (ibid.: 1/39).

here of Mansfield's narrative performance of Peacock's tired simile. "But of all those splendid things he had to say, not one could he utter. For some fiendish reason, the only words he could get out were: 'Dear lady, I should be so charmed – so charmed!'" (152)

"Her First Ball" and "The Singing Lesson", published in *The Garden Party and Other Stories* (1922), both make adroit use of the contrasting emotions inspired by music to construct narratives that hinge on a turn of feeling for the protagonist. In "Her First Ball", Leila, who has lived all her life in the country, with nothing more glamorous than all-girl dancing lessons in a corrugated iron mission hall, is so excited that she feels as though it is impossible to say "[e]xactly when the ball began […]. Perhaps her first partner was the cab" (336). This is a comic, momentary, yet expressive instance of the stream-of-consciousness animation of the material and animal world which Mansfield pioneered well in advance of Virginia Woolf, and which in her early writing produces some stunning sound-imbued performances such as an invocation, in an early Vignette, of a sensuous, personified London which, as crowds throng out of the theatre, is orchestrated as an "intoxicating madness of night music" and "the penetrating rhythm of the hansom cabs" ("Vignettes I"; 1989: 4). Leila, in "Her First Ball", remains ecstatic for her first few dances, but her state of elation is punctured when she dances with a cynical fat man who warns her that in no time at all she will be one of the frustrated chaperones with fat arms who are consigned to sit in black velvet at the end of the hall:

> Was this first ball really only the beginning of her last ball after all? At that the music seemed to change; it sounded sad, sad; it rose upon a great sigh. Oh how quickly things changed! […] Leila didn't want to dance any more […]. But presently a soft, melting, ravishing tune began, and a young man with curly hair bowed before her. She would have to dance, out of politeness […]. But in one minute, in one turn, her feet glided, glided. The lights, the azaleas, the dresses, the pink faces, the velvet chairs, all became one beautiful flying wheel. And when her next partner bumped her into the fat man and he said "Par*don*" she smiled at him more radiantly than ever. She didn't even recognise him again. (342f.)

The musical repetitions "sad, sad", "glided, glided" in this passage may owe something specifically to Mansfield's experience as a cellist, echoing the physical bow-change rhythms of the instrument on which she had herself performed, leading a fellow cellist to remark that "it is almost possible to bow Mansfield's texts" (Kennedy 2010: 117)[12].

In "The Singing Lesson", Mansfield conspicuously exploits her experience of practical music-making, and the fickle emotional responses inspired by music to underpin a turning point within a brief comic narrative. Like "Her First Ball", this performs what Trev Broughton has termed a "crisp" dramatisation of "readerly suspicion" (2008: 5). And what better vehicle to dramatise "readerly suspicion" than the yet more suspect affective power of music? Miss Meadows, a singing teacher in a girls' school, begins her singing class in a state of "cold, sharp despair" (343). Her fiancé has sent a cruel letter ending their engagement. Sternly, she beats time as she makes the girls practice "A Lament":

> Fast! Ah too Fast Fade The Ro-o-ses of Pleasure
> Soon Autumn yields into Wi-i-nter Drear.
> Fleetly! Ah Fleetly Mu-u-sic's Gay Measure
> Passes away from the Listening Ear. (346)

Mansfield's story 'performs' this text – quite probably remembered from her own school days – as repeatedly sung by the schoolgirls. The "Lament" is Mendelssohn's "Herbstlied"[13] (op. 63, 1845), a two-part song for female voices which had been popular in the English-speaking world since the mid-nineteenth century[14] and which was frequently included in anthologies for girls' school choirs[15]. The 6/8

---

[12] "Mansfield has the eyes and ears of a cellist", concludes Kate Kennedy in "Sight-reading Katherine Mansfield", a brief essay for *Landfall* Magazine; Kennedy, herself a cellist, provides an evocative discussion of the "string techniques" audible in Mansfield's writing (2010: 119; 115).

[13] I am immensely grateful to Peter Dayan, who far exceeded his duties as the world's first Professor of Word and Music Studies by identifying the music for these words.

[14] Peter Ackroyd (1990: 847) speculates that "Mendelssohn's popular 'Fast, ah, too fast fade the Roses of Pleasure' might have been amongst the duets that Charles Dickens sang with Ellen Ternan at her home in Camden Town (this would obviously have involved transposing one of the melodic lines). The Purcell Consort of Voices has very recently released a CD recording directed by Grayston Burgess under the title *Music All Powerful: Music to Entertain Queen Victoria*, which includes a setting of this translation (Decca Cat. No. 480 2091, April 2011). I am grateful to Katia Chornik for drawing my attention to this recording.

[15] "Autumn Song" appears in several arrangements for girls' school choirs held in the British Library; Kate Kennedy recalls singing this piece in the translation quoted

time signature of this work is indicated by the story's typography, and the words, whilst a less literal translation of "Ach, wie so bald verhallet der Reigen" than found in Victorian and Edwardian editions with parallel German and English texts, are a poetic approximation to the German lyrics (the lines are often more literally rendered "Soon ah, too soon die the sounds of enjoyment / Spring passes fast into Wintertime"). There are five distinct performances of the song text embedded into Mansfield's story and interwoven with the text of the fiancé's letter and Miss Meadows's thoughts. It is fabulous as a satire on literary affect (and on the pathetic fallacy) and as a precise and utterly convincing dramatisation of the singing lesson of the title. What follows here is a quite heavily abbreviated quotation from Mansfield's bravura performance:

> Miss Meadows lifted her arms [...] and began conducting with both hands. "... I feel more and more strongly that our marriage would be a mistake ..." she beat. And the voices cried: *Fleetly! Ah, Fleetly.* [...] His last letter had been all about a framed bookcase he had bought for "our" books and a "natty little hall-stand" he had seen [...].
>
> *Music's Gay Measure*, wailed the voices. The willow trees, outside the high, narrow windows, waved in the wind. They had lost half their leaves. The tiny ones that clung wriggled like fishes caught on a line. "... I am not a marrying man ..." The voices were silent; the piano waited. [...]
>
> "Quite good" said Miss Meadows, still in such a strange stony tone that the younger girls began to feel positively frightened. "But [...] think of the words, girls. Use your imaginations. *Fast! Ah, too Fast* [...]. That ought to break out – a loud, strong *forte* – a lament. And then, in the second line, *Winter Drear*, make that *Drear* sound as if a cold wind were blowing through it. *Dre-ear!*" said she so awfully that Mary Beazley, on the music-stool, wriggled her spine. "The third line should be one crescendo. *Fleetly! Ah, Fleetly Music's Gay Measure*. Breaking on the first word of the last line *Passes*. And then on the word, *Away*, you must begin to die ... to fade ... until *the Listening Ear* is nothing more than a faint whisper ... [...].
>
> "Repeat! Repeat!" said Miss Meadows. ... "More expression girls! Once more!"
>
> *Fast! Ah too Fast.* The older girls were crimson; some of the younger ones began to cry. Big spots of rain blew against the windows, and one could hear the willows whispering "... not that I do not love you ..." (346–348)

The performance continues until

---

by Mansfield at her British school in the 1990s. Recent performances of "Herbstlied" by girls' choirs can be found on YouTube (for example at: http://www.youtube.com/watch?v=cHRiybd3unY, accessed 8 April, 2011).

> [t]he voices began to die, to fade, to whisper ... to vanish ...
> Suddenly the door opened [...]. (348)

Literally the hinge, this, on which the story turns. A fidgety young messenger calls Miss Meadows to the headmistress's office, by which time her class is very subdued: "Most of them were blowing their noses" (348). In short clinking phrases, Mansfield takes Miss Meadows to the headmistress's room: "The corridors were silent and cold; they echoed to Miss Meadows's steps. The head mistress sat at her desk." (348) The headmistress, kindly at the prospect of terrible news, hands her a telegram: "Pay no attention to letter must have been mad bought hat-stand today" (349). A complete reversal of mood takes immediate effect as, "[o]n the wings of hope, of love, of joy" and in a breathless tumble of sentences, "Miss Meadows sped back to the music-hall, up the aisle, up the steps, over to the piano [...]. Then she turned to the girls, rapped with her baton: 'Page thirty-two girls. Page thirty-two.'" And the girls, still solemn and melancholy, sing:

> We come here To-day with Flowers o'erladen,
> With baskets of Fruit and Ribbons to boot,
> To-oo Congratulate ...

And Miss Meadows's response:

> "Stop! Stop!" Cried Miss Meadows. "This is awful. This is dreadful." And she beamed at her girls. "What's the matter with you all? Think, girls, think of what you're singing. Use your imaginations. *With Flowers o'erladen, With baskets of Fruit and Ribbons to boot.* And Congratulate." Miss Meadows broke off. "Don't look so doleful, girls. It ought to sound warm, joyful, eager. *Congratulate.* Once more. Quickly. All together. Now then!"
> And this time Miss Meadows' voice sounded over all the other voices – full, deep, glowing with expression. (349f.)

And thus the story ends with a moment of ironic linguistic performativity, in its most exact sense, as the sung lyrics perform the act of congratulation upon Miss Meadows's continued engagement.

Despite the happy narrative turn in these two stories, they leave the reader with a sharpened sense of "how quickly things change". The story immediately preceding "Her First Ball" in *The Garden Party* collection is "Miss Brill" – the work Mansfield recorded having played over like a musical composition and in which she uses language as notation as much as narration. In one of the few critical observations of the musical specificity of Mansfield's prose, Clare Hanson and Andrew Gurr suggest that the story is "shaped specifically as a lament" with "something of the quality of a sung lament [...]

infused into it by the use of para-musical prose rhythms" (1981: 77). Without requiring the surrender of "readerly suspicion", "Miss Brill" sustains the lament that is comically forestalled in "The Singing Lesson".

Miss Brill makes her regular Sunday visit to hear the band at the Jardins Publiques one autumn afternoon. She enjoys the band which "sounded louder and gayer [...] because the Season had begun" and enjoys, too, the sense of playing her part in a performance "exactly like a play" (334) involving all those around her, even the "odd silent" old people who are there "Sunday after Sunday" and who, "from the way they stared [...] looked as though they'd just come from dark little rooms, or even – even cupboards!" (331f.). The music of the band apparently changes – from tenderness to gaiety – to follow the emotions that she perceives as people laugh, converse and greet one another. An old lady in shabby ermine is unkindly snubbed by a gentleman-acquaintance. And now, Miss Brill's imagined drama becomes a choral performance, imbued with music's (suspiciously) uncertain emotive power, as the band plays something "warm and sunny":

> [Y]et there was just a faint chill – a something, what was it? – not sadness – no not sadness – a something that made you want to sing. The tune lifted, lifted, the light shone; and it seemed to Miss Brill that in another moment all of them, all the whole company, would begin singing. The young ones, the laughing ones who were moving together, they would begin, and the men's voices, very resolute and brave, would join them. And then she too, she too, and the others on the benches – they would come in with a kind of accompaniment – something low, that scarcely rose or fell, something so beautiful – moving . . . . And Miss Brill's eyes filled with tears and she looked smiling at all the other members of the company. Yes, we understand, we understand – though what they understood she didn't know. (334f.)

The ellipsis towards the end of this quotation is Mansfield's, a silence as acute as a rest in music, a moment for the reader to register the continuing flow of Mansfield's prose, to find it as 'moving' as the music Miss Brill invokes; a space for anticipation. Also a space for lament, lament for Miss Brill, for all the *dames seules* and their war dead, for the silent old people who visit the park each Sunday. "Yes, we understand, we understand", thinks Miss Brill, an instant before her sense of unspoken choral empathy is shattered in a painful reverse-epiphany. The young couple who share her bench make it plain that they resent the existence of such unattractive old women as she. They laugh at the tatty fox-fur which she had fondly taken from its box that morning, re-enacting the snubbing of the old lady in ermine – the tiny play within a play that she has just been watching. Miss Brill returns to her own "cupboard" of a room and, the story, as all who read it remember, ends with a voicing of repressed grief as "quickly; quickly, without looking" she puts the fur away in its box, and the unrecognised sadness that earlier had made her "want to sing" emerges as disembodied anguish: "But when she put the lid on she thought she heard something crying" (336).

Mansfield's was never a narrowly aestheticist concern with performance. In Bowen's view, "[i]ndignation at injustice, from time to time, makes her no less inflammatory a writer than Charles Dickens" and, like Dickens,

> [s]he concerns herself with bad cases rather than bad systems: political awareness or social criticism do not directly express themselves in the stories. [...] Unimaginativeness, with regard to others, seemed to her one of the grosser sins. The denial of love, the stunting of sorrow, or the cheating of joy was to her not short of an enormity. (1957: 23f.)

This aspect of Mansfield's work is more amply recognised in recent criticism, which has established its receptivity to post-colonial and feminist readings (and is sometimes even in danger of forgetting, in the effort to convey its political seriousness, the aesthetic qualities – those shimmering performances – that make one want to read her stories in the first place).

That the business of art was no "escape from life" was always clear from Mansfield's identification of "*a cry against corruption*" as a primary motivation for her writing (1984–2008: 2/54). "Not a protest – a *cry*", she asserted, and it is significant (and at one with the 'speakingness' of her writing) that Mansfield insists on that vocal term, rather than the abstract and instrumental "protest" (Bowen 1957: 15). The performance and the cry against corruption are, of course, inseparable. There is no need to downplay the close affinities with aestheticism of her writing, but her literary performances frequently satirise aestheticism as much as embody it. Her famous story "Bliss" (1920) – at one level one of her most brittle, virtuosic verbal showpieces – is simultaneously a satire and an enactment, or performance, of aesthetic sensibility. The story conveys the bankruptcy of obsessive aestheticism unredeemed by artistic talent, with a satirical portrait of an aspiring poet entranced by the whiteness of his socks by moonlight, and a naïve heroine, Bertha, self-consciously bewitched by the beauty of red soup in a grey bowl – almost as much as by her mysteriously attractive guest, Pearl Fulton, and the beautiful blossoming pear tree outside her window – but only almost. The story, as Clare Hanson and Andrew Gurr emphasise, also hovers on the edge of a near tragic portrayal of a character just self-conscious enough to know her limitations (cf. 1981: 60); Mansfield described to John Middleton Murry the intended effect of the "borrowed" phrases that she gave Bertha, who, "not being an artist, was yet artist manqué enough to realise that these words and expressions were not & couldn't be hers" (1984–2008: 2/121). All this is given an intensely realised symbolic rather than discursive existence in Mansfield's prose and it depends on the degree to which readers are intuitively and emotionally engaged by this performance, as to whether they find in Bertha's final contemplation of her lovely pear-tree, at a moment of unforeseen betrayal, a genuinely cruel, if exquisite, epiphany.

Mansfield, in fact, detested literature that was lacking in emotion, asserting that even descriptions of the weather must be "passionately realised" in fiction (1930: 51). She criticized T. S. Eliot's poetry for its lack of feeling and was extremely disappointed by the failure of Woolf's novel *Night and Day* to convey what, in a letter of 1919, she calls the "tragic knowledge" brought by the First World War (1984–2008: 3/97). Mansfield's "The Fly" (1922) is unusual in that it refers directly to the war; she was certainly not merely criticising Woolf's subject matter in *Night and Day* – "I dont want G. forbid mobilisation and the violation of Belgium" (1987: 53). Rather, she was aghast at some failure in aesthetic sensibility and acuteness of vision in Woolf's novel, so unlike the "vivid and disturbing beauty" that she praised in her review of Woolf's story "Kew Gardens" in the same year. Mansfield saw the war as something that must transform writers' responses to the world, making them see the common things of life with a new intensity and illumination. Artists who failed to take this into account she described, in strong terms, as "traitors"; "[w]e have to face our war", she asserted (1984–2008: 3/82). However, for Mansfield, this transformation had to be communicated indirectly. Quoting the seventeenth-century Andrew Marvell's *carpe diem*-poem "To his Coy Mistress", she explained that the war had brought her a new consciousness of "deserts of vast eternity". Then, in a paragraph that illuminates the way in which she values the oblique expression of this consciousness (as was to be so eloquently demonstrated in stories like "Miss Brill"), she explains:

> I couldn't tell anybody *bang out* about those deserts. They are my secret. I might write about a boy eating strawberries or a woman combing her hair on a windy morning & that is the only way I can ever mention them. But they *must* be there. Nothing less will do. (Ibid. 3: 97f.)

After the death of her brother in the war, Mansfield had determined on the development of a musicalized "kind of special prose" through which she would perform an act of memorialisation – not of her brother directly, but of all that they had shared down to the "creaking of the laundry basket" at their childhood home (1997: 2/33). Her haunting NZ stories are amongst those which show her musical Modernism at its most developed, employing what Bowen called "a marvellous sensory notation hitherto undreamed of outside poetry" yet "subject to prose discipline" (1957: 15).

The stories discussed here, where accounts of musical performance exist in part-ironic parallel with Mansfield's own musical prose, highlight the more pervasive musicality of all her work. Mansfield's writing modulates from accounts of specific musical scenes and allusions to a Modernist literary technique where music is a matter of structure and style rather than of substance – but with so much more than merely style, or performance, at stake. Interestingly, it is precisely a description of a musical performance that enraged her in Virginia Woolf's *Night and Day*, where a scene in which "a charming young creature in a light fantastic attitude plays on the flute" most represents, for Mansfield, Woolf's failure to admit the "tragic knowledge" of war into her writing (1984–2008: 3/82; 97). Her declaration that writing must be "passionately realised" is echoed in the philosopher Stanley Cavell's recent assertions that J. L. Austin's conception of a performative utterance needs to be augmented to encompass the idea of a "passionate utterance" (2005: 155–191). In Mansfield, the performative power of language cannot be divorced from its affective power. Her literary performances, even at their most virtuosic, proclaim a commitment to the performative capacity of art, in this enriched sense.

References

Ackroyd, Peter (1990). *Dickens*. London: Sinclair-Stevenson.
Bowen, Elizabeth (1957). "Introduction". Katherine Mansfield. *34 Short Stories*. London: Collins. 9–26.

Broughton, Trev (2008). [Review]. *The Collected Letters of Katherine Mansfield*. Vol. 5. Vincent O'Sullivan, Margaret Scott, eds. *Times Literary Supplement* 5507 (October): 3–5.

Cavell, Sydney (2005). *Philosophy the Day After Tomorrow*. Cambridge, MA: Harvard UP.

da Sousa Correa, Delia (2011a). "Katherine Mansfield and Music: Nineteenth-Century Echoes". Eds. Gerri Kimber, Janet Wilson. *Celebrating Katherine Mansfield: A Centenary Volume of Essays*. Basingstoke: Palgrave Macmillan. 84–98.

— (2011b). "Musical Performance in Katherine Mansfield's Stories". *Katherine Mansfield Studies* 3 (September): 21–34.

Hanson, Clare, Andrew Gurr (1981). *Katherine Mansfield*. London: Macmillan.

Kaplan, Sydney Janet (1991). *Katherine Mansfield and the Origins of Modernist Fiction*. Ithaca, NY/London: Cornell UP.

Kennedy, Kate (2010). "Sight-Reading Katherine Mansfield". *Landfall* 219: 115–119.

Kosofsky Sedgwick, Eve (2003). *Touching Feeling: Affect, Pedagogy, Performativity*. Durham, NC/London: Duke UP.

Manhire, Vanessa (2011). "Mansfield, Woolf and Music: 'The Queerest Sense of Echo'". *Katherine Mansfield Studies* 3 (September): 51–66.

Mansfield, Katherine (1930). John Middleton Murry, ed. *Novels and Novelists*. London: Constable.

— (1981). *The Collected Stories of Katherine Mansfield*. Harmondsworth: Penguin.

— (1984–2008). Vincent O'Sullivan, Margaret Scott, eds. *The Collected Letters of Katherine Mansfield*. Oxford: Clarendon Press.

— (1987). Clare Hanson, ed. *The Critical Writings of Katherine Mansfield*. London: Macmillan.

— (1989). Vincent O'Sullivan, ed. *Poems of Katherine Mansfield*. Auckland: OUP.

— (1997). Margaret Scott, ed. *The Katherine Mansfield Notebooks*. 2 vols. Canterbury: Lincoln UP/Wellington: Daphne Brasell Associates.

Tomalin, Claire (1988). *Katherine Mansfield: A Secret Life*. Harmondsworth: Penguin.

Rhythmical Ambivalence of Poetry Performance
The Case of Elizabethan Verse

Walter Bernhart, Graz

The basically uncoded prosodic dimension of language in writing gives room for variations in verse delivery which may lead to highly divergent poetry performance practices. These fulfil different functions of artistic activity and reflect contrastive stylistic impulses and aesthetic positionings, ranging from more casual, 'plain', 'drab', information-oriented style variants to more formal, 'eloquent', 'golden', 'musically'-informed ones.

This paper presents a case study from the Elizabethan period, when two distinctive types of language pronunciation were practiced (which, following Kuryłowicz, can be explained in linguistic terms as 'morphological' vs. 'syllabic') and when extensive rhythmical experimentation in verse took place (e. g., Sidney's 'classical metres'). Such variations in performance style can be explained by identifying oppositional art-ideological positions that inform them. They reflect the historical transition in the Elizabethan age from humanist-inspired to rationalist conceptions of poetry, and at the same time represent more generally relevant contrastive positionings in the world of the arts.

As the programme of this conference vividly shows, there is indeed an enormous range of options to discuss performative aspects in the field of word and music studies[1]. Yet interestingly only a few are concerned with the performative dimension of poetry, that is, with the actual delivery aspect of reading poetry out loud. To the extent that nowadays poetry is read at all, it is mostly read in private, at a silent reading, the main focus of which is a search of meaning as an intellectual challenge, as an intimate, exclusively mental activity. It is true, we have public poetry readings today, and their popularity, as far as it goes, is above all a product of the cultural upheavals in the 1960s, that decisive watershed that brought music, poetry, the arts in general, out of the closet onto the street and in front of a wider general, primarily young public. And, certainly, there are recent developments in 'performance poetry' (see, e. g., Gräbner/Casas, eds. 2011; Novak

---

[1] In view of its topic, the oral character of the conference delivery of this paper, which included poetry recitation, has been preserved in this written version.

2011), and we have audio books at times also offering poetry for our ears.

The withdrawal of poetry into the private sphere was, from a historical perspective, largely a consequence of a decisive change in the conception of rhetoric as it took place in the later Renaissance period[2]. At that time, Pierre de la Rameé, or Petrus Ramus, developed his dialectic and a logically oriented view of rhetoric, which superseded the then prevailing Ciceronian school of rhetoric. Cicero had developed his well-known five-step system of rhetoric (inventio – dispositio – elocutia – memoria – pronuntiatio), and the Humanists had put a strong emphasis on 'eloquence' and 'pronunciation' in this system, i. e., on those elements that concentrate on the performative side of speaking. Ramus's innovation, by stressing the logical and dialectical side of poetry, implied a marked downgrading of the performative aspect of speaking and thereby a fundamental reorientation as to the questions of what is (the end of) poetry and what one should do with a poem. Ramist rhetoric is the source of the modern 'Lesegedicht' with its emphasis on search of meaning, introspective reflexion and meditation. Ciceronian rhetoric, by contrast, had stressed the physical delivery aspect and the aspect of effective speaking, of articulating poetry with a persuasive purpose in the public sphere. It was this performative side of poetry in the context of humanist-inspired rhetoric that lined up Renaissance poetry with contemporary music, a field where also effectiveness of delivery – mainly in terms of being able to 'move the passions' through music – had become a central concern[3].

As a consequence of this fascinating fundamental change of perspective on the function of poetry during the Renaissance period, I have chosen to talk about this interesting transitional period in my attempt to discuss performative aspects of poetry in more general terms, with a focus on the situation in England. So the question I am trying to answer is: what do we know about the way in which poetry was orally performed, in the Ciceronian context, before it turned into

---

[2] Much of the ensuing historical discussion is based on my earlier study, *'True Versifying': Studien zur elisabethanischen Verspraxis und Kunstideologie. Unter Einbeziehung der zeitgenössischen Lautenlieder* (1993), especially ch. III, "'Drowning of letters': Zur Sprachartikulation in der elisabethanischen Zeit" (204–226).

[3] For the influence of Ramism on poetry cf. Bernhart (1993: 226), and generally on contemporary performative rhetoric see Bornstein (1983).

an activity of silent meditative concentration? And we will see that more than one style of verse delivery was available at the time, and that in fact two contrasting performative principles can be identified as having been active, which reflected contrasting aesthetic principles and views of the function of poetry, and art in general.

The main problem with studying the performative side of poetry delivery in a historical context is the fact that those elements of language which constitute and shape the act of oral delivery are largely uncoded in the written texts as they have come down to us, and of course we have no sound documents from the Elizabethan period. What is missing in any written text of poems is a graphic representation of their prosodic dimension, which is largely irrelevant for a purely semantic appreciation of the poems, but essential for their oral articulation. The elements of stress, intonation, rhythm (i. e., time segmentation), timbre, sound volume and tempo – all those, in common parlance, 'musical' elements of poetry – cannot be identified in the written document, and yet they absolutely determine the oral performance. Even the most barren musical score indicates at least pitches and durations, not to speak of elaborate post-Debussy scores with their minute specifications of dynamics, tempo, tone colour and so on. But a poem on the page has none of all this.

So how can we establish evidence of the performative practice of the time? Well, there are not so very many descriptive reports on actual Elizabethan instances of performance in courtly situations or in the pastime practices of the rising middle class (but there are some interesting ones, in fact, in plays, also in Shakespeare). Yet as the humanist period was highly educative and pedagogical in its orientation, we do have quite a number of pertinent references in manuals of grammar, rhetoric, or poetry, and above all in the influential 'conduct books' of the type of Castiglione's *Cortegiano*. A main source, however, are critical essays, often written by poets themselves who in these essays defended their own positions in the aesthetic debates of the time. These essays were often surprisingly controversial and, in principle, had to do with responses to the rise of rationalism, as reflected – among a number of other features – in the Cicero-Ramus 'turn' in the world of rhetoric already mentioned. Another important source is the music of the time, in particular, the Elizabethan airs, those popular solo songs with lute accompaniment as practiced by John Dowland, Thomas Campion and many others. These airs are a valid source for studying the performance also of poetry, and not only of music, because the theoretical treatises of the time made it patently clear that poetry and music were seen as sharing the same rhetorical and aesthetic aims, and that, as a consequence, the words as articulated in the songs were expected to follow carefully the articulation of the words in a spoken utterance.

A great number of the critical essays and manuals referred to are motivated by defending a 'classical' style of word delivery in the Humanist tradition, against tendencies that neglect the observance of a correct and accurate pronunciation of every sound and syllable in the speech flow. These critics frequently resort to vivid and sometimes quite entertaining imagery in making their point. For instance, King James, in his "Schort Treatise Conteining Some Revlis and Cautelis To Be Obseruit and Eschewit In Scottis Poesie" of 1584, complains about the frequent practice of pronouncing one syllable so very "lang" (long) that it "eatis vp in the pronouncing euin the vther syllables" (1904/1971: I/212). Similarly, George Puttenham, in his well-known *Arte of English Poesie* of 1589, regrets the 'drowning' of syllables so that it "seemeth to passe away in maner vnpronounced" (1904/1971: II/74). The same idea, using the same image of 'drowning', is expressed in an anonymous grammar book of around 1600, which contains the following quite self-explanatory dialogue:

> Q. Nowe what thinges doe yee observe in reading:
> R. These two thinges.   1 *Cleane sounding*.
>
>   2 *Dewe pawsing*.
>
> Q. Wherein standeth *cleane sounding*:
>
> R. In giving every letter his just and full sounde. In breaking and dividing every worde duely into his severall syllables, so that every syllable may bee hearde by himselfe and none drownd, nor slubbered by ill favouredly. (Qtd. Attridge 1979: 34)

Particularly vivid is Stefano Guazzo's diatribe against loose pronunciation of words. In his conduct book called *The Civile Conversation*, which appeared in English in the 1580s, he gives the following instructions:

> [...] it is not meete to utter ones woordes in suche hast, that like meate, in the mouth of one almost starved, then bee swallowed downe without chewing. [...] But we must take heede above all thinges, that the last sillables be heard plainly, least we fall into the fault of some, who suffer the last letters to die betweene their teeth [...]; therefore wee must speake freely, without supping up our woordes, and bringing them but halfe foorth. (1967: I/128)

Also to quote a musician, William Byrd, the famous composer (again in the same decade, in 1588, in his *Psalmes, Sonets, & songs of sadness and pietie*), gives good advice for how to avoid such 'slubbering', 'drowning', 'supping' and 'eating up' of sounds. What he advocates is singing: singing, he says, "is the best meanes to procure a perfect pronunciation, & to make a good Orator" (qtd. Fellowes/Dart, eds. 1956ff.: 1965/vii). And the equally famous John Dowland, the world's best lutenist of the age, is particularly harsh on careless speakers and singers: "Think you that God is pleased with such howling, such noise, such mumbling, in which is no deuotion, no expression of words, no articulating of syllables?" (Ornithoparchus/ Dowland 1609/1973: 89)

Gioseffo Zarlino, one of the most important music theorists of the time, is the mastermind of the period concerning all discussions about the rhetorical function of music, and he is a main advocate of the subordination of music to language and poetry, to which I have briefly referred. Zarlino talks about a 'rhetorical' accent as an essential element of 'ornate speech' ("pronuncia ornata"). This 'rhetorical' accent works in the speech flow as an agent of "Ritenimento, ò Retinaculo, ò Freno" ('obstacle, or net, or rein') holding back the speech flow, it is an 'artificial restraint of the breath' ("un'arteficioso ritenimento dello Spirito") and supposed to guarantee in the speech "ornamento & soavità" (ornament and suppleness) (1588/1966: 322f.).

A final example of a famous poet and playwright of the period attacking a loose form of articulation in verse is Ben Jonson, who wrote a delightful satirical poem called "A Fit of Rime against Rime", in which he complains about the fact that poets who use rhyme tend to ignore the rest of the prosody of their verse. He says:

> Joynting Syllables, drowning Letters,
> Fastning Vowells, as with fetters
>   They were bound! (1947: 183)

Jonson complains that syllables are slurred over, sounds are swallowed, and vowels are 'fastened', which last phrase is not so clear. It is likely to mean that the vowels are 'fastened' to the consonants, i. e., stick to the consonants – "as with fetters" – and so lose their full sounding; it is probably a reference to a strong quality reduction of vowels in unstressed positions.

We can see that there was a full chorus of voices attacking what the period used to call the 'barbarism' of negligent pronunciation, and these critics were inspired by the classical verse models of antiquity which they conceived of in terms of a stately and dignified pace of the utterance, and this vision of a leisurely, dignified form of verse delivery triggered the period's interest in reviving classical metres for English poetry, in particular, the classical hexameter. We now know that these classical verse experiments by the Elizabethans were bound to fail because of the non-phonemic nature of syllable length in English, which implies that durational qualities of syllables, i. e., a distinction between long and short syllables, cannot become the basis of a system of versification (cf. Bernhart 1993: 219). Yet the idea of paying attention to such durational qualities of syllables, and not only to the dynamic qualities of stress accents, sharpened the poets' minds for being careful about syllable weights in the sequential order of their verse lines. It was this concern about the "waite [weight] and due proportion" of syllables, which Thomas Campion famously called for (1904/1971: II/329) and which encouraged poets and critics of the time to pay close attention to the careful articulation of syllables, as observed in all the statements quoted above. The aim was to achieve an intentionally 'artificial' (i. e., artful) style of delivery that avoided the 'barbarism' of careless articulation.

However, this propagation of an artificial, formal style of poetry performance was not universally accepted by all the critics and poets of the time. One significant voice attacking such a style was Thomas Nash, whose *Unfortunate Traveller* – tellingly so – is an ancestor of the English realistic novel. In his "Strange Newes" of 1592, Nash rejects English hexameters by saying:

> Our speech is too craggy for him [the hexameter] to set his plough in; hee goes twitching and hopping in our language like a man running vpon quagmiers, vp the hill in one Syllable, and downe the dale in another, retaining no part of that stately smooth gate which he vaunts himselfe with amongst the Greeks and Latins. (Ibid.: II/240)

It is obvious that what Nash is here defending is the natural pronunciation of everyday English, where the rhythm is predominantly structured by the strong stress accent and where unstressed syllables are slid over and strongly reduced. In a similar way, Samuel Daniel, the younger courtly lyric poet from the Sidney circle, speaks against classical hexameters in English by saying, in his "Defence of Ryme" of c. 1603: "in the reading [of such hexameters] wee must stand bound to stay where often we would not, and sometimes either breake the accent or the due course of the word" (Ibid.: II/377).

From what we have heard so far, we can draw the conclusion that in the Elizabethan age two distinct pronunciation styles were available which both found their apologists and denouncers. Research in historical linguistics has supported such a distinction. To quote one influential earlier scholar, Helge Kökeritz, eminent authority on Shakespeare's pronunciation: on the one hand, Kökeritz observes a "radical reduction of unstressed syllables and its often nonchalant treatment of the consonants" (1953: 6); yet, on the other hand, he also identifies a "formal style of delivery [...] in which sounds and syllables normally slurred tended to be more or less fully sounded" (ibid.: 14).

Such a distinction of articulatory styles found its most convincing theoretical linguistic explanation by a Polish scholar, Jerzy Kuryłowitz, who called them the 'morphological' and the 'syllabic' forms of articulation, respectively (cf. 1966: 169), because in the one form the prosodic unit is the word with its morphological accent structure, while in the other the prosodic unit is the syllable. In the one case, the syllables have different values, and the prominent accented ones are those that are also semantically prominent. In the other case, all the syllables are of equal status and form a continuity, in which word stress is still active but has lost its primary rhythmical function of time segmentation. As Kuryłowicz asserts, both styles are equally valid and historically manifest, and both are, in principle, applicable in all languages, so, of course, also in English (cf. ibid.: 164; 168). In this observation we find a justification on a theoretical level for the existence of the two styles in English poetry, and as a consequence one would not be able to claim that one of them is necessarily unacceptable in the language (as, for instance, Nash claimed). To opt for one or the other practice is a matter of stylistic choice, and not of truth or error.

What I will now try to do is to demonstrate the two ways of reading by reciting a poem by Sir Philip Sidney, who was one of the most outspoken advocates of a stylized form of verse delivery (at least early in his short life) and who was the most significant contemporary experimenter with classical metres. These experiments can mainly be found in his *Old Arcadia*, which he wrote in the 1570s and in which the individual books of the prose romance are separated by sequences of poems. One of the poems, "If mine eyes can speake", is written as a Sapphic ode, and there is clear evidence that Sidney expected the poem to be read in a way observing the durational pattern of the ancient sapphic metre, which can be transcribed as follows (— representing a long syllable, . a short syllable, and x a lengthwise undetermined syllable)[4]:

$$— . — — — . . — . — x$$
$$— . — — — . . — . — x$$
$$— . — — — . . — . — x$$
$$— . . — x$$

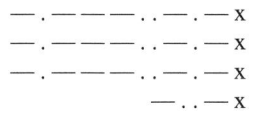

I will now try to read the poem by applying a 'syllabic' articulation in sapphics which observes the metrical durations of syllables, yet without wrenching the word and sentence accent:

If mine eyes can speake to do harty errande,
$$— . \quad — \quad — \quad — \quad . . \quad — . \quad — \quad x$$
Or mine eyes' language she doo hap to judge of,
$$— . \quad — \quad — \quad — \quad . . \quad — . \quad — \quad x$$
So that eyes' message be of her receaved,
$$— . \quad — \quad — \quad — \quad . . \quad — . \quad — \quad x$$
Hope we do live yet.
$$— \quad . . \quad — \quad x$$

But if eyes faile then, when I most doo need them,
$$— . \quad — \quad — \quad — \quad . . \quad — \quad . \quad — \quad x$$
Or if eyes' language be not unto her knowne,
$$— . \quad — \quad — \quad — \quad . . \quad — . \quad — \quad x$$
So that eyes' message doo returne rejected,
$$— . \quad — \quad — \quad — \quad . . \quad — . \quad — \quad x$$
Hope we doo both dye.
$$— \quad . \quad — \quad x$$

Yet dying, and dead, doo we sing her honour;
$$— . — \quad — \quad — \quad . . \quad — . \quad — \quad x$$
So become our tombs monuments of her praise;
$$— . \quad — \quad — \quad — \quad . . \quad — . \quad — \quad x$$
So becomes our losse the triumph of her gayne;
$$— . \quad — \quad — \quad — \quad . . \quad — . \quad — \quad x$$
Hers be the glory.
$$— \quad . \quad — x$$

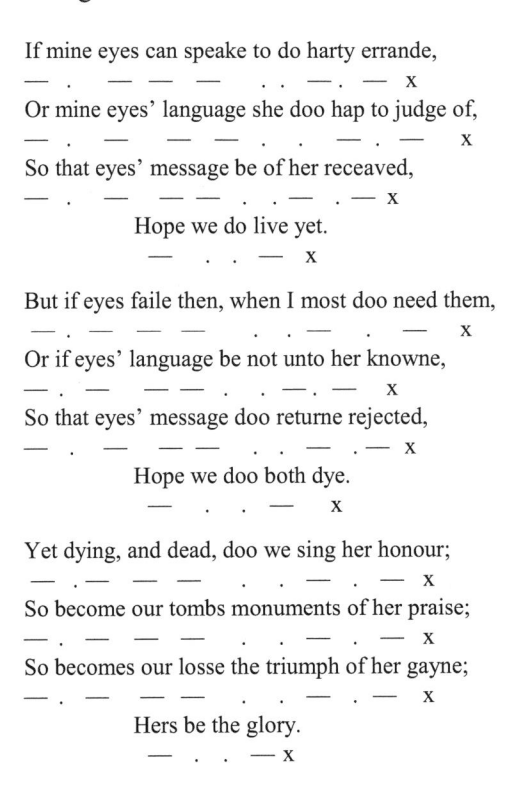

[4] For a more detailed description of the two types of reading Sidney's poem cf. Bernhart (1993: 296–303). The text of the poem is taken from Sidney (1971: 30f.).

If the senceless spheres doo yet hold a musique,
— . — — — . . — . — x
If the Swanne's sweet voice be not heard, but at death,
— . — — — . . — . — x
If the mute timber when it hath the life lost,
— . — — — . . — . — x
    Yeldeth a lute's tune,
    — . . — x

Are then humane mindes priviledg'd so meanly,
— . — — — . . — . — x
[...]

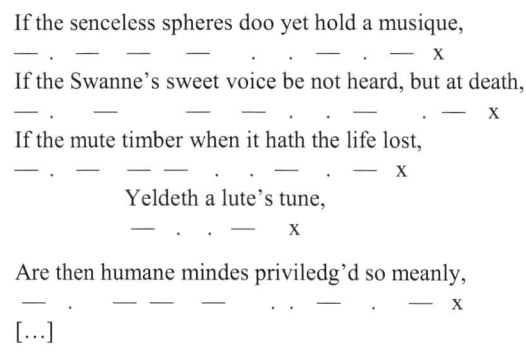

Such a 'syllabic' reading is surely quite strange in our ears and has a strongly incantatory, a very static and formalized character. But it may very well be seen as perfectly suited to the metaphysical ideas of the poem about immortal beauty beyond death and about eternal life of the soul as it is obtained by the power of love. And there is surely a strongly rhetorical, and in fact a 'musical' force in it.

As an alternative, I will now try to do a 'morphological' reading of the poem, and what will come out, in metrical terms, is a verse type in the tradition of the Skeltonics and early-Tudor poetry, as represented by Thomas Wyatt and others, i. e., a four-stress accentual metre with a break in the middle of the line and an unfixed number of unstressed syllables between the accents. The following transcription marks accented syllables as X, and unaccented syllables as x:

If mine eyes can speake to do harty errande,
x x   X x   X / x x   X x X x
Or mine eyes' language she doo hap to judge of,
x   x   X   X   x / x x   X x X   x
So that eyes' message be of her receaved,
x x   X   X x / x x X x X
    Hope we do live yet.
    X   x x X X

But if eyes faile then, when I most doo need them,
 x x X   X   x / x x X   x   X   x
Or if eyes' language be not unto her knowne,
x x X   X x/x X xx x   X
So that eyes' message doo returne rejected,
x   x   X   X x / x x X   xX x
    Hope we doo both dye.
    X   x x   X   X

```
Yet dying, and dead, doo we sing her honour;
  x  X x   x    X   /x  x  X x  X  x
So become our tombs monuments of her praise;
  x  x  X    x    X  /X  x  x  x  x  X
So becomes our losse the triumph of her gayne;
  x  x  X     x   X  /x  X  x   x  x   X
        Hers be the glory.
         X  x x  X x

If the senceless spheres doo yet hold a musique,
 x  x   X      x    X   /x  x   X  x   X x
If the Swanne's sweet voice be not heard, but at death,
 x  x    X       x     X /x   x   X      x  x    X
If the mute timber when it hath the life lost,
 x  x   X    X  x /x   x   x  x   X  X
        Yeldeth a lute's tune,
         X  x  x  X     X

Are then humane mindes priviledg'd so meanly,
  x  x    X  x    X /   Xx    x   x   X  x
[…]
```

Such an accentual, 'morphological' style of reading is obviously far more meaning-oriented than the 'syllabic' one of before and mainly by parallelisms and verbal repetitions stresses the strongly argumentative structure of the poem: 'If / Or / So that / (Then) – But if / Or / So that / (Then) – Yet / So / So / (Therefore)'. Such a reading clearly brings out the logic of the argument and makes sure that the speaker indeed presents a rational statement with a strong impulse to convince and to persuade his audience mentally by what he is saying.

We can see that, from a metrical point of view, both readings are possible in the framework of options offered by the poetic practice of the time. There is no doubt that Sidney would have favoured the first one as it answered his inclination to follow humanist ideas as they found expression in what was called the 'eloquent' style of poetry, as opposed to the 'plain', prosaic style (see Peterson 1967), or – to take up C. S. Lewis's distinction – as 'golden lyrics' in contrast to 'drab' poetry (see 1973). That Sidney was deeply concerned about a lofty conception of poetry in the context of neo-platonic humanist thinking is amply demonstrated by his "Apology for Poetrie", which is the profoundest poetological document of the period in England. There he objects to "speaking (table talke fashion […]) words as they chanceably fall from the mouth" and propagates "peyzing [weighing] each syllable of each worde by iust proportion according to the dignitie of the subiect" (1904/1971: I/160), and, further, Sidney famously contrasts the rhetorical practice of cold persuasion by merely using mechanical and conventional – as he calls them – "swelling phrases" and "fiery speeches" to the true poetic expression. True poetry is a product of what he calls a "forciblenes, or *Energia* (as the Greekes cal it), of the writer" (ibid.: I/201). This concept of 'energy', *energeia* – which goes back to Aristotle's *Rhetoric* – is central to the most refined humanist conception of poetry. I cannot go into this issue in any detail, but it is a main point that this 'energy' is a force that combines mental and physical aspects: it implies a physical manifestation and sensually experienced effectiveness of a spiritual idea. *Energeia*, according to Aristotle, is the process of establishing such an effectiveness, it is not its product: *energeia* is a bodily process of materialization, which in the neo-platonic context is related to the Christian idea of incarnation. It is on account of this its physical dimension that *energeia* manifests itself in the frame of rhetoric at the stage of *pronuntiatio* (in the Ciceronian scheme), which in turn explains why proper articulation became so important[5]. In one of his sonnets from *Astrophel and Stella* (No. 58), Sidney, again, like in his "Apology", distinguishes, on the one hand, a poet who coldly argues with "fine tropes" and "strongest reasons" and, on the other hand, the true and perfect poet who possesses "pronouncing grace, wherewith his mind / Prints his owne lively forme in rudest braine" ("Doubt there has bene"; 1971: 194; ll. 5–8).

This idea and practice of an 'artificial' articulatory performance style of verse which characterized the Elizabethan so-called New Poetry and answered the humanists' desire to revive – in Zarlino's words – the alleged 'secret and dark power of pronunciation' of ancient poetry[6] was dryly pushed aside by such late-Elizabethan 'naturalists' as Daniel, Nash, or George Gascoigne. Daniel's "Defence of Rhyme" attacks the "idle affectation of antiquitie or noueltie" (1904/ 1971: II/384) and even compares it to "a Viper" (ibid.: II/373) to be shunned and crushed. According to Daniel, sober natural and rational views of poetry must replace perverted speculations, an attitude that he wanted to be reflected in a natural style of verse delivery. It is a

---

[5] For a more extensive discussion of *energeia* in art discourse, see Bernhart 1993 ("Exkurs: Die 'energetische' Kunstauffassung": 313–331).

[6] "[…] un'ascosa & oscura forza di Pronuncia" (Zarlino 1573/1966: 320).

"deformitie", Daniel says, "to make our verse seeme another kind of speach out of the course of our vsuall practise" (ibid.: II/384). Others – like Sidney –, less soberly inclined, regretted that, on such a premise, poetry dwindled into prose.

To round off my discussion, I will only briefly point out that later poets – and great poets among them – indeed felt sympathy for a more artificial style of reciting poetry and often favoured a 'syllabic' to a 'morphological' reading of their poems. Eliot propagated an 'auditory imagination' that consisted of a "feeling for syllable and rhythm, penetrating far below the conscious levels of thought and feeling, invigorating every word" (1953: 94). D. H. Lawrence confessed: "I think I read my poetry more by length than by stress – as a matter of movement in space than footsteps hitting the earth." (1938: I/238) Pound regretted the radical change that poetry underwent in the seventeenth century and claimed: "From the Elizabethans to Swinburne, through all that vast hiatus, English poetry had been the bear-garden of doctrinaires. It had been the 'vehicle' of opinion. For Swinburne it was at least the art of musical wording." (1954/1974: 363) And Yeats, in his remarkable essay on "Speaking to the Psaltery", introduced graphic marks to characterize the syllables of his poems, but asserted that those "are not marks of scansion, but show the syllables one makes the voice hurry or linger over" (1961: 17). (Lawrence, by the way, also uses such graphic marks in the letter quoted above.)

This brings me back to the starting point of my considerations, namely, the missing codification of prosodic features in written language. If one conceives of the prosodic features of sound and rhythm as 'musical' aspects of language, and if one realizes that much of poetic language is performance-oriented (even though this aspect is widely neglected in our tradition) and that, thus, much poetry relies for its appropriate appreciation on an effective presentation of its 'musical' prosodic features, we cannot avoid drawing the conclusion that poetry performance can learn a lot from music, which of course is an art form that – ever since it has been established as, above all, *musica practica* – is centrally 'performative' in its character, and so, no doubt, poetry recitation is an ideal topic for word and music studies.

References

Attridge, Derek (1979). *Well-Weighed Syllables: Elizabethan Verse in Classical Metres*. Cambridge: CUP.

Bernhart, Walter (1986). "Castalian Poetics and the 'verie twichestane Musique'". *Scottish Language and Literature, Medieval and Renaissance. Fourth International Conference 1984: Proceedings*. Dietrich Strauss, Horst W. Drescher, eds. Scottish Studies 4. Frankfurt am Main: Peter Lang. 451–458.

— (1993). *'True Versifying': Studien zur elisabethanischen Verspraxis und Kunstideologie. Unter Einbeziehung der zeitgenössischen Lautenlieder*. Studien zur englischen Philologie, new series 29. Tübingen: Niemeyer.

Bornstein, Diane (1983). "Performing Oral Discourse As a Form of Sociability During the Renaissance". David W. Thompson, ed. *Performance of Literature in Historical Perspectives*. Lanham, MD/London: University Press of America. 211–221.

Campion, Thomas (1904/1971). "Observations in the Art of English Poesie" (1602). Smith, ed. II/327–355.

Daniel, Samuel (1904/1971). "A Defence of Ryme" (c. 1603). Smith, ed. II/356–384.

Eliot, T. S. (1953). *Selected Prose*. John Hayward, ed. London et al.: Penguin.

Fellowes, Edmund H., Thurston Dart, eds. (1956ff.). *The English Madrigalists*. London: Stainer & Bell.

Gräbner, Cornelia, Arturo Casas, eds. (2011). *Performing Poetry: Body, Place and Rhythm in the Poetry Performance*. Amsterdam/ New York, NY: Rodopi.

Guazzo, Steeven (1967). *The Civile Conversation*. George Pettie, trans. (vols. 1–3, 1581); Bartholomew Young, trans. (vol. 4, 1586). The Tudor Translations, 2nd series, vols. 7–8. New York/NY: AMS Press.

Jonson, Ben (1947). *The Works of Ben Jonson*. Vol. 8: *The Poems and the Prose Works*. C. H. Herford, Percy Simpson, Evelyn Simpson, eds. Oxford: Clarendon.

King James VI (1904/1971). "Ane Schort Treatise Conteining Some Revlis and Cautelis To Be Obseruit and Eschewit In Scottis Poesie" (1584). Smith, ed. I/208–225.

Kökeritz, Helge (1953). *Shakespeare's Pronunciation*. New Haven, CT: Yale UP.

Kuryłowitz, Jerzy (1966). "Accent and Quantity as Elements of Rhythm". *Poetics, Poetyka, ПОЗТИКА*, vol. 2. Den Haag/Paris: Mouton – Warsaw: PWN. 163–172.

Lawrence, D. H. (1938). *The Letters of D. H. Lawrence*. Vol. 1: *1909–1915*. Aldous Huxley, ed. Leipzig et al.: Albatross.

Lewis, C. S. (1973). *English Literature in the Sixteenth Century Excluding Drama*. The Oxford History of English Literature, vol. 3. Oxford: Clarendon.

Nash, Thomas (1904/1971). "From *Strange Newes*, or *Four Letters Confuted*" (1592). Smith, ed. II/239–244.

Novak, Julia (2011). *Live Poetry: An Integrated Approach to Poetry in Performance*. Internationale Forschungen zur Allgemeinen und Vergleichenden Literaturwissenschaft 153. Amsterdam/New York, NY: Rodopi.

Ornithoparchus, Andreas, John Dowland (1609/1973). *Andreas Ornithoparchus His Micrologus, or Introduction: Containing the Art of Singing*. John Dowland, trans. Gustave Reese, Steven Ledbetter, eds. New York, NY: Dover Publications.

Peterson, Douglas L. (1967). *The English Lyric from Wyatt to Donne: A History of the Plain and Eloquent Styles*. Princeton, NJ: Princeton UP.

Pound, Ezra (1954/1974). *Literary Essays*. T. S. Eliot, ed. London: Faber.

Puttenham, George (1904/1971). "The Arte of English Poesie" (1589). Smith, ed. II/1–193.

Sidney, Sir Philip (1971). *The Poems of Sir Philip Sidney*. William A. Ringler, Jr., ed. Oxford: Clarendon.

— (1904/1971). "An Apology for Poetrie" (c. 1583, printed 1595). Smith, ed. I/148–207.

Smith, G. Gregory, ed. (1904/1971). *Elizabethan Critical Essays*. 2 vols. Oxford: OUP.

Yeats, William Butler (1961). "Speaking to the Psaltery" (1902/1907). *Essays and Introductions*. London: Macmillan. 13–27.

Zarlino, Gioseffo (1573/1966). *Le Istitutioni Harmoniche*. Facsimile reprint. Ridgewood, NJ: Gregg Press.

— (1588/1966). *Sopplimenti mvsicali*. Facsimile reprint. Ridgewood, NJ: Gregg Press.

"Music will keep out temporary ideas"
W. B. Yeats's Radio Performances

Adrian Paterson, Galway

The Irish poet W. B. Yeats has been repeatedly accused of being 'tone deaf', and he himself on occasion disclaimed his musicality. However, as one of the first poets to take seriously to the radio, his intense commitment to aural communication on the medium discloses an unmistakable musical interest. The accident that most of his broadcasts do not survive has tended to obscure their significance. This paper examines what remains, discovering in the broadcasts a record of experimental musical performances. It uncovers an acute sense of melody in the poet's own readings and traces the effects of his collaborations with the composers Harry Partch and Arthur Duff. It also describes how his poetry's articulation of time is amplified and extended by the new medium's performance space, and how the intervention of music in and between poems might express the lasting of the passing moment.

"I am not musical", W. B. Yeats claimed (1966: 1008), and the world has tended to take him at his word. Evidence is usually found not in the poet's internal cognition, which must remain opaque to us, but in his attempts at performance. Unlike Thomas Hardy, James Joyce, W. H. Auden and many another poet, Yeats had no musical literacy. He could not play an instrument, and few have recognised as such his attempts to sing – least of all his father, who on hearing him at a young age banned all further musical education, profoundly affecting his musical development (cf. Yeats 1999: 54). His erstwhile editor Daniel Albright, himself a distinguished authority on literature and music, feels justified calling him "the most tone deaf of poets" (2000: 88). Yet attending seriously to the record of his radio broadcasts confronts us with a slightly different picture. The broadcasts record, primarily, Yeats's unwavering commitment to performance in poetry, to words conceived aurally and performed orally. They show a strong theatrical impulse increasingly attuned to the radio and its new possibilities, an unsung but real engagement in modernity and technology. Inextricably bound up with these impulses is, unmistakably, a fascination with music, something that persisted until the last breath of his life. Though Yeats could not repeat notes put to him, his sense of pitch, as we shall see, was not quite as it has been represented, his sense of rhythm extraordinarily acute. His lack of musical training might even have helped, leaving him open to avant-garde approaches; his frequent denials of musical knowledge often appear as disarming preludes to forthright opinions on music and words and their combination. His poetry broadcasts therefore represent a record of experimental musical performances. Viewing them alongside his other performative collaborations of the 1930s, I want to suggest here that exactly this unorthodox but indelible fascination with music not only produced these broadcasts but materially changed his conception of poetry.

By all accounts, Yeats's poetry was conditioned by its peculiar vocal genesis; its composition intricately inscribed with striking intonations, a cadence and patterning that might or might not survive the printed page, and might or might not approach something musical. With this intonation in mind, performance rather than reading seemed to best manifest its existence, although how exactly to perform it was a question never quite answered to the poet's satisfaction. A man who conducted his poetry, pacing and beating time might denounce professional musicians with abandon, but this was because he cared about how music and words were put together[1]. Nowhere is this more evident than in his broadcasts. Probably the accident that most do not survive has occasioned their neglect; although this possibility also in part conditioned their making, and indeed affected themes within the poems broadcast, as we shall see. Where original sound recordings do not survive, they can be in part reconstructed by transcriptions, musical scores, and recollections of the participants. What follows considers examples of broadcast performances authorized by Yeats to examine their approach to music; a study, to use Steven Paul Scher's distinctions, both of music *in* literature, and music *and* literature[2].

By the 1930s, Yeats's turn of the century experiments in speaking poetry to a musical instrument called the psaltery, though never forgotten, had been long in abeyance. As coming from the Nobel prize winner of 1923, many of Yeats's poems, and all six plays, had been showcased on the fledgling radio service, but although one notable

---

[1] As the actor John Stephenson remembered: "[…] it was fascinating to watch him [Yeats] beat out the rhythm he wanted to use" (Rodgers [n. d.]: 22 ["Broadcast: Poetry and the Seeing Ear", transcribed 19 June 1950]).

[2] A distinction most succinctly developed in Scher (1982/2004).

evening of readings in 1929 had featured his favourite actress Sara Allgood, Yeats had nothing to do with them – as he would drily remark, "she is now probably spoilt by Opera" (2002a: 7016)[3]. He was preceded into the studio by other modernists, although Virginia Woolf only gave three talks, Gertrude Stein's experimental broadcasts came later, and T. S. Eliot did not read his own poetry until 1941. Only Ezra Pound, who produced his revised 'melodrama' *The Testament of Francis Villon* on the BBC in the autumn of 1931 with the latest in reverberation equipment and a mix of live and recorded performance, had achieved, based on word intonations, a concentrated fusion of words, music and technology[4]. Yeats having been invited into the studio by the pioneering BBC talks producer Hilda Matheson, before long broadcasts had replaced nearly all of his public lectures and readings. In all, until 1937 he was intimately involved in twelve broadcasts and had others planned, a remarkable commitment to the new medium.

Approaching the microphone for the first time, Yeats admitted that his experience of the medium was limited to music. His first script, an account of his version of *Oedipus the King,* self-consciously noted he "had never heard a play broadcasted" (Yeats 2002b: 220)[5], and he conceded "what it feels like to listen to a man speaking over the radio I do not know for although I have heard music broadcast I have never listened to anyone speaking over the wireless" (qtd. Schuchard 2007: 339)[6]. This is a striking admission from a 'tone-deaf' poet, but telling given what was to be his expansive employment of the medium. Because from the first Yeats seems to have grasped the radio's potential: "it is a remarkable experience", he said, "to speak thus to a multitude, each member of it being alone [...]. This broadcasting may change the oratory of the world" (qtd. ibid.: 342)[7]. It might also, in Yeats's hands, change the literature, and the audience's experience of words and music. With each listener separated, there was a potential loss in communal feeling, and an impulse of many of Yeats's broad-

---

[3] W. B. Yeats's letter to Edmund Dulac, 17 July 1937.

[4] See the impressive anatomization by Margaret Fisher (2002).

[5] W. B. Yeats. *Oedipus the King.* BBC Belfast: North Ireland Programme (8 September 1931).

[6] W. B. Yeats, in *The Northern Whig and Belfast Post* (9 September 1931).

[7] W. B. Yeats, in "A Poet Broadcasts". *Belfast News-Letter* (9 September 1931).

casts would be to bridge this gap. There might be, however, a real gain in vocal intimacy. Moreover, while as here in dialogue with theatre, his broadcasts might turn the radio's lack of visual cues to advantage.

Yeats's directorial experience is manifest in his first broadcast: one great benefit was that the audience would not see the chorus of *Oedipus the King* standing immovable and "lost in shadow" in the Abbey's narrow orchestral pit, and could imagine it in movement. The limitations of the theatre might thus be transformed: "you should try to call up not the little Abbey Theatre", he said, "but an open-air Greek theatre with its high-pillared stage, and yourselves all sitting tier above tier upon marble seats in some great amphitheatre cut out of a hillside". Performing on the radio, Yeats realized, it might be possible to "call [...] into my imagination that ancient theatre", so that the audience were no longer put off by the scenery and the attitudes of the actors (2002b: 219)[8]. For the moment the play's performance itself changed little for broadcast. Still, alone together, without visual stimulus, a disparate audience might be held spellbound by the purely aural communication of words and music.

To achieve anything of this, Yeats would insist, poetry-speaking had to be rhythmical. For the first broadcast featuring his own poetry he consciously read "with great emphasis upon the rhythm", vowing not to read poems "as if they were prose" (ibid.: 224)[9]. Such a technique was perhaps instinctive, mirroring as it did his chanting of the poems during their composition, but he was also appealing to an older tradition of verse-speaking, remembering "all poets from Homer up to date" who, he claimed, "have read their poetry exactly as I read mine" (ibid.: 229).

If this sounds old-fashioned we should know that trying to describe what he calls the "articulation and rhythmic diction" of his own defiantly modern music (Stravinsky/Craft 1959: 120), Igor Stravinsky found no better example than the recordings he heard of Yeats reading his poetry. Stravinsky probably knew of Yeats through the Welsh poet Dylan Thomas, who praised him handsomely (cf. Stravinsky/Craft 2002: 241), and it seems likely he was referring to the recording of Yeats reading his greatest hit, the poem "The Lake Isle of Innisfree", one of the few recordings commercially available in the 1950s, indeed

---

[8] W. B. Yeats. *Oedipus the King*. BBC Belfast: Northern Ireland Programme (8 September 1931).

[9] See also Yeats 1931.

one of the few surviving (see Yeats 1931). Explaining himself, Stravinsky noted that "Yeats pauses at the end of each line, he dwells a precise time on and in between each word – one could as easily notate his verses in musical rhythm as scan them in poetic metres" (Stravinsky/Craft 1959: 120). In Yeats's readings Stravinsky apparently recognised the intensity and the precision of a musician.

But it was not only on rhythm that Yeats put such great emphasis. A speaker of poetry, he believed, should employ all the rises and falls of the voice. So Yeats's vocal line as he reads his poem strikes nearly identifiable notes within a range of a few semitones, producing a species of chanted melody, which rises and falls following vowel sounds and the arc of the long lines, not predictably but with a rightness borne of long practice. The method is quite deliberate: "The Lake Isle of Innisfree" is after all a poem whose subject is sound, as in this final stanza:

> I will arise and go now, for always night and day
> I hear lake water lapping with low sounds by the shore;
> While I stand on the roadway, or on the pavements grey,
> I hear it in the deep heart's core. (Yeats 1989: 74)

The closing upward intonation in Yeats's rendition of the poem's last cadence is especially arresting – in the aural attention of this last shortened line each sound takes on more resonance, while the word "core" heads upwards, denying us the dying fall we might expect. This was sometimes a habit of Yeats's when reading his most sincere early lyrical poems, as we know from musical transcriptions of his reading by the early music pioneer Arnold Dolmetsch and others. Here letting that last word be drawn out and then raised up from its depths, the intonation acts at once to prolong the attention, and perhaps to remind us that the speaker is miles away from his source: standing on "pavements grey", this sound of lake water exists only, however powerfully, in the imagination. Intonation lifts us from the memory's deep well back to life. It may be only a coincidence, but it is worth remembering that modal music of the kind that survived in Ireland often had this same upward intonation, not ending on what we might otherwise call tonic or key note, and indeed frequently closing like this on the tone above. Some have since objected to the reading as mannered, or 'sing-song', but in Yeats's performance, his voice lingering over the tone of each vowel, the intricacies of pitch and phrasing do suggest something close to a musical imperative. Just as the verses that became "Down by the Salley Gardens" and others were sung to him in cottages in the west, Yeats in turn almost *sings* his poetry. If you think that goes too far, he claimed as much himself: reading the same poem some six years later he wondered if "perhaps you will think that I go too near singing it" (2002b: 290)[10].

Yeats found the radio encouraged the careful enunciation in a low tone of his poem's "low sounds by the shore", picking up the very aural quality of the lake water that had inspired its existence: "I hear it in the deep heart's core". Until Yeats's own readings, "The Lake Isle of Innisfree" had been heard on the BBC on two separate occasions in 1927 and 1930; both times the poem was set to music, except of the kind Yeats would have abhorred, had he heard it[11]. Without the poems themselves being set to music, the readings that survive represent a conscious righting of the balance, an important statement about the poem's musical interpretation. Those that accuse Yeats of being entirely tone-deaf should note how similar the two surviving recordings of "Innisfree" are in exact pitch and intonation, though made six years apart (see 1931 and 1937). The testimony of his BBC producer George Barnes is not without contradictions but is unequivocal: "He could not hum a tune and his notion of pitch was wildly inaccurate [...] on the other hand his ear for the sound of speech was so sensitive it outran comprehension. This is the chief memory which remains with me." Consequently, concludes Barnes, "I can remember the exact intonation which he gave to every line of all the poems which he presented at the microphone". Such astonishing precision was only enhanced by the studio's capability for playing back recordings: Barnes recalls him "listening intently to the sound of his words as they come out the loudspeaker" (1940/1987: 193). Yeats's broadcast performances then were rehearsed, polished, exact, and on the evidence we have, varied only as much as the playing of a musician from one day to another. The notes sounded by the voice, unusual as they were, remained very much the same. Reviewing the latter broadcast, W. J. Turner praised Yeats's readings: "he sings them in a sort of chant which is not unmusical, though it is not music as professional musicians understand it" (qtd. McKenna 1991: 232; see Turner 1937). The

---

[10] W. B. Yeats. "My Own Poetry Again". BBC London: National Programme (29 October 1937).

[11] 12 April 1927: "The Lake Isle of Innisfree", a manuscript musical setting (BBC London station); 28 Sept 1930: "The Lake Isle of Innisfree", music setting by John Ticehurst (BBC National Programme).

poet and novelist Frank O'Connor remarked of the poet: "One of his many illusions was that he could sing. Actually, as Mrs Yeats once remarked, he had a very fine ear, but it was only for infinitesimal intervals which the average ear cannot distinguish at all" (1982: 8). O'Connor perhaps meant this to sound a species of madness. Yet if Yeats's peculiar intonation did not conform to any conventionally notated scales, it was a madness shared by others, as this letter to Margot Ruddock, an actress and verse-speaker who had just entered Yeats's life, shows:

> A Californian musician called a few days ago & is coming again to-morrow. He is working on the relation between words & music. He has made and is making other musical instruments which do not go beyond the range of the speaking voice but within that range make a music possible, which employs very minute intervals. He speaks (does not sing or chant) to this instrument. He only introduces melody when he sings vowels without any relation to words. (Yeats 2002a: 6126)[12]

The Californian musician was Harry Partch, now regarded as one of the giants of musical innovation in America and a direct forerunner of John Cage, who had come to Europe on a Carnegie scholarship to research tunings and develop new instruments, bringing with him his long-necked 'monophone' or adapted viola. Discerning such microtonal intervals and inflections in the voice was the ground upon which the composer was to build his adaptation of Yeats's *Oedipus the King*, and indeed his entire musical vocabulary. No wonder that, trying to preserve the "intrinsic music of spoken words" (1942/1995: iii), Partch meeting Yeats in November 1934 would try what Stravinsky suggested, and literally ventriloquized the poet, writing out transcriptions from his spoken rendering of the play.

On hearing from Partch the poet had been wary but enthusiastic: "so far as I can understand your methods, [they have] my complete sympathy", he confessed, later suggesting "I would of course see you with pleasure, but doubt if my unmusical mind would be of any help to you" (Yeats 2002a: 5992, 6070)[13]. Partch was disappointed to learn he could not hear the play performed in Ireland, but Yeats reassured him that in performance (and radio broadcast) the chorus gave no regard to his ideas about verse-speaking: "I made no attempt to carry out my theories [...] we used singers, I think, from the Cathedral"

---

[12] W. B. Yeats's letter to Margot Collis (née Ruddock), 17 November 1934.
[13] W. B. Yeats's letter to Harry Partch, 6 January 1934.

(ibid.: 6070)[14]. Yeats's readings once more hit home: "I made diagrams of his inflections, but my memory of his vibrant tones is more accurate than my marks" (Partch 2000: 167). Despite reservations about Partch's youth and inexperience, the excitement of each was palpable, and Yeats's protestations of being "unmusical" became less strenuous. The ideas that so appealed to Yeats are developed in Partch's compendium *Genesis of a Music* (1949), which at times, borrowing judiciously from his early prose, and drawing upon similar sources in Nietzsche, almost ventriloquizes Yeats (whom he calls a "voice in the wilderness"; 1949/1974: 38). Partch drew a distinction between what he called abstract music, instrumental and harmonic in conception, and corporeal music which at all moments remembered the body and remembered music's beginnings with words. He delighted the Yeats who had been writing scurrilous ballads by blaming the advent of Christian moralizing for corrupting ancient forms of dance and song "chok[ing] out the Corporeal attitudes, and in music, the vitality of words" (ibid.: 16). In confirming many of Yeats's instincts, the composer displays a musical sophistication well beyond the poet as his thesis is unfolded from earliest times ("he believes that he has rediscovered the foundation of Greek and Chinese music", wrote Yeats breathlessly; 2002a: 6130[15]), via Schütz, Gluck, and Musorgsky, to Janáček and Milhaud. Partch's appeal lay in combining a grasp of historical models in exacting contextualization ("just how old the 'new' philosophy actually is has been a continual revelation to me", he wrote; 1949/1974: 4) with a thoroughgoing contemporary iconoclasm. In particular the musical icons Partch wanted smashed – trained singers, overdeveloped technique, the concert platform, and the fixed scale – were those at which Yeats had been tilting for years.

Yeats had long argued that melody was not to be imposed upon the words from above but derived from within. Consonants formed sound-patterns; vowels in a poetic line had their own intrinsic intonation – what Partch calls "tonal glide", the "most salient characteristic" of spoken words (ibid.: 45). No imposed melismas were allowed, no "vowels brooding like a nemesis over three or four measures of slow music" (ibid.: 14), as Partch described them. In practical terms this

---

[14] W. B. Yeats's letter to Harry Partch, [mid-July 1934].

[15] W. B. Yeats's letter to Edmund Dulac, 21 November 1934.

demanded a close approach to spoken inflection in vocal performance together with music that should be judged by this approach. A student of Schoenberg's *Pierrot Lunaire*, Partch bemoaned the rarity of such ventures in recent musical history, and notably regretted that "Igor" (Stravinsky) and Yeats had not "encountered each other in the same decades of vitality" (ibid.: 40).

Vitality was everything. As Partch put it on the record sleeve for his *Seventeen Lyrics of Li Po* (1942),

> in this art the vitality of spoken inflections is retained in the music, every syllable and inflection of the spoken expression being harmonized by the accompanying instrument [...]. The music accompaniment, or more properly, complement, is an enhancement of the text-mood and frequently a musical elaboration of the ideas expressed. (1942/1995: iii)

Yeats's previous musical experiments had demanded one main note over which words were intoned; Partch's approach might follow and complement the voice more exactly, and more expressively. To this end, he developed new scales, including a 'just' 43-interval scale of microtones, which even now makes his work difficult to replicate. Not surprisingly, Partch's theories did not please Dolmetsch, Yeats's conservative former collaborator, particularly as he failed to bring with him his adapted viola, developed to cope with the new tunings. Even Yeats felt Partch's own voice did not always well serve what he thought was 'impressive music': "his own voice is weak and tends to be drowned by the notes. In America others spoke when he played" (Yeats 2002a: 6130)[16]. Yet Yeats, freed by his ignorance of customary musical theory, felt, according to Partch, that "a play done entirely in this way, with this wonderful instrument, and with this kind of music, might really be sensational" (2000: 167). The American left on his travels, and nothing came of the collaboration until much later, the première and recording of *Oedipus: A Music-Dance Drama*, a world away from the Abbey broadcast, taking place in 1951, in California. Yet Partch had convincingly demonstrated a palpable lack in employing vocal tone alone in performance, and gave Yeats renewed confidence, as well as renewed desire, to pursue new musical settings. Except without collaboration, with nothing more than an instinctive sense of pitch and verse rhythm, Yeats could go no further towards music. To do this, and really to intervene in modernist poetry he had

---

[16] W. B. Yeats's letter to Edmund Dulac, 21 November 1934.

to found some kind of "singing school"[17]. For this he required verse-speakers and musicians.

The obvious place to look was the theatre, although those he would find there were nothing like as radical as Partch. The Abbey Theatre's resident musical director, the composer Arthur Duff, had the job of finding music for Yeats's plays, and it was in working closely with him in Dublin that musical settings for Yeats's new play-lyrics were conceived. In principle, Duff's method was not so different from that of Partch:

> I never attempted to write a note for a line of his until I had made him recite every line a dozen times. A thing he was only too delighted to do and hearing him chant in that monotone of his I rarely left him without some line, some tune coming into my head. (Rodgers [n. d.]: 26)[18]

Duff sat at the piano on the Abbey stage, with Yeats a looming critical presence in the stalls, carefully speaking his words over the music Duff fingered:

> Rhythm was his strong point and I had a lively respect for his judgement. Every tune – he always used the word tune – every tune had to be played over to him many times. As if he were tasting it, sampling it and sizing its character. (Ibid.)

Noting Yeats's care over the process led Duff to doubt his amusia: "I was never quite sure how much Yeats knew or pretended not to know about music" (ibid.), and he quoted Yeats's own avowal: "I get the greatest pleasure from certain combinations of singing, acting, speaking, drum, gong, flute, string, provided that some or all of the words keep their natural passionate rhythm" (1966: 1008). This renewed enthusiasm about combining of words and music led to the collaboration being extended into print. Two series of remarkable *Broadsides* (1935 and 1937) would be produced at Yeats's sisters' Cuala Press. These folded sheets saw music and woodcut illustrations handprinted alongside verses of his own or which he derived from traditional sources and from approved poets like Edith Sitwell and Hilaire Belloc, who featured in his *Oxford Book of Modern Verse* (1936), and in his 1936 broadcast "Modern Poetry". Harvesting music for these publications put Yeats in renewed touch with a various group of collaborators like the poet and music critic W. J. Turner, the artist and composer Edmund Dulac, the poet Dorothy Wellesley, and the Irish poet and

---

[17] W. B. Yeats. "Sailing to Byzantium" (1927); cf. 1989: 301.

[18] Arthur Duff. "Notes for Broadcast on W. B. Yeats".

folk-song specialist F. R. Higgins. These projects also inspired new verses of Yeats's own. By the beginning of 1937, Yeats was telling anyone who would listen of his musical projects: "I have been writing endless ballads to music, and forget everything in my excitement" (2002a: 6773)[19]. He would also attack the planning of new broadcasts with intensity, and new ideas.

Having launched the *Broadside* series from the Abbey stage, at first Yeats hoped to create a coterie that could broadcast from Dublin. Yet Duff's use of a piano in transcriptions tethered the vocal line to insipid if recognisable 'tunes' in performance; his accompaniment did not of course allow any of the colourations of Partch's 'complements'. Faced with the nuances of subtle vocal delivery, Duff "could not understand & did not know how to write out the musical notes" (Yeats 2002a: 6883). From a different angle his resolutely tonal conservatism faced increasing criticism, as Yeats admitted to Dulac, who insisted on the primacy of modes: "much of what you say against 'tonal music' I have heard from Higgins. Probably Duff, who is not particularly Irish or learned knows little [of] anything else." (Ibid.: 7016)[20] Yet even with a more flexible violin playing Irish airs, and the use of accompanying rhythms, adapting stage effects to an entirely aural medium was not without hitches. The one broadcast of poetry and music from the Abbey Theatre in February 1937 became, when Yeats heard it on the radio, 'a fiasco': "Every human sound turned into the grunt roar bellow of a wild [beast]. I recognise that I am a fool & there will be no more broadcast of verse from the Abbey stage if I can prevent it." (Yeats 2002a: 6798)[21] As he explained to George Barnes, the handclaps he had put with his new ballad "Come Gather Round Me Parnellites", which in person were "very stirring", became "on the wireless [...] a school-boy knocking with the end of a pen-knife, or a spoon". "I am a humbled man", Yeats admitted. "When you get those 'records' you will know all about it." (Ibid.) No doubt the experience did not enamour Yeats to recordings; the ephemerality of broadcasts formed part of their appeal.

As Yeats returned in spring 1937 to the BBC studio in London, all the musical projects of the last few years proved to have a profound

---

[19] W. B. Yeats's letter to L. A. G. Strong, 12 January 1937.
[20] W. B. Yeats's letter to Edmund Dulac, 17 July 1937.
[21] W. B. Yeats's letter to George Barnes, 8 February [1937].

effect. Of the four broadcasts planned with Matheson and the producer George Barnes, "The Poet's Pub" is the most flamboyant and theatrical, lusting after a real communal spirit and energy. Yeats agreed with Barnes that "short rolls of the drum are better for the wireless than taps" (ibid.: 6788), so timpani assisted the hammering out of Henry Newbolt's "Drake's Drum" and Belloc's "Tarantella". But perhaps the most interesting, musically and poetically, is "The Poet's Parlour". In this broadcast Yeats intended to showcase the intimacy made possible by the medium.

Again Yeats was prescient. The radio had already altered singing techniques. Music's exponential expansion in space and volume from chamber to salon to concert hall was tempered by the presence of a microphone in a sound-proof booth. Yeats had long objected to operatic technique, observing that "the singer, shrill from conflict with the violins, loud with the strain of great concert halls, trained by some voice-producer to turn language into honey and oil, cannot sing poetry" (1966: 1008). Partch argued that new musical expression "must be intimate to provide an affirmative and individual relief from the pretentious values and standardizations, from the impersonal ubiquity of the radio (which could be very personal)" (1949/1974: 61). Yeats found with delight that the new medium could indeed be extremely personal: requiring no vibrato, no exaggerated voice-projection from speaker or singer, any verbal articulation need not be drenched with what he called the "honey and oil" of the trained singer. Deftly calling to mind a courtly troubadour tradition, with the poet on his chamber broadcast, therefore, there "are his intimate friends and fellow students. There is a beautiful lady, or two or three beautiful ladies, four or five poets, a couple of musicians and all are devoted to poetry." (2002b: 276)[22]

In practice this meant calling upon Margot Ruddock, who had "one quality Yeats valued beyond price – the ability to pass naturally and unselfconsciously from speech to song", and the actor Victor Clinton-Baddeley, with whom Yeats rehearsed intensively (Barnes 1940/1987: 192). For Ruddock Yeats had been inspired to write the poem "Sweet Dancer", and he carefully taught her the refrain on which the poem turns, a cadence long remembered by Clinton-Baddeley, as he wrote the dance rhythm out in musical notation:

---

[22] W. B. Yeats. "The Poet's Parlour". BBC London: National Programme (22 April 1937).

♩ , ♫ ♩   ♩ , ♫
Ah, dancer, ah, sweet dancer!

Example 1: W. B. Yeats, from "Sweet Dancer" (Clinton-Baddeley 1957: 49).

Subtle tunes as well as stark rhythms were involved: as Clinton-Baddeley read the verses to "I am of Ireland" Ruddock would for the chorus "glide into a melancholy tune of her own composition" (Barnes 1940/1987: 192).

Central to this musical atmosphere was a song, "The Wicked Hawthorne Tree", taken from the 1934 play *The King of the Great Clock Tower*.

> O, but I saw a solemn sight;
> *Said the rambling, shambling travelling-man;*
> Castle Dargan's ruin all lit,
> Lovely ladies dancing in it.
>
> What though they dance; those days are gone;   5
> *Said the wicked, crooked, hawthorne tree;*
> Lovely lady and gallant man
> Are blown cold dust or a bit of bone.
>
> O, what is life but a mouthful of air
> *Said the rambling, shambling travelling-man;*   10
> Yet all the lovely things that were
> Live, for I saw them dancing there.
>
> Nobody knows what may befall;
> *Said the wicked, crooked, hawthorne tree;*
> I have stood so long by a gap in the wall   15
> May be I shall not die at all.
>
> (Yeats 1966: 1004f.)

Yeats had written the short, visionary play to break a creative dry spell lasting two years; as his preface says, "that I might be forced to make lyrics for its imaginary people" (1966: 1309). The prospect of performing these with music was to shock him back into creativity. As the scenario initially conceived, the Queen does not speak but conducts a masked dance with the severed head of a poet punished by the King for praising her beauty. The poem is sung by two attendants to a tableau following this dance, the King about to strike, but kneeling and placing his sword at her feet. This is a lyric then that hovers strangely between life and death, as its two voices debate and consider the significance, the *moment* of death and time.

Just as life must be understood in relation to death, the pianist and conductor Daniel Barenboim argued in his own Reith Lectures at the BBC, musical sound can only be understood in relation to silence:

> The physical aspect that we notice first is that sound does not exist by itself, but has a permanent constant and unavoidable relation with silence. And therefore the music does not start from the first note and goes onto the second note, etc., etc., but the first note already determines the music itself, because it comes out of the silence that precedes it. (Barenboim 2006: online)

As a mouthful of air is exhaled, we return to silence. Musical notes end: that is their condition. So, as the lyric suggests, a mouthful of air, a breath, a musical note whether sung or played on a pipe, all must expire. If only because the rest is silence, we know this to be a figuration of death. (We don't have to have suffered as Yeats did from a congested lung to recognise the meaning of this expiration.) However gripping, the vision of dancers will dissipate, as the cynical, realist tree bitterly points out: such dancers expire into the air, and are now "blown cold dust or a bit of bone".

Poised thus between worlds, the song also hovers between the stage, the page, and the air. Printed in a Cuala Press *Broadside* of 1935 with a desolate illustration of the tree by Victor Brown, the tune Arthur Duff made for the poem is reproduced below:

THE WICKED HAWTHORN TREE

Example 2: W. B. Yeats. "The Wicked Hawthorn Tree". Music by Arthur Duff (1935: 1).

With just a slight suggestion of modal tonalities at the close, the tune sounds like a dance, and does not fit the words quite comfortably: we must imagine some latitude in its performance. The lyric was never printed with Yeats's collected poems. Yet on the stage the audience might be bored by the lack of a visual referent to the song's subject, and is easily distracted by the attitude of the performers. Moreover the presence or absence of the vision of dancers is exactly what the speakers dispute; on stage its inevitable absence settles the question too readily. Conversely, as printed on the *Broadside* page, the bleak illustration outweighs the accompanying notation, so the dance and breath the poem invokes becomes muted, the refrains deadened. The tree then appears to have the final word. As it turned out, the radio's aural space was the perfect forum for this visionary lyric.

Probably this was because on the radio the poem was sung following much rehearsal with simple music from a bamboo pipe played by Eva Towns inserted between the verses, the male and female voices of Yeats's collaborators taking alternate stanzas. It is not certain if Duff's tune was used at all, but crucially the words of the performance were not tethered to it. Never comfortable with accompaniments that might drown the voice and mute the words, Yeats squared the circle for his quieter lyrics by putting the music of harp, flute or violin *between* poems, and between verses. As he recalled in his first broadcast, this had been initially suggested by his attending, of all things, a Salvation Army meeting in Dublin, sermons interspersed by hymns: "I found that, rested by the change of attention made possible by the hymn [...], I listened to the exposition of one idea taken up by speaker after speaker without any sense of monotony." (2002b: 221)[23]

To Yeats this recalled the variation between chorus and dialogue in a Greek play. It was another theatrical technique, but one carefully adapted for the radio.

> When I first produced a play at the Abbey Theatre some thirty years ago I told an actor to pause to mark a change of mood, and the impression he gave me was that of a man who had forgotten his lines. Then I told him to fill up the pause with a significant movement of his body and all was well. But when you are reciting to the wireless and nobody can see your body it seems right to fill up the pauses with musical sounds. (2002b: 404)

Music must not distract from the words: at its most rhythmic it might suggest bodily excitement, at its most melodic, in pure instrumental tones, music might be at once a relief and an aid to concentration: "Why not fill up the space between poem and poem with musical notes and so enable the mind to free itself from one group of ideas,

---

[23] W. B. Yeats. "Oedipus the King". 8 September 1931.

while preparing for another group, and yet keep it receptive and dreaming?" (Ibid.: 276)[24]

Played *between* groups of words, music might represent less an access of spontaneity than a marking of time by keeping the mind "receptive and dreaming", attuned to intricacies of sound, to a sense that mere permanence was extinguished. "Music will keep out temporary ideas", Yeats was convinced: implicitly it would let in *temporal* ideas, the presence of time passing (2002a: 6894)[25].

Another musical paradigm is thus represented in Yeats's poem. As Stravinsky argued, remembering Henri Bergson's philosophy, music given to us "for the co-ordination of man and time", "is the sole domain in which man realizes the present" (1962: 53f.). In music's attendance on time, a potential for unheeding, exclusive attention to now, represented here by the dance, we might conceive the imaginative conditions for persistence: "Yet all the lovely things that were / Live, for I saw them dancing there." (ll. 11f.) In this kind of atmosphere even the rooted crooked tree hopes to sidle into immortality: "May be I shall not die at all." (l. 16) Just as the dance comes round again so do the refrains, breathed by the singers. So too does the tune, independently played between verses; because *breathed* through a pipe recalling the song's "mouthful of air" (l. 9). The persistence of music between stanzas might partially solve the question of how to fit the voice with even-tempered music. Not contradicting the breath of the sung lyric, flute music in this case allowed the dancers to continue dancing in each individual listener's imagination, even after the poem's close. Performed thus on the radio the delicate balance between the poem's two voices is preserved and it becomes credible that the tree shall not die after all.

In these musical collaborations Yeats was learning to turn broadcasting's apparent limitations to advantage. Poems could be spoken in dialogue; musicians could be unobtrusively smuggled in to accompany the speaker; speech might easily become song in a way impossible on the concert platform. Not that such projects always ran smoothly: the staged argument Yeats planned between poet and musician could become all too real. As Barnes remembered, "knowing exactly what he wanted himself, he found it difficult to express

---

[24] W. B. Yeats. "In the Poet's Parlour". BBC London: National Programme (22 April 1937).

[25] W. B. Yeats's letter to Dorothy Wellesley, 8 February 1937.

because he noticed nuances which we could hardly hear" (1940/1987: 193). In the broadcast "My Own Poetry", the BBC substituted for those poems set by Edmund Dulac a professional singer, Olive Groves, drawing savage denunciations from a furious Yeats who burned off a manifesto that recalled Partch in its announcement "no mouth trained to the modern scale can articulate poetry" (Yeats 1988: 193). Dulac considered playing music with the songs "*essential*": "the accompaniment in the case of a song is one of the means of fixing the modal character" (qtd. McKenna 1991: 226)[26]. But by now Yeats was convinced of his path. "Where the words are an object the accompaniment can but distract attention", he insisted:

> [...] sustaining notes there might be and will be again; a pause, dramatic or between verses, may admit flute or string, clapping hands or whistling mouth [...but] above all no accompaniment on a keyed instrument, because by that the public ear is nailed to the mathematician's desk. (1988: 193)

For "My Own Poetry Again" Yeats and Margot Ruddock would perform unaccompanied by any musicians. Finally however it was the illness of the protagonists rather than musical differences that curtailed the experiments: intriguing planned broadcasts like "Poems of Love and War", to feature Professor Walter Starkie on the fiddle (and no doubt further drumrolls), never took place.

Yeats's preoccupation plainly persisted to the end. He asked for Clinton-Baddeley's help with a "small book dealing with the relations between speech & song", and just days before his death he gave him his blessing to continue his experiments at the BBC, noting of a recent broadcast including one of Yeats's own poems: "it must have been well done for people keep writing to me about it" (2002a: 7375)[27]. To a degree the "singing school" survived in Clinton-Baddeley's 1941 book *Words for Music*, and in Ezra Pound's recording, in the year of Yeats's death, of "The Seafarer" to his own inimitable kettledrum accompaniment. Patently, though, the performance space of the radio had altered Yeats's poetry and the way he conceived of it, altering in turn the resonance of modern poetry. Broadcasting was made the forum for ground-breaking if unfinished experiments in words and music. This Yeats achieved by insisting upon an intense attention to sound in poetry, and a receptiveness towards music in its performance

---

[26] Edmund Dulac's letter to W. B. Yeats, 16 July 1937.
[27] W. B. Yeats's letter to V. C. Clinton Baddeley, 23 January 1939.

that prevailed even over some of his own earlier objections. Only thus could poetry achieve the articulation of the present: each passing moment might be acknowledged in its passing. From his perspective, even the sceptical Frank O'Connor concluded he had known "the most musical poet after Shakespeare" (1982: 10).

References

Albright, Daniel (2000). *Untwisting the Serpent: Modernism in Music, Literature and Other Arts*. Chicago, IL: University of Chicago Press.

Avery, Todd (2006). *Radio Modernism*. London: Ashgate.

Barenboim, Daniel (2006). "In the Beginning was Sound". *The Reith Lectures*, BBC Radio 4 (April 7). http://www.bbc.co.uk/radio4/reith2006/lecture1.shtml. [25/10/2009].

Barnes, George (1940). "Account of Yeats at B. B. C.". (May 23). National Library of Ireland (NLI MS 5919). Also: *Yeats Annual* 5 (1987): 189–194.

Clinton-Baddeley, V. C. (1941). *Words for Music*. Cambridge: Cambridge UP.

— (1957). "Reading Poetry with W. B. Yeats". *London Magazine* 4 (December): 47–53.

— (1965). "Reciting the Poems". *Irish Times* (June 10). "Yeats: A Centenary Tribute Supplement": iv.

Fisher, Margaret (2002). *Ezra Pound's Radio Operas, 1931–1933*. Cambridge, MA: MIT Press.

Matheson, Hilda (1933). *Broadcasting*. London: Thornton Butterworth.

MacKenna, Wayne (1991). "W. B. Yeats, W. J. Turner and Edmund Dulac: The Broadsides and Poetry Broadcasts". *Yeats Annual* 8: 225–234.

O'Connor, Frank (1982). *W. B. Yeats: A Reminiscence*. Edinburgh: Tragara Press.

Partch, Harry (1974). *Genesis of a Music*. 2nd ed. New York, NY: Da Capo Press.

— (1942/1995). *Seventeen Lyrics of Li Po*. CD. TZ7012. New York, NY: Tzadik.

— (2000). *Bitter Music: Collected Journals, Essays, Introductions, and Librettos*. Ed. Thomas McGeary. Champaign, IL: University of Illinois Press.

Rodgers, W. R. ([n.d.]). *W. R. Rodgers Papers*. Harry Ransom Humanities Research Centre. Austin, TX: University of Texas.

Saddlemyer, Ann (2002). *Becoming George: The Life of Mrs W. B. Yeats*. Oxford: OUP.

Silver, Jeremy (1987). "W. B. Yeats and the BBC: A Reassessment". *Yeats Annual* 5: 181–185.

Scher, Steven Paul (1982/2004). "Literature and Music (1982)". Walter Bernhart, Werner Wolf, eds. *Word and Music Studies: Essays on Literature and Music (1967–2004) by Steven Paul Scher*. Word and Music Studies 5. Amsterdam/New York, NY: Rodopi. 173–201. (Orig. publ.: Jean-Pierre Baricelli, Joseph Gibaldi, eds. *Interrelations of Literature*. New York, NY: The Modern Language Association of America. 225–250).

Schuchard, Ronald (2007). *The Last Minstrels: Yeats and the Revival of the Bardic Arts*. Oxford: OUP.

Stravinsky, Igor (1962). *An Autobiography*. New York, NY: Norton.

—, Robert Craft (1959). *Conversations with Igor Stravinsky*. London: Faber & Faber.

— (2002). *Memories and Commentaries*. London: Faber & Faber.

Turner, W. J. (1937). "Music and Words". *New Statesman and Nation* 14 (July 24): 146–147.

Wade, Allan (1951). *A Bibliography of the Writings of W. B. Yeats*. London: Rupert Hart-Davis.

Yeats, W. B. (1923). *Plays and Controversies*. London: Macmillan.

— (1931). "W. B. Yeats Reading his Poems". Broadcast recording. BBC Sound Archives, Cat. No. LP22145. (Also appears on: *The Poems of William Butler Yeats*. Spoken Arts 753. 1959).

—, ed. (1935). Broadsides: A Collection of Old and New Songs. Dublin: Cuala Press.

—, ed. (1937). Broadsides: A Collection of New Irish and English Songs. Dublin: Cuala Press.

— (1961). *Essays and Introductions*. London: Macmillan.

— (1966). *The Variorum Edition of the Plays of W. B. Yeats*. Ed. Russell K. Alspach. London: Macmillan.

— (1972). *Memoirs*. Ed. Denis Donoghue. London: Macmillan.

— (1988). *Prefaces and Introductions*. Ed. William H. O'Donnell. London: Macmillan.

— (1989). *Yeats's Poems*. Ed. A. Norman Jeffares. London: Macmillan.

— (1994a). *The Collected Letters of W. B. Yeats*. Vol. 3: *1901–1904*. Eds. John Kelly, Ronald Schuchard. Oxford: OUP.
— (1994b). *Later Essays*. Ed. William H. O'Donnell. New York, NY: Charles Scribner's Sons.
— (1999). *Autobiographies*. Eds. William H. O'Donnell, Douglas N. Archibald. New York, NY: Scribner.
— (2002a). *The Collected Letters of W. B. Yeats*. Gen. ed. John Kelly. Oxford: OUP. InteLex Electronic Edition (cited by accession number).
— (2002b). *Later Articles and Reviews: Uncollected Articles, Reviews, and Radio Broadcasts Written After 1900*. Ed. Colton Johnson. Basingstoke: Macmillan.
—, F. R. Higgins, eds. (1935). *A Broadside*. No. 2 (New Series). February 1935. Dublin: Cuala Press.

'The Invisible' / 'The Inaudible'
Aspects of Performativity in Celan and Leibowitz

Axel Englund, Stockholm

As a written poem is read aloud or performed in a musical setting, how might the transition from a visible to an audible materiality alter its meaning and its way of generating meaning? What impact does this change have on the relation between semantics and sound structure? How might the particular vocalization of the speaking or singing individual affect the interpretations of the text? The present paper approaches such questions through two late poems by Paul Celan. The poems are followed from their written existence on the page through a recorded reading by the author and, finally, into a musical setting by René Leibowitz. Not only do these texts explicitly thematize their own suspension between writtenness and orality, but they also enact the sensory disappearance and threatening collapse of their own language. Spoken and sung, moreover, the poems are subjected to the risks of misrepresentation and misinterpretation inherent in any performance, with concrete and crucial effects on their meaning as a result.

In an aphorism from *Rhumbs*, Paul Valéry succinctly defined poetry in the following way: "Le poème – cette hésitation prolongée entre le son et le sens"[1] (1960: 637). The notion of a hesitation between two things, one may note, suggests a certain incompatibility: sound and sense are at odds with each other, and the poem is the place where they vie for the attention of a recipient. This tension partially mirrors the conflictual interplay between music and poetic language that is present in the poetry of the Romanian-Jewish Holocaust survivor Paul Celan, as well as in the profusion of contemporary musical works that Celan's poetry has inspired since the late 1950s[2]. Keeping these tensions in mind, I would like to follow two of his late poems through three different material stages: as written texts, as oral performances by the author himself, and as joint musical performances by a composer, a singer, and an accompanist. The poems – entitled "In den

---

[1] 'The poem – this prolonged hesitation between the sound and the sense'. Unless otherwise indicated, all translations are mine.

[2] See Englund (forthcoming), in which I attempt a comprehensive study of Celan's interrelations with music.

Geräuschen" ('In the Noises') and "Deine Augen im Arm" ('Your Eyes Embraced') – were first printed in the 1968 collection *Fadensonnen* and recorded in Celan's own reading by Westdeutscher Rundfunk Köln in the same year. In 1969, the Polish-French composer and conductor René Leibowitz set them to music as parts of his *4 Songs for Bass and Piano Op. 86* (see 1978), subsequently recorded by Roland Herrmann (baritone) and Georges Martin (piano) to be released on CD in 1996.

1. Poetry Printed

No characteristic of Celan's poetry has been noted more often than its being marked by an intense linguistic self-awareness, constantly staging its own silence, disappearance and failure in order to raise questions about what it means for a Jew to write German-language poetry in the wake of Auschwitz. This meta-linguistic inclination entails a strong focus on the materiality of language. Celan's work often seems to be consciously situated at the crossroads of the visual and the auditory, of inscription and voice – in a "conflictual interpenetration of speech and writing", to quote one critic (Fioretos 1994: 295). The first of the two poems addressed here may serve as an illustration of this tendency:

IN DEN GERÄUSCHEN, wie unser Anfang,
in der Schlucht,
wo du mir zufielst,
zieh ich sie wieder auf, die
Spieldose – du
weißt: die unsichtbare,
die unhörbare.   (Celan 2000: II, 129)[3]

(IN THE NOISES, like our beginning,
in the chasm,
where you fell to me,
I wind it up again, the
music box – you
know: the invisible,
the inaudible.)

---

[3] Paul Celan, "In den Geräuschen", © 1983 by Suhrkamp Verlag, Frankfurt am Main. Reproduced by permission.

The poem begins with the definition of the present situation in terms of sound, or more specifically with the auditory as something primary, something akin to our beginning. The sound here is like an 'Urlaut', an unordered, original sound that withdraws from understanding. Noise is the sound that precedes patterning; it has yet to be ordered into language or music. The music box wound up by the lyric persona thus amounts to a move from unorganized to organized sound. A sonorous pattern thus appears and the sound begins to make sense, although in musical rather than linguistic terms.

This configuration of sound and sense is connected in complex ways to the notion of an addressee, the 'you', which is implicit already in the first person plural of the opening line but dissevered and thereby foregrounded in the third and fifth lines. Celan placed strong emphasis on the need in poetry of an "ansprechbares Du" ('addressable you'; 2000: III, 186) at which it must necessarily be directed, but which it could never be certain of reaching. The 'you' of this particular poem, we learn, fell into the chasm at the point of 'our beginning'. In the third and fourth lines, a linguistic game on directions is instigated as the notion of 'descent' in "zufallen" ('fall to', 'be allotted to') is juxtaposed with the notion of 'ascent' implicit in the constituents of the verb "aufziehen" ('wind up'). In this way, the 'you' that 'fell down' and the music box that is 'wound up' appear as partly overlapping. In the fifth line, this merging of the fallen and the raised is confirmed in a move entirely dependent on the poem's visual materiality: the drastic enjambments isolating the line "Spieldose – du" from its surrounding lines ("die / Spieldose – du / weißt") provoke an equation of the addressee and the music box.

But, as always in Celan, the poem simultaneously addresses its own language. Read in these terms, the lyric persona winding up the music box might also be understood as a poetological allegory corresponding to the setting in motion of a poem to make sense of noise and reach out to an addressable 'you'. From this perspective, that which is invisible and inaudible is not only the music box, but also poetry itself, which thereby seems to negate its own materiality. In an oft-quoted passage from his important poetological text *Der Meridian*, Celan noted: "[...] das Gedicht zeigt, das ist unverkennbar, eine starke Neigung zum Verstummen"[4] (2000: III, 197). Consequently, "In den Geräuschen" evokes the inaudibility of its voice and

---

[4] '[...] the poem displays, that is unmistakable, a strong inclination toward silence'.

the invisibility of its inscription, putting its own ability to communicate fundamentally in question.

In spite of this, however, communication does take place: the addressed 'you' 'knows'. The phrase "du / weißt" is certainly not limited to a designation of the particular object referred to (as in 'you know which music box I am talking of'). The knowing of the 'you' has a much greater weight: it is a knowledge resulting from the linguistic encounter of the poem. In spite of the disappearance or sensory unavailability of the music box – and, by allegorical extension, the poem – an exchange through organized sound has taken place. "Aber das Gedicht spricht ja!"[5], as Celan exclaims in another passage from *Der Meridian* (ibid.: III, 196).

If "In den Geräuschen" thematizes a visual and auditory disappearance affecting the music box as well as the addressee and the poem as such while simultaneously expressing the hope of a poetic encounter, "Deine Augen im Arm" also, in addition to such thematization, even more directly acts out the disappearance in its own language:

DEINE AUGEN IM ARM,
die
auseinandergebrannten,
dich weiterwiegen, im fliegen-
den Herzschatten, dich.

Wo?

Mach den Ort aus, machs Wort aus.
Lösch. Miß.

Aschen-Helle, Aschen-Elle – ge-
schluckt.

Vermessen, entmessen, verortet, entwortet,

Entwo

Aschen-
Schluckauf, deine Augen
im Arm,
immer.   (Celan 2000: II, 123)[6]

---

[5] 'But the poem indeed speaks!'

[6] Paul Celan, "Deine Augen im Arm", © 1983 by Suhrkamp Verlag, Frankfurt am Main. Reproduced by permission.

(YOUR EYES EMBRACED,
the
burned-apart,
rock you onward, in the fly-
ing heartshadow, you.

Where?

Put the place out, put the word out.
Erase. Measure.

Ash-brightness, ash-yardstick – swallowed.

Measured, unmeasured, located, unworded.

Unwhere

Ash-
hiccup, your eyes
embraced,
always.)

Here, vision is in focus thematically. In a strangely impenetrable image, the eyes of the 'you' are embraced, kept close and rocked in the arms of someone, as if severed from the body to which they belong. These eyes have been exposed to a trauma: burned apart, which would suggest a wounded vision or even loss of eyesight. This notion is further echoed in the poem in notions of shadow and brightness, and the dousing or putting out of a light, which merges with the notion of erasure in the verb 'löschen' ('to extinguish, to erase').

But the undermining of visual appearances is here not only a thematic matter; it is something that language *does* to, and by, its own signs. It is as if the thematically stated erasure has an immediate effect on the written text itself. The invasion of whiteness, which lets single words constitute a line and single lines constitute a stanza, is an enactment of the erasure of which the poem speaks. Even more clearly, couplings such as "Ort" / "Wort", "Helle" / "Elle" or "entwortet" / "Entwo" foreground the deletion as something that language not only is about, but something it actually does. The exhortation 'to put the word out' – "Machs Wort aus" – is carried out by the poem itself at the moment of its creation.

An intense paradox lies in this tendency. The verb 'ausmachen' may refer to the putting out or turning off of a light or a machine. But it can also mean 'to constitute' or 'to be' something, 'to span' or 'to contain'. When the 'you' is asked to extinguish the place and the word, the poem also demands that it be that place and that word. The existence in a particular place or context is equal to the deletion of that very word and place. The language of the poem is constituted by its own erasure.

The co-presence of these two senses in the word 'ausmachen' is reinforced as the poem continues. With the two imperatives of the following line ("Lösch. Miß.") the addressee is asked to erase, but also 'to measure': either to measure something in order to quantify it, but also to measure in the sense of being of a certain size, as, for instance, an area might measure a certain number of miles. To further complicate matters, the poem's tendency to blot out linguistic signs potentially subjects these single syllables to the suspicion of being themselves nothing but the remains of deleted words: read as a prefix deprived of its word, "Miß" points to notions of failure, falseness and inadequacy (e. g., 'missverstehen' / 'misunderstand').

If the burned-apart eyes and the injunction "Lösch" suggest the notion of a fire, its by-product appears in the fourth stanza with the topos of ashes, so recurrent in Celan. Here, too, the internal paradox introduced by 'ausmachen' is brought into play: "Aschen-Elle" – 'Elle' meaning a cubit or a yardstick – develops the notion of constituting, extending over or measuring something, while "Aschen-Helle" picks up the brightness suggested in the negative by "Lösch". At the same time, the erasure evoked by "Lösch" is acted out by the disappearance of the H, which turns "Helle" into "Elle".

In the four-word sequence of the fifth stanza, the notion of measuring returns, as does the conflation of 'Ort' and 'Wort'. Both are highly ambiguous: 'vermessen' means 'measured', but also 'presumptuous' (i. e. a belief in oneself beyond the appropriate measure), and 'entmessen' could be read as a neologism, signifying perhaps the bereavement of measure, but also – according to the *Deutsches Rechtswörterbuch* (see 1914–) – to quantify something with the wrong measure. The participle "verortet" suggests something having been classified or pinned down, its position decided, while the distinctly Celanian coinage "entwortet" implies the removal of words from something. The constitution or measuring of location and language, in other words, is simultaneously evoked and undermined; the comprehensive control and proportion suggested by the measuring is counteracted both by the notion of miscalculation and by the linguistic incompleteness resulting from the disappearance of words.

Next, the deletion of the word suggested by "entwortet" is acted out by the poem. On a semantic level, a word like "Entwo" seems to deny interpretation. Perhaps, its privative prefix invalidates the question "Wo?" by suggesting the removal of that very word. But its principal role is that of staging a material deletion: it is a visual manifestation of erasure in relation to the immediately preceding word "entwortet" – the four final letters have been blotted out, and the poem is itself in the process of being 'unworded'. While a language perforated by interruptions and enjambments is typical of the late Celan, the lack of a punctuation mark, leaving this fragment of a word hanging, is in fact very unusual. Celan's last collections are dominated by brief poems consisting of one or two complex but grammatically complete sentences which are spread out over a handful of lines (as in "In den Geräuschen"). Here, the poem stages an emphatic incompleteness, leaving open the question of whether it is the result of a wounded vision ascribed to the 'burned-apart' eyes of the poem's recipient, or of the erasure to which the poem itself is subjected.

While "In den Geräuschen" thematizes the material and sensorial disappearance of the poem by identifying it as invisible and inaudible, "Deine Augen im Arm" enacts this disappearance as an ongoing linguistic process by capturing language at a moment when it is about to be effaced. As I have repeatedly implied by ascribing to Celan's words the capability of 'doing', 'staging' or 'enacting' that which the poem ostensibly only speaks of, this tendency of Celan's language is a matter of performativity in the original sense of the word – the speech act theory formulated by J. L. Austin and developed by, among others, Jacques Derrida and Judith Butler. As I will now turn to the recorded reading of these poems, I hope to show how this performativity relates to an oral performance of the poems.

2. Poetry Spoken

In the printed texts discussed so far, the materiality of the poems has been a visible one. When they are read aloud, the situation changes. While in the written poem the visual marks are manifest and linguistic sound is merely implied, the hierarchy is now reversed, and the sound of language is brought to the fore in a directly palpable manner. Thus the specific visual/written meanings (such as, in the examples given, the suggested equation of 'you' with other elements in the poem in the phrases "Spieldose – du" or "den Herzschatten, dich") disappear from sight, and the timbre, rhythm, intonation and pronunciation become active agencies in the poem. Recalling Valéry, one may note that this shift in materiality changes entirely the conditions of the relation between sound and sense: even if the phonetic structures of language are implied in the written text, they gain in force when the poem enfolds as a voice in linear time. Celan's carefully conceived phonetic patterns are emphasized and potentially shift attention away from the text's semantic stratum.

Similar to the way in which the enjambments of the text repeatedly force the reader to a halt, Celan reads the poems in a hesitant, slow and laboured manner, perforating it with pauses as if held back by something. Long silences correspond to the whiteness surrounding the single words of the poem. But even more important are the alliterations of "weiterwiegen", the internal rhyme of "[-]wiegen, im fliegen-", the repetitions of "dich", the phonetic permutations of "Mach den Ort aus, machs Wort aus", "Aschen-Helle, Aschen-Elle", and a line like "Vermessen, entmessen, verortet, entwortet" – as the poem is heard rather than read, all these aspects come to the fore as strongly enforced patterns of sound. These are naturally implied in the printed text as well, yet they become manifest only in Celan's oral performance, through the particularities of his articulation.

There can be no doubt that both pitch and rhythm are important elements in Celan's reading. Although he is certainly speaking rather than singing, his voice alternates between clearly placing a fixed pitch, which produces an almost chant-like effect, and a more relaxed pronunciation. There is a marked audible element of pitch stability to his intonation, and the latent rhythmical correspondences of his language are foregrounded by his articulatory phrasing. Whether consciously so or not, his reading thus exploits pitch and rhythm as means of highlighting linguistic structure, which will presently be exemplified.

The repeated phrases of "Mach den Ort aus. Machs Wort aus" are both pronounced approximately on the level of A sharp in the great octave, with a slight descent on the final "aus". Rhythmically, the words "Ort aus" and "Wort aus" are exact equivalents and carry the main stress weight to which the preceding words lead up. Similarly, the single words of the eighth line – "Lösch" and "Miß" – are held together by a stable intonation, both being pronounced on the level of a small octave C (the former word somewhat less unambiguously so as the intonation starts at a lower level).

After this a gradual descent can be observed. "Aschen-Helle" is intoned approximately a semitone lower than the preceding line, and "Aschen-Elle" another whole tone lower. Venturing to force on Celan's reading the constraints of traditional musical notation, one will get something like what is shown in *Example 1* (with a slight hesitation before the bar line and a rather high A).

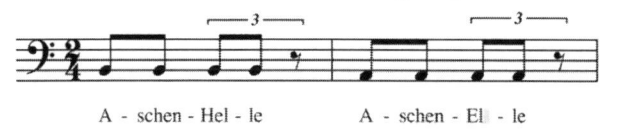

A - schen - Hel - le   A - schen - El - le

Example 1: Approximate notation of Celan's pronunciation of "Aschen-Helle, Aschen-Elle".

A similar tendency towards sequentiality can be heard in the line "Vermessen, entmessen, verortet, entwortet", where the first and third words are marked by a continuative intonation, while the second and fourth words descend into a terminative one. Rhythmically, too, the four words are very close in Celan's pronunciation, with a slight ritardando and some extra stress on the first syllable of "entmessen", which foregrounds the sounds that distinguish it from the preceding word.

The point of approaching Celan's reading in musical terms is not to imply that his reading is actual 'singing' or something similar to it, but merely to illustrate how the oral performance brings new acoustic structures to the text, which affect the interplay between sound and sense. Through the reading's tendency toward sequentiality, the poem comes to be marked by a high degree of acoustic organization involving both rhythm and intonation. This organization is not prescribed by the phonetic patterns of the text but superimposed upon them at those points where they most conspicuously govern the poem's language. The oral performance of the poem thus highlights the predominance of sound as the dominant principle of linguistic organization.

All spoken language depends on organization of sound in order to communicate. What is important in the present context, however, is a particular kind of organization. In Celan's poem, we hear a patterning of sound that seems motivated to a high degree by the sound itself. This patterning is precisely what Valéry's aphorism places in opposition to linguistic sense: the structure of sounds that disrupt and counteract meaning. Phonetic organization comes across less as a consequence of grammar and syntax than as a governing principle. Repetition and permutation of linguistic sounds take precedence over the syntactical completeness aiming at semantic reference. As the poem is perceived through the materiality of an oral performance, the 'hesitation', in Valéry's terms, between sound and sense begins to slant more decisively in favour of the former.

Surely, much the same could be said about a lot of other poetry when it is read aloud, such as the concrete poetry so much in vogue in the 1960s, or many works by the Dadaists. However, the particularity of Celan's language lies in the way in which the foregrounded sound structures relate to the thematic traces that still remain in language, and at this point the two senses of performativity referred to before converge. In terms of speech act theory, it is the locutionary aspect of language that is diminished as sound becomes the governing principle. But when locution begins to be threatened, an illocutionary force, peculiar to Celan's poetry, takes precedence: namely, the performance of its own failure of linguistic communication. Since what Celan's language enacts, through its phonetic structure, is its own difficulty, or even incapability, of communicating traumatic experience, this illocution depends precisely on the ongoing disappearance of locution. The poem communicates by staging its own difficulty to communicate as a dominance of sonic organization over semantic reference. This is not to say that all reference is lost, it is merely transferred: as sound takes precedence over sense, the meaning of Celan's language is increasingly situated in the performative sphere.

"Deine Augen im Arm" explicitly situates these difficulties of communication in its oral as well as in its written materiality. I have already pointed to the notions of visual erasure that pertain to the poem as an inscription, but the poem's self-thematization as a vocal performance is equally fraught with hindrance and disruption. The fourth stanza – "Aschen-Helle, Aschen-Elle – ge- / schluckt" – talks about something being swallowed. On the one hand, this something might be ashes – the brightness of ashes or a cubit of ashes – but, more directly, it might be an element of language itself: the [h], a consonant as unobtrusive as a breath, which disappears between "Aschen-Helle" and "Aschen-Elle". Just as the poem's exploitation of the visual materiality is directed at the disappearance of its visual traits, the increased emphasis on aural materiality, paradoxically, points to the poem's inclination towards silence, thus echoing the double dissolution of the poem into "die unsichtbare, / die unhörbare".

The ashes appear again in the final stanza: "Aschen- / schluckauf". The construct is an unsettling one, especially if one considers the fact that the crematories of Auschwitz form a constant background to Celan's writing: the notion of having ashes in one's throat thus becomes a painfully concrete image of damaged poetic speech in the wake of the Holocaust. The notion of a poetic voice affected by hiccups also has other implications, however. Placed in the tension between sound and sense, a hiccup is of course a disturbance of the latter by the former. It is an unwanted sound that interrupts communicative speech. More than that, it is essentially unruly and paradigmatically unexpected; the voice is subjected to an involuntary spasm of the diaphragm, and its own sound is out of control. In this image, the notion of sound as organized, ordered or measured is unhinged by sonic chaos more akin to noise than music. If the hiccup is read as a meta-thematization, it becomes an image of the poem's vocality, and of its oral performance as subjected to the influence of essentially uncontrollable sound, potentially disrupting linguistic meaning.

An oral performance does not literally have to be interrupted by hiccups for its meaning to be distorted, of course. The susceptibility of oral performance to (productive) misinterpretation can be illustrated by an experience of mine as I was preparing this essay. As I first listened to the recording of "In den Geräuschen", I did not have access to the printed text. As a result, I misheard a crucial word in the final line ("die unhörbare"). The mistake, however, was not entirely my own. If one listens carefully to Celan's pronunciation, one may note that he has a tendency sometimes to pronounce the alveolar plosive with a short preceding nasal when it appears as the first sound after a caesura, thus adding a very short [n] before the [d]. The two consonants have exactly the same initial tongue position; the difference is only in the manner of articulation. This articulatory peculiarity can be heard, for instance, in the first stanza of "Deine Augen im Arm", on "*die* / auseinandergebrannten" and "*dich* weiterwiegen" (my emphases). But in one particular place, namely the final line of "In den Geräuschen", it is exaggerated: the [n] is prolonged and the [d] virtually disappears. The result is an entirely different meaning: instead of "die unsichtbare, / die unhörbare", I heard 'die unsichtbare / nie unhörbare'.

In this version, instead of an equal disappearance of visible and audible materiality, the conclusion of the poem signals the complete dominance of the latter. The music box, the addressable 'you' and the poem are invisible, but they are never inaudible. Precisely when perceived as an audible artefact, this singular poem spoken by this singular voice becomes an affirmation of the audibility of poetry. In a double meaning, then, sense has been overthrown by sound. The poem speaks, and it speaks through a voice that affirms the crucially oral and aural quality of poetic communication. Moreover, this example can be understood as an empirical illustration of Derrida's transcendent argument on performativity: any linguistic act is a priori conditioned by the possibility of its own misfiring, since it is repeatable in different contexts and thus radically severed not only from its recipient but also from its author[7]. This severance, Derrida holds, is no less true of speech than of writing: the notion of speech as presence and unhindered conveyance of meaning is one of the prime tenets of the deconstructive position. Celan's ambiguous pronunciation effectively makes the point: even when the poem is spoken by the author himself, it speaks beyond the intentions of that author. When the visible materiality of the printed text disappears the audible materiality adds ambiguities specific to the spoken performance, thereby changing the interplay between sound and sense and opening it up to reinterpretations beyond the control of the authorial subject.

3. Poetry Sung

In the final part of this essay, I address the question of how these issues – the agonistic relation between sound and sense, the dialectic between organization and disorganization, the illocutionary force of the poem – are affected as Celan's poems are set to music and performed as songs. The songs in question are by René Leibowitz, a composer and conductor who was born in Poland in 1913 but moved to Paris in his teens and spent the rest of his life there. Leibowitz is perhaps best known for his 1961 recording of Beethoven's sympho-

---

[7] See Derrida 1988. Much more could be said about Celan's poetry and the Derridean interpretation of performativity, in particular with respect to Derrida's own influential essays on Celan's poetry (see Derrida 2005). Such a discussion, however, would exceed the limits of this essay.

nies and his role as apologist for the Second Viennese School. He was an ardent supporter of Schoenberg and Webern and did much to make their music known in postwar Paris: through performances, through teaching (well-known pupils include Pierre Boulez and Hans-Werner Henze) and through his books on the topic, such as *Schoenberg et son école* (1947). He even claimed to have studied with Webern and to have met Schoenberg in Vienna, a claim that for a long time was accepted as true but which has been seriously questioned by recent research (cf. Meine 2000: 29–36). In the 1940s, he corresponded with Adorno, who showed great enthusiasm for his work:

> Es ist kein Zweifel daran, daß Ihre Stücke das höchste Kompositionsniveau repräsentieren, das heute überhaupt gefunden werden kann – von einer Reinheit, Unbestechlichkeit und Konzessionslosigkeit, und zugleich einer so vollkommenen Verfügung über die Mittel in allen ihren Dimensionen, daß man Ihre Stücke allem, was heute zu komponieren sich unterfängt, als ein verpflichtendes Paradigma vorhalten möchte.[8] (Qtd. Meine 1996: 6)

Like many other commentators, however, Adorno was also bothered by the derivative character of Leibowitz's music, which sometimes borders on pastiche of the Viennese icons (cf. ibid.: 8). Leibowitz remained stubbornly convinced of the merits of the classical twelve-tone method, even as it came to be unfavourably viewed by contemporary musical life, superseded by its extension into serialism and, later on, by entirely different compositional paradigms. There was an element of dogmatism to his musical aesthetics, as can be illustrated by his critique of Schoenberg himself, in a 1945 letter, for lack of consistency in his use of the dodecaphonic technique – to which Schoenberg sardonically replied that he wrote music, not principles (cf. Meine 2000: 163–165).

---

[8] "There can be no doubt that your works represent the highest compositional standards that can be found anywhere today – so pure, unerring and uncompromising, and with such a consummate mastery of technical means in all their dimensions that one would like to hold them up as mandatory paradigms for anyone who wants to compose today." (Meine 1996: 16; trans. Roger Clément)

Example 2: René Leibowitz, "Deine Augen im Arm", bars 3–5[9].

The settings of Celan poems in *4 Songs for Bass and Piano Op. 86* from 1969 are no exception, but firmly rooted in a dodecaphonic sound world. The individual songs differ slightly in their treatment of the material, but all of them are constructed around the coupling of adjacent notes on the chromatic scale. In what follows I will focus on the second and third songs, which are based on the two poems discussed above. In both of these songs, the dodecaphonic structure is two-dimensional: generally speaking, the vocal line constitutes twelve-tone sets on its own, which stand in a complementary relation to the pitches of the piano, so that the sum of the instruments also exhausts the twelve notes in a shared set. An example from the setting of "Deine Augen im Arm" may illustrate this: the first set of the vocal line begins with D-C#, G-Ab, C-B, sung in the three first bars after the intro (see *Example 2*). Accompanying the first two notes (D-C#), the piano plays the remaining ten notes articulated as pairs of chromatically adjacent notes, concluding the shared set: F-F#, C-B, E-D#, Bb-A, G-Ab. Next, as the vocal line continues its own set with G-Ab-C-B, the piano plays the complementary eight notes arranged as D#-E, D-C#-, Bb-A, F-Gb, once more completing the shared set. As the voice continues its first set with F-Gb, Bb-A and then concludes it with D#-E, the piano part produces first C-H, D#-E, D-C#, G-Ab and then D-C#, Bb-A, F-F#, G-G#, C-H – and so on, so that the chromatic scale is continuously exhausted in the shared sets as well as in the vocal line alone.

---

[9] René Leibowitz, *4 Songs for Bass and Piano Op. 86*, © 1978 by Boelke-Bomart / Mobart Music Publications. Reproduced by permission.

In "In den Geräuschen", dodecaphonic structure is more clearly used to create a kind of perfect symmetry. The first twelve-note set of the vocal line can be thought of as constituted by four segments containing two or four notes each (labelled A-B-C-D in *Example 3*; segments B and C occur in two versions, with the two middle notes reversed, labelled B1 and C1). Thus construed, the progression of the vocal line becomes: A-B-C-D-C1-B1-A-B1-C1-D-C-B-A. The last segment of each twelve-note set (A or D) is also the first segment of the following set. In this structure, one recognizes the symmetry of the palindrome, which the composers of the Second Viennese School found so fascinating. After the two introductory bars, which consist of two instances of segment D and the three first notes of segment C1, the piano part produces a similar symmetry, except for a repetition of segment C just before the pivotal point: D-C1-D-C1-B1-A-B-A-B-C-C-D-C-B-A-B-A-B1-C1-D-C1-D.

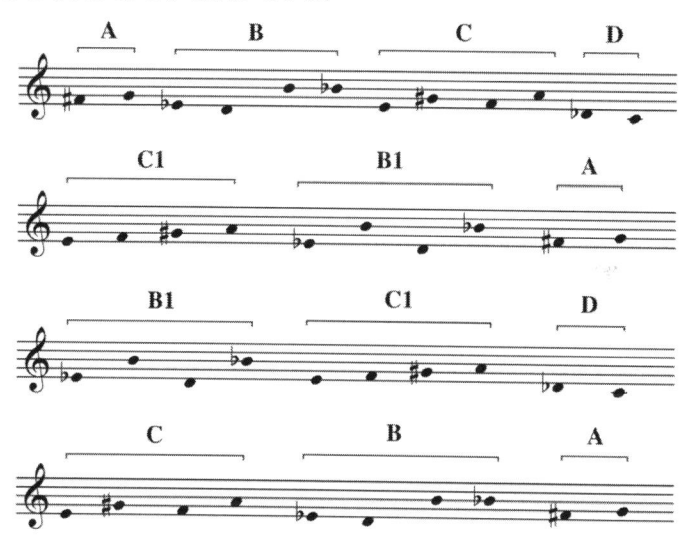

Example 3: René Leibowitz, "In den Geräuschen", pitches and segments of the vocal part.

Not surprisingly, the turning points of two palindromes (A in the vocal part and D in the piano) strictly coincide. Both occur on the first beat of the seventh bar, at the moment in the poem where the lyric persona says of the music box, "Zieh ich sie wieder auf". If one seeks to interpret text and music together, it is hard not to see in the mechanical music box a meta-critical image of the dodecaphonic principle itself. As both the voice and the piano reach the turning point of their palindromic patterns, the text tells of a music box, which, when the end of the sequence has been reached, needs to be wound backwards in order to begin again. The shift to an opposite direction, evoked in the poem by the juxtaposition of falling down and winding up, is analogically present in Leibowitz's musical palindrome. The music box that the singing persona is winding up is once again the musical structure of which he himself is a part. In his *Philosophie der neuen Musik*, Adorno, who for all his admiration of Schoenberg (and Leibowitz) was profoundly sceptical of dodecaphony as a technique, concisely captures this aspect of twelve-tone compositions: "Mechanische Muster befallen das Melos"[10] (1949/2003: 74). The chiastic symmetry of the sets in Leibowitz's "In den Geräuschen", mirrored by Celan's music box, can be read as emblematic of precisely such mechanicity.

How does this compositional strategy relate to the notion of erasure, of invisibility and inaudibility? If one conceives the interplay between sound and sense in terms of a struggle, an immediate effect of hearing a poem performed as a song might be that the predominance of sound is even more pronounced. If Celan's reading of these poems tends to emphasize acoustic patterning through elements of rhythm and intonation, a musical setting pushes these elements even further into the foreground. Insofar as the poem hesitates between sound and sense, this would amount to a downplaying of semantic meaning that is much stronger than in the spoken poem. But just as in Celan's readings, this partial disappearance of locutionary effect is related to a particular kind of upsurge of illocutionary force. This privileging of the performative over the constative is indeed an insistent characteristic of musical meaning: as Lawrence Kramer has argued, the discursive meanings of music can convincingly be approached through an Austinian-Derridean concept of performativity (cf. 1990: 1–20). In the particular case of Leibowitz's Celan settings, I would argue, the illocutionary force of music is intimately connected to the twelve-tone technique itself.

Dodecaphony depends on the saturation of chromatic space by a systematic and repeated exhaustion of the twelve available notes. The repeated use of the complete chromatic scale, in identical or intimately related constellations, is to guarantee the coherence of the musical

---

[10] 'Mechanical patterns beset the melos'.

composition in the absence of traditional tonal harmony. By subjecting every one of its pitches to a single governing principle, it becomes a manifestation of exhaustive unity and rationally organized wholeness. Herein, I would argue, lies the principal illocutionary force of Leibowitz's twelve-tone music. What, in other words, dodecaphonic music *does*, is to perform completeness and coherence. From this perspective, the act of the music is in radical opposition to the act of the poem: while the illocutionary force of Celan's reading of his poem "Deine Augen im Arm" amounts to a performance of imperfection, erasure and a threatening failure, that of the music is one of relentless perfection and symmetry, of a centrally governed coherence. Where Celan stages the crackup and erasure of a visible materiality, Leibowitz negates this tendency by letting the sounding materiality stage the essential unity and completeness of music.

But this argument needs to be relativized: the presence of such coherence and perfection in the audible materiality of a performance cannot be taken for granted. Every performance potentially distorts that which is performed. I have already mentioned my own misinterpretation of Celan's ambiguous pronunciation. Listening closely to the recording of the Leibowitz lieder by Roland Herrmann and Georges Martin, one may note some rather remarkable deviations from the written score (see Leibowitz 1996)[11].

I want to stress that these deviations are not discussed to criticize the singer. For one thing, dodecaphonic music is often notoriously difficult to sing due to the deliberate lack of points of orientation. Perfect performances of such music are very rare. Moreover, the human voice is no machine, and the practice of lied singing typically involves a good deal of portamento, and a general freedom vis-à-vis the printed music is neither uncommon nor undesirable: it serves the interest of a natural vocal expression, and the occasionally resulting compromising of exact pitch production need not be a problem at all. Having said this, there are certain moments in Herrmann's performance when the pitch deviations – much as Celan's strange pronunciation of "die" discussed above – significantly alter the identity of the composition, precisely with respect to the performative enactment of musical completeness and coherence.

---

[11] I assume that the performance is based on Leibowitz 1978, which, as far as I know, contains the only published version of this composition.

Example 4a: René Leibowitz, "Deine Augen im Arm", bars 14–17, with recorded pitches.

Example 4b: René Leibowitz, "Deine Augen im Arm", bars 20–23, with recorded pitches.

Examples 4a and *4b* show two passages from Leibowitz's score of "Deine Augen im Arm" together with the pitches actually sung by Herrmann as I hear them when listening to the recording. It is immediately striking how the melody seems to drift involuntarily towards shapes that may be understood in traditional tonal terms. The line "Aschen-Helle, Aschen-Elle" is supposed to consist of two consecutive major thirds, followed by a melodic rendering of an augmented triad. Instead, Hermann sings the same major third twice, followed by a broken major triad (see *Example 4a*). Not only that: if one interprets the repeated major third as a harmonic outline, the contours of a tonal cadence from Ab to Db are suggested.

In *Example 4b*, the pitches assigned to the word "entwortet" are transformed from B-C-Ab-G into D-Gb-Bb-A[12]. It is not hard to imagine the reason for this considerable alteration: while the correct pitches are nowhere to be found in the six-note sforzando chord immediately preceding the vocal phrase, the first three notes actually sung are a restatement of the augmented triad at the bottom of that chord. Instead of the complementary relation between voice and accompaniment called for by the twelve-tone technique, this performance gives us the rather more traditional convergence of the two. On the following word – "Entwo" – the same thing happens once again: instead of a move from C# to D, which would create a sharp dissonance with the D# and Gb of the piano on the first beat, the voice moves from a C#[13] to a D#. Not only does the voice arrive at the same note as the piano bass line, but the minor third above them and the ritardando leading into this bar give the passage a strongly cadential quality. This quality is even further emphasized by the strongly accentuated Bb (or A#) on the first beat of the preceding bar, which takes on the role of the dominant in the imaginary chordal structure. The result sounds very much like a resolution into D sharp minor.

The involuntary slip from dissonant complementarity of pitches to a harmonious agreement on a tonally flavoured phrase or chord is not a small matter in this context. In effect, it deconstructs the very cornerstone of dodecaphonic aesthetics by reinstating the harmonic levels of traditional tonality. The carefully constructed equality of the twelve pitches is dissolved, and a heavy weight is assigned to the doubled pitches and the accidentally produced cadence. In the midst of its serialized hovering, then, the song suddenly finds a place in which to land: at the word "Entwo" – into which one might now be inclined to read the suspension of tonality's search of a resting point – the ongoing denial of tonal anchorage is temporarily disrupted and the music unexpectedly finds a home. The singer's inaccuracies undermine the systematic saturation of chromatic space, and thus radically change the illocutionary force of the music. Thus disrupted, the music fails to do what dodecaphony was supposed to do.

---

[12] The D is rather high, and might perhaps be heard as a low Eb, thus producing instead a broken E flat minor triad.

[13] This is a rather shaky note, difficult to assign conclusively to either C# or D.

But even if one were to hear this composition in a flawless performance, the audibility of twelve-tone structures is far from evident. Whether the coherence and completeness aimed at by the technique can actually be accomplished is a debatable point and a matter for the individual listener to decide. Identifying and retaining a twelve-tone melody is quite possible, and the difference in character between dodecaphonic structures and their tonally suggestive distortions in *Examples 4* is not difficult to hear. The *digression* from dodecaphony, then, is very much accessible to the ear. But most of the intricacies commonly involved in this style – such as the palindromic set structure of "In den Geräuschen" or the combinations of retrogression, inversion and transposition in "Deine Augen im Arm" – are phenomena available only through vision and cognition, i. e., through an analysis of the printed score.

This fact implies a different answer to the question of how Leibowitz's compositional strategy relates to the notion of erasure, of invisibility and inaudibility. In an essay written shortly after Schoenberg's death, Adorno highlights this need for silent study of the music as one of its chief merits. His argument is based on Schoenberg's hostility toward the notion of art, which takes the form of a radical negation of music's pleasing and ornamental aspects. In Schoenberg's universe, there must be nothing but musical essence. If one pushes this argument to its extreme – which Adorno, true to his habits, does – the immediate sensual gratification belongs to that which must be banished from serious music. Appealing to the pleasure of listening, in short, is tantamount to a sell-out. By avoiding sounding performance, moreover, one would also avoid the tiresome imperfections of performing musicians:

> Stumm imaginatives Lesen von Musik könnte das laute Spielen ebenso überflüssig machen wie etwa das Lesen von Schrift das Sprechen, und solche Praxis könnte zugleich Musik von dem Unfug heilen, der dem kompositorischen Inhalt von fast jeglicher Aufführung heute angetan wird. Die Neigung zum Verstummen, wie sie in Weberns Lyrik die Aura jeden Tones bildet, ist dieser von Schönberg ausgehenden Tendenz verschwistert. Sie läuft aber auf nicht weniger hinaus, als daß Mündigkeit und Vergeistigung der Kunst mit dem sinnlichen Schein virtuell die Kunst selber tilgen.[14] (Adorno 1952/2003: 177)

---

[14] 'Silent imaginary reading of music could make loud playing as superfluous as reading a text by speaking it, and such practice could, at the same time, rescue music from the mischief to which the compositional content is subjected by almost every performance today. The inclination toward silence, which constitutes the aura of every

Interestingly, Paul Celan owned a copy of this essay, which shows traces of careful reading: many passages are underlined and marked in the margin (see Seng 1995). Many of the themes discussed and enacted by "In den Geräuschen" and "Deine Augen im Arm" can be found there. The "Neigung zum Verstummen" (Celan 2000, III: 197; 'inclination toward silence') that Celan famously ascribed to contemporary poetry seems to have emanated from Adorno's characterization of Webern and Schoenberg, and the erasure of the sensually perceptible materiality of which Adorno writes is thematized in "In den Geräuschen" and enacted in "Deine Augen im Arm". If Schoenberg's musical aesthetic, to which Leibowitz held on with such unrelenting enthusiasm, in itself entails a negation of sensual appearance, and if Celan willingly connected this notion to his own poetry, the tension between the illocutionary forces of structural wholeness and material erasure also contains an element of concordance. After all, "In den Geräuschen" does suggest its own affinity with the mechanical music box. The complexity, completeness and coherence of the dodecaphonic score reach their full significance only when its audible materiality is erased, while the spoken poem foregrounds its own audible materiality, giving sound precedence over sense, only to act out its withdrawal from the world of the senses. From this perspective, Celan's poems and their settings by Leibowitz are both contained in the compellingly mystical image of the music box performing its own disappearance – 'you know: the invisible, the inaudible'.

References

Adorno, Theodor W. (1949/2003). *Philosophie der neuen Musik.* Gesammelte Schriften 12. Frankfurt am Main: Suhrkamp.
— (1952/2003). "Arnold Schönberg (1874–1951)". *Kulturkritik und Gesellschaft 1. Prismen. Ohne Leitbild.* Gesammelte Schriften 10/1. Frankfurt am Main: Suhrkamp.
Celan, Paul (2000). *Gesammelte Werke in sieben Bänden.* Frankfurt am Main: Suhrkamp.

---

tone in Webern's lyricism, is intimately related to this tendency coming from Schönberg. It is aimed at nothing less than letting the maturity and intellectualization of art, by erasing its sensual appearance, virtually erase art itself.'

— (2004). *Ich hörte sagen: Gedichte und Prosa*. CD. München: Der Hörverlag.
Derrida, Jacques (1988). *Limited Inc*. Trans. Samuel Weber, Jeffrey Mehlman. Evanston, IL: Northwestern UP.
— (2005). *Sovereignties in Question: The Poetics of Paul Celan*. Eds. Thomas Dutoit, Outi Pasanen. New York, NY: Fordham UP.
Deutsches Rechtswörterbuch: Wörterbuch der älteren deutschen Rechtsprache (1914–). Heidelberger Akademie der Wissenschaften. Weimar: Böhlau.
Englund, Axel (forthcoming). *Still Songs: Music In and Around the Poetry of Paul Celan*. Aldershot: Ashgate.
Fioretos, Aris (1994). "Nothing: History and Materiality in Celan". Ed. Aris Fioretos. *Word Traces: Readings of Paul Celan*. Baltimore, MD/London: The Johns Hopkins UP. 295–341.
Kramer, Lawrence (1990). *Music as Cultural Practice, 1800–1900*. Berkeley, CA: University of California Press.
Leibowitz, René (1947). *Schoenberg et son école: l'étape contemporaine du langage musical*. Paris: J. B. Janin.
— (1978). *Ten Songs for Low Man's Voice and Piano*. Hillsdale, NY: Mobart Music Publications.
— (1996). *René Leibowitz: Chamber Music*. CD X-29303. Basel: Appassionato.
Meine, Sabine (1996). "René Leibowitz". Booklet. *René Leibowitz: Chamber Music*. CD. X-29303. Basel: Appassionato. 6–27.
— (2000). *Ein Zwölftöner in Paris: Studien zu Biographie und Wirkung von René Leibowitz (1913–1972)*. Augsburg: Wißner.
Seng, Joachim (1995). "Von der Musikalität einer 'graueren Sprache': Zu Celans Auseinandersetzung mit Adorno". *Germanisch-Romanische Monatsschrift* 45/4: 419–430.
Valéry, Paul (1960). *Oeuvres complètes, II*. Paris: Gallimard.

Romantic Opera and the Virtuoso

Simon Williams, Santa Barbara, CA

The late Romantic Age saw the advent of singing-actors, whose impact upon audiences depended as much, or more, upon the virtuosity of their acting and the dramatic use of the voice than it did upon pure vocal beauty. Three singers are central to the development of operatic acting in this period. The acting of Giuditta Pasta, who made her name as the first interpreter of some of Bellini's major roles, recalled the statuesque and fixed style of opera seria, though with greater refinement and more attention to the inner aspects of the role. Maria Malibran, who enjoyed a meteoric career, primarily on the stages of London and Paris, appealed through the originality and, quite often, the shock value of her performances; although her voice had its beautiful aspects, the dramatic dimension of the performance was clearly the salient one. Adolphe Nourrit, the first tenor of the Paris Opéra, acted economically and with discipline; like Pasta his name was often linked with that of Talma, the great French tragic actor. His performances were marked, however, by a sense of struggle, as if he could not achieve the vocal freedom he longed for, a struggle that in real life led to his early death by suicide.

Romanticism and performance – two concepts that, initially at least, seem to be incompatible. If there is one theme that virtually all works of European romanticism possess in common, it is a deep belief in the subjective experience of the world and in privacy as a natural, preferred state for human beings. Performance, however, is not an ideal conduit for the subjective vision. Performance implies that the world is best apprehended through social interaction and display, and, through the inevitably public context in which it takes place, it seems to deny the preeminence of the subjective. Performance, according to that great progenitor of romanticism, Jean-Jacques Rousseau, is the fons et origo of every vice that corrupts the state of harmony between the social world and the feeling, subjective individual. Performance invites display, while the romantic impulse is primarily inward, even hermetic. For Rousseau, the most authentic desire for artistic experience arises from "[un] gout […] pour la solitude" ('a taste for solitude') in which spectators become readers, who are "plus recueillis avec eux-mêmes, se livrent moins à des imitations frivoles, prennent mieux le gout des vrais plaisirs de la vie, et songent moins à paroî heureux qu'à l'être"[1] (Rousseau 1856: I/233).

The Romantic age is not, however, marked by a decline in instances of performance in Europe. On the contrary, it stood at the threshold of a century that saw a widespread proliferation of performed art, as theatre expanded to meet the increasing demands for entertainment in the growing cities of an industrializing society. Furthermore, in the decades that followed the defeat of Napoleon, much romantic art was marked by an intensely performative quality as the purpose of the work seemed to be as much to display the unique virtuosic skills of the artist-performer as to reveal that artist's inner world, be it in literature (Byron), pictorial art (Delacroix), musical composition (Berlioz), musical performance (Liszt and Paganini), or acting (Edmund Kean, Ludwig Devrient, and Frédérick Lemaître). One of the principal sites for the display of romantic virtuosity was the performance of opera, notably from the mid-1820s to the late 1830s, a span of time in which the last operas of Rossini, the entire bel canto output of Bellini, the defining works of French grand opera, and many of Donizetti's major works received their first performance. But the period is noted too for the advent of operatic performers who were celebrated as much for their virtuosic acting as for their singing.

In the performance of opera, singing and acting have not always coexisted happily. As opera is a theatrical art, the possession of histrionic skills has normally been acknowledged as desirable for the complete singer. Indeed, from the earliest days of operatic performance, voices could be heard arguing that acting should take precedence over singing. As an early-17th-century writer put it: "Sopra tutto per esser buon recitante cantando bisognerebbe esser anche buono recitante parlando, ondi aviamo veduto che alcuni che hanno avuto particolar grazia in recitare hanno fatto meraviglie quando insieme hanno Saputo cantare." He even claims that "al co[mun] del teatro sodisfazione maggiore hanno dato I perfetti istrioni con mediocre voce e perizia musicale"[2] ([Anon.] 1985: 91). But in later times, if a choice

---

[1] "[...] withdrawn more into themselves, give themselves less to frivolous imitations, get more of a taste for the true pleasures of life, and think less of appearing happy than of being so" (Rousseau 1960: 82).

[2] "To be a good actor-singer one should above all be a good speaking actor, since we have seen that some who have particular grace in acting have worked wonders when they have also been able to sing. [...] the common run of theatrical audiences

had to be made between the two, the actor in the singer usually went to the wall. "Non so se un perfetto Vocalista possa anch'essere perfetto Attore", wrote the 18th-century teacher Pier Francesco Tosi. "Essendo però assai più difficile di cantar bene che di ben recitare, il merito del primo prevale al secondo"[3] (Tosi 1723/1904: 113), a sentiment with which generations of singers and their teachers have agreed. Many singers have not cared for acting at all, leading George Bernard Shaw to claim that "operatic actors [...] wholly substitute mannerisms of the feeblest sort for acting" and "even the few singers [...] who are specially celebrated for their acting, would be celebrated for their deficiency if they were placed in an equally prominent position in [the performance of spoken] drama" (Shaw 1981: I/435). Not all would agree with Shaw's slighting view of acting in opera. Each operatic generation has its theatrical stars – its Chaliapins, its Callases, its Dessays; nevertheless each has also been rife with singers who claim, often with a note of defiant pride, that acting in opera does not matter.

Early in the 19th century, however, it came to matter. In part this was because the system of acting that had been in place for well over one hundred years in the performance of opera seria was beginning to fall apart. From the 17th century on, acting in opera seria had been tied so closely to the music that music and gesture might come to seem inseparable. According to Marco da Gagliano, "[e] sopra tutto il canto sia pieno di maiesta più ò meno secondo l'altezza del concetto gesteggiando, auuerten do però ch'ogni gesto, e ogni passo caschi sù la misura del suono e del câto"[4] (Gagliano 1608: [n. p.]). An illusion of nobility arose from the harmonious unity of the body with the music, through the incorporation of a complex language of gesture, stance, and posture that had its origins in the rhetorical practices of ancient Rome. It was a refined system in which character was represented in ideal form; decorum, harmony, and beauty were the prime

---

takes greater satisfaction in perfect actors with mediocre voice and little musical skill" (Savage/Sansone 1989: 501).

[3] "I do not know if a perfect Singer can at the same time be a perfect actor [...]. It being, however, much more difficult to sing well than to act well, the Merit of the first is beyond the second" (Tosi 1743/1926: 152).

[4] "Above all, [the actor's] singing and gestures should be full of majesty, more or less in accordance with the loftiness of the music. He must take care that every gesture and step follow the beat of the music and singing" (Gagliano 1979: 190).

markers of the performer's excellence, while 'nature' was never raw but always under the controlling influence of 'art'. This system of gesture and movement, which is still available to us today in Dene Barnett's exhaustively detailed catalogue drawn from major acting treatises from the 17th to the early 19th centuries, served as a precise code that communicated an extensive range of human emotions and motivations and was easily understood by audiences. As performers in opera seria were customarily costumed in heavy drapes, often with large plumes on their helmets, gestures had to be executed with the utmost care, so that acting may have been more akin to ballet than to the comparatively realistic mimesis of spoken drama, comedy, or opera buffa. Essentially this was a theatre in which performance was not subject to change and implicitly articulated an unchanging truth. Originality in acting was discouraged and improvisation allowed only in the vocal line.

The dismantling of the formalistic acting of opera seria did not take place overnight; indeed, vestiges of it can still be detected in operatic acting today. But the French Revolution erased the structure of values upon which the system was built, and as the focus of serious opera shifted from authenticating a progressively outworn social and political system to other matters, a new mode of theatrical representation became necessary. In Italian opera, seria was largely replaced by bel canto, by operas that centered increasingly on the emotional life of the characters. Theatrical developments, however, tended to move in a direction antithetical to that suggested by the operas themselves. In contrast to seria, bel canto seemed to invite an intimate performance environment, but the rapidly growing audience for opera in the post-revolutionary period led to the expansion, not the contraction of the auditorium. The more personal dimensions of the action suggested the need for quietness and subtlety in vocal production and acting, but the expansion of the orchestra, which could throw a wall of sound between the singer and the audience, encouraged a corresponding enlargement in performance. Then the personal dimensions of action in bel canto opera often touch upon the domestic or invite a lyrical setting, but the expansion of the stage and development of a sophisticated scenic technology sanctioned the tendency in opera production to greater and greater spectacle. French grand opera, the other generic heir to seria, thrived on noise and the pageant of history, and so it adapted with greater ease than bel canto did to the new theatrical circumstances.

It was in the performance of bel canto, and secondarily in grand opera, that a mode of acting different than that of opera seria first became evident and the acting-singer, who had previously followed a set code of gestures, began to take on the function of an interpretative artist who performed less as a servant of the music, more as an interpreter whose contribution was required to complete the work initially imagined by the composer. As the unified practice of the seria style of acting gradually disappeared, the imagination of the performer became the primary force in developing the role and created a persona not only for each role but for the performer as a performer. As in the early 19th century, operatic performance was documented primarily through chronicling the work of major soloists, this change may best be understood through the careers of three singers who dominated the operatic stage in the 1820s and '30s – Giuditta Pasta, whose career ran from 1818 to her effective retirement in 1835; Maria Malibran, who was the toast of Europe from her debut in London in 1824 to her bizarre death in Manchester in 1836; and Adolphe Nourrit, who for more than a decade was the First Tenor at the Paris Opéra until his sudden retirement in 1836. All three singers were able to convince their listeners that their powers of creativity were equal to those of the composer whose music they were singing. Stendhal interrupts his *Life of Rossini* with an encomium to Pasta in which he claims that it is through her singing that Rossini's music acquires a new freshness and luster. Her voice could even, he argues, serve as an inspiration to the composer so that his dormant energies might once again spring to life. "Inspiré par les talents sublimes de sa prima donna, Rossini retrouverait l'ardeur qui l'enflammait à son début dans la carrière, et les chants délicieux et simples qui commencèrent sa gloire."[5] (Stendhal 1968: II/138) Meanwhile Rossini himself considered Malibran to improve upon his music: "When she was to appear in *Semiramide, La gazza ladra, Cenerentola, Il barbiere*, above all in *Otello*", he told Wagner, "nothing could have kept me from going to hear her. The fact was that each time her creative genius inspired her in a stupefying, always different way with unexpected effects, both vocal and declamatory. [...] Each time, too, she taught me how I

---

[5] "Inspired by the sublime gifts of such a *prima donna*, Rossini would recover the ardour which burned like a bright flame in his soul at the outset of his career, and win back the secret of those delicious and simple melodies which laid the first foundation of his reputation." (Stendhal 1970: 372)

could have done *better* than I had done" (Michotte 1968: 127). Meyerbeer himself acknowledged that Nourrit's contribution both as a performer and musician to the love duet in act 4 of *Les Huguenots*, perhaps the most celebrated passage Meyerbeer ever wrote, was an important component in its success (cf. Becker 1999: I/19f.).

The ways in which Pasta, Malibran, and Nourrit achieved their artistic autonomy were quite different. Although all three were, by most accounts, superior actors, they were so in unlike ways. For a start, two of them, Pasta and Nourrit, were noted primarily as initiators of major roles; Bellini wrote *La sonnambula*, *Beatrice di Tenda*, and *Norma* for Pasta, while Nourrit was the first to sing Arnold in *Guillaume Tell*, Masaniello in *La muette de Portici*, Robert in *Robert le diable*, Eléazer in *La juive*, and Raoul in *Les Huguenots*. They were therefore looked upon as creating models. Malibran, in contrast, made her name mainly by playing roles that were already familiar to audiences and by challenging accepted models. According to Bellini's correspondent, Francesco Florimo, when Malibran first sang Amina in *La sonnambula*, it was like "una seconda creazione [...] fu tale e tanta l'impressione prodotta sugli animi, da far quasi porre in dubbio se gli onori del trionfo spettasero piuttosto a Bellini [...] od all' eccezionale artista, la quale l'avea Saputo sì bene interpretare"[6] (Florimo 1981–1983: III/256). Indeed in descriptions of Malibran's performances, one senses that there was a constant sense of separation between the role and the performer, and the interest in the performance lay in its difference from all other, in contrast to the similarity that was the essence of the old style of seria.

Ernest Legouvé saw a generational difference between Pasta and Malibran. Pasta constantly recalled the aura of the neoclassical theatre, as her performances were filled with "une dignité, une gravité, une noblesse, qui se rattachaient à l'ancienne école" while Malibran he considered the harbinger of romanticism in the theatre, as "[t]out dans son genie était spontanéité, inspiration, effervescence"[7] (Legouvé

---

[6] "[...] a second premier [...] the impression produced was so great and so profound that one could almost question whether the honors and the triumph belonged to Bellini or to the exceptional artist who interpreted it so well" (qtd. Bushnell 1979: 166).

[7] '[... Pasta:] a dignity, seriousness, nobleness of expression, which was linked to the old school [...]. Everything in her [Malibran's] genius was spontaneity, inspiration, effervescence' (my translation).

[1880]: 9f.). Henry Pleasants refers to Nourrit as the "greatest singing actor among all dramatic tenors" (1995: 152), but gives few reasons why. The only extended analysis of his acting is available in the biography of Louis Quicherat, who consistently uses Talma as the foil to Nourrit (cf. Quicherat 1867: 268–285). It is from the older actor that Nourrit acquired a taste for simplicity and restraint, especially in the delivery of recitative. But his powers of characterization seem to have been even more formidable, based as they were on a strong conception of each character as a unique creation, which was consistently anchored in concrete detail. Indeed, the care and balance with which Nourrit constructed his characters as much prefigures the dramatic realism of the later 19th century as it does the high classicism of Talma's days with the Comédie Française. Indeed Nourrit's strengths as an actor may well have compensated for the primary weakness of Meyerbeer and, perhaps, other grand opera composers as well, by giving their rather pallid and weakly limned heroes substantial stage presence, thereby augmenting the personal drama and giving the action a compulsion it might not have in the hands of lesser performers.

Pasta was also claimed by many of her contemporaries to be a tragic actor of the stature of Talma (cf. Stendhal 1968: I/65), whose flawless technique filled the often inflated tropes of French tragic acting with natural speech and carefully modulated gestures and whose grandiose presence on stage and in Parisian society led Napoleon to adopt him as a symbol of his imperial rule. Pasta avoided all political baggage, but grandeur, combined with "a sense for the measurement and proportion of time [...] and absence of flurry and exaggeration [...] and depth and reality of expression", was the hallmark of her acting (Chorley 1862: 129f.). Leigh Hunt, who saw her as Meyr's Medea at the King's Theatre in London, described her style as "epic" in that "she hits great points and leaves you to feel the rest" (Hunt 1949: 268). Malibran, in contrast, seems to have left nothing to the imagination. The figure in the spoken theatre to whom she was constantly compared was the English actor Edmund Kean, and, like him, she stimulated torrents of largely adulatory praise over her exceptionally detailed characterization, her powers of transformation, the sense of constant change, the ingenuity of her improvisation, and her breathtaking vocal technique. While Pasta, who never changed a gesture once she had found the one she considered right for the moment, drew audiences into a state of sublime, rapt concentration,

Malibran, one senses, kept them constantly on the verge of a nervous breakdown. As Legouvé put it: "With her the audience was always in an excited state, under the influence of some kind of surprise" (1893: 169f.). Pasta made the arc of the role abundantly clear, in contrast to Malibran, whose attention to detail often confused one's overall comprehension of the role. According to the *Musical Times*, her main failing was "a tendency to bring every point into equally high relief. The unwearied activity of her mind leads her to make even the minutiae of her part over-important" (Rutherford 2006: 240). With Pasta one senses that there was a unity between the singing-actor and the role, while with Malibran one was always aware of her as a performer, one for whom the role provided opportunities for endless variation and improvisation. Pasta recalled the sublimity of early romanticism and of late-18th-century neoclassicism and in doing so seemed to cover the widening spaces of the theatre with ease; Malibran looked forward to the psychological drama of our own age, but was possibly led to exaggeration and enlargement by the size of the theatres in which she had to sing.

It was in Bellini that the differences between Pasta and Malibran emerged most clearly. Both had made their names in the leading roles of Rossini, but his music did not always allow the actor in the singer to come to the fore. Stendhal comments that Pasta's voice often sounded as if it were imprisoned in Rossini's score, as if the obligation to sing the embellishments he had written into the role suppressed her powers of improvisation. The only Rossini role which both Pasta and Malibran made their own was Desdemona in *Otello*; the pathos of the death scene being the touchstone of this role. Pasta, who portrayed Desdemona as a mature woman, met her death with stoic fortitude; in contrast Malibran, who portrayed her to be a teenager, shocked audiences with the indecorum of her desperate panic and the comparatively graphic display of her sexual desire for her husband. Bellini's operas, however, provided a more congenial milieu for both women. In the extended strains that open "Casta Diva" in *Norma*, we can, perhaps, gain some inkling of the rapt, elevated pathos that was Pasta's particular specialty on stage. Bellini's slowly unfolding melodies provided the acting-singer with the freedom that Rossini's music did not and they suited Pasta's neoclassicism perfectly. The role of Norma requires no adoption of the gestural practice of opera seria, but a refinement of it, with its specificity reduced, but with an aura of sublimity retained. William Hazlitt identified this quality best. He considered Pasta, along with Sarah Siddons and Edmund Kean, to be one of the great tragic performers of the age. Only while Siddons commanded "every source of terror and pity" and Kean did not achieve "elevation of character", Pasta delivered totally consistent interpretations that never aimed to surprise or shock, but displayed "absolute and unbroken integrity of purpose", an approach that would have suited well with Bellini's flowing melodies. "In a word", Hazlitt concluded, Pasta "is the creature of truth and nature, and joins the utmost simplicity with the utmost force" (1933: 18/408f.). Malibran, however, as the operatic equivalent to Kean, searched for the psychological, and, in modern terms, unconscious motivations. There is room to find these in Bellini's strangely dislocated characters, who appeared totally different than when Pasta performed them. Bellini never had the opportunity to write a role for Malibran, so we have no extended passages that might allow us to surmise the quality of her voice through his music. His last opera, *I puritani*, was composed for Giulia Grisi, but he rewrote it for a performance that Malibran was to have given in Naples. It never came off and Malibran never sang the lead role of Elvira, but one passage from this version, the cavatina "Son vergin vezzosa", written for Malibran, has survived in the regularly performed score. From this brief extract it is impossible to come to any conclusions about Malibran as a performer, though clearly it was written for a voice of uncommon agility with an undertow of melancholy.

Pasta, Malibran, and Nourrit all possessed a quality that gave an unusual texture to their performances; none of them were natural singers. Pasta, as Chorley tells us, was born to be neither a singer nor an actor, but had to work to turn her "natural deficiencies into rare beauties" (1862: 1/125); her performance on stage was therefore as much a moral as an artistic triumph. Her singing was not always easy to listen to. Stendhal wrote that she did not possess "une voix également argentine et inaltérable dans toutes les notes de son extension"[8] (1968: 2/143); in fact, she had two voices, alternating and contrasting head and chest tones, which made old music sound fresh, while the through-line of her performance might be understood as the strenuously won unification of these two voices.

---

[8] "[...] it is not the perfectly pure, silvery voice, impeccably accurate in tone throughout every note of its compass" (Stendhal 1970: 375).

The tales of Malibran's vocal training at the hands of her obsessive, violent, and possibly incestuously driven father, Manuel García, are part of the myth of her life, but all evidence suggests that she had an unruly and difficult voice that, although it achieved moments of beauty, was never secure in its range. Indeed, beauty was not always a prime consideration in evaluating her singing. As the London *Athenaeum* put it, "her almost boundless voice ebbed and flowed alternately, sometimes dying away in soothing murmurs and then suddenly advancing in an irresistible volume and lashing the various cliffs at pleasure. This gifted creature's voice is surely the American sea serpent of music. It is to be met with in folds, in coils, in wreaths; but nobody seems to know where either the head or the tail of it is to be found" (qtd. Bushnell 1979: 160).

Malibran's boundless voice was as much the site of dramatic conflict as were her body and gestures. The same was probably the case with Nourrit. He too had been trained by García and his voice had none of the light lyrical quality that was expected of the tenor in bel canto. Rather, from the roles written for him in grand opera, it would appear he had a mellow, powerful voice, but from the passage in the love duet of act 4 of *Les Huguenots*, which Meyerbeer wrote virtually at Nourrit's instruction, it is apparent that he also had an extraordinarily expanded head tone, which allowed him to sing remarkably high without going into falsetto. From the tension between these two voices, there arises a suffocated quality in many of the roles written for Nourrit, as if the sounds to be expressed in the upper range are struggling to escape from below. What is clear is that with both Malibran and Nourrit, singing itself was a dramatic act and the impact of the performance depended not upon the sheer virtuosity of the voice but on a sense of struggle, either within the voice or between the singers and the voice, or, in the case of Malibran, an illusion of a voice that was constantly changing and never had a firm identity.

If we place these three singers on a historical spectrum, Pasta seems to fit period categorization most easily; she recalled the imagined grandeur of a classical theatre by casting an air of sublimity over the stages on which she performed. Nourrit is a more transitional figure. He too had been strongly influenced by Talma, but more in the way of finding exact means to represent the uniqueness of his characters. His early retirement arose mainly, perhaps even exclusively, from his incapacity to master the 'tenore di forza', the specialty of his rival Duprez, whose famous chest tones would provide the basis for the performance of Verdi in the middle decades of the century. In the 1830s, however, such voices were a rarity, and Nourrit retired specifically to train his voice in the style of Duprez, an enterprise which catastrophically failed. Nourrit fell prey to the forces of historical change in singing. In contrast, Malibran fully met the needs and tastes of her time. She was the romantic virtuoso and, like almost all of this type, she had little influence on those who came after her. One of the key attributes of the myth of romantic virtuosity is that the performer is inimitable, is one who does not provide models from which others learn. Ludwig Devrient, Franz Liszt, Niccolò Paganini were all celebrated by their public for the uniqueness of their work. The same is true of Malibran. "Boundless as were Malibran's resources", wrote Henry Chorley, "keen as was her intelligence, dazzling as was her genius, she never produced a single type in opera for other women to adopt. She passed over the stage like a meteor, as an apparition of wonder, rather than as one who, in her departure, left her mantle behind her for others to take up and wear." (1862: 1/15)

Is there any way in which these singers fit in to the broader mythology of the romantic artist as a figure driven to self-destruction, which became one of the commonest and longest-lived tropes of the late Romantic period? Pasta had no part in this; she enjoyed a long and prosperous retirement. But the energies that drove Malibran could summon up in the imagination of those who heard her associations of a Gothic realm of decay and gloom. Malibran figures prominently in Hans Christian Andersen's immensely successful first novel, *The Improvisatore*, published in 1835, in which she features as the singer Annunciata whose singing and beauty mesmerize the hero, Antonio, and drive him to ecstatic heights and corresponding depths. Circumstances separate him from her for years and, eventually, he comes across her performing in a run-down theatre in Venice, but where she appears as nothing but a "painted corpse" (Andersen [n. d.]: 306), having lost her voice due to a long and severe illness some years previously, as if the very energies that drove her also preyed on her very health. Interestingly Andersen's imagination came nowhere close to the macabre reality of Malibran's death, which occurred in the year after his novel was published. In a way, even Malibran's death was performed. She experienced a terrible fall while riding in London, suffering severe concussion and internal injuries, but she refused to modify her hectic opera and concert schedule. She died a few months later soon after giving a concert in Manchester, during which she was visibly ailing yet still completely in control of her voice and powers of improvisation; nevertheless, at the end she had to be carried, unconscious, from the stage. There is a studied quality to this death, as if she had known from the moment of her accident six months previously that it was imminent so that it might indeed be considered to have been her last performance. Adolphe Nourrit committed suicide the following year, apparently in despair that in the search for a 'tenore di forza', he had ruined whatever voice he had had. Evidence suggests he was wrong; indeed, he had enjoyed a considerable success at a concert only the night before he threw himself from the roof of his Neapolitan hotel. But for the romantics the subjective apprehension of reality is of far greater weight than any objective evidence that may counter it. Nourrit died, a victim of the illusion that his voice had been destroyed for good.

The virtuosic singers of the Romantic age were not the first operatic stars; opera seria, with the fearsome demands it made upon singers' vocal equipment, produced generations of singers who had aroused the adulation of audiences and enjoyed widespread social celebrity. Furthermore, these singers were not required slavishly to follow the music. Indeed, successful performances in seria depended, to some degree, on the capacity of the singer to improvise imaginatively; singers were even free to substitute arias of their own choice for those indicated by the composer. While singers of seria may have been constrained by a fairly rigid system of gestures, they enjoyed considerable musical freedom. It was during the Romantic period that the situation began to reverse itself. In the course of the 19th century, while the composer's score became increasingly sacrosanct, the performer acquired the stature of an imaginative, interpretative artist whose contribution to the performance was valued to the extent that it was unlike those of predecessors. This could have a revivifying impact on the score. The effect of Pasta on the roles she sang was a transformative one to the extent that, according to Stendhal, she could instil into them a significance and beauty they had so far not been understood to possess (cf. 1968: 2/146). Malibran to a more spectacular degree had the same capacity, and in her case, more than in Pasta's, this was due to her formidable histrionic skills, so that her acting drew as much attention as her singing. However, as in the spoken theatre, there was in opera no school of romantic performance. Originality, which is based upon the assumption that each individual's subjective experience of the world is different, became a prevailing value in the theatre in the course of the nineteenth century, though its advance was a process that advanced by fits and starts as originality, by its very nature, has to operate free from influence and therefore from dominant artistic modes and movements. It was not until the turn of the 19th into the 20th century, a period in which the separate components of theatrical performance were identified and developed independently of their context in the overall performance, that continuous attention was focused by performers and critics on the artistic contribution of the performing artist. However, in operatic performance as in so many other artistic genres, the Romantic era provided a foretaste of things to come.

References

Andersen, Hans Christian ([n. d.]). *The Improvisatore*. Mary Howitt, trans. Boston, MA/ New York, NY: Houghton Mifflin.

[Anon.] (1985). *Il corago: o Vero alcune osservazioni per metter bene in scena le composizioni drammatiche*. Paolo Fabbri, Angelo Pompilio, eds. Florence: Leo S. Olschki.

Barnett, Dene (1987). *The Art of Gesture: The Practices and Principles of 18th-Century Acting*. Heidelberg: Winter.

Becker, Heinz (1999). "Foreword". *The Diaries of Giacomo Meyerbeer*. Robert Ignatius Letellier, ed. and trans. 4 vols. Madison, NJ: Farleigh Dickinson UP – London/ Cranbury, NJ: Associated University Presses. I/19f.

Bushnell, Howard (1979). *Maria Malibran: A Biography of the Singer*. University Park, PA/London: Pennsylvania UP.

Chorley, Henry F. (1862). *Thirty Years' Musical Recollections*. 2 vols. London: Hurst & Blackett.

Florimo, Francesco (1881–1883). *La scuola musicale di Napoli e I suoi conservatorii*. 4 vols. Bologna: Forni.

Gagliano, Marco da (1608). *La Dafne*. Florence: Marescotti.

— (1979). "Preface to *Dafne*". Carol MacClintock, ed. *Readings in the History of Performance*. Bloomington, IN/London: Indiana UP. 187–194.

Hazlitt, William (1933). *The Complete Works of William Hazlitt*. P. P. Howe, ed. 21 vols. London/Toronto: Dent.

Hunt, Leigh (1949). *Leigh Hunt's Dramatic Criticism, 1808–1831.* Lawrence Houston Houtchens, Carolyn Washburn Houtchens, eds. New York, NY: Columbia UP.

Legouvé, Ernest ([1880]). *Maria Malibran.* Paris: Hetzel.

— (1893). *Sixty Years of Recollections.* Albert D. Vandam, trans. 2 vols. London/Sydney: Eden, Remington & Co.

Michotte, Edmond (1968). *Richard Wagner's* Visit to Rossini *(Paris 1860) and* An Evening at Rossini's in Beau-Sejour *(Passy 1858).* Herbert Weinstock, trans. Chicago, IL/London: The University of Chicago Press.

Pleasants, Henry (1995). *The Great Tenor Tragedy: The Last Days of Adolphe Nourrit.* Portland, OR: Amadeus Press.

Quicherat, Louis Marie (1867). *Adolphe Nourrit: sa vie, son talent, son caractère, sa correspondence.* 3 vols. Paris: Hachette.

Rousseau, Jean-Jacques (1856). *Ouevres complètes de J.-J. Rousseau.* Charles Lahure, ed. 8 vols. Paris: Hachette.

— (1960). *Politics and the Arts: Letter to M. D'Alembert on the Theatre.* Allan Bloom, trans. and ed. Ithaca, NY: Cornell UP.

Rutherford, Susan (2006). *The Prima Donna and Opera, 1815–1930.* Cambridge: Cambridge UP.

Savage, Roger, Matteo Sansone (1989). "*Il corago* and the Staging of Early Opera: Four Chapters from an Anonymous Treatise circa 1630". *Early Music* 17: 494–511.

Shaw, Bernard (1981). "Palmy Days at the Opera". *Shaw's Music: The Complete Music Criticism in Three Volumes.* Dan H. Laurence, ed. London/Sydney/Toronto: Bodley Head. I/432–437.

Stendhal (1968). *Vie de Rossini.* Henry Prunières, ed. 2 vols. Paris: Cercle du Bibliophile.

— (1970). *Life of Rossini.* Richard N. Coe, trans. and ed. New York, NY: Orion Press.

Tosi, Pier Francesco (1723/1904). *Opinioni de' cantori antichi e moderni.* Bologna: Forni; repr. Naples: Gennaro & Morano.

— (1743/1926). *Observations on the Florid Song.* London: Wilcox; repr. London: Reeves.

Sexing Song
Brigitte Fassbaender's *Winterreise*

Lawrence Kramer, New York, NY

Schubert's *Winterreise* represents its wandering hero's desire and despair in forms long regarded as prototypically masculine. The historical result has been that performances of the full cycle by women – always rare; the first public instance had to wait nearly a hundred years – have seemed both transgressive and fraught with anxiety. Around 1990 Brigitte Fassbaender recorded what became by far the most controversial of such performances. By both performing *with* her voice and performing her voice itself, Fassbaender unapologetically embraces the idea of transgression while dismissing the burden of anxiety. Her strategies of performance not only transform the substance of the cycle by insisting on a feminine presence that both the texts and the music efface, but also expose the network of associations linking masculinity, mourning, and expressive authority in Schubert's world and still, to a surprising degree, in ours.

By convention, art songs with a male persona may be sung by either a man or a woman but art songs with a female persona must be sung by women only. With popular song this asymmetry does not arise; the singer simply changes the relevant pronouns. But in art song, where changing the text is normally prohibited, the asymmetry is part of the genre. This rule has not always been firm; in the nineteenth century private performances often ignored it and it was sometimes even ignored in public. The baritone Julius Stockhausen gave public performances of Schumann's *Frauenliebe und -leben*, the ne plus ultra of a song cycle with a female persona. But the more professionalized the performance of art song became, the more the rule of gender asymmetry prevailed. By the turn of the twentieth century it had become rigid.

This rigidity is symptomatic of the accelerating rise of modernity, which by disrupting traditional gender roles provoked a persistent anxiety about them. Modernity in its twentieth-century form was constantly haunted by the specters of disfigured gender. It is possible, even likely, that modern popular song began rising to prominence after the turn of the century in part because it gave voice to those specters and played both with and against the anxieties they induced.

The art song was obviously far less influential, if influential at all, but in its rules governing who sang what, as well as in its traditional content, it seems to have offered those concerned with it a small island of refuge from modern gender trouble.

At stake was the familiar principle, also becoming rigid at the time, that the human subject as such is masculine. The subject of songs with a female persona is always a woman; the subject of songs with a male persona is always a person. In art song, the gender of the persona acts as a gatekeeper for the gender of the singer. A woman singing as a man re-enacts the mimetic relationship of femininity as such to subjectivity as such, but a man singing as a woman would surrender the normative identity between subjectivity and masculinity.

This priority might seem to reinforce the privileges of masculinity: men are above songs for women. But in one respect the principle of superiority is self-defeating: it limits what a man can do. The art song allows any singer to take on a grand multiplicity of roles, but it limits this subjective mobility by invoking a boundary with broad cultural force – even today, when gender-enlightenment and a postmodern proliferation of gender-types are supposed to be routine. Hence the gender paradox: in singing these songs, a man is constrained to impersonate a man, but a woman is free to impersonate anyone.

Or is she? There are exceptions to the restriction on men, for example in comic songs. But what about exceptions to the license for women? Are there not cases in which it is no joke if a woman sings in the place of a man?

Indeed there are. A woman's license to sing for a male persona does not mean that the gender of the singer is irrelevant. It does not mean that her cross-gender performance is neutral or, better, neuter, nor that it can be trusted to leave intact the norms of gender and the fantasy-structures that support them. The sex of song is not nearly as easy to control as the prevailing conventions make it seem.

Perhaps for this reason there are some songs in the male repertoire that appear to resist performance by a woman so as to exempt certain forms of masculine experience from feminine appropriation. The real rule is that women are free to impersonate *almost* anyone. Some women, however, take exception to this limit and decide to perform – the exceptions. When they do, the dichotomies of gender have a tendency to falter. They get confused; they wander off.

Schubert's song cycle *Winterreise* is a prime example. Conventional wisdom regards it as the premiere work of its kind. But the iconic status of this cycle is intimately bound up with its possession by male voices. When Christine Schäfer ventured a performance at Lincoln Center in January 2008, the advertisement in the *New York Times* proclaimed the recital a "rare opportunity to hear *Winterreise*" – no need to name the composer – "performed by a woman" (2008: B.4). The performance would thus be an exception, for as any interested reader is presumed to know, *Winterreise* is as absolutely written for a man as *Frauenliebe und -leben* is for a woman. The first full public performance of *Winterreise* by a woman – Elena Gerhardt – did not take place until 1928, a hundred years after the music was written. Lotte Lehmann followed suit in 1940 and then recorded the cycle in unequal halves for Victor in 1940 and Columbia in 1941 (see Stalker 1999: online).

There have been other recordings since, but each one counts as an exception, which is the norm for a woman in *Winterreise*. Both Gerhardt and Lehmann wrote retrospectively about their decisions to perform the cycle, justifying in very similar terms – even similar words – what they clearly regarded as an act of appropriation: "Why should a woman, who is capable of experiencing these emotions, not be able to perform [these songs]?" (Gerhardt); "Why should a singer be denied a vast number of wonderful songs if she has the power to create an illusion, which she makes her audience believe in?" (Lehmann)[1] The defensive tone of these rhetorical questions is a sure sign that these women knew they were crossing a line. When Christa Ludwig subsequently decided to follow their lead, she actually sought the permission of Dietrich Fischer-Dieskau to do so[2]. The text of the *Times* ad for Schäfer's performance suggests that today's sensibility is more open to the feminine exception, but only so long as it remains exceptional. The ad admits as much by quoting a review of an earlier *Winterreise* by Schäfer, of whom we're told that "[her] bright, agile voice brings new focus to the song cycle, like the glint of sun on an icicle" (*New York Times* 2008: B.4).

It is not immediately clear why coldness should be desirable in the performance of an extended series of laments, particularly this one:

---

[1] Gerhardt's and Lehmann's remarks are quoted (and their sentiments reiterated) in the liner notes to the Fassbaender/Reimann CD (1990); Lehmann is speaking in general about songs with male personae, but her groundbreaking recording of *Winterreise* (however truncated) is obviously part of what is at stake.

[2] My thanks to Sylvia Mieszkowski for providing this information.

the cold is precisely what Schubert's protagonist is lamenting. But one possibility is that a voice like ice has no sex. The reviewer is presumably thinking of the ice imagery in many of the songs ("Auf dem Flusse", "Gefror'ne Tränen", and "Der Leiermann", among others) and admiring Schäfer for what he takes to be an appropriate combination of purity and reserve, almost a maidenly modesty, a vocal virginity.

In his *Times* review of the Lincoln Center performance, Allan Kozinn goes a step further. He explicitly identifies the lightness and purity of Schäfer's voice with gender neutrality: "If any soprano seems likely to make the sex change seem incidental, it is Christine Schäfer, who [...] has proved adept at using her supple tone to get at the emotional core of a text, rendering its surface meaning almost secondary" (2008: B.8). This neutrality or neutering is progressive. It follows a course of decline from the first song, when the rejected protagonist abandons his home for a life of aimless wandering, to the last song, when he halts to stare at a ragged hurdy-gurdy man who stands barefoot on the ice: "You could feel the wanderer's energy fading from song to song as Ms. Schäfer's voice became quieter, lighter and more velvety." Ice remains the leitmotif of this process: "In 'Auf dem Flusse,' which likens the rejected lover's heart to a frozen stream, Ms. Schäfer produced a gentle, nuanced sound that seemed scarcely more than a whisper"; "[i]n 'Das Wirtshaus,' a song about a graveyard, likened to an inn, [she] projected a sense of being almost frozen." (Ibid.)

Nothing remotely similar could be said of an earlier performance by a woman, Brigitte Fassbaender's 1990 recording. Fassbaender seeks out the emotional core of the texts precisely by singing as a woman, and she cuts through the ice like a laser. As an exception, her performance represents not purity but transgression, even defiance. It is always intense, often extravagant, and sometimes fierce. It does not treat gender as a 'surface meaning' to be transcended but as a source of depth.

With Fassbaender's performance we have arrived at the principal topic of this paper. Fassbaender's *Winterreise* transforms Schubert's drastically male-centered song cycle into an immanent critique of the cycle's representation of desire. Or, more exactly, of the way that that representation has traditionally been received; as we will see, Schubert too has a critique to offer. He can be understood to have enveloped the music with overtones that Fassbaender's performance renders more audible in the course of its own pursuits.

Those pursuits involve repeal as well as critique. The performance aims beyond rendition and beyond appropriation to *performativity* in the sense of illocutionary force. It seeks to reverse the cycle's removal of the feminine subject and her desire to a distance, an impossible distance, just so they might be mourned; to reject the identification of desire with masculine subjectivity; and to refuse the grounding of desire in a certain tragic heterosexuality. The performance does all this, moreover, not by negating the cycle's thematic investment in endless wandering as endless mourning, but by changing the terms on which that investment may be understood.

Such endlessness is a distinctly masculine theme within the culture of early Romanticism, which understands the persistence of masculine attachments as heroic and associates feminine mourning, in contrast, with ritualistic, cathartic discharge. The measure of the aggrieved man's stature is precisely his refusal of this discharge. *Winterreise* is a textbook case of what Freud a century later would describe as the "overestimation of the object" typical of masculine desire. The "peculiar state of being in love" originates in this libidinally charged skewing of judgment, "the impoverishment of the ego in respect of libido in favor of the love object", the "flowing-over of ego-libido onto the object" (1914/1963: 69; 80). The fit is especially close as regards the protagonist's self esteem, which, as Freud suggests, becomes more depleted the more that the wandering lover esteems his forever-distant beloved. "He who loves has, so to speak, forfeited a part of his narcissism, which can only be replaced by his being loved" (ibid.: 78). As a result, life for the wanderer, his whole life story, becomes a state of never-completed mourning. One peculiar state foments another as the wanderer mourns not only his beloved but also, in her, his own beloved self.

Another century later, Derrida would describe the same state with reference to both Freud and Jean-Luc Nancy. "Mourning autobiography", he suggests, "is not just any mourning among others" (2005: 52). It is a literally unimaginable activity, something that can be performed but not represented. "It is mourning itself. It is an absolute mourning, mourning of life itself, but mourning that can no longer be *worn* and *borne* [...] nor go through the 'work' of mourning" (ibid.: 50). This 'mourning without mourning' takes the form of a haunting, though whether by oneself or others remains unknowable: "One might as well say that, unimaginable, [mourning autobiography] can only give rise to images, phantasms, and specters. [...] And so this mourning without mourning will never be overcome" (ibid.: 52). In particular the Freudian 'work of mourning' will be of no avail, so that Freud's famous distinction between mourning and melancholia, one finite, the other not, inexorably breaks down. The intention to mourn, the activity of mourning, continues, but like a wanderer it goes nowhere because it goes everywhere; it does not and cannot have an end. It continues even after the subject becomes aware of its futility and even after the lost "object" has completely disappeared from view.

Derrida's description applies remarkably well to *Winterreise*, for whose protagonist the figure of the beloved is a specter, a succubus, and one who disappears just after the midpoint of the cycle. But there is a telling exception. The figure on which Derrida concentrates, following Nancy, who follows Freud, is feminine, namely Psyche, the name of the soul and the image of the beloved. Somehow the definitively masculine character of wandering-as-mourning has turned into its feminine opposite. Psyche, we may remember, was supposed to embrace Eros but never to see him; the same rule applies to the wandering lover, whose Psyche is forever out of sight. But not because she is too far: rather because her distance is a form of uncanny proximity, a telescopic inversion in which she becomes the eye by which he sees himself – at a distance.

One way to describe Fassbaender's *Winterreise* is to say that it seeks to dramatize these reversals. The result would not be a simple feminizing but an absolutizing, enunciated in the nonetheless feminine voice of "mourning itself". In a narrow sense, Fassbaender's voice would be that of a woman claiming her own right to wander; in a wider sense, it would be the voice of the mourner channeling her traditional keening or wailing into the song of Psyche. Either way, this is an effort that could hardly have failed to meet resistance in 1990, even if the resistance was about to prove no more durable than ice in a thaw.

It is the necessity of a foundational masculinity that dominates Matthew Gurewitsch's *New York Times* review of Fassbaender's performance as represented on CD (see 1990)[3]. The interest of this

---

[3] There is also a DVD which I will not discuss here, partly because Gurewitsch does not, partly because I want to focus on questions of voice, and partly because the

review is not conceptual but symptomatic. The review was a plea for the preservation of certain gender differences at just about the last moment – already too late – that such a plea could plausibly be made in a Western society. Gurewitsch's argument ostensibly turns on a question of authenticity: because the songs of *Winterreise* are close to the bone of a great composer's anguish, they cannot tolerate the artifice involved in substituting a woman's voice for a man's; they must "be real". There is no need to dwell on the precritical naiveté of this argument because the argument is only a pretext. What really worries Gurewitsch is a woman's performative assumption of certain extreme states of feeling. Although he does offer some praise for this extremity, and although he brushes off Christa Ludwig's earlier recording as "rather matronly", Gurewitsch has clearly been made anxious by the uncontrollable subjective force that Fassbaender claims as illocutionary force. Her accompanist, the avant-garde composer Aribert Reimann, makes matters worse by mirroring the singer's extravagance with extravagances of his own that Gurewitsch hears as "brutal", as if the voice and piano were acting not in partnership but in collusion.

The reviewer's anxiety shows itself most clearly where his review lapses into some outright misogyny. At this point we need an extended quotation:

> Miss Fassbaender, to give her credit, [...] has imagined her way deep into the dark heart of Wilhelm Müller's texts and Schubert's settings. The performance displays a brave ferocity that many male duos would do well to emulate. The price, it must be said, is steep. Mr. Reimann's pianism is often brutal, and the list of Miss Fassbaender's vocal blemishes is long: savage timbres, wild wobbles, sobs fetched – heaved – from the chest.
>
> But no one could accuse Miss Fassbaender of prettifying the cycle's relentless despair. [...] The dyspeptic note she strikes in "Irrlicht" is distinctive. She goes at "Der greise Kopf" in accents that are grand and tragic. [...] Miss Fassbaender needs no instruction in the hues of gloom.
>
> Still, nothing works. Where we seek to be lost in raw experience, she offers a performance. It is not a failure of imagination; it is the nature of the instrument. In full cry, Miss Fassbaender evokes the adolescent hysterics of Octavian toward the end of "Der Rosenkavalier's" first act. The emotion is not wrong. But Octavian is a boy – a boy still smooth-cheeked enough to masquerade as a girl. The wanderer of "Winterreise" has crossed that threshold. His voice has changed. (Ibid.: A.31)

---

addition of gesture and video editing would add layers of complexity that, though interesting in themselves, would not make much difference to my argument.

Gurewitsch's condescension about the 'boy's' voice barely bothers to mask his discomfiture by the woman's. The traits that make him so unhappy – Fassbaender's ferocity, her dark intensity, her relentlessness, and above all the audible traces of her body in her singing – affect him as they do partly because he hears them (and with them Reimann's pianistic 'brutality') as an involuntary expression of the singer's feminine condition. He does *not* hear them as a series of aesthetic choices supporting a coherent representation of the cycle. They are, ironically, too real for him, even though what he hears in them is the artifice of performance. They break out like blemishes on a face. But taken on their own terms – and they are really there; Gurewitsch, to give him credit, is right about that – these traits can form the basis for a series of global observations about Fassbaender's performance independent of how she uses the gender of her voice to affect the form and meaning of specific songs.

First observation: the excesses of Fassbaender's *Winterreise* suggest an attempt to flout the rules of cross-gender performance. The persona of this version is a woman even if in some sense the same persona also remains a man. The gender of the voice usurps upon the gender of the persona rather than consenting to represent the masculine persona by default. But if this is so, the female voice immediately renders the persona of the cycle an impossible one, an identity with no identity. For the wanderer is not a man by accident; he is a quintessentially masculine figure in the culture of the period. To the extent that wandering fixes roles for both sexes, they are the roles paradigmatically articulated by Goethe's famous lyric "Nähe des Geliebten", also set by Schubert: the man wanders, the woman waits.

The woman waits, that is, if there is a woman at all. Her position may be filled by a mere personified absence, a tradition recalled a century later by Rilke: "Du im Voraus / verlorne Geliebte, Nimmergekommene, / nicht weiss ich, welche Töne dir lieb sind. / Nicht mehr versuch ich, dich, wenn das Kommende wogt, / zu erkennen" (1966: 2/79). And if there is a woman, as there is in Goethe's poem, her waiting is not only a social and, if you like, an existential condition, but also a condition of perception bordering at times on hallucination: "Ich sehe dich, wenn auf dem fernen Wege / Der Staub sich hebt, / In tiefer Nacht, wenn auf dem schmalen Stege / Der Wandrer bebt" (1994: 128). In the poetry of the time, women who wander are outcasts: madwomen, unwed mothers, prostitutes. So the protagonist of Fassbaender's *Winterreise* exists in not existing. She is not even an exception, but the embodiment of a wandering more radical than any postulated by Schubert or Müller, the wandering of everything that must remain in place, in its place, the wandering of identity itself or the identity of wandering itself. This persona is not a wanderer; she is Wandering personified.

Schubert, meanwhile, can also be understood to disrupt a normative mode of identity, only from within rather from without. His wanderer represents a dissent from the restriction imposed on masculine subjectivity by the overproduction of desire for the opposite sex. This dissent appears in the drastic under-specification of the lost beloved, who is already absent even before she is lost. She is never invoked in person, but only as an abstraction. After all reference to her disappears, the wanderer turns entirely to a landscape of pure fantasy, half spectral, half psychical. He wanders *from* the beloved; he becomes himself where (wherever) she is not. His sense of her presence never shapes what he sings. Only her absence does that. The poetic under-specification of her identity allows the musical over-specification of his.

This is not to say, apropos the formerly hot topic of Schubert's sexuality, that Schubert's *Winterreise* tries to homosexualize the Lied tradition. But given the openness to variations in identity and desire, the sympathy with the non-normative that I have elsewhere identified as the driving force behind Schubert's Lieder (see Kramer 1998), it is to say that his *Winterreise* both exposes and questions the gendered logic of the Lied world. Unable to stop wanting his nameless, faceless, 'beloved', if she can even be called beloved, the masculine protagonist of the cycle must constantly renegotiate the boundary between his survival and his extinction as a subject.

Schubert's *Winterreise* expropriates the gender of the beloved on behalf of this effort. Fassbaender's version does the same thing in reverse; it expropriates the gender of the lover. In this mirror-inversion the two versions of the cycle become each other's complements, interlocutors, doppelgänger. The two versions are like the identical doors in Jacques Lacan's famous anecdote of gender formation, rendered intimately different by being marked with the inscriptions *Hommes* and *Femmes*:

> A train arrives at a station. A little boy and a little girl, brother and sister, are seated in a compartment face to face next to the window through which the buildings along the station platform can be seen passing as the train pulls to a

stop. "Look," says the brother, "we're at 'Ladies'!"; "Idiot!" replies his sister, "Can't you see we're at 'Gentlemen'?" (1977: 152)

Once both versions are in play, the expropriation becomes general. It is no longer simply *the* gender *of* the lover or beloved that is expropriated, but gender as such that is expropriated *from* either and both. It no longer matters which door one goes through.

Second observation: according to Friedrich Kittler, the German-speaking world in the early nineteenth century connected masculine sexuality with discursive authority; those who had power over language also had power over desire (cf. 1990: 3–69). *Winterreise* takes exception to this scheme. The cycle claims discursive authority on the basis of the protagonist's *lack* of both gratified and gratifying desire. The second lack is the stronger: the cycle rejects the gratification inherent in Romantic desire itself, as embodied, for example, in the quintessentially masculine figure of Goethe's Faust. Desire becomes a burden that the cycle's wanderer refuses to throw off but instead allows to proliferate, like the three suns that seem to fill the sky in the penultimate song, "Die Nebensonnen".

The song portrays the wanderer's desire as a plural self-mirroring that is also a self-blinding. Its destructive bedazzlement operates beyond the reach of the subject's will or knowledge:

Drei Sonnen sah' ich am Himmel steh'n,
hab' lang und fest sie angeseh'n;
und sie auch standen da so stier,
als wollten sie nicht weg von mir.[4]

Though the wanderer wishes the suns away, he mimics and exceeds their multiplication by dwelling on multiple statements of a single rhythmic figure (see *Example 1*). He re-enacts in sound what he rejects in sight. He translates the phenomenology of perception into the psychology of obsession.

This dissemination of desire also has the effect of breaking the continuity between desire and the feminine. The beloved in this cycle is emptied of gender, not only because she – it – is manifest mainly by absence and evaded reference, but also because the desire is no longer *for* her, indeed is no longer *for* anything, including itself. To invoke Lacan again, desire in this cycle becomes a kind of automatism that borders on sheer drive. The cost of Schubert's need to privilege mas-

---

[4] 'Three suns I saw in the heavens stand, / stared at them long and hard; / and they too stood there so fixedly / as if they willed never to part from me.' (My translation)

culine subjectivity in these terms is the systematic erasure, even the symbolic murder, of the feminine beloved, the beloved as such, the feminine as such. "Auf dem Flusse" makes this act explicit: it reduces the beloved to a name scratched on the ice. The name remains unread and unpronounced; the wanderer cancels it by drawing a broken ring around it; the music marks the cancellation by dwindling away to silence after the ring is drawn. For a moment it seems as if the song too is broken and cannot go on.

Example 1: Franz Schubert, "Die Nebensonnen", bars 4–9.

Fassbaender's *Winterreise* undoes this erasure by reanimating the feminine as a surplus of female voice, made audible in the wobbles and sobs that so troubled Gurewitsch. This surplus cannot be assimilated to either vocal or social norms. By insisting on it, Fassbaender supplants the masculine subjectivity that Schubert has tried so hard to sustain. The voice that emits the surplus, that identifies itself with its excess, re-sexes the cycle's beloved. Although this voice is not quite that *of* the beloved, it enables the beloved's femininity to make itself heard in the voice of the wanderer, and so to become part of the subjectivity that desires rather than to remain an abstract receptacle for a desire in which femininity has no share.

Third observation: the wanderer in Schubert's *Winterreise* is the opposite of the wanderer-hero of Romantic quest romance. He lacks not only a goal but even the will to wander; he is determined without being resolute. His condition is an extreme instance of Schubert's tendency to situate the protagonists of his songs, and especially of the song cycles and sequences, in what might be called the passively resistant zone of the Romantic ego, wherein one's identity consists of the realization that, however sorely pressed, one will never consent to one's nullification as a subject[5]. The quest for positive knowledge or pleasure is thus decentered, parodied, dispersed. Self becomes measured by the capacity for suffering, 'selflessness', the ability to accept abjection.

The peculiar thing about this development is its gender orientation. Its terms of negation carry a prominent tradition of feminine identification, the model of the patient Griselda, the self-abnegating woman, mater dolorosa, and the like, but here this tradition is annexed to a certain ideal of masculine subjectivity. When Fassbaender takes up the cycle she both restores the feminine identification and rejects its abject terms. She tries to sing the abjection away *as a woman* with the effects of voice, breath, and body that Gurewitsch deplores.

Fourth observation: the format of the Lied may offer a socially sanctioned chance for the listener-spectator to dwell desirously on the desiring singer, the desire of the singer, rather than to join the singer in dwelling on a usually absent or rejecting object of desire. This would be especially true of *Winterreise*. Even a song that fills in the image of the beloved rather than emptying it out can be listened to from a standpoint in which the strength of desire, not the mode or object of desire, is paramount. When the image of the beloved is indeed emptied out, the result is to intensify focus on the singer's subject position at the expense of the object.

This economy of desire is the key to the role of Fassbaender's own sexuality, that is, her public lesbianism, in her performance, something that Gurewitsch either does not recognize or chooses to ignore. Fassbaender is no more interested in a homosexual *Winterreise* than Schubert is (and I am well aware that this way of putting it is equivocal). But in her performance Fassbaender does, for those inclined to hear her, sing *as* a lesbian even though the desire she voices is entirely nonspecific. For Terry Castle, Fassbaender's singing is "homovocal"

---

[5] On this mode of Romantic subjectivity, see Kramer (1987/2006).

(1995: 41); it communicates "exaltation in the presence of the feminine" (ibid.: 44); and it does so, paradoxically, "to the precise degree that [she] seems to enter 'into' [...] male roles" such as operatic trouser parts or Schubert's winter wanderer (ibid.: 43).

Heard in these four contexts, Fassbaender's *Winterreise* sounds less like a series of discrete utterances than like a single enormous speech act. Each separate song forms the momentary tip of the iceberg. But since ice has been one of our themes, let me close with a brief reflection on breaking it.

Example 2: Franz Schubert, "Auf dem Flusse", bars 66–70.

"Auf dem Flusse" divides roughly in two. Its first half makes a simple equation between singing *piano* or *pianissimo* and feeling the frozen brook and frozen heart; the second half equates singing *forte* with exposing the passion that lies beneath. *Forte*: never louder. Each impulse to rise to *fortissimo* – and Schubert writes out the impulses in the score – is immediately pulled back, as if the protagonist were fearful of triggering a catharsis that would empty rather than relieve him (see *Example 2*, which occurs toward the end of the song and marks its climax).

But Fassbaender will not be restrained. She quickly rises to *fortissimo* at the start of her closing statement and stays at that level until she ends it. Her articulation is monolithic. She projects no fear of catharsis because she does not seek catharsis; she voices the protagonist's passion as a protest, not a question. She does not simply accept that the lover's work of mourning can never be completed; she embraces this impossibility with a courage and defiance that Schubert, at least, sought to withhold.

Fassbaender's performance almost explains what the wanderer finds inexplicable, the reason for his rejection. "If I", she seems to say, "a woman, were in your place I would not preserve myself in ice to protect myself from my loss. I would live it; I would become who I am rather than refuse to be anyone at all." Thus Schubert's poor wanderer is rejected all over again – not for having too little manhood, but for having too much.

References

Castle, Terry (1995). "In Praise of Brigitte Fassbaender: Reflections on Diva Worship". Corinne E. Blackmer, Patricia Juliana Smith, eds. *En Travesti: Women, Gender Subversion, Opera.* New York, NY: Columbia UP. 20–58.

Derrida, Jacques (2005). *On Touching: Jean-Luc Nancy.* Trans. Christine Irizarry. Stanford, CA: Stanford UP.

Fassbaender, Brigitte, Aribert Reimann (1990). *Franz Schubert: Winterreise*, EMI CDC 7-49846-2.

Freud, Sigmund (1914/1963). "On Narcissism: An Introduction". Trans. Cecil M. Baines. *General Psychological Theory.* Philip Rieff, ed. New York, NY: Macmillan. 56-82.

Goethe, Johann Wolfgang (1994). *Selected Poems* (bilingual edition). Christopher Middleton, ed. Princeton, NJ: Princeton UP.

Gurewitsch, Matthew (1990). "Recordings View: Can a Woman Do a Man's Job In Schubert's *Winterreise?*". *The New York Times* (Oct. 28): A.31.

Kittler, Friedrich (1990). *Discourse Networks 1800/1900.* Trans. Michael Metteer, Chris Cullens. Stanford, CA: Stanford UP.

Kozinn, Allan (2008). "A Passionate Yet Light Voice for Icy Songs by Schubert". *The New York Times* (11 January): B.8.

Kramer, Lawrence (1987/2006). "Decadence and Desire: The Wilhelm Meister Songs of Wolf and Schubert". *19th-Century Music* 10: 229–242. (Rpt. Lawrence Kramer. *Critical Musicology and the Responsibility of Response: Selected Essays.* Aldershot: Ashgate. 21–34.)

— (1998). *Franz Schubert: Sexuality, Subjectivity, Song.* Cambridge: CUP.

Lacan, Jacques (1977). "The Agency of the Letter in the Unconscious, or Reason Since Freud". *Écrits: A Selection.* Trans. Alan Sheridan. New York, NY: W. W. Norton. 146–178.

New York Times (2008). Advertisement Christine Schäfer (Jan. 11): B.4.

Rilke, Rainer Maria (1966). *Werke in drei Bänden.* Frankfurt am Main: Insel.

Stalker, Douglas (1999) [online]. "Lehmann's *Winterreise*". *American Record Guide* (Nov./Dec.). http://voxnovamedia.com/lehmann/llf/news/reviews/llf_reviews2.html [09/08/2010].

Vocal Embodiment and Performing Language in *Waiting for the Barbarians*
Philip Glass's Adaptation of J. M. Coetzee's Novel

Michael Halliwell, Sydney

The body and voice are central to opera, yet the purely vocal aspect of opera performance, as opposed to the use of voice in its capacity for linguistic signification, has not been prominent in much scholarly work in this area. The voice is both material and abstract, and is central to the performance of literature in its operatic adaptation, yet the words in opera have received much more attention than the actual materiality of the voice itself which can both support or disrupt the ultimate 'meaning' of opera: voice often distorts the linguistic basis of opera. Music in opera suggests interiority achieved through analyzable complex harmonic, melodic and rhythmic structures in combination with the words characters sing as well as through the staging and *mise-en-scène*. The operas of Philip Glass offer a challenge to this perception both in terms of dramaturgy as well as musical idiom. This paper explores Glass's recent (2005) adaptation of Nobel laureate J. M. Coetzee's influential 1980 novel, *Waiting for the Barbarians*. The novel is told from the first-person perspective of the central character of the Magistrate and has at its thematic core issues of alterity, physical violence and moral accountability where the body itself literally becomes a site of exploration of the darker recesses of the human soul. A pervasive duality present in much of Glass's music gives a sense of abstraction to what is occurring on stage; while at the same time suggesting empathy for the characters, there is often a tension between voice as both linguistic signifier as well as material presence. His work often combines a distancing, quasi-allegorical element with the immediacy of vocal dramatic representation. The possibility of linguistic signification as well as its 'silencing' is central to both novel and its operatic embodiment.

The study of opera from a performance perspective is a relatively recent phenomenon in musicology and current trends have been strongly influenced by aspects of performance studies. Opera, once the exclusive domain of musicology, has been embraced by a wide variety of interdiciplinary scholars who have brought an impressive range of critical approaches to the art form. There has been an ever increasing movement away from a purely score-based approach to a much more comprehensive view of opera, reflecting the hybrid art form that it is.

Michelle Duncan observes that opera studies needs to "examine what a performance *does*; that is, how a performance generates or disrupts levels of meaning by doing" (2004: 288)[1]. She argues that the performative utterance as formulated by J. L. Austin concerns the notion that to 'say something is to do something', but she observes that Austin was silent on the role of voice, noting that his project is "explicitly concerned with linguistic effect, not vocal effect" (ibid.: 291). She poses the question: "how does the status of the utterance change according to the register of resonance? And what exactly does the vocal utterance *do* if this doing is not a linguistic act?" (Ibid.: 289) If "the force of vocal resonance does violence to anything, it is to the absolute sovereignty of language and thus the absolute intentionality of the speaking subject" (ibid.: 291).

Of course these observations are fundamental to word/music debate itself. The apparent sovereignty of language is problematised in any staged adaptation of a literary work, particularly a novel; the 'silent' and 'un-voiced' language of fiction will literally be given both 'voice' and physical embodiment in a dramatic adaptation. This is further complicated in a musical dramatisation where sung speech is combined with instrumental music in a synthesis of vocal and instrumental sound emanating from 'real' and very present physical bodies, both singers and instrumentalists. The nature of dramatic performance presupposes that any intrinsic 'meaning' in the performance will vary from production to production; indeed from single performance to single performance. Language and sonority, as observed in the adaptation of a particular work of fiction to opera, is the subject of this paper.

Nobel laureate J. M. Coetzee's celebrated early novel, *Waiting for the Barbarians* (1980), obliquely reflects the political situation in South Africa during the 1970s. The novel is profoundly concerned with oppression, particularly physical and mental torture, and the deaths of political prisoners depicted in the novel have strong resonances with the deaths of political activists in South Africa at the time. The ambiguous but ominous threat that the barbarians pose in the

---

[1] Duncan argues that "hermeneutic readings of opera have tended to overlook issues of performativity because they search for an ultimate truth that can be either represented or somehow excavated through a live staging. Being attentive to performativity means looking for ways that performance may expose 'truth' by disruption as well as complementarity." (2004: 288)

novel had its parallels with the all-pervasive 'communist threat' that was often advanced for the gradual dismantling of the legal system as well as the increasingly restrictive media and other laws that were imposed.

It is not surprising that this novel attracted Philip Glass, particularly after the attacks of September 11, 2001, and the USA's continuing controversial response to the threat of terrorism. However, Glass observes that he had already contacted Coetzee in 1991 to see whether he was willing to give his permission for an adaptation, and actually began preliminary work at that time. Glass, in a brief foreword to the recording of the opera, notes:

> I'd begun to do this kind of social/political opera in 1979 with *Satyagraha* [...]. My aim then, as it is now, was to preserve Coetzee's bold allegorical approach while dramatizing the classic themes of confrontation, crisis and redemption so the audience itself is left weighing the meaning of good and evil in their own lives. To reduce the opera to a single historical circumstance or a particular political regime misses the point. That the opera can become an occasion for dialogue about political crisis illustrates the power of art to turn our attention toward the human dimension of history. (2008: 4)

The first performance of the opera, with its concise and pithy libretto by Christopher Hampton, took place at the Erfurt Opera on September 10, 2005. Critics and audiences immediately identified thematic links with the USA's role in Iraq, and made connections with the notorious Iraqi prison Abu Ghraib. It can be argued that both novel and opera can be 'read' in this more direct and specific way without diminishing their broader allegorical power.

The first-person narrative mode of the novel – homodiegetic simultaneous present – is significant for its operatic transformation. This is a narrative strategy, James Phelan argues, which places the reader in

> a very different relationship to the magistrate and to the events of the narrative than would any kind of retrospective account. The strategy takes teleology away from the magistrate's narrative acts: since he does not know how events will turn out, he cannot be shaping the narrative according to his knowledge of the end. Consequently, we cannot read with our usual tacit assumptions that the narrator, however unselfconscious, has some direction in mind for his tale. Instead, as we read any one moment of the narrative we must assume that the future is always – and radically – wide open: the narrator's guess about what will happen next is really no better than our own. (1994: 223)

This distinctly limited narrative mode, with its sense of simultaneity and open-endedness, allows only a form of heavily mediated communication for all characters apart from the narrator, and access to characters is, in turn, mediated through his subjective perspective. While the novel is concerned with notions of 'interpretation' and the exploration of alterity, both of which are intricately linked to the themes of language and writing, this deliberately restricted narrative form limits giving voice to the 'other' either in the form of speech or writing. This is naturally subverted in an operatic adaptation where all characters are given equivalent sung speech, and undercuts the novel's restrictive narrative mode: the immediacy of the human voice, and, in particular, the trained operatic voice, has a visceral impact which is denied the heavily mediated other voices in the novel. All characters have a roughly equivalent vocal presence on stage.

The singing voice has the potential for providing 'meaning' far beyond the semantic meaning of the actual sung text. Duncan notes that if there is a

> certain 'truth' revealed about a text through its performance, a 'truth' revealed through the act of singing, then in opera this 'truth' is revealed through the performance of the voice, a performative 'force' beyond both music and libretto, beyond the hermeneutics of performance. (2004: 297)

Of course, in musical adaptation much more than the particular characteristics of the speech of a character can be represented. Definition of character can be achieved by the shape of the vocal line itself, and emotional states can be suggested by rhythmic and pitch variations as well as the actual sonorous materiality of the voice itself. Surrounding and encompassing this is the 'commentary' on character and situation suggested by the orchestra which can provide contradictory 'information' about that character, or information of which that character is unaware. The production of 'meaning' in opera is a complex process, and the materiality of the voice is certainly a crucial aspect of the phenomena that Hans Ulrich Gumbrecht describes as "contributing to the constitution of meaning without being meaning themselves" (1994: 398). Meaning in opera is not just contingent on the libretto, or on the dramatic impetus provided by the music, but on crucial performative aspects of the actual performance itself.

Carl Dahlhaus observes that the "story underlying an opera does not exist independently of the music; and the story in the libretto as such is not the story of the opera as a musical drama" (1989: 101). In effect, what Dahlhaus argues is that one cannot actually 'tell' the story from the libretto alone as the dramatic thrust of an opera occurs essentially in the music and not in the verbal text; what can be adapted effectively is that which can be adapted into music. While what Dahlhaus maintains is compelling, it perhaps undervalues the crucial role of the libretto in underpinning the ultimate form of the operatic work, but it would generally be accepted that musical development in opera shapes our sense of character, dramatic architecture and dramatic impetus.

Owing to its intrinsic nature Philip Glass's music problematises the representation of subjectivity in his operas. While his music has changed significantly over the years, in general terms it is characterized by repetitive, rhythmic musical cells underpinned by often slowly-changing harmonies. These underscore what seems at times almost a 'detached' vocal line which often does not appear to have much connection to the harmonic or rhythmic orchestral palette which supports it. However, his vocal lines frequently also reveal a 'traditionally' operatic expressivity and rhythmic and melodic shape that reflect the emotional and physical action represented on stage. What Glass achieves in his work is a larger and somewhat detached sense of the character in a particular context rather than portraying any particular musical distinctiveness of character. This is unlike more 'mainstream' opera where a composer will strive to create the character as much through the orchestral music as the dramaturgy; where through musical development we have a sense of a parallel process of character development, both in the words and actions of the character, but also through the orchestral 'commentary' surrounding and informing our perception of that character.

Glass's characters resemble emblematic figures in a tableau or pageant rather than typical subjective operatic figures, and much of the dramatic 'action' is provided by this endlessly 'busy', yet slowly-changing musical accompaniment. This is often radically different to the musical development of the kind that is found in much post-Wagnerian opera. What Glass does, in effect, is to stylize the operatic performance mode even further. There is a continual tension between the 'realistic' situations represented in the staging as well as the idiomatic and 'natural' cadences in the vocal line which seem to be in conflict with the surrounding, 'detached' musical accompaniment which appears at once to 'contain' the characters, but who, through their physical presence and, in particular, through their sonorous voices as performers as well as characters, attempt to break through this apparently 'disconnected' web of music. The seeming disconnect between the vocal line and the orchestral accompaniment accentuates this tension as the vocal line appears to 'float' above the music. Obviously the question arises whether the minimalist idiom in its various manifestations can convey the range of psychological subjectivity that more 'mainstream' opera sees as its raison d'être.

Glass's operatic structures have shown an increasing tendency to narrative linearity, particularly as he has used fiction as the basis for many of his new operas while at the same time moving towards 'traditional' opera production techniques, and indeed, into standard opera theatres. In structural terms there has been a move away from extended, seemingly unconnected scenes in the earlier pieces, to a structure characterised by shorter and more inter-connected scenes, departing from what has been described as 'landscape drama' (cf. Ashby 2005: 252).

As Glass moved from the non-linear, often circular structures of his early stage works to more literary and narrative-based ones, his focus on the words has become more acute. Therefore, in these later works the words sung by characters allied to the visual aspects of performance take on an added importance which was not fore-grounded in the earlier, perhaps more experimental works. Understanding character through the music that surrounds them, however, is not the primary focus as it is in more 'mainstream' opera where the orchestra is employed in a dual capacity, both as a commentary on the events portrayed on the stage, as well as providing access into the thoughts of the characters. Carolyn Abbate memorably described minimalism as music with "no past tense", and the devices of harmonic development and transformation as well as leitmotivic techniques common in opera have little place in operas written in this idiom (1991: 52). However, critics have argued that these later works of Glass's reveal a composer attempting to speak through his characters, very much in the standard operatic tradition[2].

Glass himself has observed that "it is surely no coincidence that it was at the moment that I was embarking upon a major shift in my music to large-scale theater works that I began to develop a new, more expressive language for myself" (qtd. Ashby 2005: 256). However, what frequently occurs is that in musical terms there are large, often

---

[2] Discussing Glass's 1992 opera, *The Voyage*, Arved Ashby comments that none of his other stage works gives "quite the same impression of a composer speaking and emoting through his characters – a ventriloquism that lies at the heart of opera conventionally defined" (2005: 253).

slowly evolving harmonic and rhythmical gestures which are not directly related to the text that is being sung, but more directly related to creating the mood of the broad dramatic situation: in a sense, perhaps, closer to what often occurs in the deployment of film music. The repetitive circularity of the musical structures is particularly suited to the circularity of this particular narrative as the story ends much where it began, but a year later. Sandra Corse sees a fundamental tension within operatic works in the minimalist idiom, arguing that although one of the

> revolutionary intents of minimalist music was to create a new intersubjective stance for music, to suggest […] a type of music in which the expressive impulse is shared among a group of performer/composers, in actual practice such an ideal has largely proven impractical for larger works such as operas. Instead, minimalist music has reverted to the service of a kind of psychologizing tendency not completely different from that explored by Wagner. The radical intersubjectivity and objectivity promised by minimalist music have not always materialized, partly because composers such as Glass and Adams remain obliquely dependent on tonality in that their music bases much of its appeal on the audience's allegiance to traditional tonal structures. The critique of subjectivity intended by these works is partially diluted by their dependence on historically venerable musical and dramatic forms. The effort to subvert the subject fails and the individual audience member emerges […] more locked into individuality than ever. (2000: 191)

Certainly this tendency is characteristic of Adams's recent opera, *Doctor Atomic,* as well as some earlier works.

Glass's operas employ a quasi-Brechtian approach to theatrical representation. He described his early work in the theatre in terms of being

> encouraged to leave what I call a "space" between the image and the music. In fact, it is precisely that space which is required so that members of the audience have the necessary perspective or distance to create their own individual meanings. (Qtd. Ashby 2005: 254)

This strongly recalls Brecht's desire to make audiences think about the characters rather than empathise with them. *Waiting for the Barbarians* is surely a work that incorporates and develops these trends and approaches, and perhaps it is better to speak of this work in post-minimalist terms. John Adams's operas perhaps best encapsulate these trends: works that use the repetitive and tonal aspects of minimalism with a freedom "to underline the dynamics and surface emotions experienced on stage" (ibid.: 260). Ashby observes that in regard to all major operatic reforms, "realism has been invoked in the name of modernity" but operatic minimalists have "remade conceptions of reality itself [through] contravening basic ideas of narrative and refuting breath-based conceptions of musical utterance [turning] opera into something that might seem more, rather than less, theatrical" (ibid.: 265). Glass regards realism as "a matter of faithfulness towards dreams as the true, perhaps post-Freudian reality" (qtd. ibid.: 254).

There is a pronounced sensual quality in Coetzee's physical descriptions in his novels, and one could argue that in any musical dramatization of a text this quality is represented primarily by the music. The musical dramatization of the story inevitably takes it out of the realm of the somewhat abstractly allegorical into something much more concrete and visceral. Music's essential capacity to enhance and magnify character also lends itself to the move away from the allegorical into the immediate and direct. We are, as the audience, acutely aware of the physical presence and, particularly, the voices of the operatic performers in front of us. Thus, Glass's music theatre works display a duality more extreme than works written in a more standard operatic idiom; perhaps what could be described as a 'tension' between the abstract nature of the orchestral music which is in constant conflict with the immediate, visual and visceral aspects of the performers' voices and bodies. There is a sense of abstraction and detachment regarding what is occurring on stage, while at the same time there is a striving for empathy with the characters; it combines a distancing allegorical element with the immediacy of dramatic representation. Glass's *Waiting for the Barbarians* is a work that incorporates and develops these trends and approaches into what might be termed post-minimalism with all its inherent tensions and contradictions.

* * *

The nature of language and writing and its representation is prominent in both Coetzee's novel and Glass's adaptation. Coetzee's first-person narrator of the novel, the Magistrate, meditates on the link between writing and civilization:

> Do I really look forward to the triumph of the barbarian way: intellectual torpor, slovenliness, tolerance of disease and death? If we were to disappear would the barbarians spend their afternoons excavating our ruins? Would they preserve our census rolls and our grain-merchants' ledgers in glass cases, or devote themselves to deciphering the script of our love letters? Is my indignation at the course that the Empire takes anything more than the peevishness of an old man who does not want the ease of his last years on the frontier to be disturbed? (1981: 52)

It is not only writing that is examined, but also the concept of language's capacity to articulate thought. At one point in the opera, the Magistrate muses:

> I've often thought
> What few ideas we put into words
> Are never clearly expressed
> And what we cannot clearly express
> We are condemned to live through. (Glass 2005: 150)

It is a Hegelian notion that the distinction between civilization and barbarism lies in writing, and this is given thematic prominence in the novel as exemplified in the attitude of the Magistrate. Michael Valdez Moses argues that the novel suggests that "writing – and we may include legal codes and historical narratives under this rubric – is necessarily implicated in and complicit with the worst excesses of Empire. Most distressingly, Coetzee renders writing (inscription and interpretation) as a form of torture" (1993: 120). Moses comments that Coetzee's fiction

> offers a meditation on the question of whether all civilizations are not necessarily founded upon some arbitrary distinction between the civilized and the barbarian, a historical distinction that seems to require an element of force and compulsion, an act of discrimination that has no moral basis. Coetzee is the bad conscience of postmodern fiction in the postcolonial world. (Ibid.: 116)

The novel depicts a year in a desolate outpost of an unnamed Empire. The narrator is the Magistrate of this town and the events focus on his relationship with a 'barbarian' girl who is captured in a military raid and whom he befriends; it is the ambiguous nature of his relationship with her that is explored at length in the novel. The head of the military forces in the town, the enigmatic Colonel Joll, comes into conflict with the Magistrate, particularly after the Magistrate undertakes what appears to be an unnecessary journey to return the girl to her nomadic people. In the novel, the Magistrate has excavated some ruins close to the town where he has found a cache of wooden slips bearing an indecipherable script. These slips precipitate several confrontations between the Magistrate and Colonel Joll in the novel, and are dramatised in two extended scenes in the opera.

In Scene 5 of Act One, while the relationship between Joll and the Magistrate is still on reasonably good terms, the Magistrate explains the origin of these slips:

> My hobby is archaeology
> There's a site a few miles from our walls

> These have been well preserved in the sand
> Some archaic system of communication
> Used in some ancient time now lost to us
> Destroyed perhaps, who knows, by the barbarians.
> *(Joll replaces the slips, not rising to the bait.)* (Glass 2005: 76f.)

The implication in the stage direction is that the Magistrate is taunting Joll through his reference to the barbarians, the threat of whom he perceives with great scepticism. There has already been a confrontation in Scene 3 where Joll describes the information that he has obtained from one of the prisoners after he has been tortured – something Joll does not admit. Joll will use this suspect information as the spurious pretext to "launch a short sharp war to safeguard the peace" (ibid.: 48f.).

The main confrontation concerning these wooden slips occurs after the Magistrate's un-sanctioned journey to return the girl to her people. He has been imprisoned after his return and has been further humiliated as a result of his attempted intervention to prevent the public torture of prisoners in the town square. He is summoned to Joll and his assistant, Mandel, and is requested by Joll to explain the meaning of the script. The thought processes of the Magistrate are expressed in his first-person narration in the novel:

> I look at the lines of characters written by a stranger long since dead. I do not even know whether to read from right to left or from left to right. In the long evenings I spent poring over my collection I isolated over four hundred different characters in the script, perhaps as many as four hundred and fifty. I have no idea what they stand for. Does each stand for a single thing, a circle for a sun, a triangle for a woman, a wave for a lake; or does a circle merely stand for "circle", a triangle for "triangle", wave for "wave"? Does each sign represent a different state of the tongue, the lips, the throat, the lungs, as they combine in the uttering of some multifarious unimaginable extinct barbarian language? Or are my four hundred characters nothing but scribal embellishments of an underlying repertory of twenty or thirty whose primitive forms I am too stupid to see? (Coetzee 1981: 110f.)

In the opera the Magistrate is humiliatingly left standing in front of his own desk where he is requested by Joll to explain the meaning of the script. Joll describes them as being coded messages passed between the barbarians and the Magistrate who counters by seemingly interpreting them:

> In this one he sends greetings to his daughter
> He hopes the lambing season has been good
> He hopes to see her soon and sends his love.
> *(He looks at another slip; Mandel has his pencil poised over a notebook, not quite*

sure whether to take note)
Here he tells her his son has been arrested
Taken away by the soldiers
He searched for days and found him in a barracks
Wrapped in a winding-sheet
His ankles broken and his eyes torn out.
(Mandel puts down his pencil and half-rises to his feet; but Joll gestures for him to sit down again; meanwhile, the Magistrate has reached for a third slip)
This one is interesting
A single symbol
The barbarian word for "war"
But if you hold it on its side ...
(He does so)
It means justice.
(He puts the slip down and stares truculently at Joll) (Glass 2005: 221–223)

What he does is to deliberately taunt Joll with his knowledge of the events that had previously occurred in this 'interpretation' of the supposed indecipherable script. This causes a furious reaction from Joll and leads to the accusation that the Magistrate is aiding the enemy to which he violently retorts: "You are the enemy [...]. History will not forgive you!" (Ibid.: 230) Joll's reply is chilling in its implications both for the Magistrate and for everyone else: "There is no history / Not out here on the dusty fringe of Empire" (ibid.: 231).

However, actual inscription such as that on the wooden slips and the letter written by the Magistrate is not the only form of 'writing' that is subjected to critical scrutiny in the novel and opera. One of the most horrific instances occurs when the prisoners brought back by Joll's expedition are paraded and tortured in front of the townsfolk. The stage directions describe it as follows:

> As [the guard] leads the Magistrate across the courtyard and through the barracks gate into the main square, the first four Prisoners have been moved into the center of the square. As they turn, it becomes clear that the word "Enemy" has somehow been etched on their backs. They are made to kneel in front of a kind of low hitching post, to which they are secured by a rope which passes in and out of the loops of wire through their cheeks and hands. (Ibid.: 208)

These prisoners are beaten until the word "Enemy" becomes illegible. Here one sees bodily mutilation and torture overtly presented as a form of inscription: an aspect of the significant trope of erasure developed in both novel and opera. This horrific scene has the Magistrate confronting Joll, who it appears is about to strike the prisoners with a hammer. He finally cries out in anguish as he is beaten by the guards:

> I remain the Magistrate
> Responsible for justice in this town!
> This is not justice!
> Man is the great miracle of creation
> And you dare degrade him in this way?
> A hammer!
> You would not use a hammer on a beast
> Not on a beast!
> This is the black flower of civilization!
> Cruelty corrupts
> You are depraving these people
> You bring shame on all who witness these atrocities. (Ibid.: 211–213)[3]

Duncan makes the point that "the singing voice has moments when it tears language apart, or tears itself apart from language. Certainly the voice as well as and in addition to the body, says more, or says differently, than it means to say" (2004: 294). Immediately after the scene previously discussed where the Magistrate 'reads' what is on the wooden slip, he is taken out into the public square and tortured. Here the theme of language and voice is directly interrogated as he is made to "bellow" and "roar". Moses observes that it is this

> "language" that connects the civilized magistrate with the barbarian victims of the Third Bureau [which] proves indistinguishable from the subhuman roar of a tortured animal body. The unmediated language and prehistorical language of men and beasts naturally contains no discrete or articulate words; in such a tongue the name of justice cannot be spoken. (1993: 127)

As this torture occurs, and to the repeated syllabic chanting of the chorus – they sing words which are fragmented and syntactically unintelligible – Mandel makes the intensely ironic comment: "That's the barbarian language!" (Glass 2005: 248f.) The language of the cry is, in fact, the language of Empire.

This is, of course, a moment where verbal signification completely breaks down and all that is left is the raw materiality of the human voice in extremis. Paradoxically, this could be seen as a fundamentally 'operatic' moment where, what Michel Poizat has called the "autonomisation" of the musical aspect of the voice, occurs; where there is a "total erosion of all concern for dramatic and textual intelligibility" (1992: 53). It is a moment when "language disappears and is gradually superseded by the cry, an emotion arises which can be expressed only

---

[3] The link is made explicit between writing and civilization and how writing (and civilization) can so easily become corrupted.

by the irruption of the sob that signals absolute loss" (ibid.: 37). In these moments the materiality of the voice completely subsumes the denotative function of words, where language cannot express what cannot be articulated, but where the sound of the voice carries any ultimate 'meaning'.

* * *

In many ways the most interesting and subtle use of language and writing as a trope is found in the representation of the relationship between the Magistrate and the girl. Coetzee refuses to 'name' her – indeed, he does not name the Magistrate either – thus increasing the alterity that both characters share: she remains an enigmatic object rather than a subjective consciousness. The marks that torture has left on the girl's body have obvious thematic links to the wooden slips and hold the same mixture of fascination and frustration for the Magistrate. A prominent trope in the novel is the erasure of features as one would erase writing and is reflected in the opera where actual text is erased literally through the beating of the prisoners, as we have seen, but also metaphorically through the combination of words and music which, of course, is opera's essence. In the novel the Magistrate muses: "So I begin to face the truth of what I am trying to do: to obliterate the girl. I realize that if I took a pencil to sketch her face I would not know where to start. Is she truly so featureless?" (Coetzee 1981: 47) In the dreams of the Magistrate, the girl often appears to him with a blank, featureless face.

This trope is expanded in the opera in the important series of 'dreamscapes', suggesting another mode of communication which 'erases' both the need for writing and, indeed, language itself. Dreams are a form of 'silent language' and the featureless face is emblematic of a lack of communication; but the visual and the musical combine to provide 'meaning' without the need for language. Indeed, these scenes take place in the form of mime where the novel's intensely subjective and 'wordy' narrative is stripped of all verbal signification and is reduced to its narrative essence in gesture and music. The Magistrate, in fact, makes no effort to learn the girl's language and comments in the novel that "in the makeshift language we share there are no nuances" (ibid.: 40). The novel itself problematises the ability of language to convey meaning, while the opera represents this through its generic obliteration of language through the processes of staged performance.

In a sense the journey of the Magistrate and the girl is mirrored in microcosm by the Magistrate's exploration of her body which is distinctively couched in the colonial 'language' of exploration with the Empire and its surrogate, the Magistrate, as the colonial intruder. This is a reflection of his guilt and sense of complicity in her torture, and these marks exert a powerful fascination for the Magistrate as they seem emblematic of a hidden story which he cannot penetrate, just as he cannot penetrate the mysteries of the text on the wooden slips. Through its generic problematising of language, the opera expands this theme; like the marks on the girl which could be seen as emblematic of writing, but which are not decipherable, so too the characters in the opera sing text, but it is not so much any semantic meaning of this text which conveys 'real' meaning, but it is in the actual sonority of the voices uttering these 'sounds' where real meaning resides. Indeed, through verbal and musical repetition the importance of the semantic meaning of the sung text is thoroughly marginalised.

The intensely physical, though sexless, relationship between the Magistrate and the girl is depicted in the opera and conveyed in sometimes very striking music. However, the ambiguities of the Magistrate's changing attitudes to the girl which form such a crucial part of the novel are not, and perhaps cannot, be depicted to nearly the same extent in the opera. We are not offered anything near the same kind of detailed access to his 'tortured' psyche. It could be argued that this is not Glass's intention, but his musical idiom by its very nature does not allow this to anywhere near the same extent as might be attempted in a more 'traditional' operatic idiom. It could be argued that the objective of the opera is to represent the individual subjective character subordinated to the social aspect of character at both an individual level as well as the level of the state. This, then, is a thematic departure from the novel where much of the 'action' occurs within the psyche of the narrator.

Both the Magistrate and Joll are complicit in the damage that the girl has suffered; in a sense they have both left the 'language' of the colonizers on her body. As he lies imprisoned after returning the girl to her people he reflects on the torture that has occurred in his cell, including that of the girl and her father, and he articulates his awareness of complicity: "She smelled on me the odour of collusion" (Glass 2005: 177). Of course, there are 'internal marks' as well – she says to the Magistrate in one of their early scenes in the opera: "Those things they did to me ... and other things I haven't told you ... which left no outward mark" (ibid.: 137). Her whole body has become a history and a map of Empire, despite Joll's claims that there is no history on the 'dusty fringes' of Empire. Both novel and opera emphasise alterity through the Magistrate's fetishisation of her body rather than through any real understanding which he might achieve through learning her language. However, when the Magistrate himself is subjected to extreme physical torture, he reaches a sense of commonality with the 'barbarians' through the discovery of a shared humanity where, in his agony as he is tortured, he is described as speaking the language of the barbarians. This is achieved through that basic element of shared humanity, the human voice, but voice shorn of any overt verbal signification.

In the novel the Magistrate meditates on the futility of attempting a written account of what has happened during the last year; he has "wanted to live outside the history that Empire imposes on its subjects", but although having lived through "an eventful year" he understands "no more of it than a babe in arms". Of all the people of the town he is the one "least fitted to write a memorial" (Coetzee 1981: 154f.). Towards the end of the novel the Magistrate again reflects on the girl's body as a repository for script. In the dark, outside the town, he bumps into a woman, which causes his thoughts to turn once more to the barbarian girl:

> There is no limit to the foolishness of men of my age. Our only excuse is that we leave no mark of our own on the girls who pass through our hands [...]. Our loving leaves no mark [...]. Though I cringe with shame, even here and now, I must ask myself whether, when I lay head to foot with her, fondling and kissing those broken ankles, I was not in my heart regretting that I could not engrave myself on her as deeply. (Ibid.: 134f.)

Earlier, during their journey, the Magistrate reflected on his obsession with the marks on her body:

> [I]t has not escaped me that in bed in the dark the marks her torturers have left upon her, the twisted feet, the half-blind eyes, are easily forgotten. Is it then the case that it is the whole woman I want, that my pleasure in her is spoiled until these marks on her are erased and she is restored to herself; or is it the case (I am not stupid, let me say these things) that it is the marks on her which drew me to her but which, to my disappointment, I find do not go deep enough? Too much or too little: is it she I want or the traces of a history her body bears? (Ibid.: 64)

These marks exert a powerful fascination for the Magistrate as they seem emblematic of a hidden story which he cannot penetrate, just as he cannot penetrate the mysteries of the text on the wooden slips, and, indeed, cannot or will not penetrate her during their sexual encounters. The marks reflect his sense of complicity in her torture.

The ending of this opera is equivocal (as is that of the novel). The soldiers and bureaucrats from the Third Bureau have gone and the town returns to a sense of normality. The stage directions suggest that aspects of the Magistrate's various dreams which have been played out on the stage now take on a sense of heightened reality. He now sees an actual child with distinct facial features rather than the range of distorted or erased images that have previously emerged in the 'dreamscapes'. The open-ended and 'incomplete' nature of the music here strongly reflects and underscores this combination of dream and reality: there is no sense of a musical resolution through any harmonic development, progression or conclusion. Significantly, the dying sounds of the opera are the fading wordless syllable 'ah!'. Just as in previous scenes where the chorus sings elements of distorted language, it is as if the final moments of the opera re-emphasise the view that the meaning of opera lies ultimately in the sound of the human voice, particularly when stripped of semantic meaning.

Of course, operatic adaptation of literature by its very nature disrupts language. In the adaptation of this novel, where the interrogation of language is thematically so central, Glass deliberately problematises the function of text in his musical representation; his idiom is particularly well suited for this purpose. In writing the opera after the Iraq war and the atrocities of Guantanamo Bay, the focus is even more directly than in the novel on language and its corruption by the state. We see that by destroying language the Empire destroys the individual as well – in fact, the individual is 'erased'. The most overt manifestation of this occurs in the disruption of syntax and even verbal comprehension in Glass's use of the chorus in particular, and in this his musical idiom is perfectly suited with its characteristically repetitive short musical cells. During his torture, the Magistrate cries out in the most brutal corruption of language: the human is reduced to the non-verbal cry. Perhaps this is the essence of what opera fundamentally is – emotion expressed in vocal sound without dependence on syntactical signification? This is arguably the moment when the emotional core of the opera is most manifest; the sound and materiality of the singing voice itself becomes its own subject! Not only the 'meaning' of the opera emerges, but it is through the sonority of the human voice that final 'truth' is made clear. Glass embraces the novel's themes of the instability and ineffectual nature of language to convey meaning, but it is the very medium he employs which itself fulfils this function – his post-minimalism disrupts, perhaps even ultimately destroys, language: the medium itself becomes the subject of his opera!

References

Abbate, Caroline (1991). *Unsung Voices: Opera and Musical Narrative in the Nineteenth Century*. Princeton, NJ: Princeton UP.

Ashby, Arved (2005). "Minimalist Opera". *The Cambridge Companion to Twentieth-Century Opera*. Ed. Mervyn Cooke. Cambridge: CUP. 244–266.

Coetzee, J. M. (1981). *Waiting for the Barbarians*. Johannesburg: Ravan Press.

Corse, Sandra (2000). *Operatic Subjects: The Evolution of Self in Modern Opera*. Cranbury, NJ: Associated University Presses.

Dahlhaus, Carl (1989). "What is Musical Drama?". Trans. Mary Whittall. *Cambridge Opera Journal* 1/2: 95–111.

Duncan, Michelle (2004). "The Operatic Scandal of the Singing Body: Voice, Presence, Performativity". *Cambridge Opera Journal* 16/3: 283–306.

Glass, Philip (2005). *Waiting for the Barbarians*. New York, NY: Dunvagen Music Publishing.

— (2008). "Note from the Composer". *Waiting for the Barbarians*. CD: OMM0039. New York, NY: Orange Mountain Music B0018C6QYB. 4.

Gumbrecht, Hans Ulrich (1994). "A Farewell to Interpretation". Trans. William Whobrey. *Materialities of Communication*. Eds. Hans Ulrich Gumbrecht, K. Ludwig Pfeiffer. Stanford, CA: Stanford UP. 389–404.

Moses, Michael Valdez (1993). "The Mark of Empire: Writing, History, and Torture in Coetzee's *Waiting for the Barbarians*". *The Kenyon Review* 15/1: 115–127.

Phelan, James (1994). "Present Tense Narration, Mimesis, the Narrative Norm, and the Positioning of the Reader in *Waiting for the Barbarians*". *Understanding Narrative*. Eds. James Phelan, Peter J. Rabinowitz. Columbus, OH: Ohio State UP. 222–245.

Poizat, Michel (1992). *The Angel's Cry: Beyond the Pleasure Principle in Opera*. Trans. Arthur Denner. Ithaca, NY: Cornell UP.

Operatic Hyperreality in the Twenty-First Century Performance Documentation in High-Definition Quality

Bernhard Kuhn, Lewisburg, PA

This article studies the new phenomenon of high-definition (HD) broadcasting of opera performances, which the Metropolitan Opera initiated in its 2006/07 season with enormous success. It situates this new hybrid form within the spectrum of screen opera ranging from film operas to internet broadcasts of operas performed in historical settings in real time. This paper examines the HD broadcast of selected scenes from *La Bohème*, performed and screened on April 5, 2007, which serves as a case study. Using the concepts of intermediality developed by Werner Wolf and Irina Rajewsky, in particular the concepts of 'medial transposition' and 'plurimediality', this article analyzes the live HD broadcast of *La Bohème* comparing it to the stage performance. It concludes that while HD opera broadcasts seek to offer an encounter as close as possible to a theatrical opera event, it supplies in fact only the illusion of being present at a live stage performance and instead provides the audience with what Umberto Eco or Jean Baudrillard would call a 'hyperreal' experience.

Introduction

Intermedial relationships between opera and screen media have existed at least since the beginning of the twentieth century when early cinema began creating short adaptations of operatic scenes[1]. In addition, many films began also incorporating operatic references. The relationship between the two media, however, worked both ways and opera soon began incorporating filmic references into performances[2]. The bond between opera and the audio-visual media has continued to develop in a symbiotic manner throughout the twentieth century until today. One relatively new phenomenon is the live transmission of

---

[1] Examples of early opera adaptations include Edwin S. Porter's *Parsifal* (1904), George Méliès's *Faust aux enfers* (1903), and *Damnation du Docteur Faust* (1904). *Faust aux enfers* is based on Hector Berlioz's *La damnation de Faust*, *Damnation du Docteur Faust* on Charles Gounod's *Faust*.

[2] Examples include Alban Berg's *Lulu* (unfinished, first performance 1937) and Bohuslav Martinů's *Les trois souhaits ou les vicissitudes de la vie* (1929).

opera in high-definition quality into movie theaters, also known as 'high-definition opera' or 'HD opera', which will be the focus of this article. As HD opera broadcasts have been initiated only in 2006, scholarly attention on this phenomenon is currently still sparse. This article attempts to contribute to the research by offering an initial aesthetic analysis of this new hybrid form of opera also with an eye towards potential consequences for performers as well as the audience. I will situate HD opera transmissions in the intermedial context of screen opera and focus on the 2008 version of Puccini's *La Bohème* produced by Franco Zeffirelli. I will argue that this new form of live-transmitted opera is a spectacle on its own and that the event can best be described as 'hyperreal' in that the operatic performance mediated through cameras seems and, at least to large parts of the audience, feels more real than the opera being watched on a theater stage.

What is High-Definition Opera?

On December 30, 2006, the Metropolitan Opera began broadcasting the images and sounds of some of its operas live via satellite and in high-definition quality into about 150 movie theaters around the world[3]. Using cutting edge technologies, these first HD transmissions usually employed up to 14 cameras, including remote-controlled dollies and telescopic lenses. The first opera performed for such a live broadcast was an English language version of Mozart's *The Magic Flute*, which reached an audience of about 30,000 spectators in one showing (see Metropolitan Opera 2006: online). The commercial success of the first season was significant, and in the 2007/08 season the number of participating movie theaters more than tripled reaching over 600 venues across North America, Europe, Asia, and Australia (see Metropolitan Opera 2008a: online). The performance of *La Bohème*, which was broadcast on April 5, 2008, for example, sold about 136,000 tickets worldwide (see Wenzel 2008: online). During the 2008/09 season, with a total of 11 transmissions, the Met sold more than 1.6 million tickets in movie theaters (see Metropolitan Opera 2008a: online). Of course, these numbers do not say anything about quality of either the performance or the transmission of the

---

[3] In addition, these HD performance recordings from the Metropolitan Opera are available on the Metropolitan Opera's web page as well as on DVD.

performance, but they document that HD operas have a significant following. Observing the commercial success of these HD transmissions, European opera houses, such as Milan's La Scala or London's Covent Garden, or festivals, such as the Glyndebourne festival, followed the Met's example and started live HD broadcasts of their own performances.

Most relevant for understanding HD operas is the development of the medial transposition of opera, and in particular the presence of opera in audio-visual media. *Figure 1* illustrates the possible medial transpositions of opera.

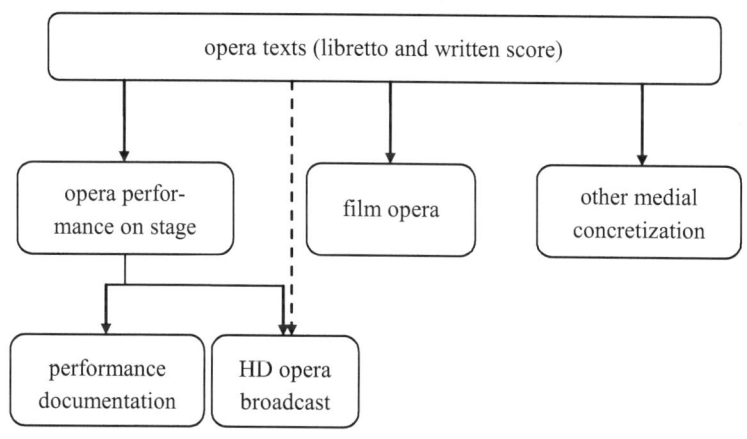

Figure 1: Forms of medial transposition of opera[4].

Regarding audio-visual transpositions of opera texts, the most obvious form is the film opera, the filmic realization of an opera. The genre 'film opera' originated after the Second World War in Italy and was very popular during the postwar period. In the early examples of the genre, the performers were sometimes actors who lip-synched the opera singer's voice, and the camera typically took on a strong narrative function. In the 1970s and 1980s, international auteurs, such as Ingmar Bergman, Franco Zeffirelli or Francesco Rosi, further developed the genre (see Citron 2000 and Kuhn 2005). The genre is still alive today, and directors continue to experiment with film operas. Most recently, on March 5, 2011, the film opera *Carmen 3D*,

---

[4] This is an updated version of a figure depicting the medial transpositions of opera published in WMS 9 (cf. Kuhn 2008: 79). Regarding the intermedial category of 'medial transposition', cf. Wolf (2002: 178) and Rajewski (2005: 51).

which is indeed filmed in 3D format, opened at the Santa Barbara Film Festival. The category 'other medial concretization' refers to further results of medial transpositions of opera texts, for example an opera created exclusively for being broadcast over the internet. Also 'spoken opera films' may be put in this category[5]. In contrast to a film opera, 'performance documentation' and an HD opera broadcast present audio-visual transpositions of an opera presentation. The dotted line in *Figure 1* illustrates that while an HD opera broadcast is typically based on a performance, it may also transpose elements of opera texts that are not presented in the performance[6].

Since the HD opera broadcast has strong ties to the other forms of screen opera, it is useful to take a closer look at the development of these forms. With the invention and growing popularity of television in the 1950s, the practice of broadcasting opera performances on television developed (see Kühnel 1998). This form of opera for television, which appropriately has been defined as 'performance documentation', typically employed five to seven stationary cameras. The broadcasts were rarely transmitted live, and there was usually a time lag between performance and broadcasting[7]. The social functions of these recordings were twofold: first, to give the audience a possibility to watch a performance which otherwise they would not have been able to see, and second, to preserve a particular performance to enrich the cultural memory (cf. ibid.: 166f.). From an aesthetic point of view, most of these operas produced in the second half of the twentieth century for television have shortcomings. Specific deficits are preferences for medium shots over long shots[8], change of colors

---

[5] Spoken opera films transform the operatic voice into a speaking voice and incorporate parts of the opera score into the film's soundtrack (see Kuhn 2008).

[6] The HD opera broadcast of Wagner's *Tristan und Isolde* on March 22, 2008, for example, includes zoom shots to illustrate the movement of Tristan's ship. See below.

[7] There are several possibilities of producing opera for television. A television broadcast may be based on one or several performances of one production, either with or without an audience. Typically, opera broadcasts for television are created from a combination of recordings with and without an audience. Another possibility is the new production of an opera in television studios. This option was popular in the 1950s and 1960s but became very rare after that (cf. Kühnel 1998: 170f.).

[8] The relatively small screen and the relatively weak resolution of television screens made the use of long shots problematic. The dominance of medium shots, on the other hand, often caused difficulties to relate the cinematic images to the whole theatrical

between the stage production and the broadcast[9], and recording techniques and editing choices that are technically and not aesthetically motivated[10]. Jürgen Kühnel defines the ideal 'performance documentation' as a document in which the camera functions as "servant" to the performance by following primarily the aesthetic code of opera and not the aesthetic code of television (ibid.: 169f.).

With the further development of technology, new forms of screen opera developed, which can be characterized by a general quest for realism. At least since the late 1980s, opera videos have been produced using prerecorded music, real locations as sets, and physically suitable actors. This method highlighted the problem of lip-synching (known from earlier film operas) and caused a medial balance shift towards the visual aspect thereby diminishing the role of music (orchestral music as well as vocal music) of the opera as a plurimedial art form. This development towards a visual realism continued: from the early 1990s, Giuseppe Patroni Griffi produced two opera performances at real locations in real time and broadcast them live on television or the internet. Examples include the 1992 version of *Tosca* performed in Rome and directed by Brian Lange (see Hoff 1994), and a 2000 version of *La Traviata*, filmed in Paris. We may of course disagree on the results, which according to Jürgen Kühnel smack a bit of reality television (cf. 1998: 174), but these forms of screen opera signal a trend in the direction of visual realism, a trend which cannot be denied in today's opera practices on stage as well as on screen[11].

---

mise en scène (cf. Kühnel 1998: 168f.). While the quality of the television screens has improved, the deficits are still often recognizable.

[9] The reason for this was inappropriate lighting or an unfortunate color scale for TV recording.

[10] Before the invention of high-definition television and surround sound, the quality of image and sound in television was usually not the greatest. In order to compensate for the imperfect quality and the size of the images, television developed a general tendency to frequent cuts and a dominance of close-ups and medium shots. Adopting such a visually dominant narrative style can destroy the balance, in particular between sound and image, and have a disturbing effect on the music, whose function could be degraded to an illustrative one accompanying the images (cf. Kühnel 1998: 163).

[11] It seems that the physical appearance of the performers has recently become more important. One example is Deborah Voigt, who in 2004 was fired in London because she did not have the appropriate body for the role of Ariadne. According to Danielle De Niese, this tendency is encouraged by directors who are interested in making opera more authentic (cf. Hough 2009: online).

From a media-comparative perspective, HD operas can be categorized as a hybrid form incorporating elements of opera performed on stage, performance documentation for television, and film opera. Like a stage opera, the audience observes the performance in real time and reacts to what is happening on stage. Like in a television broadcast, the spectators watch a mediatized performance and the camera functions as a 'visual narrator' selecting what will be shown on screen. Finally, the audience watches the opera in the cinema like a film opera. While HD broadcasts are by definition performance documentations, the opera transmission on the big screen in a cinema provides a communal experience where large parts of the audience behave as if they were physically present at the opera house where the performance is staged. In order to offer the audience an experience as close as possible to the actual event, the broadcasting time of the opera generally conforms to actual performance times, and the intermission schedule is respected[12]. HD transmissions offer the viewer a 'hyperreal' experience by providing not only a performance documentation in HD quality, but also showing additional materials which are not available to the audience in the theater[13]. The cinema audience gets to see the performance from different camera angles and perspectives and hears a high-quality recording of the music. Typically, the opera is introduced by an opera host, such as Renée Fleming, who also conducts interviews with opera singers, stage directors or other people working in the performance, before the show begins and during intermissions. Frequently, the viewer gets a glimpse behind the curtains and can observe the changes of the stage or the preparation of the singers. But the adjective 'hyperreal' is also appropriate for describing the reaction of the spectators, who to some degree behave as if they were in an opera house and not in a cinema. The most obvious example is that the cinema audience applauds successful solos and thus simulates the experience of being physically present in the theater where the performance is taking place. In contrast to a 'real' per-

---

[12] Concerning the different experience of attending a performance in the opera house and a HD opera broadcast in the cinema, see Sheppard (2007). The Metropolitan Opera offers also encore HD screenings.

[13] By calling HD opera broadcasts 'hyperreal', I am referring to Umberto Eco and Jean Baudrillard, who define as 'hyperreal' things that seem more real than reality, such as American wax museums, fake art, and Disneyworld (cf. Eco 1986: 1–58; Baudrillard 1994: 22).

formance in the theater, the performers of course cannot hear the reactions of the audience in the cinema.

The Metropolitan Opera's webpage defines HD operas as 'live' experiences, which is an accurate description considering recent theoretical reflections in the field of performance studies. While, traditionally, physical and temporal co-presence of performer and audience and their immediate exchange used to be the defining criterion, Philipp Auslander has recently questioned what should be considered as a 'live' experience and argues for a historical redefinition and for placing less weight on the immediate spatial relationship. While there are phenomenological and ideological distinctions between 'live' and 'mediatized' performances, the differences are not ontological. In the light of new technological developments[14], there is a fluid continuum between 'live' and 'mediatized' performances rather than a polar opposition between them. In addition, in order to define 'liveness', we ought to take into account the affective side by considering what feels 'live' to the audience (cf. Auslander 2008: 112). Concerning the reactions of the typical spectator of an HD opera, it is obvious that large parts of the audience expect to be captured by the illusion of being present at a live performance.

It seems that HD opera seeks to visually and aurally present an opera performed on stage as much in detail as possible and to create with screened images and transmitted sound an operatic experience that is as effective as possible. Achieving such effectiveness requires more than mechanical filming, since medial differences and conventions of opera and film cause aesthetic challenges, and it might be necessary to compromise between an audio-visually effective presentation and one which is most appropriate for opera. Consequently, HD opera ought to be considered as a hybrid art form that is placed between opera and film. For it to be aesthetically successful, it needs to find the right balance between the various sign systems of an audio-visual transmission, which are different from a performance on stage. Works in both media, performance on stage and the transmission in the cinema, are plurimedial artifacts, which can be categorized according to Werner Wolf's terminology as 'intermedial fusions' since the single media involved cannot be separated (cf. 2002: 22). A

---

[14] Considering interactions with 'live' websites or virtual entities, even relationships between living human beings are no longer essential for defining a live experience (cf. Auslander 2008: 112).

typical opera performance incorporates the semiotic sign systems of the opera's text, its music, and the staged performance. A performance documentation, on the other hand, further includes the sign systems of the camera.

Particular challenges for opera on screen are arias, big chorus scenes, and orchestral pieces. An aria would certainly deserve a close-up, but such a close-up of the singer's face might aesthetically be problematic since the sight of each muscle of a singer's face or the sweat on the diva's brow might destroy the theatrical illusion. A crowd scene, on the other hand, would deserve a long shot, but this could easily render things unrecognizable on screen, creating a feeling of medial imperfection. During orchestral pieces usually nothing happens on stage, but conventionally the camera has to visualize something. The HD broadcast of *La Bohème* can demonstrate how a typical HD opera deals with these challenges.

La Bohème (Franco Zeffirelli, April 5, 2008)

A representative example for an HD opera produced by the Metropolitan Opera is the 2008 high-definition broadcast of Puccini's *La Bohème*, directed by Franco Zeffirelli. Zeffirelli is known for his historical reconstructions and his focus on realistic detail, and it is my goal to determine whether such a traditional approach on the stage can as well work on the big screen. Zeffirelli's version of *La Bohème* has been performed since the 1981/82 season and has been on the Met's program 347 times sofar. It is the most often performed production of the Metropolitan Opera until now, and it has been very successful with large parts of the audience. This, of course, does not mean that Zeffirelli's 'realistic' form of presentation is the most creative or innovative approach, but it is one that seems to work perfectly with *La Bohème* at the Met.

The following analysis of the HD transmission of *La Bohème* reflects in detail on three scenes of the opera performance and their screened versions: Rodolfo's aria "Che gelida manina" from the first act of the opera, the beginning of the second act as an example for a big chorus scene, and the last scene of the opera. The problem of the visualization of solo orchestral pieces does not present itself in *La Bohème*, since the opera does not include such extended solo orchestral passages. I will, however, refer to the cinematic presentation of the brief orchestral passage at the beginning of the second act.

In the first act, after the presentation of the bohemians, the Benoît episode, and the departure of Rodolfo's friends, Mimì enters, and while looking for her lost key, Rodolfo touches her hand and subsequently sings his famous aria, "Che gelida manina", which can by and large be described as a presentation of himself as a poet and dreamer. The aria is divided into four parts: it starts in D flat major, followed by a short recitative-like section beginning with the question "Chi son?" ('Who am I?'). Then the theme that has introduced Rodolfo at the beginning of the act (18 before 2[15]) starts the third part where Rodolfo refers to his poverty ("In povertà mia lieta"). In the last part, which is the most lyrical section that begins with "Talor dal mio forziere", he tells Mimì that her eyes have stolen all his dreams and that he has hopes for the future.

In accordance with Zeffirelli's traditional approach, Rodolfo and Mimì are on the floor when he touches her hand. The HD opera transmission presents the complete aria in 26 shots varying in length, mostly between medium and medium-close-ups. Some shots include panning as well as zooming and the cuts are very subtle. By and large, the technicians follow the rules of the classical Hollywood style, which deemphasizes the transitions between the shots so that the audience perceives the presentation on screen as one continuous action. Most of these cuts, however, are not aesthetically motivated and exclusively serve to lighten the visual discourse and create a more natural feeling[16].

Critical for the evaluation of the audio-visual interpretation is the way in which the different media involved work together. Arias are typically rather static elements where time seems to stop, which is also the case with "Che gelida manina". Nothing is really happening on stage, and it is the aria's function to express Rodolfo's thoughts and inner feelings. Film directors usually try to compensate static moments of the mise en scène with active camera movements or editing. In so doing, the visual narrative can easily become dominant and

---

[15] The score is quoted after Puccini (1920).

[16] For the average viewer of the twenty-first century, a film scene presented with few long takes and without much action would cause a visually disturbing effect, since such a technique is rarely used on today's television or in contemporary popular feature films.

degrade the operatic music to a role secondary to the visual narrative. Evaluating the audio-visual presentation of this aria, however, I would argue that this is not the case and that the producers get the balance right by presenting a scene that is visually neither annoying nor dominant and is rather sensitive to the music so that the musical discourse can be effective. Helpful in this respect is the fact that the cuts often take place in synchrony with the music, for example at the beginning of a new theme or in connection with a particular action on stage. The first cut takes place in measure 12 after 30, after Rodolfo's first two lines ("Che gelida manina, se la lasci riscaldar. / Cercar che giova? Al buio non si trova.") at the moment when Rodolfo and Mimì get up from the floor. At this point in the score, the harp sets in and plays until Rodolfo continues to sing in measure 16 after 30.

The visual presentation of the scene also includes cinematic elements, such as different angles, zoom and pan shots. In synchrony with the beginning of Rodolfo's theme (32[17]), for example, the camera changes to a low angle and presents the scene by zooming in on Rodolfo and Mimì, who are standing behind a table. This camera movement, however, is subtle enough not to disturb the musical discourse and has no other function than avoiding a static impression. Later in the aria, the camera several times switches briefly to Mimì, highlighting Mimì's reaction to Rodolfo's words (12 after 32, 2 after 33, and 1 before 35). Here the function is different. The first time, the camera occupies a narrative function, since Mimì's cameo appearance somewhat visualizes the text referring to her eyes ("gli occhi belli"; 'the beautiful eyes'), but almost immediately the camera switches back to a medium shot portraying both Rodolfo and Mimì. The second appearance is in synchrony with the music, and its function is exclusively to avoid a static state. The third appearance, at the end of the aria, visually foreshadows the beginning of Mimì's aria.

During the whole aria, the camera by and large stays away from close-up shots of the singer's face, which would highlight the physical strain of singing and thus create a conflict with the theatrical illusion. It can therefore be concluded that Zeffirelli's visual presentation of

---

[17] Rodolfo's theme accompanies the text "In povertà mia lieta scialo da gran signore" ('In my happy poverty I squander like a fine gentleman'). The musical reference to 18 before 2 points also to the burning of Rodolfo's manuscript (cf. Girardi 2000: 125).

"Che gelida manina" focuses on Rodolfo and Mimì and that medium and medium close-up shots are dominant. With cinematic technology such as zoom or pan shots, as well as with editing, the producers are able to create a rather unobtrusive visual narrative which does not overpower the music. Following Kühnel's critical assessment of performance documentations, we could even say that for the most part the cameras are "servants" to the opera (1998: 169f.).

The second act begins with a brief orchestral introduction. Here, the camera presents first the conductor, Nicola Luisotti, in a medium close-up (Act II, mm. 1–4), and then the orchestra in a high angle long shot panning over the orchestra. During this second shot (mm. 5–23 [= 5 after [1]]) the camera slowly turns towards the stage, which, eventually, is first presented in a long shot. Although *La Bohème* does not include extended passages performed by the orchestra with the curtain closed, this short introduction can be seen as a representation of orchestral passages typical for HD operas. The two shots show that the camera takes an active role in presenting the orchestra and thus avoids a static impression[18].

The first scene of the second act in this performance, which follows the introduction, can be described as a typically Zeffirellian spectacle. During this scene, the chorus is divided into small groups on the very crowded two-level stage. Thematically, the second act is a direct continuation of the first act, Rodolfo and Mimì joining their friends and the crowds for the celebration of Christmas Eve in the Latin Quarter in Paris. According to Michele Girardi (cf. 2000: 127), Puccini and his librettists intentionally imagined the scene in an almost cinematic manner by creating nearly simultaneously a series of events happening in a short amount of time in the manner of brief film shots.

In general, the camera does an excellent job of communicating the content of the scene in harmony with the atmosphere created by the music. In detail, the camera presents vendors selling their goods, town people talking to each other, children running around, Schaunard buying a musical instrument, Colline purchasing a coat, Marcello flirting with women, and Rodolfo and Mimì buying a bonnet. Comparing the presentation in the theater with the screening, the joyful atmosphere is well transmitted in both versions. Zeffirelli's Latin Quarter

---

[18] During other introductions, in addition to pans, the visual presentation includes cuts and zoom shots to communicate a dynamic and natural impression.

scene is unique in that it involves a very crowded stage including many spectacular elements, such as a clown on stilts, an artist wearing a bear costume and playing with children, or Parpignol arriving in a carriage pulled by a real donkey. While spectacular elements can distract from the essence of a scene, here they add to the festivities communicated.

The manner in which Zeffirelli presents the scene on stage might be visually confusing, since it is difficult to figure out where things happen on stage. On the big screen, however, this is not the case thanks to the camera action focusing on the appropriate elements on stage according to the textual and musical meaning. The camera presents Schaunard in a medium shot during measure 5 before [4]. At that moment, he is in the process of buying a horn. In 13 after [4], the camera switches to Colline (medium close-up), who is buying a coat, before presenting Rodolfo and Mimì in a medium close-up (14 after [4]). These brief visual cameo-like appearances of the opera's protagonists are in harmony with the score, the text, and the scenic action. In addition to concentrating on these and other details[19], however, the cameramen make sure that the spectators can also see the whole stage by switching between these medium shots or medium close-ups and long shots visualizing the whole stage (for example during mm. 15 after [4] – 17 after [4]). Similar to the cinematic realization of "Che gelida manina", the changes in shot length, the incorporation of zoom and other camera movements are frequently in synchrony with changes in the score or incorporated in an otherwise relatively unobtrusive manner. The main difference between the visual presentation of the stage production and the HD broadcast, from the audience's point of view, can therefore be defined as 'visual simplification', since the camera highlights the details of the large scene in accordance with the score.

Considering the very delicate musical narrative, the opera's last scene presents a particular challenge for the cameras, since the lyrical essence can easily be destroyed by a visually over-dominant narrative. *La Bohème* ends with Mimì's death and the suffering of the

---

[19] Other details visually emphasized are: Marcel (13 before [5] – 5 before [5]), the plum seller (4 before [5]), Schaunard, Marcel and two women (3 before [5] – 1 before [5]), Colline and Schaunard (5 after [5] – 8 after [5]), Rodolfo and Mimì (9 after [5] – 9 after [6]), Parpignol (10 after [6] – 19 after [6]), and a man in a bear costume (1 after [7] – 8 after [7]).

bohemians, but the ending of the opera is not exclusively about lost love. It also reflects about the end of a stage in life, about lost youth, and the utopian past (cf. Groos 1986: 79). Musically, this is emphasized by ending the opera the same way as Colline's aria "Vecchia zimarra", which points to happier moments in the past by depicting the philosopher's farewell to his coat. The danger in filming the opera's last moments thus lies in visually ignoring this broader meaning and to focus in a melodramatic way exclusively on Mimì's death and the end of the love story.

It cannot be denied that the ending is cinematically presented in a sentimental way by Zeffirelli, but I would argue that it is successful in avoiding a pathetic soap opera ending. What makes this last scene of the HD opera broadcast work are the moments of visual distance which open the space for the musical discourse. The camera mostly uses medium shots and only a few medium close-ups or close-ups. This is appropriate since more or longer close-ups would suffocate the music. The last scene (Act III, |27| – end) is cinematically divided into 41 shots. During the first half (shots 1–17, mostly medium or medium close-up, act III, |27| – 1 before |29|), the focus is mostly on Musetta's muff, which she gives Mimì to keep her hands warm, and on Rodolfo's and Mimì's last exchange. Towards the end, the camera breaks the visual flow twice with a long shot (9 before |29| and 2 before |29|). In similar fashion, long shots are included in the second half of the final scene (7 after |29|, 14 after |29|, 18 after |29|, 3 after |30|, and 6 after |30|). The thematic focus is first on Mimì's death and then on the bohemians' realization that she has died. In addition, the camera underscores significant objects or actions, such as Musetta's muff or Colline giving Musetta the money he has received for selling his coat. Of particular significance is the last medium close-up (7 after |30| – 8 after |30|), which visually emphasizes Mimì's bonnet. The camera's focus here is on Mimì lying in her bed. When Rodolfo takes Musetta's muff away, we see that Mimì holds it in her hands. Like Colline's coat, the bonnet was acquired on Christmas Eve in the Latin Quarter scene of Act II and like no other object symbolizes the happy past. By visually highlighting the bonnet at the end of the opera, the film cinematically underscores the larger meaning of the scene. The possibility to create with ease visual references to the past is of course an advantage of the audio-visual technology. Here it reinforces the musical meaning of the opera's ending.

Overall, it can be concluded that the HD transmission of Zeffirelli's *La Bohème* can by and large be evaluated as aesthetically successful. We can of course find aspects to criticize. In Mimì's aria "Sì mi chiamano Mimì", for instance, the interplay between music, scene, and camera does not produce a positive result at first because the camera focuses in a medium close-up frontally on the performer sitting at a table (in particular 8 after |35| – 3 after |36|). At this moment, it is difficult to imagine Mimì as 'femme fragile', since the visual focus is on the face of the performer (Angela Gheorghiu), who understandably has difficulty singing and smiling at the same time[20]. By employing a rather static and dominant visual narrative, the camera draws attention to the art of singing, which distracts from the performance and the music. As the aria continues, the visual presentation, however, gets better and the camera avoids the static frontal medium close-up and incorporates a more fluid technique, including unobtrusive low angle shots and zooms comparable to the visual representation of "Che gelida manina".

Like in all HD operas, the cinema audience of the HD opera broadcast of *La Bohème* sees more than the audience in the Metropolitan Opera House and thus has a 'hyperreal' operatic experience. As opposed to watching the opera from one specific seat in the opera house, the cinema audience is able to observe the presentation through different camera perspectives and with perfectly balanced sound quality[21]. This includes the highlighting of relevant details on stage, such as the bonnet in the last scene or the visual simplification during the crowded Latin Quarter scenes. In the opera house, these performance elements might be difficult to see. In addition to the performance, the cinema audience is able to watch Renée Fleming's introduction before the first act as well as back stage interviews with

---

[20] A general problem with too many close shots of the performers is that it might highlight the age or the physical constitution of the singer. Neil Kurtzman noted that, in *La Bohème*, "the close-up was not her [Angela Gheorghiu's] friend" since she is not at an age "where she can sustain a point of view a few feet from her face" (2008: online). The critic points here to the undesirable effect of the close-up to underscore the singer's age. Nonetheless, Kurtzman acknowledged that Angela Gheorghiu's voice and experience are perfect for the part of Mimì.

[21] While in the opera house the sound might at some points be disturbed by whispers or other noises caused by the audience, the transmitted sound in the cinema is free of disturbing elements.

technical director Joe Clark, Angela Gheorghiu and Ramón Vargas during the intermissions after Acts II and III. Furthermore, at the end of Act I, the camera shows the exit of the performers from behind the curtain and the actual set change, which hence the audience in the cinema can follow in detail. The HD opera, thus, offers the interested audience not only the occasion of experiencing an operatic performance in the cinema but also the possibility of taking a look behind the stage and becoming informed about some details of the actual performance. Although we are in fact not in the opera house and might in reality be watching the performance on a different continent, with modern technology we not only get the sensation of being there, but actually get the hyperreal impression to be closer to the performance than an audience in the opera house can ever be.

Conclusions: Opera and HD Opera in the Twenty-First Century

It is fairly safe to say that HD transmissions will continue to exist and probably be further extended. It is also likely that this will involve not only operas presented in a traditional Zeffirellian manner. The Met's HD broadcasts of the last few years demonstrate that many other directorial approaches have been adopted for the screen. Examples include Penny Woolcock's production of John Adams and Peter Sellers's *Doctor Atomic* (November 8, 2008), Robert Lepage's production of Berlioz's *La damnation de Faust* (November 22, 2008), Nicholas Joël's production of Puccini's *La Rondine* (January 10, 2009), and Mark Morris's production of Gluck's *Orfeo ed Euridice* (January 24, 2009). Comparable to the HD transmission of *La Bohème*, also these HD opera broadcasts typically choose a rather neutral form of visual presentation and attempt to present the performance in synchrony with the score and according to the actions on stage. Depending on the set of the performance, this can cause particular challenges. The set of Lepage's *La damnation de Faust*, for instance, consists of a four-tiered wall subdivided into 24 cubicles, which simultaneously is used as screen. During the performance, at times, one large image is portrayed on the whole screen, at other moments the wall is used to present 24 different scenes or 24 identical images. Here, the difficulty for the HD broadcast director resides in choosing between long shots capturing the whole set or medium shots or medium close-ups focusing on performance details. In addition, this production not only included a substantial amount of video imagery[22], but the performance also incorporated metareferential elements eliciting reflections, for example on the recordings of performances or the role of the diva in today's media society[23]. In general, I would argue that the broadcast was basically successful in finding the right balance in shot length and kept the filmic presentation rather unobtrusive.

This cinematically rather neutral approach seems to be typical for HD operas so far. One exception to this general tendency is the HD opera broadcast of Wagner's *Tristan und Isolde* of March 28, 2008. The HD opera transmission director, Barbara Willis Sweete, incorporated framing techniques to visually simplify what is narrated through orchestra and scenic performance. At the beginning of the first act, for example, she uses the zoom and a slowly enlarging frame of the mise en scène to demonstrate the movement of Tristan's ship. In addition, she frequently presents different frames on the screen in order to simultaneously show the whole stage and the performers in medium close-up. While this is certainly a new way for HD opera broadcasts of presenting the singers in a visually appropriate manner without ignoring the scenic context, it also has a (probably undesired) illusion-breaking effect. Even by incorporating this rather unusual technique, however, the broadcast does not offer a significantly different interpretation of the opera on the cinema screen than the one presented on stage.

Considering the history of HD opera up to now, it is still not clear what consequences, if any, this new form of high-definition performance documentation will have on the art form of opera. HD

---

[22] Some of the video imagery responds to the performers on stage by monitoring their movements, changes in vocal or orchestral pitch, and body temperature. Lepage says in an interview that he was interested in "finding a meeting point between the theatricality of opera and the cinematic world". The interview is published on the Metropolitan Opera's webpage (Metropolitan Opera 2008b: online).

[23] Examples of metareferential elements include the set itself, which serves simultaneously as screen and performance space. During the "Marche Hongroise", soldiers march backwards on the wall in a stylized manner reminiscent of the rewind option of a video. During the performance of the aria "D'amour l'ardente flame", the mezzo-soprano's (Susan Graham's) simultaneously filmed image appears in medium close-up surrounded by flames on the screen behind her. Although the HD broadcast does not particularly reinforce these metareferential elements of the stage performance, they are highly recognizable in the HD opera as well and thus have the power to cause a metareflection also in the cinema audience. Cf. also Moore (2009: 185–213).

opera certainly offers people living in remote areas or who do not have enough money to afford an opera ticket the possibility of seeing the broadcast of a high-quality performance. Peter Gelb, the general manager of the Met, originally defined HD operas primarily as a marketing tool hoping to create more interest in opera (cf. Metropolitan Opera 2006: online). While this might indeed be one of the positive outcomes, it remains to be seen what consequences HD operas will have for smaller opera companies and whether parts of their audience might choose to visit an HD opera broadcast instead of attending a performance in a smaller theater[24]. For the performers, it is certainly a challenging difference to know that they are constantly being filmed. Whether the selection of photogenic singers benefits from this, however, is questionable. While it is true that some opera impresarios seem to be obsessed with the looks of their singers, such physical realism has started before the invention of HD opera[25]. On the contrary, HD opera might even make life less difficult for large or older singers in the long run. Considering the history of stage opera, we know that voice and physical appearance do not always match, and until recently it did not seem much of a problem. Although critics notice discrepancies in this regard, looking at the recent HD performances produced by the Met, it is refreshing to see how the impresarios seem to ignore those critical voices and continue to present the best singers on stage and screen disregarding their physical appearance. The positive response from the audience demonstrates that this resonates well with the public. If this trend continues, even opera directors currently obsessed with physical realism might change their minds. Hyperreality in the form of HD operas could thus result in a move away from exaggerated physical realism on stage.

---

[24] According to Rosenberg (cf. 2010: online), some regional companies seem to have been negatively affected by HD opera transmissions. Opera Cleveland, for example, takes a break from performances in 2011 to get reorganized.

[25] Because of her robust figure, Deborah Voigt was not allowed to sing in a performance at Covent Garden in 2004 (cf. Hough 2009: online). Dominique Meyer, the director of the Wiener Staatsoper, supposedly said that he would not again hire the star tenor Johan Botha because of his robust figure (cf. Sinkowitz 2008: online).

References

Auslander, Philipp (2008). "Live and Technologically Mediated Performance". Tracy C. Davis, ed. *The Cambridge Companion to Performance Studies*. Cambridge: CUP. 107−119.
Baudrillard, Jean (1994). *Simulacra and Simulation*. Ann Arbor, MI: University of Michigan Press.
Cavassilas, Pierre (2000). *La Traviata*. TV. France/Italy: NVC Arts/ Rada Film.
Citron, Marcia (2000). *Opera on Screen*. New Haven, CT: Yale UP.
Eco, Umberto (1986). *Travels in Hyperreality*. New York, NY/ London: Harcourt Brace & Company.
Girardi, Michele (2000). *Puccini: His International Art*. Trans. Laura Basini. Chicago, IL/London: University of Chicago Press.
Groos, Arthur (1986). "The Libretto". Arthur Groos, Roger Parker, eds. *La Bohème*. Cambridge Opera Handbooks. Cambridge: CUP. 55−79.
Hoff, Peter (1994). "Die Ergreifung, Folterung und Exekution des Malers Mario Cavaradossi auf der Engelsburg in Rom im Morgengrauen des 12. Juli 1992 vor einem Publikum von 2 Milliarden Menschen oder ein Versuch zur Errettung der Aura der 'Grossen Oper' im Fernsehen durch das 'Prinzip Live'". Joachim Paech, ed. *Film, Fernsehen, Video und die Künste: Strategien der Intermedialität*. Stuttgart: Metzler. 190−213.
Hough, Andrew (2009: online). "Fat Lady Sings her Last Song as 'Thinner Opera Divas Take Over Centre Stage'". *The Telegraph*. 17 August. http://www.telegraph.co.uk/culture/music/opera/60379 56/Fat-lady-sings-her-last-song-as-thinner-opera-divas-take-over-centre-stage.html. [25/09/2010].
Kuhn, Bernhard (2005). *Die Oper im italienischen Film*. Fora: Studien zu Literatur und Sprache 9. Essen: Die Blaue Eule.
— (2008). "The Spoken Opera-Film *Fedora* (1942): Intermedial Transposition and Implicit Operatic References in Film". *Essays on Word/Music Adaptation and on Surveying the Field*. David F. Urrows, ed. Word and Music Studies 9. Amsterdam/New York, NY: Rodopi. 75−92.
Kühnel, Jürgen (1998). "Oper im Fernsehen". Inga Lemke, ed. *Theaterbühne − Fernsehbilder: Sprech-, Musik- und Tanztheater im und für das Fernsehen*. Anif: Müller-Speiser. 159−188.

— (2001). "'Mimesis' und 'diegesis' – szenische Darstellung und filmische Erzählung: Zur Ästhetik der Oper in Film und Fernsehen". Peter Csobádi et al., eds. *Das Musiktheater in den audiovisuellen Medien: '... ersichtlich gewordene Taten der Musik'. Vorträge und Gespräche des Salzburger Symposions 1999*. Anif: Müller-Speiser. 60–79.

Kurtzman, Neil (2008: online). "La Boheme [sic] in HD – April 5, 2008". *Medicine & Opera*. http://medicine-opera.com/2008/04/la-boheme-in-hd. [25/09/2010].

Lange, Brian, dir. (1992). *Tosca*. TV. Italy: Rada Film/RAI Uno.

Metropolitan Opera (2006: online). "'Metropolitan Opera: Live in HD' Makes its Debut". December 30. http://www.metoperafamily.org/metopera/news/press/detail.aspx?id=2709. [25/09/2010].

— (2008a: online). "The Metropolitan Opera Announces Expansion of Life, High-Definition Transmissions to Eleven in 2008-09". April 22.
http://www.metoperafamily.org/metopera/news/press/detail.aspx?id=3810. [25/09/2010].

— (2008b: online). "The Auteur of Opera". http://www.metoperafamily.org/metopera/news/interviews/detail.aspx?id=5806. [25/09/2010].

— (2009: online). "Metropolitan Opera Hits Box Office Goal of 8% for the 2008–09 Season". May 8. http://www.metoperafamily.org/metopera/news/press/detail.aspx?id=8786. [25/09/2010].

Moore, Frances Claire (2009). *A Night at the (Imaginary) Opera: The Visual Dimension in Hector Berlioz's* Lélio, Roméo et Juliette, *and* La damnation de Faust. Master's thesis, New Zealand School of Music. http://hdl.handle.net/10179/1830. [15/03/2011].

Morris, Christopher (2010). "Digital Diva: Opera on Video". *The Opera Quarterly* 26/1: 96–119.

Napier, Julian, dir. (2011). *Carmen 3D*. Film. UK: Royal Opera House.

Puccini, Giacomo (1920). *La Bohème: Partitura*. Milano: Ricordi.

Rajewsky, Irina O. (2005). "Intermediality, Intertextuality, and Remediation: A Literary Perspective on Intermediality". *Intermédialités/Intermedialities* 6: 43–64.

Rosenberg, Donald (2010: online). The Met's Live HD Performances Widen Opera's Audience". *Cleveland.com*. October 3. http://www.cleveland.com/musicdance/index.ssf/2010/10/the_mets_live_hd_performances.html. [15/03/2011].

Senici, Emanuele (2010). "Porn Style? Space and Time in Live Opera Videos". *The Opera Quarterly* 26/1: 63–80.
Sheppard, Anthony W. (2007). "Review of the Metropolitan Opera's New HD Movie Theater Broadcasts". *American Music* 25/3: 383–387.
Sinkowitz, Wilhelm (2008: online). "Wie dick dürfen Sänger sein?". *Die Presse*. July 18. http://diepresse.com/home/kultur/klassik/399512/Wie-dick-duerfen-Saenger-sein. [25/09/2010].
Wenzel, John (2008: online). "How Can Arts Thrive in Increasingly Digital World?". *The Denver Post*. June 8. http://www.denverpost.com/ci_9494414. [25/09/2010].
Wolf, Werner (2002). "Intermediality Revisited: Reflections on Word and Music Relations in the Context of a General Typology of Intermediality". *Word and Music Studies: Essays in Honor of Steven Paul Scher and on Cultural Identity and the Musical Stage*. Suzanne M. Lodato, Suzanne Aspden, Walter Bernhart, eds. Word and Music Studies 4. Amsterdam/New York, NY: Rodopi. 13–34.

Jazz Novels and the Textualization of Musical Performance

Emily Petermann, Göttingen

> This paper examines the role of performance in jazz novels – novels that not only deal with jazz on the level of content, but use it as a structural model in their narrative construction. It considers several aspects of the performance situation in jazz music and their evocation in the novels, beginning with the relationship between the performer and composer, which is reflected in the novels by the tension between dramatized narrators and implied authors. Elements borrowed from oral storytelling are used to link text and music, bridged by orality as an intermediate stage. Several oral devices are imitated in these texts, from aspects of language and deictic references to the speech context, to topics and styles reminiscent of gossip, to a strong focus on the figure of the narrator as an individualized voice. After a discussion of first-person narration and the tenses used to convey immediacy, the paper concludes with an analysis of the 'solos' by some of those narrators and the way they attempt to 'improvise on the break'.

The present paper concerns the jazz novel, by which I mean a novel that is not necessarily, or not only, *about* jazz, but attempts *to be like* jazz by imitating[1] various aspects of the music, whether of the surface (i. e., rhythm, timbre), structure (i. e., riffs, call and response patterns), or context (i. e., live performance, improvisation). The focus in this analysis is on the imitation of the musical performance situation in jazz novels. Gunther Schuller's *Early Jazz* provides a concise introduction to the central importance of performance in jazz music:

> Whereas we are interested primarily in the *Eroica* and only secondarily in someone's performance of it, in jazz the relationship is reversed. We are only minimally interested in *West End Blues* as a tune or a composition, but primarily interested in Armstrong's rendition of it. Moreover, we are obliged to evaluate it on the basis of a single performance that happened to be recorded in 1928 and are left to speculate on the hundreds of other performances he played of the same tune. (1986: x)

A genre of music like jazz that relies so fundamentally on improvisation is by necessity different from one performance to the next. The transient nature of all music is further emphasized by this practice in

---

[1] The term 'imitation' is Werner Wolf's, who distinguishes between the modes of 'thematization' or 'telling' and 'imitation' or 'showing' (see 1999).

jazz. Jazz has been described as "defying notation" (ibid.) as much of the music is played without the aid of a score, and its use of a wide range of timbres, for example, is also difficult to capture in conventional musical notation. Together with the central role of improvisation, this relative lack of notation in jazz music helps to create "an aesthetic of sheer presentness" (Rice 2000: 170) to an extent that is not found in other genres. Of course a performance of classical music is also evanescent, but there isn't the same emphasis on presence as in jazz since a performance is perceived as being to a much larger extent repeatable. The difference between classical music and jazz is above all the *culture* that emphasizes the transience and changeability, the newness of jazz, as opposed to fidelity to a score in classical music.

This reflects a fundamentally different ideology and approach to musical performance in these two traditions. Where the classical musician most often aims at a faithful reproduction of the composer's ideal as indicated in the score, a jazz-musician places the emphasis on a creative and innovative treatment of a starting tune or harmonic framework. The idea of the composer is thus secondary to that of the performer, who is expected to display not only his technical proficiency, but also his originality and individuality. The jazz performer and his individual style take precedence over the content of the piece – *how* he or she plays is more important than *what* is being played, the process of performing is privileged over the product of composition.

The following analyses consider a few of the various aspects of the performance situation in jazz music and their evocation in the novels, beginning with the relationship between the performer and composer, which is reflected in the novels by the tension between dramatized narrators and implied authors. I argue that elements borrowed from oral storytelling are used to link text and music, with orality serving as an intermediate stage. Several oral devices are imitated in these texts, from aspects of language and deictic references to the speech context, to topics and styles reminiscent of gossip, to a strong focus on the figure of the narrator as an individualized voice. After a discussion of first-person narration and the tenses used to convey immediacy, the paper concludes with an analysis of the 'solos' by some of those narrators and the way they attempt to 'improvise on the break'.

1. The Narrator as Performer: Imitating Orality

The role of the performer and his or her relationship to the composer is mirrored in the relationship between narrator and implied author in a text. Indeed, the 'composer' here should be understood as the 'implied composer', as his or her intentions can only be inferred from the piece of music. The Bach of the *Goldberg Variations*, like the Ellington of "Mood Indigo", is a construction distinct from the historical person of either J. S. Bach or Duke Ellington. A primary strategy for emphasizing performance aspects in a jazz novel is thus the foregrounding of the narrator role. A prominent narrator function, often with a highly individualized personality, is common in jazz novels. Rather than relating events from the perspective of an omniscient and anonymous narrator, these novels frequently draw attention to the individual who fills that narrator role. This often occurs through the use of the first person, whether as an autodiegetic (I-protagonist) or heterodiegetic (I-witness) narrator (cf. Genette 1972/1983: 245). The main thing is for the narrator's voice to be distinctive and individual, not discreet and anonymous.

In those jazz novels that do not make use of a first-person narrator, the third-person narration is still prevented from appearing anonymous, given an individual flavor through strong internal focalization (cf. ibid: 189–194). In such cases, though the character is described in the third person, the perspective is overwhelmingly that of an individual character, and the style of language used corresponds to that of the character in the manner Gordon Collier has called "subjectivized third-person narration" (1999: 9), "in which the discourse of the narrator is infiltrated by language typical of the character being described" (Richardson 2006: 9). My claim is that a powerful strategy for evoking the performance situation – and especially for privileging the role of the performer over that of the composer – is the use of a distinct voice by the narrator, either in the first person[2] or as focalized through a character's perspective[3].

---

[2] Examples of jazz novels told in the first person include *Jazz* by Toni Morrison, *Train Whistle Guitar*, *The Spyglass Tree*, and *The Seven League Boots* by Albert Murray, *Be-bop, Re-bop* and *Muse-Echo Blues* by Xam Wilson Cartiér, and *Invisible Man* by Ralph Ellison.

[3] Examples of jazz novels that focalize a third-person narration through the consciousness of a particular character include *Be-bop* and *Un soir au club* by Christian Gailly, and *Don't the Moon Look Lonesome* by Stanley Crouch.

In addition to the frequent use of homodiegetic narrators in the first person, there are several other devices that contribute to the individual voice and spontaneous feel of these texts. These include dialect or slang, informal or conversational sentence structure and punctuation, deictic expressions that emphasize the importance of context, noticeable use of the present tense, and attempts to draw in the reader, whether through direct address by means of the second person pronoun or through metafictional devices that challenge the reader to participate actively in the production of textual meaning. These techniques combine to produce the impression of a story that is embedded in a performance situation, unfolding as it is told, just as a jazz solo is developed and modified during the process of improvisation.

Though distinctive narrative voices in the first person are hardly restricted to novels based on jazz, this is one means of evoking the performer's role that is quite common in jazz novels. In these cases, the prominence of the narrator's personality and relative absence of the implied author serve to evoke the dominance of the jazz performer over the composer. Indeed, these narrators often seem to usurp the author's role, claiming to determine or produce the text themselves, as in Xam Wilson Cartiér's novels *Be-bop, Re-bop* and *Muse-Echo Blues*, in Albert Murray's *Train Whistle Guitar* and other novels in the 'Scooter' series, and in Toni Morrison's 1992 novel, *Jazz*.

From the opening line, the narrative voice of *Jazz* conveys an aura of immediacy, intimacy, and above all, orality. The language used is that of spoken gossip, as discussed by Esther Fritsch in her study of gossip in ethnic American writing (see 2004). In addition to evoking oral rather than written language, this gossipy style creates closeness, combating the distance typical of writing (cf. ibid: 39). Language of closeness[4] presumes a shared context in place and/or time, in which more emphasis can be placed on the means and process of communication, in contrast to language of distance, which privileges a higher density of information and focuses on the product or results of communication, rather than the process itself. In the following, I will argue that the use of gossip and other oral forms of storytelling in

---

[4] Like Deborah Tannen (1982), Peter Koch and Wulf Österreicher (1985) propose replacing the distinction between orality and literacy with differentiations in features that are traditionally assigned to the one or other pole. A graphic representation of their categories of language of distance and of closeness is printed in Goetsch (cf. 1987: 209).

Morrison's and other jazz novels serve as a bridge between the traditionally static written novel and jazz music as embedded in the performance situation and the process of improvisational artistic creation. The novels use linguistic means to imitate a musical context, as both media – language and music – share the distinction between process and product. An evocation of oral language by the written text is thus a linguistic imitation of a generalized performance situation.

Some of the oral devices used in *Jazz* – which can be seen as exemplary for the jazz novel written in the first person – include: 1) informal language and slang, shorter or incomplete sentences typical of speech; 2) frequent use of deictic expressions that emphasize the role of context in communication; 3) choice of topics and style typical of gossip; 4) prominence of the speaker/narrator, who may also employ the present tense to convey immediacy; and 5) active involvement of the listener/reader. A more comprehensive forthcoming study of mine[5] will discuss each of these devices in greater detail. Here I can concentrate only on the prominence of the speaker/narrator and his or her use of the present tense and tense switching.

2. First-Person Narration: The Case of *Jazz*

The first-person narrator in *Jazz* establishes herself[6] from the outset as a source of information. She claims to know the characters, to know

---

[5] My Ph. D. thesis on "The Musical Novel: Imitating Musical Structure in Contemporary Fiction" (Petermann forthcoming) has been submitted to the University of Konstanz in 2011. The present paper is based on the chapter of that study entitled "The Performance Situation in Jazz Novels".

[6] Though it is never explicitly stated in the novel, the narrator of *Jazz* is often presumed to be a female voice, due in part to her diction and partially also through the stereotypical association of women with gossip. If extra-textual information is taken into account, Morrison's assertion that the narrator is female can confirm this assumption: "Toni Morrison sprach bei einer Lesung im Amerikahaus Köln (13. 5. 1993) vom weiblichen Geschlecht der Erzählinstanz." (Fritsch 2004: 176, fn. 203. 'Toni Morrison spoke during a reading in the Amerikahaus Köln [13 May 1993] of the female sex of the narrative instance.' My translation.) Although later in the novel it would seem that the narrator is not a 'person' at all, but a personification of the novel or its discourse, the narrator's opening emphasis on her role as an observer suggests that she may be a neighbor or other witness to the events related. I use the female pronoun for the narrator, with the caveat that this is more out of convenience than narratological necessity.

their histories, and to be reasonably well informed as to their motivations. Even her speculations, while serving as warnings that not all of this information is certain, lend an air of authenticity to what she claims to know: "Whether she sent the boyfriend away or whether he quit her, *I can't say*. [...] *But I do know* that mess didn't last two weeks" (Morrison 1992/1993: 5; my emphasis). The logical assumption on the part of the reader is that this gossipy, intimate voice belongs to that of a neighbor or other witness to the events she describes, and that we as readers are privileged recipients of this inside information. The narrator thus seems to inhabit the same diegetic level as the characters Joe, Violet, and the rest, as an intradiegetic narrator, while the implied reader is also drawn in as a listener, rather than as a reader. As a character herself, then, the narrator's point of view is expected to be limited to her observations and opinions, as she speculates on what she does not know for certain.

The narrator slowly and unobtrusively extends the boundaries of what she tells, however, going beyond her own observations to relate events she could not have witnessed, as well as the thoughts of other characters. The intradiegetic first-person narrator thus seems to have morphed into an omniscient third-person narrator, though this role also remains in flux. She continues to insert herself into the story, expressing her opinions and preferences and dropping hints at her own unreliability and the impossibility of knowing anyone else's mind[7]. By the end of the novel, her seeming omniscience has been revealed as a fraud, as she admits to having 'misread' her characters. Indeed, they are not the objects of her observation, but have been watching the narrator instead:

> I thought I'd hidden myself so well as I watched them through windows and doors, took every opportunity I had to follow them, to gossip about and fill in their lives, and all the while they were watching me. [...] I was the predictable one, confused in my solitude into arrogance, thinking my space, my view was the only one that was or that mattered. [...] It never occurred to me that they were thinking other thoughts, feeling other feelings, putting their lives together in ways I never dreamed of. (Ibid.: 220f.)

---

[7] See for example this statement by the narrator: "Risky, I'd say, trying to figure out anybody's state of mind. But worth the trouble if you're like me – curious, inventive and well-informed. [...] So he didn't know [about True Belle]. Neither do I, although it's not hard to imagine what it must have been like." (Morrison 1992/1993: 137)

The narrator has thus shifted diegetic levels. No longer on the same level as the characters, observing them as a fellow resident of the City, no longer with a claim to omniscience on a diegetic level above the story being told, the narrator is now seen and observed by her own inventions, is no longer in control of the story but controlled by it. In fact, the narrator seems to have become not the creator of the story, but the story itself[8], as becomes clear in her appeal to the reader – in the vein of reader-response criticism reminiscent of Wolfgang Iser (see, e. g., 1974 and 1976) – to "make me, remake me. You are free to do it and I am free to let you because look, look. Look where your hands are. Now" (Morrison 1992/1993: 229). Not only has the role of the narrator changed, yielding what is quite literally a "speakerly text" (Gates 1988: 181), but the narratee/implied reader/reader role has also become ambiguous. Not only is the narratee explicitly addressed – the pronoun "you" is first used on page 4 to draw in the listener/reader – but also the actual reader, whose hands are on the book, with "*fingers on and on, lifting, turning*" (Morrison 1992/1993: 229; emphasis in the original) the pages as he or she reads these lines.

By claiming that the actual reader is the same as the narratee, the text/narrator collapses diegetic levels in a distinctly postmodernist fashion. This use of second-person address corresponds to Brian Richardson's category of the "autotelic"[9]:

> [...] the direct address to a 'you' that is at times the actual reader of the text and whose story is juxtaposed to and can merge with the characters of the fiction. It is a narrativization of a form of address, and as such appears in relatively 'pure' instances only in extremely short texts [...]. In more extended works, it alternates with third or first person narration. (2006: 30)

In this case, the majority of the novel is narrated in the third person, in which the narrator relates the events surrounding the characters, or in the first person, either in the narrator's own voice or in the voices of Joe, Violet, Dorcas, and Felice speaking for themselves. It is only in

---

[8] Cf. the following remark: "If jazz is a music the performer composes himself, then this novel she calls *Jazz* is a book that composes itself." (Leonard 1992/1993: 37; qtd. Gutmann 2000: 71) A more accurate parallel, obviously, would be a book that the narrator composes herself.

[9] One of the most distinctive examples of this type of address cited by Richardson is Italo Calvino's *Se una notte d'inverno un viaggiatore* (1979), in which both the actual reader and the implied reader are addressed at different points, blurring the borders of diegesis.

the transition of the narrative voice to that of the text itself at the end of the novel that the autotelic function becomes significant.

This unusual transformation from narrator to speaking text suggests a model of artistic creation in which the art 'product', the text, creates itself with the help of an audience. It is constantly in a state of coming into being, rather than already existing. This is yet another way of suggesting the model of oral cultures, in which a story unfolds only as it is being told or a piece of music comes into existence only as it is being played. There is no recourse to the 'original', as there is "'no concept of a "correct" or "authentic" version'[10] [...] but the text is variable and dependent on the occasion of performance" (Gutmann 2000: 63).

The idiosyncracies of the narrator in *Jazz* become even more pronounced when compared with other examples of first-person narration such as those in Albert Murray's 'Scooter' series. In contrast to *Jazz*, there the narrating voice remains fairly constant. The four novels are all told in memoir form, in the voice of the adult 'Scooter' relating stories and memories from his youth. While this narrative form is quite conventional[11], the personality of the narrator is in fact the main subject of the novels, and there is a blurring of boundaries between the narrator and the implied author. Though the musician Scooter is of course not equivalent to the writer Murray, the numerous parallels in their biographies encourage an identification of Scooter's ideals and attitudes with those espoused by Murray in his non-fiction works. Also, these parallels encourage the reader to view comments on music and on literature in a similar light, as the two media are presented as sister arts and related forms of expression. Such an association of the narrator and author – like that of the jazz performer and composer – is reinforced on the level of content in *The Seven League Boots* by images of jazz musicians like Scooter and The Boss Man who are both composers and performers.

The first-person novels by Morrison and Murray thus present two different models of narration. In one case, the narrator merges with the text to form a "speakerly text", a product that is also a process, a piece of music that is always developing, never completed. In the other, the

---

[10] Gutmann here cites Finnegan (1988: 89).

[11] The novels clearly partake of the 'Bildungsroman' tradition, even down to the division in *The Seven League Boots* into sections labeled "The Apprentice", "The Journeyman", and "The Craftsman".

narrator merges with the implied author, or the performer with the composer, to suggest creation-in-performance in a manner that is typical both of the oral storyteller and the jazz musician.

3. The Present Tense and Tense Switching in Performed Texts

In addition to person, another relevant aspect of the narrative situation that conveys a sense of performance is the tense used. While Murray's novels are rather conventionally related in the past tense, several other examples use the present tense as part of their dramatization of the storytelling situation. Christian Gailly's *Be-bop*, for example, is narrated entirely in the present tense, which suggests spontaneity in the relating of events only as they unfold. Other jazz novels use tense switching between past – telling the story – and present – acting it out. Suzanne Fleischman's detailed study of oral patterns in literature elucidates the influence such orally conveyed stories have had on written texts. She cites studies on "performed narratives" in which the use of the present tense is a marker for performance:

> [...] tense switching is virtually always a mark of orally performed narratives of the type Nessa Wolfson [...] has labeled performed stories, on the basis of certain features that such texts share with theatrical presentations. These features include direct speech, asides, repetition, expressive sounds and sound effects, and motions and gestures. Not all but at least some of them must be in evidence for a narrative to constitute a performed story and not merely an oral report of past events. [...] The more fully a story is performed, Wolfson asserts, the more likely it is to exhibit tense switching[12]. [...] In her data, tense switching occurs only in those narrations in which the speaker 'breaks through' into performance (cf. Hymes 1974). (Fleischman 1990: 8f.)

Xam Wilson Cartiér's novels *Muse-Echo Blues* and *Be-bop, Re-bop* are clear examples of this practice of switching between stories told in the past tense and the use of the present tense to lend immediacy and an air of 'showing' to the 'telling' of the tale. Within the same paragraph or even the same sentence, the narrator will switch between the past and the present tenses. Fleischman argues that this tense switching is "linked to a particular 'style' of narration, [...] the 'performed story'" (ibid.: 68)[13]. Though the present tense is used, it relates

---

[12] Fleischman here cites Wolfson (1978 and 1979), and later Hymes (1974).

[13] The term "performed story" is taken from Nessa Wolfson.

events that are clearly contiguous with those related in the past tense. It has thus been classified as the "historical present", the "narrative present", the "diegetic present", or "dramatic present", "a neutral tense which behaves like a P[ast]"[14], or a "device for introducing the 'present of the living speaker' into the past story-world (and thereby ostensibly collapsing the distance between the two)" (ibid.: 78)[15]. The present tense thus evokes a storyteller who ceases merely to report events, but instead acts them out for his or her audience in the present tense.

In Cartiér's novel *Be-bop, Re-bop* (1987), some events are presented in the past tense, as having already occurred, while others begin to be told in the present tense, sometimes alternating between the two tenses within the space of just a few sentences. In other cases, the narration is conducted primarily in the past tense, but sudden bursts of present tense lend immediacy and drama to the tale, very much as Fleischman observes in oral storytelling:

> There *was* strange restless silence before Vole replied. "Is that what's scaring you to death? What have you got to lose?" She *stopped* for a while, then *threw* out in a rush as if dammed up too long with a gush of her feelings now at high tide [...]. [= past tense]
>
> With this last, I*'m* aghast; I*'ve* never heard Vole talk like this before – something*'s* up here that*'s* new and it*'s* out of control – but wait, listen up, Double*'s* speaking again –. [= present tense]
>
> (Cartiér 1987: 21; my emphases)

In this example, the narrator's sudden use of the present tense places her back at the scene of the events she relates, much as someone telling a story orally will use expressions like "So then he says ..." or "and I go ..." to dramatize or act out the scene rather than simply giving a factual report. In this way, the listeners seem to witness the events rather than merely hearing them second-hand. Of course, in an actual oral situation there would also be nonverbal elements like facial expression, tone of voice, and gesture to support this dramatization, which can only be implied in a written text. The use of tense switching is thus a crucial device for indicating this oral situation in the absence of other such oral means.

---

[14] Paden (1977) qtd. Fleischman (1990: 78).

[15] Fleischman includes a detailed overview of philological and linguistic work on tense usage. The embedded quotation is from Ollier (1978).

4. Improvising on the Break: Performing *Train Whistle Guitar*

I will conclude my discussion of performance aspects of jazz novels with an example taken from Albert Murray's first in the series of 'Scooter' novels, *Train Whistle Guitar*, published in 1974. Improvisation is one of the most central aspects of jazz performance, and one that distinguishes it from many other genres of music. Significantly, improvisation is one of the features of the music that are most central for novels that seek to imitate jazz, with its associations with freedom, self-definition, heroism, and individual creativity.

There are a number of different ways that a jazz novel can attempt to create the impression of improvisation, corresponding to different levels of the text's construction. A particular style of emphasizing the sound of language as well as inventiveness in forming new words and compounds can yield a playful effect. As I have argued, a narrator's use of oral elements (i. e., imitating the style of a gossip, use of speech patterns, and direct address of the reader) can create the impression of spontaneity, of a story that is being made up as it is told. These narrators also revise their stories as they tell them, such as acknowledging that their story has turned out differently than expected, as in Toni Morrison's *Jazz*, as discussed above[16].

Perhaps the most striking imitation of improvisation, however, involves the structural device of the 'break', which Albert Murray explains as follows:

> Another technical device peculiar to blues music is the break, which is a very special kind of ad-lib bridge passage or cadenzalike interlude between two musical phrases that are separated by an interruption or interval in the established cadence. Customarily there may be a sharp shotlike accent and the normal or established flow of the rhythm and the melody stop [...]. Then the gap, usually of not more than four bars, is filled in most often but not always by a solo instrument, whose statement is usually impromptu or improvised even when it is a quotation or a variation from some well-known melody. Then when the regular rhythm is picked up again [...] it is as if you had been holding your breath. (1976: 99)

Such interruptions of the choral progression in jazz can be seen in novels in passages that 'break' the flow of narrative. The action of the plot is suspended for a few pages, while the narrator goes off on a

---

[16] The narrator of *Jazz* also explicitly acknowledges changing the events and characters of which she speaks: "Not hating him is not enough; liking, loving him is not useful. I have to alter things." (Morrison 1992/1993: 161)

tangent, develops a theme, or inserts other material. Such passages have a pronounced air of playfulness and often strike the reader as a free play of associations. Wordplay is often prominent, serving yet again to foreground the sound of the words used and remind the reader of the auditory element of language that it shares with music.

Train Whistle Guitar is a memoir-like jazz novel notable for its use of poetic passages that interrupt the flow of the protagonist's reminiscing to evoke an improvisatory solo. The first such passage comes early in the novel and is graphically set apart from the main narrative by being printed in italics. When the first short chapter has introduced the place of the protagonist's childhood and concluded by calling it "the briarpatch" and introducing his nickname Scooter[17], the first 'solo' takes up the theme of naming and its connection to home. I quote this passage in full as it exemplifies several features of the improvised solo:

> *I used to say My name is also Jack the Rabbit because my home is in the briarpatch, and Little Buddy (than whom there was never a better riddle buddy) used to say Me my name is Jack the Rabbit also because my home is also in the also and also of the briarpatch because that is also where I was also bred and also born. And when I also used to say My name is also Jack the Bear he always used to say My home is also nowhere and also anywhere and also everywhere.*
>
> *Because the also and also of all of that was also the also plus also of so many of the twelve-bar twelve-string guitar riddles you got whether in idiomatic iambics or otherwise mostly from Luzana Cholly who was the one who used to walk his trochaic-sporty stomping-ground limp-walk picking and plucking and knuckle knocking and strumming (like an anapestic locomotive) while singsongsaying Anywhere I hang my hat anywhere I prop my feet. Who could drink muddy water who could sleep in a hollow log.* (Murray 1975/1999: 4f.; italics in the original)

Much as a solo may be structured around a preexisting melody, this passage picks up the themes of name and place from the previous section, introducing the additional nicknames of "Jack the Rabbit", which is a product of place – "because my home is in the briarpatch" – and "Jack the Bear", whose home is "nowhere and also anywhere and also everywhere". This passage does not merely restate the theme, however, but experiments with it and strings it out, using a series of

---

[17] As will be discussed in the following, the actual name of the narrator is never mentioned in this or any of the following novels. He is most often referred to as 'Scooter', but will also receive numerous other nicknames from the outset and as the series of novels progresses.

licks or motifs – repeated short phrases as used in motivic improvisation to structure a solo[18] – to connect the various ideas. The first repeated phrase is "I used to say My name is", which appears with a slight variation three times in this first paragraph. Ironically, the reader never learns Scooter's actual name in this novel[19], so this emphasis on introducing oneself and determining one's own identity strikes a slightly strange note, either as seemingly ingenuous, or, more likely, as a claim that heroic self-naming is more important than official or legal names.

The many repetitions of the word "also", particularly in the unusual combination as a noun phrase "the also and also", are further examples of such a lick. The plethora of uses in this passage serves to sensitize the reader to this word, such that it becomes much more striking throughout the remainder of the text(s).

Murray's use of "also and also" is highly idiosyncratic, and it forms a piece of his individual vocabulary that makes connections with his uses of it in other contexts. For example, in an interview with Tony Scherman that appeared in 1996, Murray used the phrase in discussing the picaresque plot structure of his 'Scooter' novels:

> My narrative structure is not geared to a tightly knit plot. It is a picaresque story, more a matter of one thing following another than one thing leading to another. To me, the 'and then and then and also and also and next after that' of a picaresque reflects a sensitivity consistent with contemporary knowledge of the universe. The connection between that and the requirements of ongoing improvisation in the jam session should be easy to see. (Scherman 1996: [un-paginated])

---

[18] Cf. Kernfeld, ed. 2002: 2/315–321. In motivic improvisation, just a few motifs form the basis of the improvisation, but unlike the formulaic type, these motifs draw attention to themselves and connect the various sections of a piece through their repetition and variation. In all these approaches, the improvisation oscillates between fidelity to a predetermined basis in a theme or harmonic and rhythmic structure and imagination or creativity.

[19] The protagonist-narrator, while clearly sharing many biographical features with the implied author, Albert Murray, remains unnamed (with the exception of nicknames like "Scooter", "Mister Man", and "Schoolboy") throughout the trilogy. This is reminiscent of the first-person narrator of Ralph Ellison's *Invisible Man*, who likewise refers to his changed name without ever revealing it to the reader. See also Murray's statement in an interview with Charles Rowell: "Scooter is a fictional representation of my consciousness. *He is not, of course, a documentary image of me; rather he is a literary device for dealing with my consciousness.*" (Rowell/Murray 1997: 399; italics in the original)

Here, "also and also", like "and then and then", has non-hierarchical or non-causal connotations. Murray aims at a plot that is serial or episodic rather than causal or climactic[20]. The word "also" can thus be seen as a renunciation of formal structure, or more accurately, as a demonstration that such formal structures are imposed from the outside upon material that is inherently chaotic. Elsewhere, Murray refers to the "ultimate actuality of entropy (repeat, entropy) *of the void*, upon which we impose such metaphorical devices as AND, as in (andoneandtwoandthreeandfourand) [...]" (2005: 237f.; emphasis in the original). "And", like "also", conjoins two or more entities, whether those are people or things, attributes, or actions, proclaiming their simultaneous existence. This is suggestive of Murray's concept of the United States as a "mulatto culture" made up of "composite" identities (Scherman 1996: [un-paginated])[21], but it also corresponds to his ideal of the blues idiom, in which a piece of music can say multiple things at once. The lick "and also" thus alludes to elements of the wider episodic structure of jazz at the same time as it functionally serves to link elements of an improvised solo.

5. Conclusion

In this paper, I have only been able to touch on a few of the aspects of the performance situation in jazz music that are imitated or evoked in jazz novels – the emphasis on a distinctive narrative voice as a means of privileging the performer over the composer; the use of the present tense as a way of dramatizing the tale, of showing it as it unfolds rather than telling it retrospectively; and especially the emphasis on

---

[20] Cf. the entry for "picaresque" in the *Oxford Concise Companion to English Literature*: "[...] nowadays it is commonly, and loosely, applied to episodic novels [...] which describe the adventures of a lively and resourceful hero on a journey" (Drabble/Stringer, eds. 1996: 454).

[21] See Murray's interview with Tony Scherman: "[...] the United States is a mulatto culture. First, let's put things in a world context. Go back to what [the French poet] Paul Valéry called Homo europaeus, a composite of Greek logic, Roman administration, and Judeo-Christian morality. That's what makes a European different from somebody in India, Japan, or Africa. Now send him across the Atlantic. You get [...] a new composite: of the ingenious Yankee, the frontiersman, who's part Indian, and the Negro. All Americans, I don't care if it's a neo-Nazi, are part Yankee, part backwoodsman, part Negro." (1996: [un-paginated])

improvisation as a central feature of jazz performance. Improvisation represents an ideal to which such written texts aspire, something they approach but cannot actually reach. This tension between the fixed text and the ideal of spontaneity becomes a point on which the jazz novel pivots, a fruitful field for exploration of the mediality of both text and music.

References

Primary Sources

Cartiér, Xam Wilson (1987). *Be-bop, Re-bop*. New York, NY: Ballantine.
— (1991). *Muse-Echo Blues*. New York, NY: Harmony.
Crouch, Stanley (2000). *Don't the Moon Look Lonesome*. New York, NY: Pantheon.
Ellison, Ralph (1952/1994). *Invisible Man*. New York, NY: Modern Library.
Gailly, Christian (1995). *Be-bop*. Paris: Les Éditions de Minuit.
— (2001). *Un soir au club*. Paris: Les Éditions de Minuit.
Morrison, Toni (1992/1993). *Jazz*. New York, NY: Penguin.
Murray, Albert (1975/1999). *Train Whistle Guitar*. New York, NY: Vintage.
— (1991). *The Spyglass Tree*. New York, NY: Pantheon.
— (1995). *The Seven League Boots*. New York, NY: Pantheon.
— (2005). *The Magic Keys*. New York, NY: Pantheon.

Secondary Sources

Collier, Gordon (1999). "Apparent Feature-Anomalies in Subjectivized Third-Person Narration". John Pier, ed. *Recent Trends in Narratological Research*. GRAAT Anglophone Studies 21. Tours: University of Tours. 129–152.
Drabble, Margaret, Jenny Stringer, eds. (1996). *Oxford Concise Companion to English Literature*. Oxford/London: OUP.
Finnegan, Ruth (1988). *Literacy and Orality: Studies in the Technology of Communication*. Oxford: Basil Blackwell.
Fleischman, Suzanne (1990). *Tense and Narrativity: From Medieval Performance to Modern Fiction*. Austin, TX: University of Texas Press.

Fritsch, Esther (2004). *Reading Gossip: Funktionen von Klatsch in Romanen ethnischer amerikanischer Autorinnen*. Trier: Wissenschaftlicher Verlag Trier.

Gates, Henry Louis, Jr. (1988). *The Signifying Monkey: A Theory of Afro-American Literary Criticism*. New York, NY/Oxford: OUP.

Genette, Gérard (1972/1983). *Narrative Discourse: An Essay in Method*. Trans. Jane E. Lewin. Ithaca, NY: Cornell UP. (French orig.: "Discours du récit". *Figures III*. Collection Poétique. Paris: Éditions du Seuil, 1972. 71–273).

Goetsch, Paul (1987). "Fingierte Mündlichkeit in der Erzählkunst entwickelter Schriftulturen". *Komparatistische Hefte* 15/16: 202–218.

Gutmann, Katharina (2000). *Celebrating the Senses: An Analysis of the Sensual in Toni Morrison's Fiction*. Tübingen/Basel: Francke.

Hymes, Dell (1974). "Breakthrough into Performance". *Folklore, Performance, and Communication*. D. Ben Amos, K. Goldstein, eds. The Hague: Mouton. 11–74.

Iser, Wolfgang (1974). "The Reading Process: A Phenomenological Approach". *The Implied Reader: Patterns of Communication in Prose Fiction from Bunyan to Beckett*. Baltimore, MD/London: Johns Hopkins UP. 274–294.

— (1976). The *Act of Reading: A Theory of Aesthetic Response*. London: Routledge and Kegan Paul.

Kernfield, Barry, ed. (2002). *The New Grove Dictionary of Jazz*. 2nd ed. 3 vols. London: Macmillan.

Koch, Peter, Wulf Österreicher (1985). "Sprache der Nähe – Sprache der Distanz: Mündlichkeit und Schriftlichkeit im Spannungsfeld von Sprachtheorie und Sprachgeschichte". *Romanistisches Jahrbuch* 36: 15–43.

Leonard, John (1992/1993). "On *Jazz*". Henry Louis Gates, Jr., K. A. Appiah, eds. *Toni Morrison: Critical Perspectives Past and Present*. New York, NY: Armistad. 36–49. (Orig. publ.: *The Nation*, 25 May 1992).

Murray, Albert (1976). *Stomping the Blues*. New York, NY: Da Capo.

Ollier, Marie-Louise (1978). "Le Présent du récit: Temporalité et roman en vers". *Langue Française* 40: 99–112.

Paden, William D., Jr. (1977). "L'Emploi vicaire du présent verbal dans les plus anciens textes narratifs romans". *XIV Congresso internazionale di linguistica e filologia romanze* 4: 545–557.

Petermann, Emily (forthcoming). "The Musical Novel: Imitating Musical Structure in Contemporary Fiction". Phil. Diss. University of Konstanz.

Rice, Alan (2000). "'It Don't Mean a Thing If It Ain't Got That Swing': Jazz's Many Uses for Toni Morrison". Saadi A. Simawe, ed. *Black Orpheus: Music in African American Fiction from the Harlem Renaissance to Toni Morrison*. New York, NY/London: Garland. 153–180.

Richardson, Brian (2006). *Unnatural Voices: Extreme Narration in Modern and Contemporary Fiction*. Columbus, OH: Ohio State UP.

Rowell, Charles, Albert Murray (1997). "'An All-Purpose, All-American Literary Intellectual': An Interview with Albert Murray". *Callaloo* 20/2: 399–414.

Scherman, Tony (1996). "The Omni-American". *American Heritage* 47/5: 68–77. [Accessed through EBSCO Host; un-paginated].

Schuller, Gunther (1986). *Early Jazz: Its Roots and Musical Development*. New York, NY/Oxford: OUP.

Tannen, Deborah (1982). "The Oral/Literate Continuum in Discourse". Deborah Tannen, ed. *Spoken and Written Language: Exploring Orality and Literacy*. Advances in Discourse Processes 9. Norwood, NJ: Ablex. 1–16.

Wolf, Werner (1999). *The Musicalization of Fiction: A Study in the Theory and History of Intermediality*. Internationale Forschungen zur allgemeinen und vergleichenden Literaturwissenschaft 35. Amsterdam: Rodopi.

Wolfson, Nessa (1978). "A Feature of Performed Narrative: The Conversational Historical Present". *Language in Society* 7: 215–237.

— (1979). "The Conversational Historical Present Alternation". *Language* 55/1: 168–182.

Charles Mingus and Performative Composing

Mario Dunkel, Dortmund

In European and Anglo-American culture, musical composition is closely linked to the use of musical notation. Over centuries, musical notation has been regarded as the most efficient way of fixing and transmitting musical ideas. In the mid-1950s, however, African-American jazz musicians increasingly questioned the use of musical notation and started to explore alternative ways to convey their compositions. Charles Mingus was one of the pioneers of alternative ways of composing. Instead of writing his music on paper, he turned to more performative ways of composing, often using his body as a compositional medium: he sang and played parts of his music to musicians in his groups and used wild gestures to express his intentions. Sometimes he would stand behind instrumentalists while singing melodic phrases and gesticulating wildly until he felt that the musicians had fully absorbed his music. Mingus's method to communicate his complex compositions is unique and has hardly been explored by jazz scholars. As I will demonstrate, performative composing is an invention which can best be understood contextually. During the time of its emergence, it served as a facilitator of existentialist self-expression[1], spontaneity, and immediacy, and as a device that suited the democratic interests of the African-American counter-culture.

1. Jazz and Performative Composing

As Emily Petermann observes in "Jazz Novels and the Textualization of Musical Performance", the actual performance of music is more central to jazz music than to most other musical genres (see her essay in this vol.). The performative character of jazz music has led jazz scholars to describe the jazz aesthetic as an "aesthetic of sheer

---

[1] Self-expression is a very problematic term, as it presupposes the existence of an individual's essence that can indeed be externalized. It is, however, impossible to find out what constitutes the self. How can one distinguish between the expression of the self and of something else which is outside the self? Yet, I decided to use the term, as the belief in the authenticity of the self was immensely important for Mingus and for the culture of the 1950s as a whole. As Martin Halliwell points out in *American Culture in the 1950s*, many artists during the 1950s saw authenticity as an anti-pole to 1950s mass culture (cf. 2007: 10).

presentness" (Rice 2000: 170; see Petermann in this vol.). Yet, jazz music is too diverse to reduce its general character to its performative nature. The music of some jazz artists has been much more concerned with the performance than the music of others. The bebop revolution of the early 1940s, for example, was a revolt against the automation of jazz production by musicians who often had to reproduce pre-composed commercial songs in swing big bands. It is therefore important to pay closer attention to the degree of performativity in jazz music. In order to differentiate between various degrees of performativity in music, a distinction has to be made between composition and performance. If a symphony orchestra plays for instance Maurice Ravel's *La Valse*, one would generally say that *La Valse* is the composition while the actual concert is the performance of the musicians' interpretation of the composition, which is often judged by its ostensible proximity to the composer's ideal. In jazz music, however, the composition is oftentimes a very simple twelve to 32-bar song. In a concert, the musicians would also interpret this composition, but the proximity to the composer's ideal would be insignificant. Rather, what matters in jazz music is the musicians' rendering and appropriation of the composition.

> Classical musicians generally aim to reproduce the music, rather than to make it completely new; a dress rehearsal allows the coordination of tempi, dynamics, and other features that can thus be reproduced in essentially the same way in the performance. The difference between performances of classical music and jazz lies primarily in a culture that emphasizes the transience, changeability, and newness of jazz, as opposed to fidelity to a score in classical music. (Petermann forthcoming: 109)

During the 1950s, composer and bass player Charles Mingus blurred this traditional distinction between composition and performance, developing an art genre that I call performative composing. With his Jazz Workshop, Mingus revolutionized the ways in which complex compositions could be composed, drawing inspiration from sources as diverse as abstract expressionism, the literature of the beat generation, and the African American cultural legacy. In his arguably most creative period during the late 1950s and early 1960s, Mingus challenged traditional conceptions of the composer and of composing, embodying what Jason Toynbee in his description of a composer who leaves extended room for other musicians to express their own ideas called the "social author" (2006: 73). Musicians playing with Mingus were encouraged to not just solo over a familiar tune, or to play the changes, but to actually co-compose. At the same time, the process of composing was moved from a usually private realm to a public space – it became part of the show. In Mingus's music, composition is therefore performative: it is a staged process that is influenced by each performer of the composition and subject to continual change.

2. Charles Mingus's Jazz Workshop

In 1955, Charles Mingus was a leading figure in jazz music. Within four years, he had become one of the most celebrated jazz bassists in New York City. Additionally, he now began to earn recognition as a composer and band leader. In order to advance as a composer, he co-founded the Composer's Workshop – a collaboration of musicians and composers who worked on and played one another's compositions. However, Mingus was not quite satisfied with the Composer's Workshop, although it was, as he said, "musically successful in many ways" (Mingus 1956). According to the Mingus, the Composer's Workshop had two main drawbacks:

> First, that a jazz composition as I hear it in my mind's ear, although set down in so many notes on score paper and precisely notated, cannot be played by a group of either jazz or classical musicians. Secondly, jazz, by its very definition, cannot be held down to written parts to be played with a feeling that goes only with blowing free. A classical musician might read all the notes correctly but play them without the correct feeling or interpretation, and a jazz musician, although he might read all the notes and play them with jazz feeling, inevitably introduces his own **individual** [emphasis in the original] expression rather than what the composer intended. (Ibid.)

In this excerpt from the liner notes for his album *Pithecanthropus Erectus* Mingus hints at the general insufficiency of music scores to convey the composer's intention. He then proceeds to argue that this drawback of music notation is particularly true for jazz music, where improvisation is indispensable. Music scores tend to keep a composition fixed and inflexible – qualities that Mingus was strongly opposed to.

Consequently, Mingus began to look for new possibilities of conveying his compositions to his band mates. His solution to the problem of music notation was the Jazz Workshop: a group of musicians, varying in size and personnel, that he lead for almost ten years. Instead of using music scores, Mingus decided to communicate his compositions orally.

> My whole conception with my present Jazz Workshop group deals with nothing written. I 'write' compositions – but only on mental score paper – then I lay out the composition part by part to the musicians. I play them the 'framework' on piano so that they are familiar with my interpretation and feeling and with the scale and chord progressions to be used. Each man's own style is taken into consideration, both in ensemble and in solos. For instance, they are given different rows of notes to use against each chord but they use their own notes and play them in their own style, from scales as well as chords, except where a particular mood is indicated. In this way I find it possible to keep my own compositional flavor in the pieces and yet to allow the musicians more individual freedom in the creation of their group lines and solos. (Ibid.)

For Mingus, composition became a public performance rather than an activity carried out in seclusion. During live performances he would stand behind musicians, sing melodic phrases in their ears, gesticulate wildly, and sometimes even switch instruments in order to show other musicians how to use their instruments to realize certain ideas. His use of mimicry was hardly ever planned or ordered. Quite the contrary, Mingus's methods originated spontaneously (cf. Santoro 2001: 116). Naturally, a compositional style that demanded a lot of group interaction was loaded with tension between group members. Some musicians therefore experienced Mingus as authoritarian. 'Sweatshop' became a common nickname for the Jazz Workshop, and John Handy, who worked with Mingus as a saxophonist in 1959, for example, felt that "Mingus was in the way so much, you couldn't play for it. The man 'd stop your solos – he was totally tyrannical" (qtd. Priestley 1983: 99). However, many of the musicians who played in Mingus's Jazz Workshop disagreed with John Handy, arguing that working with Mingus was a great creative stimulation which " helped [them] grow" (Jackie McLean; qtd. Hersch 1996: 109).

The creative stimulus that many musicians experienced while working with Mingus stems from another major invention concerning the role of the composer. In addition to making composition a performative practice, Mingus also transformed the act of composing from an individual act into a collaborative project. While Mingus created the framework of a composition, he demanded that his musicians actively participate in the compositional process. By that he did not just mean that his band mates should alternately take solo flights – this would have been common during the 1950s and was notoriously practiced by musicians such as Charlie Parker, Dizzy Gillespie, or Miles Davis. Charles Mingus wanted his musicians to engage in the rest of the composition as well.

Mingus found several ways to increase the contribution of his band mates to his compositions. First, he considered the musicians' idiosyncratic styles for his compositions and included them in the creation of musical ideas – a method which was inspired by Duke Ellington. Second, he invented what he called the "extended form" (Mingus 1956), in which, according to Scott Saul, "sections of a composition would be elongated, compressed, or recombined, their underlying rhythms radically altered through stop-time, background riffs [and] new bass-vamps" (2003: 162). Often the cues to jump from one part of the composition to the next were given by his band mates so that each musician had the opportunity to decisively change the direction in which a composition was going. Third, Mingus left a lot of space for spontaneous interaction in his compositions. Thus he would sometimes only compose a rhythmical pattern and chord changes, leaving the rest open for improvisation. In contrast to the music of many of his contemporaries, Mingus's compositions were based on the principle of collaborative improvisation. His role as bass player during performances allowed him to make sure that collective improvisation was indeed taking place and that musicians would not fall back into standard phrases. Mingus goaded every musician in his workshop to express his own ideas rather than copying the music of others.

3. "Pithecanthropus Erectus" and "Folk Forms, No. 1"

Charles Mingus employed the new concept of the extended form for the first time in his composition "Pithecanthropus Erectus", recorded in 1956 (see Mingus 1981). The extended form is obvious in various ways: the melody consists mainly of whole notes that can alternatively be interspersed with quarter triplets or eighth notes. It thus leaves plenty of room for improvisation. Additionally, the main theme does not have a previously composed ending. On the contrary, it ends with a 4-bar A flat and jumps right into an improvisatory part that is played until someone in the band signals the end: "vamp until cue". It is therefore completely uncertain where the melody goes by the end of part A. On the first recording of the song, this part is used for collaborative blues-based improvisation. The instruction "on cue" subsequently introduces the interlude, which consists of three fermatas on different chords and a solo break. The extended form is obvious here:

the length of the fermatas depends on the musicians and the performance, and the solo break offers additional room for improvisation. The outcome of the composition is thus unforeseeable (cf. Mingus 1991: 108). Charles Mingus, usually cited as the composer of "Pithecanthropus Erectus", becomes a pre-composer. He gives up complete control over his composition and hands a great part of his authority over to his band mates, who figure as co-composers and whose contributions add to the final product created during the performance itself.

A second example of Mingus's new, performative compositional style is "Folk Forms No. 1", a piece that was first recorded in 1960 for the album *Charles Mingus Presents Charles Mingus*. The composition illustrates how Mingus creates simple compositional units that are intended to be further developed in live performances. As Mingus explained to his friend, record producer, civil rights activist, and jazz critic, Nat Hentoff, the musicians were first given a basic rhythm pattern.

> Then they had to listen to what I do on the bass. If I changed it, they'd have to go a different way. This is a very flexible work. About the only other guidance I give them is that if I hear them doing something particularly good one night, I remind them of it next time we play the number and suggest they keep it in. But as a whole, it never comes out the same. (Qtd. Hentoff 1960)

"Folk Forms, No. 1" is a 12-bar blues in F. The main theme is introduced by the solo bass in a 24-bar introduction. It differs slightly in rhythm and melody from other live recordings (for example the 1963 *Mingus at Antibes* recording), which shows that even the main theme is subject to re-interpretation. A sense of coherence is provided by the repetition of a rhythmic figure: a pair of eighth starting on the beat followed by an eighth note rest and an offbeat eighth. It is a recurrent rhythmic pattern, first introduced by the bass in the introduction. Drummer Dannie Richmond takes it up when he enters the composition toward the end of the introduction, and saxophone player Eric Dolphy paraphrases it playfully a few seconds later. It is also the first motif trumpet player Ted Curson plays when he enters the piece. It recurs throughout the piece in alternating pitches and in different voices – most notably Dannie Richmond makes it a main recurring motif of his drum solo starting at 8:50. All musicians are free to alter the pitch of the different notes that comprise the motif and are equally involved in the process of composing. Especially the bass and the drums are noteworthy here, because it was unusual for these instruments to get such crucial roles in a composition. Their roles by far exceed those of mere accompanists. While bass and drums freely join the process of composing, the function of the horns is extended to the role of occasional accompanists, providing a rhythmic basis in addition to their lead roles in many other parts of the composition. As Salim Washington remarks, "the quartet is broken into various combinations of duets and trios, where all instrumental voices assume differing roles. The relationship between horn and rhythm instrument is frequently inverted here, the horn providing accompaniment to the drum or bass melody" (2004: 40). There are no inferior roles of instruments in this recording.

In addition to the equalization of instrumental voices, there is an extraordinarily high amount of group interaction in "Folk Forms, No. 1". In Todd Jenkins's words, "the four men bounce ideas off of one another like a constant barrage of ping-pong balls, altering the intensity and volume of the music at individual will and following as they see fit" (2006: 76). Especially Eric Dolphy and Charles Mingus are outstanding in their abilities to quote and further develop their band mates' ideas. Simultaneous improvisation is prevalent in "Folk Forms, No. 1". The citations and similar developments in mood and tone show how carefully the musicians listen to one another's creative impulses and how they use them as stimulants for their own musical expressions. Citing their fellow musicians is more than just showing the mastery of ear and instrument. If music is to some extent self-expression, citing represents an echo, showing that the comments of the individual are heard and even answered; it expresses empathy and community based on the importance and dignity of the individual.

The notion of musical interaction is even increased when Mingus begins to use his voice in order to scream and shriek partly undecipherable utterances toward the end of "Folk Forms, No. 1". While Curson and Dolphy are soloing simultaneously over a background provided by a driving rhythm group, there is a third leading voice entering their solo. It is a long shrieking sound coming from Mingus's voice, starting on the sound [u:] slowly shifting to an [a:] sound. It is a clearly identifiable melody that starts on a D and then frequently alternates between D and C until it goes back via an A to F, the tonal root of the piece. The scream is not a strong, 'manly' scream that would involve the diaphragm or any of the vocal techniques of singers, as one might expect of a man as vigorous as Mingus was. Rather it sounds thin, although it is passionate and at full volume. It is a very instinctive expression, which suggests a sense of self-loss; as if Mingus himself hadn't known that he was going to scream immediately before the moment when he opened his mouth. Mingus's screams show how his music is an immediate emotive expression.

His screams and shouts, however, are more than just self-expression. At other moments of the composition, Mingus's utterances are decipherable. For example, he shouts empathetically, "Yes I know", at 8:52, or, "Oh yeah", during the last blues chorus. His spontaneous utterances are especially audible during a drum and bass solo and during Dannie Richmond's drum solo. The fact that Mingus shouts passionately during a drum solo – a moment when he is usually not musically involved at all – illustrates that Mingus's screams also function to spur on his band mates. He signals that he is listening to what they communicate, and, by yelling "Yes I know", reaffirms that the things they are saying mean something to him. He demonstrates that he understands and sympathizes with his band mates. Mingus's vocal utterances are part of the musical interaction in the song and illustrate his emphasis on individuality within the community of a jazz band, they have both a self-expressive and an affirmative interactive function.

In conclusion, I will emphasize three elements of "Folk Forms, No. 1" which are particularly striking: first, each of the four instruments is *equally* important – there is no hierarchy between instrumental voices; second, *individual* expression of each performer is a major element of the music; and third, the composition is a *collaborative* process and is to a great extent created in the performance. Similar to Ralph Ellison's novel *Invisible Man*, which narrates the main protagonist's process of identity formation in the form of a 'Bildungsroman', the Jazz Workshop is a staged identity formation of each musician. Corresponding to Mingus's maxim that musicians should play themselves, his band mates are encouraged to voice their own ideas. Like the nameless protagonist of *Invisible Man*, they have to form their identity by negotiating their ideas with the outside world – by testing and transforming their ideas in accordance with, or in rejection of, those of other musicians.

4. Performative Composing in its Historical Context

The contextualization of Mingus's innovations is complex as they can be analyzed from very different angles. Mingus's eclecticism as a composer and musician complicates the use of approaches to his music. Mingus drew inspiration from sources as diverse as be-bop, New Orleans Jazz, German Romanticism, French Impressionism, Latin American music, Duke Ellington, and Ludwig van Beethoven. It would therefore be inaccurate to view his music solely in an African-American cultural context; neither should it be regarded as merely part of an avant-garde movement that was influenced by the experiments of modern classical musicians during the 1950s. Yet, these examples provide important frames of reference in the light of which an understanding of Mingus's innovations can be increased. Only an investigation from many different perspectives can provide an adequate assessment of the emergence and development of performative composing.

The fact that Mingus's innovations are closely related to concurrent art movements outside of jazz music has often been overlooked by jazz scholars. Spontaneity and experimentation were substantial elements of 1950s avant-garde art and of the literature of the beat generation. Moreover, the insufficiency of music scores was not only felt by jazz musicians; it was also recognized by composers of classical music. In the late 1950s, a circle of European composers, including Karlheinz Stockhausen and Luciano Berio, experimented with indeterminacy regarding the notation of time, not yet dissolving the prearrangement of other parameters such as form and pitch. In the 1950s, American composers of classical music were even more audacious than their European counterparts, extending the concept of indeterminacy to all parameters. John Cage's compositions – in which chance is introduced as a major constituent of composing – are prominent examples for new compositional experiments. By the mid-1960s, many classical composers would have disagreed with Maurice Ravel's statement that musicians were "the composer's slaves" (qtd. Stegemann 1996: 54) and should exercise precisely what the composer demanded; rather, they would have agreed with Pierre Boulez that total organization in music was an illusory goal.

To some extent, Charles Mingus was influenced by the trend toward experimentation by avant-garde composers of classical music. He was similarly fascinated by the new experiments in literature and painting; he read the literature of the beat generation and befriended and performed with Allen Ginsberg (cf. Santoro 2001: 271). His innovations as a performative composer have to be seen against the background of the shifts in concurrent art movements towards spontaneity and immediacy. Similar to Jack Kerouac, who was dissatisfied with the limitations of language and tried to overcome them in his novels, Mingus attempted to transcend the boundaries of the composer and of musical forms in his art to create additional room for individual expression.

The importance of the idea of self-expression during the 1950s can hardly be overestimated. As Martin Halliwell remarks, "one of the strongest themes of the decade was that of authenticity, the difficulty of preserving genuine experience in the face of commercial and ideological pressures" (2007: 10). In these post-WWII years of increasingly subtle marketing strategies, subliminal advertising, and large-scale mass production, the pursuit of authenticity represented a protest against the synchronization of experience and the blind acceptance of a technocratic society. The image of the so-called phoney, popularized in J. D. Salinger's *Catcher in the Rye* (1951), pervades 1950s literature as authenticity's antidote, as the image of those who conform to the mandates of America's mass cultural market. Mingus's concept of performative composing has to be seen in the context of this pursuit of authenticity. It was a means to increase the space for self-expression, to make room for the possibility of 'authentic' expression. This belief in the possibility of authentic expression distinguishes Mingus's concept of music from those of many other experimental composers during the 1950s. One of the most striking differences between Mingus's innovations and those of John Cage and the Black Mountain school, for instance, is Mingus's emphasis on individuality. Whereas Cage replaced the determinacy of compositions with chance, thereby creating chance-controlled music, Mingus created new room to be filled with spontaneously and cooperatively developed ideas. These ideas were regarded as the musicians' spontaneous self-expression.

The writers of the beat generation were inspired by bebop, which they regarded as essentially African American, as "the language from America's inevitable Africa" (Kerouac 2007: 556). The importance of individuality and collaboration in Mingus's performative compositions must therefore also be viewed against the background of African-American culture and the atmosphere of impending change during the Civil Rights Movement. In the 1940s and early 1950s, bebop musicians such as Charlie Parker and Dizzy Gillespie had extensively exercised the idea of musical self-expression, evident in Parker's famous aphorism, "If you don't live it, it won't come out of your horn" (qtd. Santoro 2001: 78). In the early 1950s, Mingus performed with bebop musicians and adopted their style and maxim that the expression of individuality was one of the most important aspects of jazz. However, for Mingus, musical collaboration was similarly important. This shift of emphasis from individualism to collaboration and solidarity parallels the Civil Rights Movement with its emphasis on equal rights and the democratization of US society.

Moreover, there are analogies between African-American literature of the 1950s and Mingus's innovations. As Bernard W. Bell points out, African-American literature of the 1950s is marked by "a rediscovery and revitalization of myth, legend, and ritual as appropriate sign systems for expressing the double consciousness, socialized ambivalence, and double vision of the post-WW II experiences of African Americans" (2004: 125). Rather than succumbing to the mandates of European-American-controlled mass culture, many African-American artists identified with and stressed their African-American cultural heritage. Rejecting a clearly European-American cultural practice, such as the use of music scores, and embracing an African-American cultural code, such as the oral method of communication, signified resistance against the dominant culture. The transmission of information via the oral method was of course limited, as it increased the difficulty of conveying fixed musical ideas. This disorderly way of composing was part of Mingus's countercultural concept of music, however. From his studies of child and adult games, Brian Sutton-Smith concluded that through being "disorderly" humans have to learn "the possibility of alternate orders" (qtd. Carlson 2004: 19). The performances of the Jazz Workshop can thus be decoded as liminal activities – as anti-structure that is countercultural or, according to Sutton-Smith, "a source of new culture" (qtd. ibid.).

The countercultural character of Charles Mingus's performative composing also had a political dimension. The equalization of instrumental voices, the increased space for individuals to express themselves, the abundance of collective improvisation – all these elements resemble a societal process that calls for a fulfillment of democratic promises. "Folk Forms, No. 1" can be interpreted as a democratic utopia in which the American constitutional promise that all people are equally valuable is fulfilled. To some extent, the ideal state that the

Civil Rights Movement and Martin Luther King, Jr. promoted and pursued in the late 1950s and early 1960s is reflected in Charles Mingus's music. In this context, the fact that composing became a staged process is particularly important: by staging composition, Mingus created a space in which musicians could show an audience that they were creators and innovators rather than mere imitators. Almost all of the musicians in Mingus's Workshop considered themselves African Americans. Demonstrating that African-American jazz musicians could do more than just plagiarize – that they were engaging in a creative process – was part of the Jazz Workshop's political agenda. The academic discovery of performative composing thus entails a necessary reconsideration of the impact jazz musicians and their music had on the Civil Rights Movement. Whereas Mingus's political activism is self-evident in his lyrics to songs like "Fables of Faubus", where he criticizes and mocks racist governor Orval Faubus and other politicians for denying African- American children access to an all-white American high school, an investigation of performative composing illuminates the political dimensions of Mingus's instrumental music.

Mingus's performative composing can be seen as a result of both the composer's interest in avant-garde art and beat literature of the 1950s, and his participation in an African-American cultural and political movement that saw an increasing interest of African Americans in their cultural legacy. These circumstances, Mingus's attitudes, and his outstanding talent as a musician and composer led to a new performative approach to composing. Instead of trying to convey via paper a complex composition whose meaning would ultimately have to get lost (as musicians would have to play music which in its solidity contradicted his idea that creativity was immediate and subject to continuous change), Mingus decided that it would be advantageous to convey compositions orally, and to engage the performers in a staged compositional process. This would allow the musicians to express themselves, and it would accord with his idea that things change permanently and that music thus has to keep on changing if it wants to portray reality and truth as Mingus defined them. By making the composition part of the performance he thus blurred the distinction between composition and performance.

> Each jazz musician when he takes a horn in his hand [...], each soloist, that is, when he begins to *ad lib* on a given composition with a title and improvise a new creative melody, this man is taking the place of a composer. He is saying, 'Listen,

I am going to give you a new complete idea with a new set of chord changes. I am going to give you a new melodic conception on a tune you are familiar with. I am a composer.' That's what he is saying. (Mingus 1991: 97)

References

Bell, Bernard W. (2004). *The Contemporary African American Novel: Its Folk Roots and Modern Literary Branches*. Amherst, MA: University of Massachusetts Press.
Carlson, Marvin (2004). *Performance: A Critical Introduction*. New York, NY: Routledge.
Ellison, Ralph (1952/2001). *Invisible Man*. London: Penguin Books.
Halliwell, Martin (2007). *American Culture in the 1950s*. Edinburgh: Edinburgh UP.
Hentoff, Nat (1960). "Original Liner Notes". *Charles Mingus Presents Charles Mingus*. Candid. CCD 79005.
Hersch, Charles (1996). "'Let Freedom Ring!': Free Jazz and African American Politics". *Cultural Critique* 32: 97–123.
Jenkins, Todd (2006). *I Know What I Know: The Music of Charles Mingus*. Westport, CT: Praeger.
Kerouac, Jack (1959/2007). "The Beginning of Bop". Ann Charters, ed. *The Portable Jack Kerouac*. New York, NY: Penguin Books. 555–559.
Mingus, Charles (1956). "Original Liner Notes". *Pithecanthropus Erectus*. Atlantic. SD-8809-2.
— (1991). *More Than a Fakebook*. New York, NY: Jazz Workshop.
Petermann, Emily (forthcoming). "The Musical Novel: Imitating Musical Structure in Contemporary Fiction". Unpublished doctoral dissertation. University of Konstanz.
Priestley, Brian (1983). *Mingus: A Critical Biography*. New York, NY: Da Capo Press.
— (1998). "Liner Notes". *Mingus Ah Um / Re-Release*. CD. Columbia. 01-065145-10.
Rice, Alan J. (2000). "'It Don't Mean a Thing If It Ain't Got That Swing': Jazz's Many Uses for Toni Morrison". Saadi A. Simawe, ed. *Black Orpheus: Music in African American Fiction from the Harlem Renaissance to Toni Morrison*. New York, NY: Garland: 153–180.

Salinger, J. D. (1951/1973). *Catcher in the Rye*. London: Penguin Books.
Santoro, Gene (2001). *Myself When I Am Real*. London: OUP.
Saul, Scott (2003). *Freedom Is, Freedom Ain't: Jazz and the Making of the Sixties*. Cambridge, MA: Harvard UP.
Stegemann, Michael (1996). *Maurice Ravel*. Berlin: Rowohlt.
Toynbee, Jason (2006). "Making Up and Showing Off: What Musicians Do". Andy Bennett, ed. *The Popular Music Studies Reader*. New York, NY: Routledge. 72–77.
Washington, Salim (2004). "All the Things You Could Be by Now: Charles Mingus Presents Charles Mingus and the Limits of Avant-Garde Jazz". Robert G. O'Meally, ed. *Uptown Conversation: The New Jazz Studies*. New York, NY: Columbia UP. 27–49.

Discography

Mingus, Charles (1963/1986). *Mingus at Antibes*. Atlantic. 90532-2.
— (1981). *Pithecanthropus Erectus*. Atlantic. 8809-2.
— (1989). *Charles Mingus Presents Charles Mingus*. Candid. CCD 79005.
— (1998). *Mingus Ah Um*. Columbia. CK65512.

Wittgenstein and Schoenberg on Performativity of Music as Method for Philosophy

Katrin Eggers, Hannover

This paper focuses on performativity as a 'therapy' for philosophical thinking as it is developed in Ludwig Wittgenstein's later writings. Wittgenstein develops this 'therapy' by distrusting any method at all. I compare his attacks on philosophical systems with critical remarks by Arnold Schoenberg on the same matter. This paper deals with their criticism and sketches out how both of them agree in special reservations regarding philosophy coming to conclusions about art, especially about music. It seemed to be clear for both the philosopher and for the composer alike that new approaches had to be found for what could be truly called a 'philosophy of music'. From that Wittgenstein developed a 'musical way' of dealing with this matter, which this paper in its final section is engaged with.

"My style is like bad musical composition." (CV: 45e)[1]

Ludwig Wittgenstein and Arnold Schoenberg most likely never met. It is also not established that they ever read each other's writings. However, one cannot rule out the possibility as both have strikingly similar philosophical ideas on music (see Eggers 2011 and Wright 2007), such as their thoughts on methodological questions dealing with music, which led them to a specific understanding of performativity.

In his search for "aesthetic meaning", Peter Faltin claimed that doubtlessly the "most severe problem" in this issue would be a

> problem of method. [...] Because all mysteries, prompted by the phenomenon of aesthetic meaning, are not so much a problem of the ontology of meaning, but in fact a problem regarding a proper method, to gain proper control over a phenomenon that eludes itself from semantic language so that it becomes part of scholarly discourse.[2]

---

[1] Abbreviations in this text refer to the works of Wittgenstein, see "References" below.

[2] "Das zweifellos schwierigste Problem bei der Untersuchung der ästhetischen Bedeutung ist ein methodisches Problem. [...] Denn all die Rätsel, die das Phänomen ästhetischer Bedeutung aufwirft, sind nicht sosehr ein Problem der Ontologie von

Indeed it was Wittgenstein's aim to find a methodological answer to what he repeatedly called a complex net of language games (cf. PI: § 66), especially concerning music. Yet, in contradiction to Faltin, it was not Wittgenstein's intention to make musical phenomena a matter of scholarly debate. Instead he chose a completely different approach, one musical in itself. With some side glances to Schoenberg, I am going to sketch this specific Wittgensteinian performative method in musical philosophy.

Nowhere in the entire work of Wittgenstein does one find a passage that explicitly engages with methodology (cf. Schulte 1990: 31–42). Instead, there are a couple of questions dealing with method(s) that are widely spread throughout his later works. From this perspective it seems all the more astonishing that Wittgenstein himself considered his method (of all things) to be his most important contribution in philosophy:

> He [Wittgenstein] went on to say that, though philosophy had now been 'reduced to a matter of skill', yet this skill, like other skills, is very difficult to acquire. One difficulty was that it required a 'sort of thinking' to which we are not accustomed and to which we have not been trained – a sort of thinking very different from what is required in the sciences. And he said the required skill could not be acquired merely by hearing lectures: discussion was essential. As regards his own work, he said it did not matter whether his results were true or not: what mattered was that 'a method had been found'. (Moore 1955: 26)

In other words: philosophical problems can only be solved with a special ability, namely by learning a technique. And this particular technique, or way of thinking, cannot be learned through the usual normative or, respectively, deductive operations, which are commonly taught in philosophy classes. Instead they are trained and improved in continuing engagement and conversation with the surrounding world. This 'method', as Wittgenstein admits, differs categorically from the usual scientific methods.

If we take seriously Wittgenstein's claim that 'a method had been found' (see above), this method is indeed completely different from what is usually conceived of being a 'method'. This paradoxical issue results from the fact that Wittgenstein himself shows his method in his later writings without discussing it. In his later works he attempts to

---

Bedeutung als vielmehr ein Problem der geeigneten Methode, ein Phänomen, das sich der Wortsprache entzieht, so in den Griff zu bekommen, daß es wissenschaftlich diskutierbar wird." (Faltin 1985: 112f.; unless otherwise stated, translations are mine.)

write a text without operative layers, by using the viability of language to illuminate its use in itself (cf. Hiltmann 1998: 15). This is a complex performative practice, which becomes apparent only if the reader has already been acquainted with it. Wittgenstein developed an "operational aspect" against the backdrop of a "thematic layer" of his texts (ibid.). This operational aspect – metaphorically speaking – constitutes the invisible texture of a fabric which at the same time forms the texture of a surface layer, while the thematic layer determines design and colour. In this radical act Wittgenstein performs what he simultaneously demands: the continuing restlessness which works subliminally throughout every part of the text becomes a semantic impact in itself and as such performs being a method (see Schobinger 1992).

In a way this is not an entirely new way of writing. There are some outstanding texts in poetological discourse which are especially valued for their potential of producing meaning in an almost 'musical' way. In Wittgenstein's younger days, for example, it was the so-called Chandos-Brief (1902) by Hugo von Hofmannsthal, where a young poet describes his loss of language, which is being visibly executed in the text. However, this way of writing was strictly reserved for poetic texts. Wittgenstein's claim that this poetic performativity is the 'new method' for philosophy implies an unsurpassable break-up with philosophical traditions, especially with the German tradition. This is the non-trivial background for Wittgenstein's famous remark: "I believe I summed up where I stand in relation to philosophy when I said: really one should write philosophy only as one writes a poem." (CV: 28e)

But this leaves us with a big problem: how can this way of thinking – which is at best 'only composed' – lead at all to insights or knowledge?

For Wittgenstein this complete change in thinking and writing is the only acceptable consequence of his philosophical ideas. According to him, 'philosophical problems' emerge through our way of using words. Their linguistic structures are "like a pair of glasses on our nose, through which we see whatever we look at" (PI: §103). The change of our use of language does not solve these problems. The problems disappear if one changes one's manner of expression. If Wittgenstein therefore focusses on language use as an object on the one hand and uses language as an instrument of research on the other hand,

> he lets the problems disappear that arise within his investigations of using language, by changing his own speech. [...] The change of language discloses

differences within language itself and makes it possible to reflect on it without being forced to take a so-called metaperspective.[3]

As in other instances where Wittgenstein discusses complex thoughts, it is typical for him to do so by using simple pictures. Originally used to explain his theory on 'seeing aspects', this figure can also be used to show the implied interaction between the operative structure and the thematic layer of a text, therefore performing and embodying ambiguous thought through a picture puzzle ('Vexierbild').

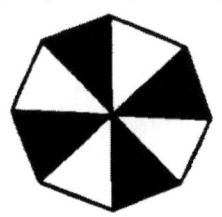

Illustration 1: The double cross.

Wittgenstein called this picture puzzle a "double cross", "as a white cross on a black ground and as a black cross on a white ground" (PI xi: 207e). The two crosses can be perceived as figures or as a surface on which the black respectively white cross can be seen. This display of looking at two different aspects in one picture is related to the technique of seeing the same material in different ways.

Though not specifically described as such, this picture illustrates the relationship between language and forms of life ("Lebensform", as Wittgenstein calls it; PI: §23). The latter is the implied setting for the former and therefore cannot be entirely translated into language. Let's have a look at the puzzle: if the white and black areas could be seen as figures simultaneously, the whole picture would be impossible because it lacks a background, an operational basis for each figure. Wittgenstein is especially interested in this implied background or surface structure of language. He is interested in the parts of utterings that operate clearly, yet unintentionally, by the speaker, which in his view actually creates meaning. As early as in 1931, Wittgenstein

---

[3] "[...] kann er die Probleme, die sich in der Untersuchung des Sprachgebrauchs stellen dadurch zum Verschwinden bringen, daß er seinen eigenen Sprachgebrauch ändert [...]. Die Änderung des Sprachgebrauchs eröffnet im Sprachgebrauch selbst Differenzen, in denen die Reflexion auf den Sprachgebrauch möglich ist, ohne dafür eine sogenannte Metaebene einnehmen zu müssen." (Hiltmann 1998: 19)

claimed this thought to be essential: "The inexpressible (what I find enigmatic & cannot express) perhaps provides the background, against which whatever I was able to express acquires meaning." (CV: 23e)

For Wittgenstein, this ever present but usually unperceived surface structure molds into the backdrop, against which music can enfold meaning in the first place:

> I say to myself: "What is this? What does this phrase say? Just what does it express?" – I feel as if there must still be a much clearer understanding of it than the one I have. And this understanding would be reached by saying a great deal about the surrounding of the phrase. As if one where trying to understand an expressive gesture in a ceremony. And in order to explain it I should need, as it were, to analyse the ceremony. E. g., to alter it and show what influence that would have on the role of that gesture.[4]
>
> The question is really: are these notes not the best expression for what is expressed here? Presumably. But that does not mean that they aren't to be explained by working on their surrounding.[5]

This 'working on their surrounding' or 'alteration of a ceremony' are only two examples for the perception of the surface structure or operational basis of a musical phrase, melody or parameter. Hearing is always 'hearing as (if)': if a piece of music is heard as music, the listener is usually not aware of the specific background of his impression, but without these impressions the sounds would appear to be just noise. As the white cross in the figure is only visible if one does not focus on the black cross, it is not possible to perceive all layers of expression in a musical phrase simultaneously. After some practise in listening to music and after one has learned enough about music in general – in other words, listening to music as an "insider", as Wittgenstein calls it (VÄ: I §19) – it is possible to hear a special musical phrase as an expression of an era or in the context of its history of reception or one can concentrate on its specific interpreta-

---

[4] "Ich sage mir: 'Was ist das? Was sagt nur diese Phrase? Was drückt sie nur aus?' – Es ist mir, als müßte es noch ein viel klareres Verstehen von ihr geben, als das, was ich habe. Und dieses Verstehen würde dadurch erreicht, daß man eine Menge über die Umgebung der Phrase sagt. So als wollte man eine ausdrucksvolle Geste in einer Zeremonie verstehen. Und zur Erklärung müßte ich die Zeremonie gleichsam analysieren. Z. B. sie abändern und zeigen, wie das die Rolle jener Geste beeinflussen würde." (RPP: § 34)

[5] "Die Frage ist eigentlich: Sind diese Töne nicht der *beste* Ausdruck für das, was hier ausgedrückt ist? Wohl. Aber das heißt nicht, daß sie nicht durch ein Bearbeiten ihrer Umgebung zu erklären sind." (RPP: § 36)

tion. But like with the picture puzzle, it is impossible to comprehend all of this simultaneously.

In most cases this is not a problem at all. But if the recipient focusses on the operational basis of a text or a piece of music, the materiality of this layer itself has to be questioned. It consists of an unperceivable abundance of factors and informations, and it is the structure of a theory of interpretation, the actual musicological categories, which result in a semantic hierachy. This consists of historical targets in theories, which are written down in textbooks, treatises or aesthetic writings. But it also contains social implications, as reported for example in letters, diaries or travel books. All of these implications indicate specific changes in the 'languages game' that surrounds a piece of music at a specific point in history, and they are attached to its surface structure, whether the listener is aware of them or not. Therefore it is not enough to work out the changes of conceptualization, but it is equally important to know that the understanding of music as such underlies constant change. Without doubt it is impossible to consider each and every factor important for an operational basis of just one piece of music. However effective the best theory of understanding and interpretation seems to be, we are always, as Wittgenstein puts it, back to the starting point: "I don't know my way about" (PI: §123), and we can never be familiar with it. This is because we can never adopt a starting point or become a firm object of reflection because "[u]nderstanding is essentially an historically effected event" (Gadamer 1972/2006: 299). As an observer one is oneself part of the hermeneutic process. One can never overcome language via language, the operational basis of one's speech is nothing one can handle autonomously.

Seeing this invariably subjective constitution, Wittgenstein tries a new perspective on the problem of understanding:

> A main source of our failure to understand is that we do not *command a clear view* of the use of our words. – Our grammar is lacking in this sort of perspicuity. A perspicuous representation produces just that understanding which consists in 'seeing connexions'. Hence the importance of finding and inventing *intermediate cases*. The concept of a perspicuous representation is of fundamental significance for us. It earmarks the form of account we give, the way we look at things. (Is this a 'Weltanschauung'?) (PI: §122)

The term 'Weltanschauung' indicates that Wittgenstein does not trust the "perspicuous representation" to solve the problem of 'not knowing one's way about' (see above). On the contrary: every firm theory automatically involves the danger of creating what seem to be 'facts' of musical meaning, which actually result from the current 'Weltanschauung'. For Wittgenstein the longing for "perspicuous representation" is nothing else than the convenience of thinking. The more inapprehensible and 'mysterious' a phenomenon becomes, which is undoubtedly the case with musical meaning, the more well-arranged we would like its components to be presented.

Interestingly, Wittgenstein is not the only thinker of his time struggling with the comfort of his fellow men in their 'Weltanschauung'. Arnold Schoenberg accuses his time of searching for answers – he does not accuse them of looking for wrong answers, but he accuses them of searching for answers in a misleading way –, and he does so far more vigorously than Wittgenstein. 1911 Schoenberg writes in the preface to his *Theory of Harmony*:

> We solve problems to remove an unpleasantness. But, *how* do we solve them? And what presumption, even to think we have really solved them! Here we can see most distinctly what the prerequisite of comfort is: superficiality. It is thus easy to have a 'Weltanschauung', a 'philosophy', if one contemplates only what is pleasant and gives no heed to the rest. The rest – which is just what matters most. In the light of the 'rest' these philosophies may very well seem made to order for those who hold to them, whereas, in that light, the tenets which constitute these philosophies are seen to spring above all from the attempt at self-vindication. [...] The thinker, who keeps on searching, does the opposite. He shows that there are problems and that they are unsolved. [...] Comfort as a philosophy of life! The last possible commotion, nothing shocking. Those who so love comfort will never seek where there is not definitely something to find. (1911/1978: 2)

Both, Schoenberg and Wittgenstein, demand this pattern to be broken. But how? Schoenberg is very clear about this: a method will lead to congealment of thought. Only constant movement can be productive in this case, as Schoenberg continues:

> [A]n Idea lurks behind this method. Namely, that movement alone can succeed where deliberation fails. Is it not the same with the learner? What does the teacher accomplish through methodology? At most, activity. If everything goes well! But things can also go badly, and than what he accomplishes is lethargy. Yet lethargy produces nothing. Only activity, movement is productive. Then why not start moving right away? But comfort!? Comfort avoids movement; it therefore does not take up the search. (Ibid: 2f.)

Our scientific culture tends to ever greater abstraction, leading to a system of terms and definitions, dicta, paradigms and axioms that claim to be as enduring as possible. The common discursive way of thinking leads away from experience to more general phenomena, one thing stands for the general principle. It is Wittgenstein's aim, by contrast, to prove that there is no anchor in thinking due to the endless variety of language. There are only numerous situations which Wittgenstein wants to expose:

> It is all one to me whether the typical western scientist understands or appreciates my work since in any case he does not understand the spirit in which I write. Our civilization is characterized by the word progress. Typically it constructs. Its activity is to construct a more and more complicated structure. [...] I am not interested in erecting a building but in having the foundations of possible buildings transparent before me. So I am aiming at something different than are the scientists & my thoughts move differently than do theirs. (CV: 9e)

This attitude is especially important in dealing with art: on the one hand, science tends to a higher degree of generalization. On the other hand, a composer is doing just the opposite: he creates a singular position within an endless variety of choices, a subjective objectivation. In other words, a composer creates "the foundations of possible buildings", whereas scientific consideration tends to establish a closed system. Wittgenstein had a problem with this and asked: how can global and abstract terms ever explain the magnitude of unsystematic singularities in music? Schoenberg, too, keeps asking himself the same question:

> Art is different from science. While science requires systematically *all* characteristic cases, art is satisfied with a lesser number of interesting ones: as many as fantasy demands in order to produce for itself an image of the whole, in order to dream about it. For this reason even development should never be understood here to mean all cases must come into being, but rather just a few, the interesting ones – 'More of this another time', the artist can say – 'for today enough of it'. (1995: 93)

Like Wittgenstein, Schoenberg deeply mistrusts the scientific desire for generalization and methods leading to established doctrines. In line with Wittgenstein, he states programmatically:

> These Systems! Elsewhere I will show how they have really never been just what they still could be: namely, systems of presentation (*Darstellung*). Methods by which a body of material is coherently organized and lucidly classified, methods derived from principles which will assure an unbroken logic. I will show how quickly this system fails, how soon one has to break into it to patch up its holes with a second system (which is still no system), in order even halfway to accomodate the most familiar facts. It should be quite different! A real system should have, above all, principles that embrace all the facts. Ideally, just as many facts as there actually are, no more, no less. Such principles are natural laws. And only such principles, which are not qualified by exceptions, would have the right to be regarded as generally valid. Such principles would share with natural laws this

characteristic of unconditional validity. The laws of art, however, consist mainly of exceptions! (1911/1978: 10)

The affinity of both approaches, especially towards their criticism of what both call 'systems', can easily be detected if one looks at their remarks, taking turns. For example, Wittgenstein declares in his *Philosophy of Psychology*:

> Above all, someone attempting the description lacks any system. The systems that occur to him are inadequate, and he seems suddenly to find himself in a wilderness instead of in the well-laid-out garden that he knew so well. Rules will occur to him, no doubt, but the reality shows nothing but exceptions.[6]

> And the rules of the foreground make it impossible for us to recognize the rules in the background. For when we keep the background together with the foreground, we see only jarring exceptions, in other words *irregularity*.[7]

If irregulaties and exceptions are the basis, there can only be one consequence, as Schoenberg puts it:

> Nor have I been able to discover such principles, either; and I believe they will not be discovered very soon. [...] Efforts to discover laws of art can then, at best, produce results something like those of a good comparison: that is, they can influence the way in which the sense organ of the subject, the observer, orients itself to the attributes of the object observed. In making a comparison we bring closer what is too distant, thereby enlarging details, and remove to some distance what is too close, thereby gaining perspective. No greater worth than something of this sort can, at present, be ascribed to laws of art. Yet that is already quite a lot. [...] For, once again, the laws of nature admit no exceptions, whereas theories of art consist mainly of exceptions. (1911/1978: 11)

Instead of looking at something from a great distance and losing important details, we are in fact looking for something else, as Wittgenstein constantly emphasizes: we are looking for 'good comparisons' and images, enlightening aspects of this very object or this very music we are momentarily in touch with. From the usual bird's eye view of positivistic science, we are, as Wittgenstein states, "like savages, primitive people, who hear the expression of civilized men,

---

[6] "Vor allem fehlt dem, der die Beschreibung versucht, nun jedes System. Die Systeme, die ihm in den Sinn kommen, sind unzureichend; und er scheint plötzlich sich in einer Wildnis zu befinden, statt in dem wohlangelegten Garten, den er so gut kannte. Es kommen ihm wohl Regeln in den Sinn, aber die Wirklichkeit zeigt nichts als Ausnahmen." (RPP I: §557)

[7] "Und die Regeln des Vordergrunds machen es uns unmöglich, die Regeln im Hintergrund zu erkennen. Denn, wenn wir ihn mit dem Vordergrund zusammenhalten, sehen wir nur widerliche Ausnahmen, also *Unregelmäßigkeit*." (RPP I.: §558)

put a false interpretation on them, and then draw the queerest conclusions from it" (PI: §194). This is exactly what Schoenberg criticizes:

> If art theory could be content with that, if it could be satisfied with the rewards afforded by honest searching, then one could not object to it. But it is more ambitious. It is not content to be merely the attempt to find laws; it professes to have found *the eternal* laws. It observes a number of phenomena, classifies them according to some common characteristics, and then derives laws from them. That is of course correct procedure, because unfortunately there is hardly any other way. But now begins the error. For it is falsely concluded that these laws, since apparently correct with regard to the phenomena previously observed, must then surely hold for all future phenomena as well. And, what is most disastrous of all, it is then the belief that a *yardstick* has been found by which to measure artistic worth, even that of future works. (1911/1978: 8)

Again, for Wittgenstein there can only be one consequence deriving from this dilemma:

> The difficulty here is not to dig down to the bottom, but to identify the bottom before our eyes as the bottom. For this bottom consistently pretends to be of greater depth, and when we try to reach this depth, we always find ourselves back in our initial position.[8]

According to Wittgenstein, talking of 'solutions' in music, they have to be completely different from those that are derived at in discursive sciences. They rather resemble a result of calculation, which cannot be reasonably scrutinized without questioning the whole architecture of the mathematical system:

> Take a theme like Haydns Choral of S. Anthony, take that part of one of Brahms's variations that corresponds to the first part of the theme and set the task to construct the second part of the variation in the style of its first part. This is a problem in the fashion of mathematical problems. Once the solution is found, like Brahms has it, there remains no doubt; – this is the solution.[9]

Surely, a specific variation is just one of many possibilities a composer could think of. But 'one of many possibilities' is a solution

---

[8] "Das Schwere ist hier, nicht bis auf den Grund zu graben, sondern den Grund, der vor uns liegt, als Grund zu erkennen. Denn der Grund spiegelt uns immer wieder eine größere Tiefe vor, und wenn wir diese zu erreichen suchen, finden wir uns immer wieder auf dem alten Niveau." (BGM: VI, Nr. 31)

[9] "Nimm ein Thema wie das Haydnsche (Choral St. Antons), nimm den Teil einer der Brahmsschen Variationen, der dem ersten Teil des Themas entspricht, und stell die Aufgabe, den zweiten Teil der Variation im Stil ihres ersten Teils zu konstruieren. Das ist ein Problem von der Art der mathematischen Probleme. Ist die Lösung gefunden, etwa wie Brahms sie gibt, so zweifelt man nicht; – dies ist die Lösung." (BGM: VII, Nr. 11)

where the basis, as mentioned above, is reached. Trying to achieve a deeper level of justification, following Wittgenstein, means to follow a wrong approach:

> Our mistake is to look for an explanation where we ought to look at what happens as a 'proto-phenomenon'. That is, where we ought to have said: this language-game is played. (PI: §654)

A method dealing with this kind of solution, namely, works of art, can never lead to a system, as Wittgenstein and Schoenberg claim (see above). Wittgenstein insists on taking precautions:

> You must again not let yourself be deceived by the generic term. Don't take comparability, but rather incomparability, as a matter of course. (CV: 84e)

Wittgenstein can only escape the danger of solid methods of whatever kind by exposing himself to the flow of language itself. Thus, his philosophical writings are consequently drawn to poetry:

> When I don't want to teach a more accurate way of thinking, but a new movement of thought, my purpose is an "Umwertung von Werten" (reevaluation of values) and I come to think of Nietzsche, also because I take the view that a philosopher should be a poet.[10]

Like a poet, a composer never provides a method exceeding his own works of art. Exactly in this sense, Wittgenstein refuses to provide the reader with clearly arranged thoughts, which entail the danger of alluring normativity.

> Instead, we now demonstrate a method, by examples; and the series of examples can be broken off. – Problems are solved (difficulties eliminated), not a *single* problem. (PI: §133; emphasis in the original)

In the end, all philosophical problems result from the simple fact that we "do not *command a clear view* of the use of our words" (ibid.: §122; emphasis in the original). We are simply misled by our "grammatical disorientation" (ibid.: §123). As an author, Wittgenstein himself reacts to this disorientation with a "a number of sketches of landscape" (ibid.: Preface), to cast an ever different light on what he called the "deep structure of grammar" ('Tiefengrammatik'; PI I: §446).

So instead of using a word without reflection, we must be aware that we are not, and can never be, fully familiar with its deep struc-

---

[10] "Wenn ich nicht ein richtigeres Denken, sondern eine neue Gedankenbewegung lehren will, so ist mein Zweck eine 'Umwertung von Werten' und ich komme auf Nietzsche, sowie auch dadurch, daß meiner Ansicht nach der Philosoph ein Dichter sein sollte." (BEE: MS 120 [23/03/1938]: 145)

tures, which lead us to wrong conclusions (for instance, interpret the term 'understanding' "as the expression of a queer *process*"; ibid.: §196; emphasis in the original), and coming from this misunderstanding to the construction of 'philosophical problems', Wittgenstein takes a radical step:

> It was true to say that our considerations could not be scientific ones. [...] And we may not advance any kind of theory. There must not be anything hypothetical in our considerations. We must do away with all *explanation,* and description alone must take its place. And this description gets its light, that is to say its purpose, from the philosophical problems. These are, of course, not empirical problems; they are solved, rather, by looking into the workings of our language, and that in such a way as to make us recognize those workings: *in despite of* an urge to misunderstand them. The problems are solved, not by giving new information, but by arranging what we have always known. Philosophy is a battle against the bewitchment of our intelligence by means of language. (PI: §109; emphases in the original)

Likewise Schoenberg:

> It is indeed our duty to reflect over and over again upon the mysterious origins of the powers of art (*Kunstwirkungen*). And again and again to begin at the beginning; again and again to examine anew for ourselves and attempt to organize anew for ourselves. Regarding nothing as given but the phenomena. (1911/1978: 8)

This last remark, "Regarding nothing as given but the phenomena", is a hint that leads to Wittgenstein's research into music: like the Brahms variation mentioned above, we can describe aspects of a special work, or find "good comparisons", according to Schoenberg (ibid.: 11). But we are not able, for example, to explain why a specific musical solution pleases us when another does not:

> Think, for example, of certain involuntary interpretations that we give to one or another passage in a piece of music. We say: this interpretation forces itself on us. [...] And the interpretation can be explained by purely musical relationships. – Very well, but our purpose is, not to explain but to describe.[11]

Wittgenstein purposely transgresses the common path of linear argumentation. Schoenberg's attempts, on the other hand, lead towards a textbook which is full of exceptions to enable his pupils to learn and to develop their own creativity. Wittgenstein was not a teacher in the

---

[11] "Denk z. B. an gewisse unwillkürliche Deutungen, die wir der einen oder anderen Stelle eines Musikstücks geben. Wir sagen: diese Deutung drängt sich uns auf. [...] Und die Deutung kann aus gewissen rein musikalischen Beziehungen erklärt werden. – Wohl, aber wir wollen ja nicht erklären, sondern beschreiben." (RPP I: §22)

sense Schoenberg was. He did not have to guide pupils carefully into creating actual works. And, as is well-known, wherever possible he withdrew from his teaching duties. This is why it was possible for Wittgenstein to develop a far more radical denial of any method than Schoenberg ever could:

> It is not our aim to refine or complete the system of rules for the use of our words in unheard-of ways. [...] There is not *a* philosophical method, though there are indeed methods, like different therapies. (PI: §133; emphasis in the original)

This is where Wittgenstein and Schoenberg differ. Schoenberg's attempts, despite his disrespect for any system, had to lead into some kind of system at last: namely his own teaching system – and his success as a teacher speaks for itself. In the end, he actually had clear principles and ideas on composition, and had pupils and colleagues who were influenced by his ideas. Therefore he is looking forward to 'gaining perspective', as cited above, and herein lies the difference between Wittgenstein and Schoenberg: for Schoenberg, 'good comparisons' lead to a 'perspective'. For Wittgenstein, 'good comparisons' lead to a multiperspective approach, in methods instead of 'a method', or as claimed in the quote above, lead to "different therapies". Wittgenstein makes his denial of every system clear not only in the context of his philosophy, but also in the very form of his writings. His Tractatus "is therefore not a text-book" (TLP: 27), and with his *Philosophical Investigations* he did not want "to spare other people the trouble of thinking. But, if possible, to stimulate someone to thoughts of his own." (PI: Preface) This can only be done by becoming completely engaged with his anti-systematic way of thinking, by following every meander and variation of Wittgenstein's way of looking at things. And the reader must be prepared not to look for solutions or answers. Wittgenstein does not want to create a new school of thought, he wants to change the common ways of thinking. As cited above, he wants to achieve an 'Umwertung der Werte' and claims 'propaganda for a style of thinking as opposed to another'[12]. And he explains how this change of style could look like:

> I [Wittgenstein] show that it [the expression] has kinds of uses of which you had not dreamed. In philosophy one feels *forced* to look at a concept in a certain way. What I do is to suggest, or even invent, other ways of looking at it. I suggest possibilities of which you had not previously thought. You thought that there was

---

[12] "Propaganda für einen Stil des Denkens im Unterschied zu einem anderen" (VÄ III: 37).

one possibility, or only two at the most. But I made you think of others. Furthermore, I made you see that it was absurd to expect the concept to conform to those narrow possibilities. Thus your mental cramp is relieved, and you are free to look around the field of use of expression and to describe the different kinds of uses of it. (Qtd. Malcolm 1966: 50)

In order to design one's own language (and one's ability to speak about music) in such a way that hidden aspects are revealed as much as possible, language would have to interpret itself. But language is not a subject, it cannot analyze itself, it is interpreted by speaking subjects. In the end, this makes the interpretation of language subjective. Multiperspective language that would allow more points of view demands more than one speaker. This is why Wittgenstein, ultimately, had to let go of the position of the author in order to come close to this goal. In his later remarks he is no longer talking to a reader – in contrast to his *Tractatus* – but only to himself. Wittgenstein tries out questions, rejects them, brings them up again in countless variations and tries several tentative answers, which lead to new questions, and so on. He never seems to prefer one point of view over another or he reverses an initial point of his thoughts. Thus he creates numerous 'language games' that are only loosely tied together, more like an accumulation than a continuing text, and within these games he tries out new perspectives, like 'I', 'you', 'we', 'one', etc. This culminates in the remark: "Almost the whole time I am writing conversations with myself. Things I say to myself tête-à-tête." (CV: 88e)

In a sense, Wittgenstein acts like a composer: he does not only constantly implement new quasi-musical themes or phrases by varying them or contrasting them against one another or by placing them in entirely new contexts, but he also introduces them within a symphonic setting, like a musical score. His way of multi-perspective speech therefore becomes truly polyphonic. The distinct parts of this 'score', their individual 'timbres', act like personae of their own within the thematic process. They make their appearance, fade away, and almost immediately come back later in entirely new connections and environments. Yet, it is specific for this Wittgensteinian 'score' that it does not lead anywhere. It does not interpret itself and does not follow an apparent plan. He just lists what comes to his mind, so that his themes, phrases or parts never become something like a 'developing variation' (cf. Eggers 2011: 229f.).

With this attitude, Wittgenstein leaves his reader almost entirely on his own. Whenever one thinks one might get a firm grip on all the phrases and parts and establish what might be a philosophy of art, the airy, hardly palpable leitmotif falls apart. Wittgenstein never allows his reader to follow him on one of his improvised examples up to the point where hints of a theory appear to the reader. What follows, is asserted by Margolis: 'I have to say, that the report on the 'application' of Wittgensteinian thought to the philosophy of art is, to a large extent, a report on constant failure.'[13] It is therefore very important not to confound this description of what is sometimes called Wittgenstein's 'morphological method' (see Schulte 1990), an implicit thread or background of the operative structure on which the thematic layers are performed, with the preparation of an application or a method[14]. 'The truth is that there *is* no method at all, and wherever we could expect instructions, Wittgenstein obliterates the traces guiding his own design as much as he can.'[15] So we finally have to reject everything that could be called a 'Wittgensteinian aesthetic', everything that exceeds mere inspiration (cf. Margolis 2006: 484). Like in a piece of music, described as a 'solution' above, it is not possible to separate aesthetic concerns from sheer forms of composition (cf. Cavell 2006: 39). As Michael Nedo, the editor of the so-called 'Wiener Ausgabe' of Wittgenstein's works, points out:

> He [Wittgenstein] wrote completely differently from the academic, more like a fugue with repetitions of themes reappearing in changing circumstances. [For Wittgenstein] this is how you understood something, by looking at it again and again, first this way, then that, as you do a musical theme. Philosophers translating him could not understand that, and had to use their own language, which is

---

[13] "Der Bericht über die 'Anwendung' Wittgensteins auf die Philosophie der Kunst ist, wie ich sagen muss, weitgehend der Bericht über ein ständiges Versagen." (Margolis 2006: 473)

[14] In fact, I came in contact with just three 'applications' of Wittgensteinian thoughts to music. Ingolf Max attempts to ascribe complex tonal and polyphonic structures under the term of 'family resemblance' to logical operations (see 2003). Judith Etzion and Susana Weich-Shahak also deal with "Family Resemblances", but with quite a different approach, analyzing sephardic musical traditions (see 1993). Finally there is a deconstructionist attempt by Brian Kane to analyze a piece of Mathias Spahlinger by means of the Wittgensteinian 'seeing aspects' (see 2008).

[15] "Die Wahrheit ist, dass es gar keine Methode *gibt,* und dort, wo wir Anleitung durch eine Lehre fordern könnten, verwischt Wittgenstein die expliziten Spuren seiner Lehren, die seine eigene Darstellung gelenkt haben, sosehr er nur kann." (Margolis 2006: 473; emphasis in the original)

why he has become unreadable. His heirs made the mistake of striking out the repetitions so the changing nature of his writing was lost. (Qtd. Tait 2003: online)

Following this is a completely different kind of aesthetic approach: there is no method at all, but in fact, there is an indoctrination or instruction. A piece of music – necessarily – is no method although it is based on careful methodological work. A piece of music is a singular case of indoctrination through the performed objectivation on the basis of the process of creation – like a language game between composer, performer and recipient. This explains another quote of Wittgenstein:

> People nowadays think, scientists are there to instruct them, poets, musicians etc. to entertain them. *That the latter have something to teach them*; that never occurs to them. (CV: 42e; emphasis in the original)

A piece of music has "*something to teach*". For Wittgenstein the counterpart in language to 'musical instruction' was the aphorism. For it is the aphorism that is able to show that paradoxa, gaps, disruptions and sudden turns of thinking, the wits and intellectual surprises, belong inherently to the articulated thought (cf. Kroß 1993: 10). His way of writing does not follow a deductive or linear scientific mindset, but it is intrinsically performative: it shows what it means rather than talking about it. His 'solutions' in their aphoristic, pointed way, are similar to the 'solutions' Brahms chose for his variations. This is a basic musical principle, as Schoenberg, too, pointed out (see Danuser 1975: 125–144):

> If science provides facts that it orders according to common principles, art produces images in which facts are freely joined to common principles, so that the sense of what is to be stated can be clearly grasped and at once. It thus works like the proverb, which abstracts from many experiences an often meager bit of wisdom but a wisdom whose meaning becomes immediately and unquestionably comprehensible. And the aphorism, too, operates in a similar way, in which usually a certain imbalance – a not-being-brought-into-balance – of contrasting elements, a certain exaggeration of contrasts and a rudimentary presentation of conflict, aims at an excitement that, as with intuitive knowledge, lifts us above the necessity of examining details, or secondary circumstances, and produces the effect of a revelation. (1995: 115)

It was never Wittgenstein's intention to create a method – especially not one for dealing with art. According to his belief, only something that shows something can shed light on another showing structure, he created these very performative structures, language compositions via musical principles. Going on from this, there is a new aspect to be pointed out in the famous paragraph 43 in Wittgenstein's *Philo-*

sophical Investigations, saying, "the meaning of a word is its use in the language": if "Words are also deeds" (PI: §546), this is not only a hint at the generally performative dimension of language but also the Wittgensteinian way of acting through language: without considering the eminently musical aspect of this, Hiltmann concludes: 'The argumentative gesture of the matter in question and its relation to 'thematic' evidence may become traces that can lead to a possible approximation to instrumental layers of the matter. It can be fruitful to read the 'thematic' evidence [...] as a description of the line of thought, i. e., in a way bending the content back to the form.'[16] Whenever Wittgenstein is talking about music or whenever he is talking 'musically' (and he did both a great deal), this serves to enlighten special aspects of a philosophical thought *and* – like in the figure of the double cross – shows the immanent performative structure in the line of thought itself.

References

Cavell, Stanley (2006). "Einführende Bemerkung zur Alltagsästhetik der *Philosophischen Untersuchungen*". *Wittgenstein und die Literatur*. Martin Suhr, trans. John Gibson, Wolfgang Huemer, eds. Frankfurt am Main: Suhrkamp. 33–38.

Danuser, Hermann (1975). *Musikalische Prosa*. Studien zur Musikgeschichte des 19. Jahrhunderts 46. Regensburg: Bosse.

Eggers, Katrin (2011). *Ludwig Wittgenstein als Musikphilosoph*. Reihe Musikphilosophie 2. Freiburg: Alber.

Etzion, Judith, Susana Weich-Shahak (1993). "'Family Resemblances' and Variability in the Sephardic Romancero: A Methodological Approach to Variantal Comparison". *Journal of Music Theory* 37/2: 267–309.

Faltin, Peter (1985). *Bedeutung ästhetischer Zeichen: Musik und Sprache*. Aachener Studien zur Semiotik und Kommunikationsforschung 1. Aachen: Rader.

---

[16] "Der argumentative Gestus eines auszulegenden Gegenstandes und sein Verhältnis zu 'thematischen' Aussagen können Spuren bilden, denen zur Annäherung an instrumentale Schichten dieses Gegenstandes gefolgt werden kann. Es kann fruchtbar sein, eine 'thematische' Aussage [...] als Beschreibung des Denkgestus zu lesen – d. h. den Inhalt gleichsam auf die Form zurückzuwenden." (Hiltmann 1998: 20)

Gadamer, Hans-Georg (1972/2006). *Truth and Method*. Joel Weinsheimer, trans. London: Continuum. (German orig.: *Wahrheit und Methode: Grundzüge einer philosophischen Hermeneutik.* Tübingen: J. C. B. Mohr, 1960; 3rd extended ed.).

Hiltmann, Gabrielle (1998). *Aspekte sehen: Bemerkungen zum methodischen Vorgehen in Wittgensteins Spätwerk.* Epistemata. Würzburger Wissenschaftliche Schriften. Reihe Philosophie 235. Würzburg: Königshausen & Neumann.

Kane, Brian (2008). "Aspect and Ascription in the Music of Mathias Spahlinger". *Contemporary Music Review* 27/6: 595–609.

Kroß, Matthias (1993). *Klarheit als Selbstzweck: Wittgenstein über Philosophie, Religion, Ethik und Gewißheit.* Berlin: Akademie Verlag.

Malcolm, Norman (1966). *Ludwig Wittgenstein: A Memoir*. London et al.: Clarendon Press.

Margolis, Joseph (2006). "Unwahrscheinliche Aussichten für die Anwendung von Wittgensteins 'Methode' auf die Ästhetik und die Philosophie der Kunst". *Wittgenstein und die Literatur.* John Gibson, Wolfgang Huemer, eds. Frankfurt am Main: Suhrkamp. 471–507.

Max, Ingolf (2003). "Zur Familienähnlichkeit von Begriffen und Akkorden". *expressis verbis: Philosophische Betrachtungen. Festschrift für Günter Schenk zum fünfundsechzigsten Geburtstag.* Matthias Kaufmann, Andrej Krause, eds. Halle: Hallescher Verlag. 385–415.

Moore, George Edward (1955)."Wittgenstein's Lectures in 1930–1933". *Mind* 64: 1–27.

Schobinger, Jean-Pierre (1992). "Operationale Aufmerksamkeit in der textimmanenten Auslegung". *Freiburger Zeitschrift für Philosophie und Theologie* 39/1–2: 5–38.

Schoenberg, Arnold (1911/1978). *Theory of Harmony*. Roy E. Carter, trans. Berkeley, CA/Los Angeles, CA: University of California Press. (German orig.: *Harmonielehre*. Vienna: Universal Edition, 1911).

— (1995). *The Musical Idea and the Logic, Technique, and Art of Its Presentation.* Patricia Carpenter, Severine Neff, eds. and trans. New York, NY: Columbia UP. (German orig.: *Der musikalische Gedanke und die Logik, Technik und Kunst seiner Darstellung.* Ms. fragment [1934–1936]).

Schulte, Joachim (1990). "Chor und Gesetz: Zur 'morphologischen Methode' bei Goethe und Wittgenstein". *Chor und Gesetz: Wittgenstein im Kontext.* Joachim Schulte, ed. Frankfurt am Main: Suhrkamp. 11–42.

Tait, Simon (2003: online). "Mind over Music". *The Independent.* 12/11/2003. http://www.independent.co.uk/arts-entertainment/music/features/mind-over-music-735389.html [01/10/2010].

Wittgenstein, Ludwig:

BEE: (2000). *Wittgenstein's Nachlass: The Bergen Electronic Edition.* The Complete Edition on CD-ROM. Oxford: OUP.

BGM: (1984). *Bemerkungen über die Grundlagen der Mathematik.* G. E. M. Anscombe, Rush Rhees, Georg H. von Wright, eds. Frankfurt am Main: Suhrkamp.

CV: (1998). *Culture and Value: A Selection from the Posthumous Remains.* Georg H. von Wright et al., eds. Oxford: Blackwell.

PI: (1953/1998). *Philosophical Investigations.* G. E. M. Anscombe, ed. Oxford: Blackwell.

RPP: (1980). *Remarks on the Philosophy of Psychology.* Vol. I. G. E. M. Anscombe, G. H. von Wright, eds. Oxford: Blackwell.

TLP: (1922/2005). *Tractatus logico-philosophicus.* C. K. Ogden, ed. London: Routledge. (German and English orig.: *Tractatus logico-philosophicus.* London: Kegan Paul, Trench, Trubner & Co.).

VÄ: (2000/2005). *Vorlesungen und Gespräche über Ästhetik, Psychoanalyse und religiösen Glauben.* Ralf Funke, trans. Yorick Smythies et al., eds. Frankfurt am Main: Fischer.

Wright, James K. (2007). *Schoenberg, Wittgenstein and the Vienna Circle.* Bern: Lang.

Surveying the Field

Seeing Words and Music as a Painter Might
The Interart Aesthetic

Peter Dayan, Edinburgh

Both word and music studies and word and image studies have tended to concentrate on the specific interactions between the two arts that they work on. However, rather than focusing on the peculiar character of words, music, and visual art, and the distinctive modalities of their interactions, one might interrogate the interart phenomenon as such. Why is it that, at least since the romantic era, creators in each art have so generally presented their own art in terms of other arts? What are the implications of this general intermediality for the development, over the past two centuries, of art itself, perceived as a general category including works in many different media? This essay suggests that the best way to acquire a proper perspective on what is at stake is to examine how creators in one medium have seen the relationship between their own art, and *two* other arts. As a first step, I offer an analysis of how Whistler and Braque viewed music and poetry, and why they presented painting in terms of those other arts, before suggesting that the dynamic of the interart appeal, as it may be deduced from their writings, remains surprisingly constant across the arts.

I shall begin from a simple observation. 'Word and Image Studies' has been a recognised and organised field of academic enquiry for a quarter of a century. The International Association of Word and Image Studies was founded in 1987; the term 'Word and Image' is one that academics throughout the world use to designate a recognisable, widespread, and well respected approach to research and, increasingly, to teaching. 'Word and Music Studies' is more recent, but it, too, has had an institutional identity since 1997, when (as anyone likely to be reading this essay will know) the International Association for Word and Music Studies (WMA) was founded; that identity is now similarly generally recognised. 'Image and Music Studies', on the other hand, does not exist in the same way. There is no 'International Society for Image and Music Studies'. There is a journal for the study of music *in* art[1]; research is certainly carried out on the iconography of music in

---

[1] *Music in Art* is a journal produced by the Research Center for Music Iconography at the City University of New York; the remit of that centre is to study musical subject-matter represented in works of visual art.

painting; but that is a very different matter. Music *in* art is not the same as music *and* art. The essential identity of word and image studies, as of word and music studies, the fundamental rule of their game, is that the distinctiveness of the two media, their difference, their separation, should be respected and taken into account, at the same time as their interactions. In the WMA, we do not simply describe, for example, how music is depicted in novels; rather, we also ask why it should be music that is depicted in this way, and what happens when the reader considers it as music, as an art which functions according to principles that cannot be straighforwardly assimilated to those of the novel itself. To give a particularly clear and successful recent example: Regula Hohl Trillini, in *The Gaze of the Listener* (2008), does not content herself with showing how novelists describe piano-playing; she teases out of those descriptions a rich cultural sense of what the music means, as music, to the characters and authors involved, and brings her own critical distance to bear on the question of what happens to music in this literature. It seems to me that the exemplary sensitivity of Steven Paul Scher to this necessary distance between the arts is one of the reasons for his unique position in the founding of word and music studies.

Why, then, do we have word plus both music and image, but not music and image without word? Is this because of a fundamental dissymmetry in the relationship between the arts? The aim of this paper is to present a point of view from which the answer to that question is no. There is no fundamental dissymmetry between the three arts, of 'word', 'music', and 'image'. There is, however, a fundamental dissymmetry between the media that they use. It is a dissymmetry between media, not between arts, that renders 'Music and Image Studies' relatively difficult for academics to conceive. My argument, then, hinges on a distinction between medium, and art. That distinction is itself highly problematic, simply because the term 'art' is highly problematic, for us as 21st-century academics; far more problematic than 'medium'. It only acquires a meaning stable enough to be used in critical discourse such as mine, here, when it is carefully pinned to a historicised context, to an aesthetic that lends it an identifiable sense by contrast with its Other, with non-art. The primary aim of this paper, given above, is therefore inseparable from a secondary aim: to define an aesthetic, which I shall call the 'Interart Aesthetic', whose aim is to give to the word 'art' a meaning according to which there is no fundamental dissymmetry between the arts; whereas, according to that same aesthetic, within 'non-art', fundamental differences between the media pertain.

To begin with media, rather than arts: there is undoubtedly a privilege of the word in academic studies of intermediality. I am certainly not the first to observe that words are the substance of which the academic theory of all the arts is made up. Music, painting, and literature are all approached, by academics, through words. In the academic view of intermedial relations, words thus occupy one specific type of position, which the other media cannot take. Music and painting are, one might say, more alien to our discourse than literature, in that they use a medium which we cannot use. It is inevitable, in accordance with the fundamental rule of the intermedial game which I proposed above, that in word and music studies as in word and image studies, we should bring out the implications of that alien nature of image and of music, their heterogeneity to our own verbal language. Hence, the focus of intermedial studies has often been on the ways that non-verbal arts operate as markers of something that words cannot do. Most typically, music serves as the emblem of what cannot be explained, represented, or said. In this way, our contemporary intermedial studies link back to a perspective on the relationship between words and music that was created by poets in the 19th century. Words, which are the matter of literature, are also the matter of explanatory discourse. Music is different, because it is never explanatory. If one assumes, as the romantics and post-romantics generally did, that art itself is not explanatory, then it follows that there are two ways to use words: one is explanatory, and the other resembles music in its refusal to explain. And what of painting? I think it is fair to say that as a medium, for most of the 19th century at least, it seemed to come between the two, between words and music, because unlike music, it could represent, but unlike words, it could not put forward discursive arguments.

This focus on the distinctive characteristics of media, and particularly on the unique position of words in relation to music and painting, is certainly important from a certain theoretical perspective. But what I would like to suggest here is that from another point of view, it is a red herring. It tends to obscure another perspective, a more important one for poets, painters and composers since the 19th century; a perspective in which arts in all media must have the same value and the same function. I am going to try to sketch a view of intermediality in which poetry, music, and painting, considered as arts (rather than simply assimilated to their media), must all relate to one another in the same way.

This view corresponds, in my opinion, to the way that a high proportion of European composers, poets, and painters thought between the Romantic period and the 1960s. (I shall not attempt to comment on what happens before or after those dates.) My method, in expounding that view, can only be to tease it out of what was written by those artists at the time. I shall have to concentrate here on two examples, no more, because this understanding of what constitutes art can only be constructed through careful textual analysis. Naturally, this inductive method does not prove that the aesthetic I describe really was widely shared; it will be up to my readers to relate it to what they know of other artists in the period, and then to judge for themselves whether this aesthetic has the general force I claim for it[2].

I have chosen two artists, one from the middle and one from the end of the period in question. They were both painters who published books about their view of art. Furthermore, music is an important presence both within those books, and in the iconography of their paintings (as well, incidentally, as having been a powerful presence in their lives). Hence they offer clear connections to all three arts. They are James McNeill Whistler (1834–1903); and Georges Braque (1882–1963).

As I have said, my argument, in this essay, rests on a distinction between medium, and art. There are, I suggest, essential differences between media; as a result, each medium relates to the others in a distinctive way. Words do not relate to music in the same way that painting relates to music. However, between the arts, there are no such distinctions; all the arts relate to one another in the same way. The hallmark of the aesthetic that maintains this distinction between medium and art is a willingness to generalise about art, to provide definitions of art that transcend the medium. The most general characteristic of those definitions, in the period under consideration, is that they must be able to serve to separate the art of words (usually called 'poetry') from the medium of words. The latter – the medium of

---

[2] My book *Art as Music, Music as Poetry, Poetry as Art, from Whistler to Stravinsky and Beyond* (Dayan 2011), which takes as its central theme the same aesthetic as this essay, provides rather more examples. However, it does not address the question of the distinction between medium and art; nor does it investigate critical approaches to 'word and music', 'word and image', and 'music and image'.

words – is conceived of as the medium which allows for rational, academic, critical, and scientific thought, in a word for that which can be explained. Poetry is levered away from its medium by means of its refusal to explain; and this refusal of explanation is presented as a universal feature of art. As Braque put it in his *Cahier*:

> Il n'est en art qu'une chose qui vaille: celle qu'on ne peut expliquer.[3] (1956/1994: 21)[4]

This is certainly clear enough, on one level. However, it begs the question of the relationship between the inexplicable valuable thing, and the work of art itself as a material object. In one way, a painting by Braque is entirely explicable. I can tell you exactly what it is made of, what shape and size it is, what colours are used, and so on. Where, then, is the inexplicable thing to be found? Braque's favourite image to explain this mystery is one that I have not come across elsewhere; nonetheless, it is one that I think many poets, painters, and composers of his time would have been happy to adapt or adopt.

> Le tableau est fini, quand il a effacé l'idée.
> L'idée est le ber du tableau.[5] (Ibid.: 88)

I have translated "ber" as 'cradle', since that is the proper technical term in English; but 'ber' has a specific meaning. It is the wooden structure, the mould, so to speak, in which the hull of a ship was traditionally built. When the boat is launched, it leaves the cradle. In the same way, the painting must leave behind the idea on which it was formed.

Georges Braque thinks in ideas; he cannot help it. When he begins work on a painting, he has ideas about it. These ideas are quite explicable. I should say that it would be a mistake to suppose that the painter's ideas are necessarily abstract or verbal concepts, such as a writer might have in mind. As we will shortly see, a painter thinks in forms and colours; his ideas can be visual ones. Nonetheless, they can

---

[3] 'There is in art only one thing which is of value: that which one cannot explain.' (All translations from the French throughout this essay are mine.)

[4] Braque's *Cahier*, which he elaborated over a period of nearly forty years, is a book of aphorisms, intertwined with often mysterious line drawings. The 1994 edition, to which reference will be made throughout this essay, reproduces in facsimile Braque's handwriting, as well as the drawings.

[5] 'The painting is finished, when it has erased the idea.
The idea is the cradle of the painting.'

be called ideas, in Braque's terminology, and they resemble the writer's conceptual ideas, because they exist within the mind of an individual, and could in principle be communicated to another individual. It is from such ideas that the painting must slip away. It has to escape from Braque's own ability to contain, retain, understand, or explain it. In the process, it has to escape from the reach of representation in words as well as in images. And he follows a good century of tradition by repeatedly using musical vocabulary to stand for what, if one follows the 'ber' analogy, might be thought of as the boat once it is afloat on the sea, freed from its cradle. What escapes from the cradle is music.

It was common enough at the time to think of paintings as accessible to two types of interpretation. One concentrated on the painting as image, on what painting represented. The object of this type of interpretation can quite readily be assimilated into the category of what Braque calls ideas, and is translatable into the medium of words: we can say what the painting represents. The other type of interpretation focused its attention on the elements of the painting that did not work by representation: the inexplicable effects of colours, lines, forms, considered independently of the images they might contain. The latter perspective is the one habitually described as musical. Here, for example, is how Braque, in conversation with Dora Vallier, evoked his cubist period, when he was working alongside Picasso:

> Tenez, vous mettez une tache jaune ici, une autre à l'autre bout de la toile et aussitôt un rapport s'établit entre elles. La couleur agit comme une musique, si vous voulez. [...] C'est de là que nous avons pris le départ, mais aussitôt que la réalisation a commencé, il fallait que le calcul cesse – et c'est la seule raison pour laquelle ça vit.[6] (Vallier 1982: 37)

When painting is seen as an art whose value does not derive from representation or from calculation, it becomes analogous to music. This analogy corresponds to such a widespread topos of the 19th and 20th centuries that in itself it is hardly worth commenting on. What does seem to me worthy of note, however, is that Braque uses the quality of the poetic in the same way as he uses music, as an analogon

---

[6] 'You see, you put a patch of yellow here, another patch at the other side of the canvas, and immediately a relationship appears between them. The colour operates like music, if you like. [...] That is where we started from, but as soon as we began to realise this, calculation had to stop – and that is the only reason for which there's life in what we did.'

for painting beyond representation. Remembering the process of composition of his series of 'Ateliers', Braque said:

> J'étais dans l'état heureux de quelqu'un à qui se révèle l'harmonie des choses entre elles et entre les hommes. Or ces choses s'effaçaient pour ne me laisser que l'empreinte et l'écho de leurs poétiques rapports. Elles n'existaient plus.[7] (Qtd. Verdet 1978: 24)

What these two passages have in common is the description of a process in which the focus on the thing represented is replaced by a sense of 'rapports' whose relationship to representation cannot be calculated. These 'rapports' are brought into being through painterly means, obviously. But the effect cannot be analysed by painterly means. To explain this effect of painting that is not explicable within the means of painting, Braque describes these 'rapports' in terms of music – *or of poetry*, and it makes no fundamental difference which. When Braque uses them to express the quality of painting that escapes explanation, poetry and music are strictly equivalent. Either can stand for the voyage of the boat freed from the measurable cradle of the idea. Either can stand for the universal quality of art, independent of medium.

But for the reciprocity between the arts to be perfect, it is necessary, not only for any one of them to be able to stand in the same way, and to the same extent, for the universal quality of art, but also for each of them to be able to point back in the same way, through their medium, to non-art. Painting, music, and words can all be vehicles for art; but they can also be seen to operate in a medium that serves as a vehicle for the idea that art is not. To return to the obvious and essential question: what is the medium of Braque's idea, the idea from which his painting must escape? Is it words? Does Braque's idea necessarily begin in words, which he then attempts to translate into images? The answer is no: Braque's idea was in the first place an image. If the painting does not escape from that idea, the image remains; and that image is not art. Bad painting, non-art painting, is not necessarily the translation of words into images. It can just as well be the copying of an image. As Braque said in an interview with Georges Charbonnier:

---

[7] 'I was in the happy state of someone to whom is revealed the harmony of things, between things and between people. But these things faded away, to leave me with nothing but their imprint and the echo of their poetic relationships. They themselves no longer existed.'

> Dans le tableau, ce qui compte, c'est l'imprévu. C'est lui qui reste. Si je pouvais concevoir un tableau mentalement, je ne me donnerais jamais la peine de l'exécuter. Certains artistes exécutent leurs conceptions mentales. Quand ils peignent, c'est absolument comme s'ils faisaient une copie. Aussi l'esprit est-il absent du tableau. Le peintre a imité son idée.[8] (Charbonnier 1980: 26f.)

It is not, then, the medium that determines whether or not a work is art. It is the perceived relationship between the work and the process of reproduction. That process of reproduction in painting works in the same way as explanation in words: it is an ever-present possibility, indeed a vital principle of the medium, without which the artwork cannot be structured; but the artwork must escape from it, must escape from its own structuring principle, before it can be received as art. Word as explanation, then, and painting as copiable image, provide such principles; and in music? The commonest answer is: harmony. Harmony, like explanation, like the image, is a structuring principle accessible to reason, whose rules can be learned, and which is in itself inadequate to create works of art; indeed, the musical work must disturb harmony, just as the painting must disturb image and the poem must disturb explanation. All three arts possess, then, within their media, analogous principles which can figure, like Braque's idea, the cradle from which art is born, but from which it must escape.

Among the many lapidary intermedial formulations of Braque's *Cahier*, there is one that, for me, stands out by virtue of its condensation of the relations between the two arts it evokes:

> Le peintre pense en formes et en couleurs, l'objet c'est la poëtique.[9] (1956/1994: 19)

The painter does not think in poetry, he thinks in the medium of his own art, in form and colour, as the composer, doubtless, thinks in sounds, notes, or harmonies. But the *object* is not in form or colour. It must be conceived from within each art *in terms of* another art, of an art that uses a different material. Conversely, the poet must know that his work is made of words. No formulation concerning the nature of the poet's art in the 19th century is more celebrated than Mallarmé's

---

[8] 'In the painting, what counts is the unforeseen. That is what remains. If I could conceive a painting in my head, I would never bother to paint it. Some artists paint what they have conceived in their heads. When they paint, it's exactly as if they were making a copy. When that happens, the spirit is absent from the painting. The painter has imitated his idea.'

[9] 'The painter thinks in forms and colours, the object is poetics.'

reported response to Degas, when Degas complained to him that he had plenty of ideas for poems, but was having difficulty finding the words; it is not with ideas that one makes a poem, Mallarmé is supposed to have replied, it is with words. And yet what the poet makes out of his words must be something beyond words. The Mallarméan poem is, of course, as we all know, just like the Braque painting, music. Or is it? Mallarmé roots his own poetics in a movement towards something beyond language by describing his use of words as creating 'rapports' – in exactly the same way as Braque writes of 'rapports' in his paintings, since these 'rapports' are *between* rather than *within* the elements that make up the painting or the poem, and cannot be defined by any scientific or rational analysis rooted in their media. The importance in our contemporary appreciation of Mallarmé's aesthetics of these 'rapports' is, I think, sufficiently established by the long-standing celebrity of the letter to Edmund Gosse dated 10 January 1893, in which he describes them most simply and directly:

> Je fais de la Musique, et appelle ainsi non celle qu'on peut tirer du rapprochement euphonique des mots, cette première condition va de soi ; mais l'au-delà
>
> magiquement produit par certaines dispositions de la parole, où celle-ci ne reste qu'à l'état de moyen de communication matérielle avec le lecteur comme les touches du piano. Vraiment entre les lignes et au-dessus du regard cela se passe, en toute pureté, sans l'entremise de cordes à boyaux et de pistons comme à l'orchestre, qui est déjà industriel ; mais c'est la même chose que l'orchestre, sauf que littérairement ou silencieusement. Les poëtes de tous les temps n'ont jamais fait autrement et il est aujourd'hui, voilà tout, amusant d'en avoir conscience. Employez *Musique* dans le sens grec, au fond signifiant Idée ou rythme entre des rapports; là, plus divine que dans son expression publique ou symphonique.[10] (Mallarmé 1998: 807)

---

[10] 'I make Music, and call by this name not the music that one can draw from the euphonic concatenation of words, that being a first condition one can take as read; but the beyond magically produced by certain dispositions of the word, in which it survives only as a means of material communication with the reader like the keys of the piano. Between the lines and above the gaze is in truth where the event takes place, purely, without the mediation of gut strings and metal valves as in an orchestra, which is already industrial; but it is the same thing as the orchestra, except literarily and silently. The poets of all eras have never done otherwise and it is today amusing, that's all, to be conscious of what is going on. Use *Music* in the Greek sense, signifying at root Idea or rhythm between relationships; there, more divine than in its public or symphonic expression.'

In his lecture "La Musique et les Lettres", Mallarmé, equally famously, maintains that "saisir les rapports" (2003: 68), 'to perceive relationships', is the only action available to us. After making this affirmation in rather abstract terms, he proceeds to elaborate on it using visual images (the arabesque, for example), musical vocabulary (referring to harmony and melody), and references to the art of letters, weaving the three together in such a way as to produce the impression that these 'rapports' are not essentially incarnated in any one medium. Their creation, in the work of art, depends on the medium; but their perception always goes beyond it, to the "au-delà". Music and letters, he concludes, are the two faces of a single phenomenon, which he calls "l'Idée" (ibid.: 69). Music and letters only? But in his very presentation of this concept, he repeatedly uses visual imagery. Both music and letters are shown to produce their effects as they are *seen*, printed, for example, on the page. The circulation between all three media never ceases. In a vital sense, in short, the 'rapports' are not actually there in the material of the work. They have left, as the boat has left the 'ber'. And the poet may well, as Mallarmé did, tell us that these 'rapports' are musical or visual in essence, just as the painter may tell us they are musical or poetic in essence. The important point is that they must not remain within the medium of any art. The object must never come to rest. There is no Mount Ararat for the ark that is launched from Braque's cradle.

Whistler and Braque never met, as far as I know. Braque certainly never read Whistler's wonderful book *The Gentle Art of Making Enemies* (first published in 1890); astonishingly, it has never been translated into French. However, though I have no direct evidence of this, it is more than likely that Braque knew, at least, of the existence of the most celebrated text in that book: Whistler's lecture on art entitled "Ten O'Clock". For that lecture was published in French translation almost immediately after it had been published in English, in 1888. The translator was Whistler's closest friend and spiritual brother among writers: Stéphane Mallarmé. And while Braque never met Mallarmé (he was only 16 when Mallarmé died), he always admired his work, read it carefully, and quoted it more frequently than any other poet's.

In his "Ten O'Clock", Whistler carefully combines a revealing parallel between the work of the visual artist and the work of the composer of music, with an assertion of the absolute distinction between the medium, and the work of art:

> Nature contains the elements, in colour and form, of all pictures, as the keyboard contains the notes of all music.
> But the artist is born to pick, and choose, and group with science, these elements, that the result may be beautiful – as the musician gathers his notes, and forms his chords, until he bring forth from chaos glorious harmony.
> To say to the painter, that Nature is to be taken as she is, is to say to the player, that he may sit on the piano.
> That Nature is always right, is an assertion, artistically, as untrue, as it is one whose truth is universally taken for granted. Nature is very rarely right, to such an extent even, that it might almost be said that Nature is usually wrong: that is to say, the condition of things that shall bring about the perfection of harmony worthy a picture is rare, and not common at all. (1890/1994: 145)

The medium of the painter is, of course, distinct from that of the composer; but his relationship to that medium is the same. He creates, not by reproducing, but by picking, choosing, and grouping. And the poet? In the lecture, Whistler seems wary of people who call themselves poets; for poets use words, and his central concern is to reject the words of those who seek to tell him what his art says. Nonetheless, the painter knows true poetry when he sees it; and that is perfectly analogous to his own art in its functioning, as it is to music. Whistler defines "the *painter's* poetry"[11] as "the amazing invention that shall have put form and colour into such perfect harmony, that exquisiteness is the result" (ibid.: 147) all three arts, painting, poetry, and music, united around the common axis, not of any medium, but of invention.

The three arts are bound together just as tightly in another article reproduced in *The Gentle Art of Making Enemies*: "The Red Rag".

> As music is the poetry of sound, so is painting the poetry of sight, and the subject-matter has nothing to do with harmony of sound or of colour. (Ibid.: 127)

I have spent many happy hours and many learned papers trying to untangle the implications of this extraordinary pronouncement. It has led me in many different directions. But for the purposes of the present essay, we need go no further than this: it is clear that for Whistler, not everything that is heard is music, and not everything that is seen is painting. The quality of what distinguishes music from non-musical sound, and paintings worthy of the name from non-painterly colour, is represented, here, by two words: poetry, and harmony; one word from the domain of word-art, one from the domain of sound-art;

---

[11] The emphasis is Whistler's, to distinguish the painter's poetry from the writer's.

and they are, I would venture to say, fundamentally interchangeable. Whistler could have written: 'As music is harmony in sound, so is painting harmony in colour, and the subject-matter has nothing to do with the poetry of sound or of sight'; and no one would have been very shocked. After all, Whistler did entitle several of his paintings 'Harmony' – and none of them 'Poetry'.

To conclude: there is, as I said at the beginning, one way in which words are certainly different from music or painting within the interart aesthetic: words are used to explain or analyse. Poets, painters, and composers all use words in the same way when they are trying to explain things. But when words are considered as *poetry*, their relationship with music or painting is precisely and necessarily reciprocal. So whenever a poet is thinking *as a poet* in words, his words appear inexplicable; they create 'rapports' which, the poet suggests, might be best understood as music or as visual art. Similarly, whenever a musician is thinking in music, his music appears inexplicable; but it creates 'rapports' which, the composer suggests, can best be understood as poetry or as visual art. And whenever a painter is thinking in form and colour, his form and colour appear inexplicable; they create 'rapports' which, the painter suggests, should be understood as music or as poetry. In every case, the evoked arts serve to save the material art from explanation, without denying us the right to think analytically about art. And that is a fundamental function of the interart appeal. Within the Interart Aesthetic, all the arts must be separate but equal; each art must serve the others in the same way, as the horizon of their explicability – or rather: as the horizon both of their explicability, and of their inexplicability.

The implication for word and music studies, when we are considering works from the era of the Interart Aesthetic, would be this. To understand properly the relationship between words and music in the arts, we should not content ourselves with looking for anything that words can say specifically about music – about music as distinct from poetry or painting. Nor is it enough to look for the distinctive presence of music in literature; nor yet for the differences between the arts. Rather, we should in a further step seek out the reasons for which each art appeals to the other; and those turn out to be the same for all the arts. What word and music studies pursued thus would end up telling us is not what words are, nor what music is, nor even what the relationship between them is, but rather, how art can be recognised. That may seem to be an impractical and unfashionable endeavour. But it is,

I think, certainly the central aim of intermediality for Braque as for Whistler – and for most (though admittedly not all) of the other poets, painters, and composers who, since the Romantic era, have defined our sense of what art is. For them, any recognition of the quality of painting, or of music, or of poetry, is necessarily dependent on an intermedial concept of art in which the distinction between medium and art is essential: the defining character of each medium is necessarily different, but the defining character of all the arts is necessarily the same. Within this view of intermediality, 'Image and Music Studies' is no more problematic than 'Word and Music Studies'. In the Interart Aesthetic, the privilege of the word as the medium of critical discourse gives no privilege to the art of words.

References

Braque, Georges (1956/1994). *Cahier de G. Braque*. Paris: Maeght.
Charbonnier, Georges (1980). *Monologue du peintre: entretiens avec Braque* [et al.]. Neuilly-sur-Seine: Durier.
Dayan, Peter (2011). *Art as Music, Music as Poetry, Poetry as Art, from Whistler to Stravinsky and Beyond*. Aldershot: Ashgate.
Hohl Trillini, Regula (2008): *The Gaze of the Listener: English Representations of Domestic Music-Making*. Word and Music Studies 10. Amsterdam/New York, NY: Rodopi.
Mallarmé, Stéphane (1998). *Œuvres complètes*. Ed. B. Marchal. Vol. 1. Paris: Gallimard, Bibliothèque de la Pléiade.
— (2003). *Œuvres complètes*. Ed. B. Marchal. Vol. 2. Paris: Gallimard, Bibliothèque de la Pléiade.
Vallier, Dora (1982). *L'intérieur de l'art*. Paris: Seuil.
Verdet, André (1978). *Entretiens, notes et écrits sur la peinture: Braque, Léger, Matisse, Picasso*. Paris: Galilée.
Whistler, James A. McNeill (1890/1994). *The Gentle Art of Making Enemies*. London: Heinemann.

Milan Kundera's Polyphonic Novels and the Poetics of Divestment

David Mosley, Louisville, KY

The Franco-Czech novelist Milan Kundera situates his work in relation to the generation of Mann, Broch, and Musil, each of whom, according to Kundera's reading, failed in the attempt to integrate music as a structuring principle in their novels. This article examines Kundera's poetics of *dépouillement radical* – an aesthetic ideal he finds manifest in the music of Leoš Janáček – and the degree to which he realizes this musical ideal in prose. Based upon this examination it is argued that those engaged in word and music studies should consider, *pace* Gianni Vattimo's *pensiero debole*, a 'weaker' definition of musicalized fiction.

It can be argued that Milan Kundera, the Franco-Czech novelist, is among the most musically literate and philosophically sophisticated writers at work today. His father, a student of the composer Leoš Janáček, was a pianist and musicologist, and the young Kundera studied piano, harmony, and counterpoint before enrolling at the Charles University in Prague. There he studied composition until, at the age of 25, he transferred to the university's film school. Furthermore, the more one reads Kundera the clearer it becomes that the nihilistic world his characters inhabit is the one Friedrich Nietzsche describes in the "Parable of the Madman" (cf. 2003: 119f.). Similarly, Kundera's conception of the novel as "nothing other than the investigation of [...] forgotten being" (1988: 4) and its singular capacity to reveal "previously unseen possibilities of existence" by "uncover[ing] what is hidden from each of us" (1993: 264) is clearly Heideggerian.

In the same way that the history of philosophy can be read as the process by which one generation pursues questions left unanswered by the previous generations, so Kundera sees each generation of novelists pursuing that which "great works of literature (precisely because they are great)" left "unachieved" (1988: 65). In this regard, Kundera identifies Kafka, Gombrich, Musil, and Broch as his literary "Pleiades" (ibid.). Of these, Kundera cites the novels of Hermann Broch, especially the last volume of *The Sleepwalkers*, as the origin of his own interest in music and the novel[1]. According to Kundera, "Broch is an inspiration [...] not only because of what he brought off but also for what he aimed for and missed". Broch's appeal to music as a structuring principle arose from the desire to "encompass the complexity of existence in the modern world without losing architectonic clarity". However Broch's failure, so far as Kundera the critic is concerned, exposes "the need for a new art of *radical divestment*" (ibid., emphasis in the original), or "*dépouillement radical*" (1986: 22), which Kundera the author adopts and adapts as a guiding principle[2]. In what follows Kundera's poetics of "*radical divestment*" and his appeal to music will be situated in the context of discussions about the extent to which literature can assimilate musical properties. It will then be argued that by thinking ontologically, rather than descriptively, about the possibility of the novel as a musical expression reveals the need to re-conceive of the so-called musicalization of fiction.

In an interview with Christian Salmon, Kundera outlines the strategy by which he tries to accomplish what Broch failed to achieve: to compose a text in which each of the lines "could be read as an independent novel" and all of the lines "evolve simultaneously" (1988: 74). When asked by the interviewer if such a novel is truly polyphonic, Kundera concedes that verbal narratives cannot achieve the simultaneity of voices according to which musical polyphony is defined, i. e., he recognizes what Calvin Brown characterized as the "insuperable barrier" in literature's effort to become musical (1948: 39). Nevertheless, the novelist argues that if these lines, which can be "an idea, a question, or an existential situation", treat the novel's overall theme equally, illuminate one another, and contribute to the work's indivisibility, then the result is "perfectly sufficient" to qualify as polyphony (1988: 75).

---

[1] If the musicalization of fiction was an aspiration not only for Broch, but also for the canonical modernists, such as Joyce, Proust, and Mann, then Kundera's claim is quite audacious.

[2] In another collection of essays Kundera observes, "every era's art has its structural problems: that is what lures the artist to search for original solutions and thereby set off the evolution of form" (1993: 154). Thus it is clear he understands the inheritance of the unachieved not only in terms of genre but in a broader, historical sense as well.

Later in the same interview, Kundera explains his musical thinking about the novel in greater detail (see *Figure 1*) and his strategy for incorporating tempo and rhythm into the text (see *Figure 2*).

theme:	e. g. Immortality; Slowness; Identity; *The Book of Laughter and Forgetting*; *The Unbearable Lightness of Being*
line:	ideas, questions, existential situations in which characters serve as vehicles for different explorations of the theme
motif:	key words, metaphors, or images that represent the theme and appear several times in the novel
counter-point:	alternating modes of discourse, e. g. narrative, poetry, essay, reportage
movements:	the large parts of the novel (often seven in number)
measures:	the brief chapters, of 1–5 pages, that comprise each part
tempo:	the number of chapters in a part
rhythm:	the relative length of each chapter (Ibid.: 91)

Figure 1: Musical/Literary Equivalencies in Kundera's Musicalized Novels[3].

	Chapters	Pages	Tempo
Part One:	11	71	moderato
Part Two:	14	31	allegretto
Part Three:	28	82	allegro
Part Four:	25	30	prestissimo
Part Five:	11	96	moderato
Part Six:	17	26	adagio
Part Seven:	23	28	presto (Ibid.: 88)

Figure 2: Kundera's Rhythmic Analysis of Life is Elsewhere[4].

Kundera identifies his prose style with the musical style of Leoš Janáček[5]. In the Moravian composer's music the author finds "the will to divest" manifested in "the total absence of mere technique" (ibid.: 73) resulting in musical compositions marked by "harsh juxtapositions

---

[3] In both his novels and essays Kundera is clear about his aversion to 'lyricism', which he sees as a literary form of totalitarianism; this may explain why he never speaks of the lines as melodies.

[4] As a reader I am most sensitive to the musical features of tempo and rhythm in the novels. Thanks to the alternation of tempi in the multiple parts of his novels, which Kundera compares to a dance suite, it can be argued that the time of the reader, the time experienced while reading, becomes musical time in an existential sense.

[5] Kundera makes his identification with the music of his countryman explicit: "My own imperative is completely 'Janáčekian': to rid the novel of the automatism of novelistic technique, of novelistic verbalism; to make it dense" (1988: 73).

instead of transitions, repetition [of thematic material] instead of variation" (ibid.: 72); the absence of "contrapuntal filler"; and the rejection of "routine instrumentation" (1993: 183). In other words, Janáček cashes out of the late-nineteenth-century market of instrumental composition. To Kundera's ears, Janáček's music is entirely expressive and, rather than exhibiting a distinction between foreground and background, it is comprised of a series of rapidly alternating passages whose musical material, tempo, rhythm, and instrumentation, are radically different from one another (see 1983).

As a consequence, Janáček's music possesses a dramatic quality that "does not suggest a narrator telling a tale; rather from a single melodic motif it evokes a stage set on which different characters are simultaneously present, speaking, confronting one another" (1993: 186)[6]. Furthermore, in Janáček's music "many contradictory emotions" coexist "in a very limited space" creating a musical "semantics that is brand new" (ibid.: 185). "What astonishes and fascinates is the[ir] unexpected juxtaposition" such that for Kundera "they sound simultaneously as a polyphony of emotions" (ibid.). Other features of Janáček's style Kundera incorporates include: the rapid alternation of contrasting tempi and tone (the latter used in a literary sense); the absence of development in his characters; the absence of transitions; and the repetition of 'theme words' as literary motifs. As might be expected, Kundera also discusses the composer's fascination with the melodic and rhythmic content of speech, and its incorporation into Janáček's instrumental and vocal works. In this regard, the author stresses that these speech melodies were never quoted verbatim, rather they served as a musical reference for melodic contours meant to reflect a speaker's psychological disposition in specific existential situations[7].

---

[6] Those familiar with the early years of word and music studies will recognize that this is the example used by Calvin Brown in his speculation on how a sort of polyphony might be realized in drama (cf. 1948: 39–43).

[7] In *Testaments Betrayed*, Kundera explains, "what most interested Janáček in his research on spoken language was not the specific rhythm of language (the Czech language) or its prosody [...] but the influence on spoken intonation of a speaker's shifting psychological state; he sought to comprehend the *semantics of melodies* [...]" (1993: 135; emphasis in the original). Might it be that in Kundera's novels he seeks to comprehend the syntax of music?

Janáček's appeal to the musical content of speech, as I have tried to conceive it, is analogous to Wittgenstein's "aspect seeing" (1953/ 2001: II, §xi).

Figure 3: Wittgenstein's Rabbit-Duck.

Put succinctly, and without doing justice to the full extent of Wittgenstein's idea, in the same way one sees either a rabbit or a duck, in Wittgenstein's famous example borrowed from Joseph Jastrow (see 1899), I would argue that Janáček's musical technique constitutes 'aspect hearing'[8]. Speaking of Janáček's transcription of a spoken sentence into music, Kundera asks: "What is the *melodic truth* of this sentence? What is the melodic truth of a vanished moment?" (1993: 138; emphasis in the original). Kundera answers his own rhetorical query with the observation, "[t]he search for the vanished present; the search for the melodic truth of the moment; [...] the wish to plumb by that means the mystery of the immediate reality constantly deserting our lives, which thereby becomes the thing we know least about". He concludes: "This I think is the ontological import of Janáček's studies of spoken language and, perhaps, the ontological import of all his music." (Ibid.)

Here Kundera's philosophical speculation is distinctly Heideggerian, he asks about the world opened by the work of art and what dwelling there might mean, i. e., might it be a world in which the question of being is not forgotten? Likewise, just as Heidegger believes the work of art opens a world in which it is possible to ask the otherwise forgotten question of being (cf. 2008: 139–212), so Kundera speaks of "asking questions of existence only the novel can

---

[8] An essential part of Wittgenstein's argument is that the viewer, even after she knows both a rabbit and a duck are represented in the single graphic representation, cannot see both simultaneously.

ask" as the genre's *raison d'être* (1988: 42f.). Like Janáček's experiments with speech melody, allowing the listener to experience music under the aspect of language, so Kundera's novels, it seems to me, are an experiment in 'aspect reading', opening a world in which the reader experiences literature under the aspect of music.

In terms of the descriptive typologies employed in word and music studies, Steven Paul Scher would classify Kundera's works as examples of music *in* literature, where formal and structural properties of music are adapted to prose (see 1970). Since there are moments in many of the novels when a specific musical composition is discussed, Scher's designation of verbal music also applies. Nevertheless, Scher emphasizes the verbal text's inability to be polyphonic for the same reason as Brown: the insuperable barrier of the simultaneity of voices (cf. Scher 1968: 8). Using Werner Wolf's elaboration and refinement of Scher's typology, Kundera's musicalized fiction is an example of "covert/indirect musico-literary intermediality" that, on the whole, "shows" rather than "tells" (Wolf 1999: 44–46). Like Brown and Scher, Wolf is skeptical that literature can attain the status of polyphony. He states, "the musicalization of fiction [...] remains a mere, and at times questionable *attempt* to imitate music" (ibid.: 55; emphasis in the original).

Yet what if we were to take Kundera at his word and accept the contention that, while his novels fail to achieve the simultaneity of voices we associate with polyphony, they are, nonetheless, polyphonic? To think in this way is to entertain the possibility that, in an ontological sense, polyphony exists differently in the novel than, say, in a string quartet. Can we imagine a polyphony for which the simultaneity of voices is neither a necessary nor a sufficient feature? To do so would mean rethinking Lawrence Kramer's Derridian observation that literature's appeal to music tends to "annex certain values" that, from the perspective of literature, are perceived as "lack" (1989: 162). Taking Kundera at his word, conceding that his novels both fail and succeed to realize polyphony in prose, demands thinking differently and deeply about the genre and its history, as Walter Bernhart recommends when he observes, "literature and music, as it were, share a common ground, i. e., they pose the same problems and can be investigated by the same tools" (1999: 33). Ultimately we would need to think about the genre, as Kundera does, when he situates his work in the "third, or overtime period of modernity" – a period of its decline, or weakening (1993: 161).

At this point, I should confess that the degree to which Kundera writes polyphonic prose, at least according to the descriptive standards of word and music studies, interests me less than the incentive his works provide for an ontological consideration of literature's appeal to music. In Heidegger's essay on "The Origin of the Art Work" he argues that art works open a "possible world" in which their existence comes into conflict with the more or less closed region of the "earth" (2008: 180). This existential conflict raises questions we typically forget to ask about the nature of art's being[9]. If Heidegger's ideas about the work of art are applied to Kundera's novels and essays, we are compelled to ask fundamental questions about a possible literary 'world' in which musical novels exist and what dwelling there might mean.

Gianni Vattimo, the contemporary Italian philosopher, finds in Heidegger a "recuperation of aesthetic consciousness [...] as an experience of Truth precisely insofar as this experience is substantially nihilistic" (1999: 115). For the postmodernist, the nihilistic experience of 'Truth' points to paradox and parology, i. e., the retreat from philosophy as a meaningful enterprise found, for example, in Lyotard or Derrida. For Vattimo, on the other hand, the nihilistic experience of Truth (note Vattimo's capitalization) permits philosophy to continue, but with the crucial acknowledgement that its tools are ultimately flawed rendering its conclusions provisional (cf. 1991: 132–135). Vattimo's philosophy, after the end of metaphysics, operates according to what he calls *pensiero debole*, or 'weak thought' (see 1983). With a nod to Heidegger, Vattimo's 'weak thought' is not concerned with the *Überwindung*, or overcoming, of metaphysics, but with *Verwindung*, a turning, or twisting, or distortion of metaphysics. Such thinking also offers healing, convalescence, resignation, and acceptance of the all-too-human, often tragic, consequences of metaphysical thought (cf. ibid.: 136; 2000: 187). Vattimo characterizes his continuation of Heidegger's work as "hermeneutic ontology" (1999: 113), a way of thinking about being interpretively, i. e., thinking about being in the same way we think about artistic expressions[10].

---

[9] For Heidegger, the work of art in general allows us to remember the 'throwness' of beings, i. e., the arbitrary nature of their historical destiny and their mortality, their "being-toward-death" (2008: 196).

[10] It is important to note than if being is a matter for artistic judgment, then any conclusion about its meaning is provisional and subject to historical contingencies.

Kundera's essays on the novel are acutely aware of the genre's history and his commitment to work in the genre despite its demise as pronounced by "the modernism of fixed rules, the modernism of the university – establishment modernism so to speak" (1988: 66). Furthermore, his novels present a philosophy of history in which historical circumstance creates not only "a new existential situation for a character" but "history *itself* must be understood and analyzed as an existential situation" (ibid.: 38; emphasis in the original). Nevertheless, Kundera writes not with a grim determination but a "blissful smile", and he reads the "obituaries of the novel" as "frivolous", because he has "already seen and lived through the death of the novel, a violent death (inflicted by bans, censorship, and the ideology of pressure), in a world […] usually called totalitarian" (ibid.: 13f.). Furthermore, "[t]he novel is incompatible with the totalitarian universe", an incompatibility "not only political or moral but *ontological*. By which I mean", Kundera continues, "[t]he world of one single Truth and the relative, ambiguous world of the novel are molded of entirely different substances. Totalitarian Truth excludes relativity […] it can never accommodate what I call the *spirit of the novel*" (ibid.: 14; emphases in the original).

When Kundera argues that his novels, written according to Janáček's poetics of divestment, both are and are not polyphonic, I hear him making a weak claim, in Vattimo's sense of the word. Just as Vattimo engages in philosophical activity while admitting its provisional status, Kundera writes novels after the genre has been pronounced moribund. When Kundera describes Janáček's poetics of divestment, I hear a description of a weak music, again in Vattimo's sense of the term. In a chapter titled "The Depreciated Legacy of Cervantes", the first chapter of *The Art of the Novel*, Kundera discusses the "inability to tolerate the essential relativity of things human" and then observes: "This inability makes the novel's wisdom (the wisdom of uncertainty) hard to accept and understand" (1988: 7). Weakness is also a more general concern for Kundera. Following an account of the Prague Spring of 1968 and Alexander Dubček's coerced radio address, Kundera describes the President's "gasp[ing] for breath, in mid-sentence" and the "awful long pauses" in the speech. He then reflects: "What this historical episode reveals for me (an episode, by the way, completely forgotten because, two hours later, the radio technicians were made to cut the painful pauses out of his speech) is *weakness* [...] as a very general category of existence" (ibid.: 38; emphasis in the original).

In an extremely interesting discussion of twentieth-century music, in which Kundera takes on Adorno's famous distinction between the paths taken by Schoenberg and Stravinsky versus the path not taken, i. e., that of Janáček, the novelist observes that Schoenberg and Stravinsky are committed to overcoming the nineteenth century's strong works. To use Heideggerian language, they are engaged in *Überwindung*. Conversely, Janáček appeals to the musical aspect of speech, its non-semantic element, to its weakness. In Heideggerian terms, Janáček chooses the path of *Verwindung*. Not surprisingly, the same can be said of Kundera's attitude toward the novel, inasmuch as he jettisons the traditional techniques of prose composition and appeals, instead, to that which is left unachieved, to novelistic polyphony.

Kundera's "Janáčekian imperative", his own poetics of divestment, his weak thinking about the novel, calls into question the unquestionable authority of polyphony, the "insuperable barrier" it poses for the novelist, and demands a weaker definition of musicalized fiction. Such a definition, based upon the phenomenological experience of the reader, would bracket the literary nature of the work and, instead, present the possibility of reading as a musical experience. Rather than being descriptive, such a definition would be based upon the ontology of the work and, like Kundera's novels which ask questions about existence that only novels can ask, a weak definition of musicalized fiction would ask a fundamental question about the experience of reading, one that it has not yet been possible to ask: might we (finally) be permitted to hear multiple voices while reading[11]?

References

Bernhart, Walter (1999). "Some Reflections on Literary Genres and Music". *Word and Music Studies: Defining the Field.* Walter

---

[11] While they are beyond the scope of this paper, such a weak definition of musicalized fiction also poses the question of whether Kundera's novels might also be read as fictionalized music in which he seeks to comprehend the syntax of music just as Janáček seeks to comprehend the semantics of melody.

Bernhart, Steven Paul Scher, Werner Wolf, eds. *Word and Music Studies 1*. Amsterdam/Atlanta, GA: Rodopi. 25–36.

Brown, Calvin (1948). *Music and Literature*. Athens, GA: University of Georgia Press.

Heidegger, Martin (2008). "The Origin of the Work of Art". *Martin Heidegger: The Basic Writings*. David Farrell Krell, trans. New York, NY: Harper Collins. 139–212.

Jastrow, Joseph (1899). "The Mind's Eye". *Popular Science Monthly* 54: 299–312.

Kramer, Lawrence (1989). "Dangerous Liaisons: The Literary Text in Musical Criticism". *19th-Century Music* 13: 159–167.

Kundera, Milan (1983). "Janáček: He Saw the Coming Night". Ladislav Matejka, Benjamin A. Stoltz, eds. *Cross Currents: A Yearbook of Central European Culture*. Ann Arbor, MI: University of Michigan Press. 371–380.

— (1986). *L'art du roman*. Paris: Gallimard.

— (1988). *The Art of the Novel*. Linda Asher, trans. New York, NY: Harper and Row.

— (1993). *Testaments Betrayed: An Essay in Nine Parts*. Linda Asher, trans. New York, NY: Harper/Collins.

— (1999). *The Book of Laughter and Forgetting*. Aaron Asher, trans. New York, NY: Harper and Row.

Nietzsche, Friedrich (2003). *The Gay Science*. Josephine Nauckhoff, trans. Cambridge: CUP.

Scher, Steven Paul (1968). *Verbal Music in German Literature*. Yale Germanic Studies 2. New Haven, CT: Yale UP.

— (1970/2004). "Notes Toward a Theory of Verbal Music (1970)". Walter Bernhart, Werner Wolf, eds. *Word and Music Studies: Essays on Literature and Music (1967–2004) by Steven Paul Scher*. Word and Music Studies 5. Amsterdam/New York, NY: Rodopi. 23–35. (Orig. publ.: *Comparative Literature* 22: 147–156).

Vattimo, Gianni (1980). *Le avventure della differenza*. Milan: Garzanti.

— (1983). *Il pensiero debole*. Milan: Feltrinelli.

— (1991). "The End of (Hi)story". *Zeitgeist in Babel: The Postmodernist Controversy*. Ingeborg Hoesterey, ed. Bloomington, IN: Indiana UP. 132–141.

— (1999). *The End of Modernity: Nihilism and Hermeneutics in Postmodern Culture*. Jon R. Snyder, trans. Baltimore, MD: Johns Hopkins UP.

— (2000). "The Death of the Decline of Art". *The Continental Aesthetics Reader*. Clive Cazeaux, ed. New York, NY: Routledge. 187–194.
Wittgenstein, Ludwig (1953/2001). *Philosophical Investigations*. London: Blackwell.
Wolf, Werner (1999). "Musicalized Fiction and Intermediality: Theoretical Aspects of Word and Music Studies". *Word and Music Studies: Defining the Field.* Walter Bernhart, Steven Paul Scher, Werner Wolf, eds. Word and Music Studies 1. Amsterdam/Atlanta, GA: Rodopi. 37–58.

Notes on Contributors

Walter Bernhart (walter.bernhart@uni-graz.at), retired Professor of English Literature at the University of Graz, Austria, is the Director of the university's "Centre for Intermediality Studies in Graz (CIMIG)" and the founding and current President of "The International Association for Word and Music Studies (WMA)". His most recent publications include "*Christophorus, oder 'Die Vision einer Oper'*: Franz Schreker's Opera as a Metareferential Work" (2010) and "Metareference in Operatic Performance: The Case of Katharina Wagner's *Die Meistersinger von Nürnberg*" (2011). He is Executive Editor of two book series, "Word and Music Studies (WMS)" and "Studies in Intermediality (SIM)", both published by Rodopi (Amsterdam/New York, NY), and has (co)edited numerous individual volumes.

Katia Chornik (katia.chornik@manchester.ac.uk) studied music and literature at the Catholic University of Chile, the Royal Academy of Music (UK) and The Open University (UK). She has published on music in Latin American literature, popular music and artistic activities in concentration camps. Her doctoral research dealt with the role of music in the novels of the Cuban writer and musicologist Alejo Carpentier (1904–1980), who coined the concept of magic realism in literature. Dr Chornik has conceptualised and developed several knowledge-transfer projects on Latin American culture with the media and museum sectors, including the BBC and the Chilean Museum of Memory and Human Rights. She is currently Postdoctoral Research Fellow at Manchester University and Visiting Scholar at Salford University. Among other awards, she is the winner of the 2011 annual Postdoctoral Research Fellowship of the Association of Hispanists of Great Britain and Ireland/WISP.

Delia da Sousa Correa (d.dasousa@open.ac.uk) is Senior Lecturer in English at the Open University. She studied at the Universities of Canterbury (New Zealand), London (King's College London), and Oxford. Her research centres on connections between literature and music. She is the author of *George Eliot, Music and Victorian Culture* (Palgrave Macmillan, 2003) and editor of *The Nineteenth-Century*

Novel: Realisms (Routledge/Open University, 2000) and of *Phrase and Subject: Studies in Literature and Music* (Legenda/Modern Humanities Research Association, 2006). She is the founding editor of *Katherine Mansfield Studies*, published by Edinburgh University Press. She chairs the Open University's English MA and is the co-editor, with W. R. Owens, of *The Handbook to Literary Research* (Routledge, 2010).

Peter Dayan (peter.dayan@ed.ac.uk) is Professor of Word and Music Studies at the University of Edinburgh, where he has taught in the French department for over twenty-five years, since completing his studies at Lincoln College, Oxford. His two most recent books, both published by Ashgate, are: *Music Writing Literature: From Sand via Debussy to Derrida* (2006), and *Art as Music, Music as Poetry, Poetry as Art: From Whistler to Stravinsky and Beyond* (2011). His research has focused not on concrete similarities or collaborations between the arts, but on the ways in which artists conceptualise the relationship between artworks in different media.

Mario Dunkel (mario.dunkel@udo.edu) is a PhD candidate and lecturer in American Studies at Technical University Dortmund. His research interests and publications range from African American cultural history, music, and literature to performative aspects in Modernism and Postmodernism. He is currently working on a dissertation project with the working title "Writing Jazz History: Emergence and Development of a Genre", funded by the German National Academic Foundation (*Studienstiftung des deutschen Volkes*). He was a student at Oglethorpe University, Atlanta, in 2005/06 and a German Teaching Fellow at Hamilton College, NY (2007/08), before completing his *Erstes Staatsexamen* in English and Music at TU Dortmund in November 2008. More recently, he was selected for the Fulbright American Studies Institute at San Francisco State University (2010) and spent four months as a Visiting Scholar at Columbia University, New York (2011).

Katrin Eggers (katrin-eggers@gmx.de), having studied musicology, philosophy and literature, took her doctoral degree in musicology at the Hanover University of Music, Drama and Media in 2010. Her dissertation, supported by a grant from the Studienstiftung des Deutschen Volkes, is on "Ludwig Wittgenstein als Musikphilosoph". Her main research interests are musical aesthetics and semiotics, narratology and pragmatics of music, as well as experimental film music. She has worked on everyday history of the early modern period and is currently writing a book on Johann Hermann Schein. Eggers lives and teaches in Hanover, Germany.

Axel Englund (axel.englund@littvet.su.se) is presently a Visiting Scholar and Anna Lindh Fellow at the Europe Center, Stanford University. He received his PhD in 2011, from Stockholm University, where he has also taught modernist exile literature and metrics. His principal research interests include the poetry and music of the 20th century, German literature, hermeneutics and aesthetics. He is the author of *Still Songs: Music in and around the Poetry of Paul Celan* (Ashgate, 2012), and co-editor (with Anna Jörngården) of a Swedish volume on aesthetics and authenticity, *Okonstlad konst? Om äkthet och autenticitet i estetisk teori och praktik* (Symposion, 2011). His articles on musico-literary interrelations have been published in *Perspectives of New Music* and *Seminar: A Journal of Germanic Studies*.

Michael Halliwell (m.halliwell@usyd.edu.au) studied music and literature at the University of the Witwatersrand in Johannesburg, and at the London Opera Centre with Otakar Kraus, as well as with Tito Gobbi in Florence. As principal baritone for many years with the Netherlands Opera, the Nürnberg Municipal Opera, and the Hamburg State Opera, he took part in several world premieres and had frequent appearances at major European festivals in opera, oratorio and song recitals and sang over fifty major operatic roles. He is Vice-President and Editorial Board Member of The International Association for Word and Music Studies (WMA) and has written and presented many TV and radio programs. At the Sydney Conservatorium of Music he has been Chair of Vocal Studies and Opera, Pro-Dean and Head of School, and Associate Dean (Research). He performs regularly in Australia and abroad, and has recorded many programs for ABC Classic FM and 2MBS FM. A double CD of settings of Kipling ballads and Boer War songs, *When the Empire Calls*, was released by ABC Classics in September 2005, and he has recently premiered several song cycles by Lawrence Kramer. His book, *Opera and the Novel*, was published by Rodopi (Amsterdam/New York, NY) in January 2005.

Tobias Janz (tobias.janz@uni-hamburg.de) is Juniorprofessor of Musicology at the University of Hamburg. He received his Ph. D. in 2005 from the Humboldt University of Berlin. He also received degrees in Music (Piano) and Music Theory from the Musikhochschule Lübeck. He has published widely on 19th- and 20th-century music and is author and editor of two books on Richard Wagner (*Klangdramaturgie: Studien zur theatralen Orchesterkomposition in Wagners* Ring des Nibelungen. Würzburg: Königshausen & Neumann 2006; and *Wagners Siegfried und die (post-)heroische Moderne.* Würzburg: Königshausen & Neumann 2011). He is co-editor of the volume *Musiktheorie/Musikwissenschaft: Geschichte – Methoden – Perspektiven.* Hildesheim: Olms 2011. His research interests are in the areas of the historiography of music, music analysis, the philosophy of music, sound and orchestration, musical modernity and musical modernism.

Lawrence Kramer (lkramer@fordham.edu) is Distinguished Professor of English and Music at Fordham University in New York, NY. He is the author of numerous books, most recently including *Interpreting Music* (2010) and *Why Classical Music Still Matters* (2007), both from the University of California Press. He is the editor of the journal *19th-Century Music.* And he is a composer; his cantata *Crossing the Water* premiered at the Santa Fe conference of the WMA in 2011 and his piano work *The Wild Swans at Coole* in New York City shortly thereafter.

Bernhard Kuhn (bkuhn@bucknell.edu) is Associate Professor of Italian Studies at Bucknell University (Lewisburg, PA). He received his doctorate degree in Romance Philology from the University of Bamberg. His current areas of research include Italian cinema, 19th- and 20th-century Italian culture, intermediality, and in particular the relationship between opera and cinema. He is the author of *Die Oper im italienischen Film* (Essen: Die Blaue Eule, 2005) and several articles concerning intermedial aspects of the relationship between stage media and film.

David L. Mosley (dmosley@bellarmine.edu) is a member of the Philosophy Faculty at Bellarmine University, where he teaches courses in Aesthetics, Modern Philosophy, 19th- and 20th-century Continental

Philosophy, Contemporary Philosophy, and the Philosophy of History. He has written about text-music relationships in Schubert, Schumann, Brahms, Wagner, Mahler, Hegel, Nietzsche, and Joyce. His publications include *Gesture, Sign, and Song: An Interdisciplinary Approach to Schumann's* Eichendorff-Lieder, Op.39 and articles in *The Journal of Aesthetics and Art Criticism, Contemporary Music Review, Analecta Husserliana, Word and Music Studies, Interdisciplinary Studies in Musicology*, and others. He is currently working on a book-length manuscript examining the role of *Stimmung* in the philosophy of Nietzsche.

Adrian Paterson (adrianpaterson@yahoo.com) is an IRCHSS (Irish Research Council for the Humanities and Social Sciences) Research Fellow at the National University of Ireland, Galway. A graduate of Worcester College, Oxford, and Trinity College, Dublin, he has published widely on nineteenth- and twentieth-century literature with a particular interest in artistic interactions (http://thebicyclops. wordpress.com). He is working on a history of poetry and music in Ireland entitled *Perfect Pitch: Music in Irish Poetry from Moore to Muldoon*; a monograph, *Words for Music Perhaps: W. B. Yeats and Musical Sense*, is in press.

Emily Petermann (emily.petermann@phil.uni-goettingen.de) is Assistant Professor of American Literature at the Georg-August University of Göttingen. She earned a Ph. D. in Literature from the University of Konstanz with a dissertation on "The Musical Novel: Imitating Musical Structure in Contemporary Fiction". She is one of the founders of the WMA Forum and is currently co-editing a volume of essays presented at that organization's first conference in 2010, on the subject of "Time and Space in Words and Music", to appear with Peter Lang in 2012.

Robert Samuels (r.samuels@open.ac.uk) is Lecturer in Music at The Open University in the UK. He studied at Robinson College, Cambridge, reading English and Music (BA, 1985), and completing a Ph. D. in Music, supervised by Derrick Puffett. He worked at Lancaster University from 1989 to 1995 before moving to his current post. His work centres on music from the 19th and 20th centuries, and is principally concerned with analytical theory, aesthetics, and the relationship between music and literature. He has written on Schubert, Schumann,

Mahler, Cage, Boulez and Birtwistle, amongst others. His book *Mahler's Sixth Symphony: A Study in Musical Semiotics* was published by CUP in 1995. A second book, *Novel and Symphony: A Study of Nineteenth-Century Genres* is in preparation. He is a co-ordinator of the Literature and Music Research Group at The Open University and Secretary of the International Association for Word and Music Studies.

David Francis Urrows (urrows@hkbu.edu.hk) is Associate Professor in the Department of Music at Hong Kong Baptist University, where he teachers music history, analysis and aesthetics. He is the editor of an ongoing critical edition of the works of the German-American composer Otto Dresel (1826–1890), and has co-edited and edited two volumes of Word and Music Studies (Vol. 7, 2005, and Vol. 9, 2008). In addition to his research on 19th-century musicological topics, he has interests in East-West musical and cultural studies, and is completing a book on the history of the pipe organ in China.

Simon Williams (williams@theaterdance.ucsb.edu) is Professor and Chair of the Department of Theater and Dance at the University of California, Santa Barbara. He possesses a Ph. D. in European Literature from the University of East Anglia and has published four books and numerous articles on the history of acting and opera. He is currently editing the forthcoming *Cambridge World Encyclopedia of Stage Actors and Acting*. He is also active as an opera critic and as a director of operatic and spoken drama.

Live Poetry

An Integrated Approach to Poetry in Performance

Julia Novak

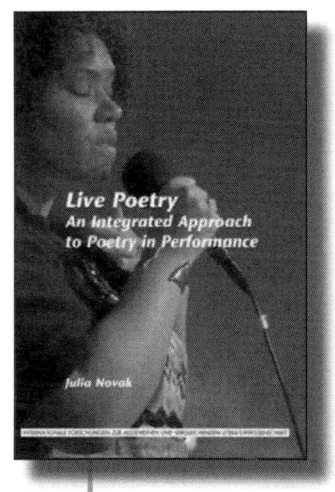

Given the increasing popularity of literary festivals, open mics, and poetry slams, one could justifiably claim that the English-speaking world is currently experiencing a 'Live Poetry' boom. Yet, despite this raised awareness for the aesthetic and social potential of performed poetry, academia has barely responded, failing in the process to update and adapt its concept of poetry to meet these recent developments.

Bridging this critical gap, this volume provides for the first time a full methodological 'toolkit' for the analysis of live poetry by drawing together approaches from diverse disciplines concerned with speech and forms of cultural performance. Most notably, these include literary studies, paralinguistics, musicology, kinesics, theatre and performance studies, and folklore studies.

This innovative methodology is demonstrated through sample analyses based on a mixed corpus of audio and video recordings of poetry performances, as well as on personal interviews with practitioners of live poetry. Of value to the scholar and poetry enthusiast alike, this volume presents an indispensable guide for anyone interested in understanding and analysing poetry's evolution through its current 'spoken word' renaissance.

rodopi
Orders@rodopi.nl—www.rodopi.nl

Amsterdam/New York, NY
2011. 271 pp.
(Internationale Forschungen zur Allgemeinen und Vergleichenden Literaturwissenschaft 153)
Paper €26,-/US$39,-
E-Book €26,-/US$39,-
ISBN: 978-90-420-3405-1
ISBN: 978-94-012-0692-1

USA/Canada:
248 East 44th Street, 2nd floor,
New York, NY 10017, USA.
Call Toll-free (US only): T: 1-800-225-3998
F: 1-800-853-3881

All other countries:
Tijnmuiden 7, 1046 AK Amsterdam, The Netherlands
Tel. +31-20-611 48 21 Fax +31-20-447 29 79
Please note that the exchange rate is subject to fluctuations

Performing Poetry

Body, Place and Rhythm in the Poetry Performance

Edited by
Cornelia Gräbner and
Arturo Casas

Orders@rodopi.nl—www.rodopi.nl

Over the past decades, the poetry performance has developed into an increasingly popular, diverse, and complex art form. In theoretical and critical discourse, it is referred to as performance poetry, spoken word poetry, and polipoesía; some theorists argue that it is an independent poetic genre, others treat it as a contemporary manifestation of oral poetry or of the poetry recital. The essays collected in this volume take up the challenge that the poetry performance poses to literary theory. Coming from a variety of disciplines, including Literary Studies, Theater Studies, and Area Studies, contributors develop new approaches and analytical categories for the poetry performance. They draw on case studies from a variety of contexts and in several languages, including Brazilian Portuguese, Dutch, Catalan, English, French, Galician, and Spanish. Essays are organized in three sections, which focus on critical and theoretical approaches to the poetry performance, on the mediatic hybridity of this art form, and on the ways in which the poetry performance negotiates locatedness through engagements with space and place. The structure of the volume intersperses essays on theory and analysis with self-reflexive essays from performance poets on their own performance practice.

Amsterdam/New York, NY
2011. 293 pp.
(Thamyris Intersecting Place, Sex and Race 24)
Paper €58,-/US$87,-
E-Book €58,-/US$87,-
ISBN: 978-90-420-3329-0
ISBN: 978-94-012-0025-7

USA/Canada:
248 East 44th Street, 2nd floor,
New York, NY 10017, USA.
Call Toll-free (US only): T: 1-800-225-3998
F: 1-800-853-3881
All other countries:
Tijnmuiden 7, 1046 AK Amsterdam, The Netherlands
Tel. +31-20-611 48 21 Fax +31-20-447 29 79
Please note that the exchange rate is subject to fluctuations

rodopi

Orders@rodopi.nl—www.rodopi.nl

The Metareferential Turn in Contemporary Arts and Media

Forms, Functions, Attempts at Explanation

Edited by
Werner Wolf
In collaboration with
Katharina Bantleon and
Jeff Thoss

One possible description of the contemporary medial landscape in Western culture is that it has gone 'meta' to an unprecedented extent, so that a remarkable 'meta-culture' has emerged. Indeed, 'metareference', i.e. self-reflexive comments on, or references to, various kinds of media-related aspects of a given medial artefact or performance, specific media and arts or the media in general is omnipresent and can, nowadays, be encountered in 'high' art and literature as frequently as in their popular counterparts, in the *traditional* media as well as in new media. From the *Simpsons*, pop music, children's literature, computer games and pornography to the contemporary visual arts, feature film, postmodern fiction, drama and even architecture — everywhere one can find metareferential explorations, comments on or criticism of representation, medial conventions or modes of production and reception, and related issues.

Within individual media and genres, notably in research on postmodernist metafiction, this outspoken tendency towards 'metaization' is known well enough, and various reasons have been given for it. Yet never has there been an attempt to account for what one may aptly term the current 'metareferential turn' on a larger, transmedial scale. This is what *The Metareferential Turn in Contemporary Arts and Media: Forms, Functions, Attempts at Explanation* undertakes to do as a sequel to its predecessor, the volume *Metareference across Media* (vol. 4 in the series 'Studies in Intermediality'), which was dedicated to theoretical issues and transhistorical case studies. Coming from diverse disciplinary and methodological backgrounds, the contributors to the present volume propose explanations of impressive subtlety, breadth and depth for the current situation in addition to exploring individual forms and functions of metareference which may be linked with particular explanations. As expected, there is no monocausal reason to be found for the situation under scrutiny, yet the proposals made have in their combination a remarkable explanatory power which contributes to a better understanding of an important facet of current media production and reception.

The essays assembled in the volume, which also contains an introduction with a detailed survey over the possibilities of accounting for the metareferential turn, will be relevant to students and scholars from a wide variety of fields: cultural history at large, intermediality and media studies as well as, more particularly, literary studies, music, film and art history.

Amsterdam/New York, NY
2011. XI, 594 pp.
(Studies in Intermediality 5)
Bound €120,-/US$180,-
E-Book €120,-/US$180,-
ISBN: 978-90-420-3370-2
ISBN: 978-94-012-0069-1

USA/Canada:
248 East 44th Street, 2nd floor,
New York, NY 10017, USA.
Call Toll-free (US only): T: 1-800-225-3998
F: 1-800-853-3881
All other countries:
Tijnmuiden 7, 1046 AK Amsterdam, The Netherlands
Tel. +31-20-611 48 21 Fax +31-20-447 29 79
Please note that the exchange rate is subject to fluctuations

Rodopi

: **rodopi**

Orders@rodopi.nl — www.rodopi.nl

Efficacité/Efficacy

How To Do Things With Words and Images?

Edited by
Véronique Plesch,
Catriona MacLeod, and
Jan Baetens

This book aims at offering a broad survey of the encounter between word and image studies and anthropology and to demonstrate the mutual benefits of this dialogue for both disciplines in the three fields of the image (Marin), the social history of writing (Petrucci), and memory (Yates). The themes discussed by the contributors to this volume, all specialists in their field, highlight each in their specific field one or more aspects of the agency of both text and image. Bridging the gap between the Anglo-Saxon and the Latin research traditions, this bilingual volume focuses on three major questions: What do we do with texts and images? How do texts and images become active cultural agents? And what do texts and images help us do? Contributions cover a wide range of topics and disciplines (from visual poetry to garden theory and from ekphrasis to new media art), and represent therefore the best possible overview of what cutting-edge analysis in word and image studies stands for today.

Amsterdam/New York, NY
2011. 320 pp. (Word & Image Interactions 7)
Paper €64,-/US$96,-
E-Book €64,-/US$96,-
ISBN: 978-90-420-3374-0
ISBN: 978-94-012-0073-8

USA/Canada:
248 East 44th Street, 2nd floor,
New York, NY 10017, USA.
Call Toll-free (US only): T: 1-800-225-3998
F: 1-800-853-3881

All other countries:
Tijnmuiden 7, 1046 AK Amsterdam, The Netherlands
Tel. +31-20-611 48 21 Fax +31-20-447 29 79
Please note that the exchange rate is subject to fluctuations

Rodopi

rodopi

Orders@rodopi.nl—www.rodopi.nl

Transfigured Stages

Major Practitioners and Theatre Aesthetics in Australia

Margaret Hamilton

Transfigured Stages: Major Practitioners and Theatre Aesthetics in Australia captures the excitement of a key period in the emergence of postdramatic theatre in Australia in the 1980s and 1990s. It is the first book to discuss work by The Sydney Front (1986–1993) and Open City (1987–), and engages contemporary cultural and aesthetic theory to analyse performances by these artists, as well as theatre productions by Jenny Kemp and others. These performance practitioners are considered as part of an international paradigm attesting to forms of theatre that no longer operate according to the established principles of drama. This book also highlights the complexity of Indigenous theatre through its analysis of the Mudrooroo-Müller project staged in 1996.

Margaret Hamilton is a lecturer in Theatre Studies at the University of Wollongong, Australia, and publishes on contemporary performance. For a number of years she developed and managed a major program of Australian arts in Berlin, and a subsidiary European touring program for the Australia Council for the Arts and the Department of Foreign Affairs and Trade.

Amsterdam/New York, NY
2011. 243 pp.
(Australian Playwrights 14)
Paper €48,-/US$72,-
E-Book €48,-/US$72,-
ISBN: 978-90-420-3356-6
ISBN: 978-94-012-0055-4

USA/Canada:
248 East 44th Street, 2nd floor,
New York, NY 10017, USA.
Call Toll-free (US only): T: 1-800-225-3998
F: 1-800-853-3881

All other countries:
Tijnmuiden 7, 1046 AK Amsterdam, The Netherlands
Tel. +31-20-611 48 21 Fax +31-20-447 29 79
Please note that the exchange rate is subject to fluctuations

Rodopi

Radical Visions 1968-2008

The Impact of the Sixties on Australian Drama

Denise Varney

Radical Visions 1968–2008: The Impact of the Sixties on Australian Drama is about a generation of Australian playwrights who came of age in the sixties. This important book shows how international trends in youth radicalism and cultural change at the time contributed to the rise of interest in alternative theatre and drama in a number of locations. It follows the career of Australia's major playwrights — Alma De Groen, Jenny Kemp, Richard Murphet, John Romeril, Stephen Sewell and David Williamson — whose early plays were first performed at La Mama and the Pram Factory theatres in Melbourne in the sixties and seventies and who continue to make new work. The book's dual purpose is to examine the impact of the sixties on playwriting and update the scholarship on the contemporary works with close readings of the plays of the nineties and the first decade of the twenty-first century. By analysing the recent plays, the book traces the continuing impact of left wing politics and cultural change on Australian theatre and society.

Associate Professor Denise Varney is in the English and Theatre Program in the School of Culture and Communication at the University of Melbourne. She is co-author of *The Dolls' Revolution: Australian Theatre and Cultural Imagination* and editor of *Theatre in the Berlin Republic: German Drama Since Reunification*.

Amsterdam/New York, NY
2011. 294 pp.
(Australian Playwrights 13)
Paper €59,-/US$89,-
E-Book €59,-/US$89,-
ISBN: 978-90-420-3354-2
ISBN: 978-94-012-0053-0

USA/Canada:
248 East 44th Street, 2nd floor,
New York, NY 10017, USA.
Call Toll-free (US only): T: 1-800-225-3998
F: 1-800-853-3881

All other countries:
Tijnmuiden 7, 1046 AK Amsterdam, The Netherlands
Tel. +31-20-611 48 21 Fax +31-20-447 29 79
Please note that the exchange rate is subject to fluctuations